Praise f

"Mark Leier has produced the fin[e] ....~ ~..g..~.. language—a tremendously witty, informative, and insightful study that restores
to Bakunin his humanity as well as his intellectual and political significance."

—PAUL MCLAUGHLIN, author of *Mikhail Bakunin: The Philosophical Basis
of His Anarchism*

"A modern biography of the father of anarchism is overdue: Mark Leier's admirable study tells the colorful, rebellious, and often outrageous story of the
eccentric Bakunin in a style that is entertaining, scholarly, and fresh, a biography that not only reassesses this fascinating and important character but
also provides the biography of the forgotten ideology of anarchism itself."

—SIMON SEBAG MONTEFIORE, author of *Stalin:
The Court of the Red Tsar*

"The time for Bakunin—the real one, not the caricature—has come again,
and Mark Leier has given us just the history that we need. Wonderfully written, scholarly but also packed with fascinating tales and fresh revelations,
Bakunin: The Creative Passion is passion with purpose."

—PAUL BUHLE, coeditor *of Encyclopedia of the American Left* and
Wobblies! A Graphic History of the Industrial Workers of the World

"The life of Bakunin (1814–1876), the Russian architect of the anarchist
movement, provides a surprisingly enjoyable introduction to the tumult of
nineteenth-century radicalism ... A chapter on the roots of Bakunin's
thought in German idealism provides a lucid eight-page precis of Hegel's
ideas that's actually fun to read. The feud between Bakunin and Marx gets
ample space . . . [Leier] brings welcome consideration to the real merits of the
movement's theory."

—*Publishers Weekly*

ALSO BY MARK LEIER

Rebel Life: The Life and Times of Robert Gosden, Revolutionary, Mystic, Labour Spy

Red Flags and Red Tape: The Making of a Labour Bureaucracy

The Light at the End of the Tunnel: The Tunnel and Rockworkers Union, Local 168 (with M. C. Warrior)

Where the Fraser River Flows: The Industrial Workers of the World in British Columbia

BAKUNIN

THE CREATIVE PASSION—A BIOGRAPHY

MARK LEIER

SEVEN STORIES PRESS
NEW YORK

Seven Stories Press
140 Watts Street
New York, NY 10013
www.sevenstories.com

In Canada: Publishers Group Canada, 559 College Street, Suite 402, Toronto, ON M6G 1A9

In the UK: Turnaround Publisher Services Ltd., Unit 3, Olympia Trading Estate, Coburg Road, Wood Green, London N22 6TZ

In Australia: Palgrave Macmillan, 15–19 Claremont Street, South Yarra, VIC 3141

College professors may order examination copies of Seven Stories Press titles for a free six-month trial period. To order, visit http://www.sevenstories.com/textbook or send a fax on school letterhead to (212) 226-1411.

Book design by Jon Gilbert

Library of Congress Cataloging-in-Publication Data
Leier, James Mark.
 Bakunin : the creative passion : a biography / Mark Leier. — 1st Seven Stories Press ed.
     p. cm.
Includes bibliographical references and index.
ISBN 978-1-58322-894-4 (pbk.)
 1. Bakunin, Mikhail Aleksandrovich, 1814-1876. 2. Anarchists—Russia—Biography. 3. Anarchism—Russia—History. I. Title.
HX917.2.Z67B34 2009
335'.83092—dc22
[B]
                                        2009018098

Printed in the United States of America

9 8 7 6 5 4 3 2 1

To the East Kings Road Commune

CONTENTS

INTRODUCTION

The war was supposed to be over. In 1989 the Berlin Wall was torn down and with it went the fabled evil empire of the Soviet Union. For many observers, this meant more than the collapse of a rival power and the end of the Cold War; it was the end of history itself. They didn't mean that the past had ceased to exist or that societies would cease to change. Their point was both more metaphysical and more banal. Simply put, history was a heroic struggle between capitalism and communism. Locked in mortal combat, the two opposing systems used ideas, ballots, bullets, even the threat of nuclear Armageddon, to seek the winning advantage. The struggle, on the high plane of ideals and literature, in steaming jungles and on dark, rain-slicked streets, sometimes open, sometimes hidden, propelled change over time—history— as humanity lurched desperately from left to right to an uncertain future. But with the collapse of the Soviet Union, the West had won, using, in the words of G. B. Trudeau in his comic strip, *Doonesbury,* "the basics: hard currency, cheap wheat, and good rock 'n' roll."[1] History as cataclysmic clash was over. There was some mopping up to be done in the hinterlands, but soon they too would be quiet. At long last the business of business could proceed smoothly, without interference or distraction, because there was no alternative to capitalism.

That illusion was shattered on the streets of Seattle in November 1999. Five days of protest against the World Trade Organization showed that dissent was possible and that resistance was not futile. Students, trade unionists, environmentalists, indigenous people, farmers, and consumers raised their fists and voices against globalization, the surveillance state, and business as usual. Seattle was a symbol that the struggle continued, and that history had begun again.

The five days that shook the world were led by a movement many thought had vanished with the flip of the switch that electrocuted Nicola Sacco and Bartolomeo Vanzetti in Boston in 1927.[2] For the first time in years, anarchism was a political force that rallied thousands under its black flag. As protest flashed around the globe, from Melbourne to Mexico City to Prague to Quebec City to Nice to Genoa to Miami, the anarchist "Black Bloc" and "White Overalls" groups generated a frisson of fear and shock. Anarchism made the six o'clock news. It even invaded American prime time as Toby Ziegler deplored "anarchist wannabes" on *The West Wing* and Tony explained Sacco and Vanzetti to the rest of *The Sopranos.* The media rushed to explore the phenomenon, and articles on anarchism appeared in *The Economist, The Washington Post, The Wall Street Journal, The New York Times, National Post, Harper's,* and *Time.* The *Utne Reader,* a sort of *Reader's Digest* for New Agers, even warned its readers that "You may be an anarchist—and not even know it."[3]

The media, however, did more to obscure anarchism than to explain it. Focusing on the street fighting and confrontations with police, mainstream commentators were unable to understand what anarchism was or why a philosophy with roots in the nineteenth century resurfaced with such power at the dawn of the new millennium. Their inability to understand anarchism is not surprising. It is often misunderstood by its opponents and even by its advocates. The word itself has long been separated from its real meaning of "rule by no one." A check of "anarchism" and its cognates in thesauruses from the 1935 *Roget's* to the one in Microsoft Word 2000 reveals misleading synonyms such as "evildoer," "destroyer," "disobedience," "disorder," and "mayhem." High and popular cultures alike have contributed to the misunderstanding. W. B. Yeats, appalled at the post-apocalyptic world of the Great War and the popular demand for sweeping social change that followed, whined that "things fall apart; the center cannot hold; mere anarchy is loosed upon the world." Since the nineteenth century, the anarchist has been pictured as a wild-eyed bohemian, clothed in a wide-brimmed, pointed felt hat and a long black cape that concealed a round bomb with a sputtering fuse. Bertram Lamb and A. B. Payne's popular comic strip in the British *Daily Mirror* newspaper of the 1920s and 1930s, *Pip, Squeak, and Wilfred,* featured such a character, named "Popski"—read foreigner, Bolshevik, evil—and the strip and the animated short films that followed popularized the portrait. Robin Williams gave a dynamite—and dynamited—performance of just such a figure in the 1996 film adaptation of Joseph Conrad's *The Secret Agent.* The old image has been updated, with anarchists now portrayed clad in black fatigues, their faces hidden by woolen balaclavas, as they trash the storefronts of McDonald's and Starbucks outlets and fight with police. Such inaccurate stereotypes persist, even in contemporary fiction.[4]

Other events, however, soon diverted attention away from demonstrations and street protests. After 11 September 2001, the experts now looked to anarchism for explanations of terrorism. David Ignatius, in a widely reprinted editorial, wrote that while "bin Laden's texts are couched in the language of Islam, they read like the flowery manifestos of the elitist bomb throwers of the nineteenth century like Prince Peter Kropotkin or Mikhail Bakunin." Lewis Lapham drew a straight line from Bakunin to bin Laden via Timothy McVeigh, who was executed for the Oklahoma City bombing, and Ted Kaczynski, better known as the Unabomber. John le Carre, in an otherwise extremely thoughtful and insightful article, concluded that "Mr. Bakunin in his grave and Mr. bin Laden in his cave must be rubbing their hands in glee" as security forces were expanded and civil liberties were curtailed in the panic that ensued in the aftermath of the WTC bombing. In Canada, the mild-tempered Ian Brown concluded in the pages of the *Globe and Mail* newspaper that Bakunin "ended up demanding terror for terror's sake, terror as spectacle, death as spectacle" and was the direct ancestor of cults such as the Solar Temple and the Kool-Aid-swilling minions of Jim Jones.[5]

Michael Bakunin[6] is now of keen interest in the twenty-first century, though the attention paid to him continues to obscure the man and his ideas. Certainly Bakunin was no pacifist, but he was no mad bomber or assassin. Typically that sort of violence has been the prerogative of the state. Two world wars, the Holocaust, Communist purges and famines, Vietnam, Nicaragua, Iraq, Afghanistan, Rwanda, East Timor, Kosovo, Chechnya, and four wars for Middle East oil since 1948 should remind us it is not the anarchists who are primarily responsible for terror and violence in the world.

If an "expert" is someone who has read one more book on the subject than you have, then many writers became instant experts on anarchism by flipping through the relevant chapter in Barbara Tuchman's 1966 book, *The Proud Tower*. It is a fine book, but it is not primarily about anarchism or even the years between 1814 and 1876 in which Bakunin lived. The would-be experts who dug a little deeper turned to some of the standard books on the subject, but these are dated. The best of them, E. H. Carr's biography, was published in 1937, and the two most influential books published in English in the 1980s are deeply flawed. Much of the newer scholarship on Bakunin is not easily accessible to the general researcher, for it is to be found in theses and scholarly journals rather than widely available books.

More important, most of the authors of the standard histories of Bakunin were interested not in understanding anarchism but in burying it. They wrote to discredit the radicalism of their own generations, using Bakunin as a stand-in for their contemporaries; they wrote to make it plain which side they were on during the Cold War; they wrote to promote orthodoxy and order, and to oppose critical thinking and protest. Their tactics were often unscrupulous: the misquote, the lack of context, the repetition of groundless stories, the impugning of motives without evidence, and most of all, the unexamined assumption that no reasonable person could take anarchism seriously. These interpretations, because they are accessible, continue to distort our understanding of anarchism and anarchists. Even when Bakunin trod the London stage in 2002 as a character in Tom Stoppard's trilogy, *The Coast of Utopia,* it was as a caricature, his ideas reduced to attitudes and platitudes.

Determined to root anarchism in individual pathology, many historians have examined Bakunin as an exercise in psychohistory. One plainly states that Bakunin's anarchism is of interest only for "what it reveals of the Utopian psychology." Several argue, without any evidence, that Bakunin's commitment to revolution was the result of sexual impotence, essentially arguing that men who can't get it up want to blow it up. There is, unfortunately, only a very short dash between a "psychohistorian" and a "psycho historian." Psychohistory has its uses, but it is rarely helpful in understanding politics or political movements. If we wish to understand anarchism and its enduring appeal, we need to go beyond the psychology of a single man, especially as it is understood by his enemies.[7]

Because of his radical critique of state socialism, some of the worst smears on Bakunin have come from the left. Sadly, Marxists have used the same shoddy tools on Bakunin that liberals and conservatives have used on Marx: innuendo, inappropriate literalism, willful misinterpretation, *ad hominem* arguments, and special pleading. Marx himself falsely accused Bakunin of being a police spy and spent much of his later career attacking anarchism. Generations of Marxists have continued to hurl abuse at Bakunin, usually without bothering to read him. Francis Wheen, in his recent delightful biography of Marx, repeats all the old canards and dismisses Bakunin as the "hairy Russian giant," an odd and particularly ironic complaint given Marx's own hirsute appearance. In an otherwise excellent and insightful play, *Marx in Soho,* left-wing historian Howard Zinn has Marx and Bakunin in a heated debate that sees the anarchist spit on the floor, urinate out the window, then fall to the floor in a drunken stupor while Marx gets most of the good lines. It makes for gripping drama, but it fails to take Bakunin's trenchant critique of Marxism seriously. Eric Hobsbawm, undoubtedly the finest historian of our time, has written sympathetically and critically about anarchism in the nineteenth and twentieth centuries, but surely is mistaken in his conclusion that anarchism has no significant contribution to make to socialist theory. By now, the Lenin Harangue Pie is pretty stale.[8]

This book starts from a different premise. I offer an interpretation of

Bakunin's life and ideas of use to those interested in understanding anarchism and social change. This is a biography that stresses the evolution of his ideas as much as the details of his life. The emphasis is less on his personality, usually described as generous, or his appetites for tobacco, food, and alcohol, inevitably described as voluminous. Carr's biography does that about as well as it can be done, right down to the color and style of the jackets Bakunin and Ivan Turgenev sported on a Berlin outing: the anarchist wore purple, the novelist green. Bakunin took part in some of the most important and exciting debates and events of the nineteenth century and his anarchism is a reflective response, rooted in philosophy and reality. For that reason, this book provides some background on the context in which Bakunin formulated his ideas.

At the same time, it does not explore and defend Bakunin's every action and idea. Some of these, such as the anti-Semitism that surfaces in some of his writing, are indefensible. But as the historian E. P. Thompson remarked of Karl Marx, the point is that Bakunin is on our side; we are not on the side of Bakunin.[9] He still has much to say to us, for the current interest in anarchism is not misplaced or irrelevant. To understand anarchism, it is necessary to go beyond the caricature presented by the media. It is a sophisticated political and ethical theory that has attracted thinkers as diverse as Mary Wollstonecraft Shelley, George Orwell, Ursula K. Le Guin, and Noam Chomsky. It is worth understanding because it is again a force in current events, and because it tells us something about our past and, possibly, our future.

The fundamental point of anarchism is critique. Anarchists have tried to show what is wrong with the world and why, but their message has been buried and distorted. Its resurgence at the "end of history" is not surprising, for anarchism has often renewed precisely when we are told that this is as good as it gets and that happiness lies in adapting ourselves to the new horrors. When the lid of the box gets screwed down tight, people start to think and act outside the box.

The blunt fact is that while our modern world has, as Karl Marx put it, "accomplished wonders far surpassing Egyptian pyramids, Roman aqueducts, and Gothic cathedrals," it has also accomplished horrors far surpassing any the world has seen before. Anarchism remains the most optimistic and hopeful of alternatives. It is worth understanding because it continues to be a political force able to inspire. It is also worth understanding because we are a long way from Utopia. If we are to do better, we need to think creatively. But the tendency in recent years has been to close off debate, to limit possibilities, to declare Utopia out of bounds. The anarchists put dreams back on the negotiating table. The anarchist critique of the state, of capital, of power, is a compelling one, and the lesson of anarchism is constantly relearned through experience: people who do not benefit from the system will organize to create alternatives.

Thus Bakunin's life and ideas are worth a thorough reexamination. He spent a great deal of time thinking about tactics and strategy, and his ruminations and actions may still be instructive, for their failures as well as their successes. He was present at the birth and early adolescence of industrial capitalism and the modern state, and thus he had a unique vantage point from which to observe these creations. Despite all their changes, the state and capital still look and function much as they did in the nineteenth century, and so by studying Bakunin we can learn a great deal about our own time. Our ability to examine the world critically has been impaired by 150 years of propaganda and practice. We often mistake technology for capitalism, profit for freedom, parliamentary procedure for democracy. Too often we assume blindly that modernization is good and that economic growth is progress. The effect is to push us to believe that this is the best of all possible worlds and to shrink our dreams about what is possible and desirable. Clearly this benefits some while harming most. The practitioners of power, of pragmatism and practicality, have had their chance, and it is difficult not to conclude that they have botched it. In examining Michael Bakunin, we begin to recover a world of possibility and promise.

1

WEREWOLVES, NOBLES, AND THE IDYLL OF PRIAMUKHINO

There was little in his family background or his early childhood to suggest that Mikhail Aleksandrovich Bakunin would grow up to be anything other than a loyal officer and subject of the Tsar of All the Russias. As a young man, he even looked the part. He stood six feet four inches tall and filled out his gaudy Russian military uniform splendidly. His thick blond hair, startling blue eyes, strong nose, and chin complete with a dimple made him perfect for a recruiting poster.[1] As an officer in the artillery, the most prestigious arm of the military, his future seemed assured: a good war or two to provide quick promotion, then early retirement to run the family estates, where the lands and serfs would provide a comfortable income as he pottered about the gardens and read the classics of literature and science.

Instead Michael Bakunin became the most notorious radical of the nineteenth century. He devoted his adult life to the destruction of the tsar and feudalism, of capitalism, the state, even God. He inspired armed revolutionaries from Auguste Vaillant, who lobbed a bomb into the French parliament in 1893, to Eldridge Cleaver, a founder of the American Black Panthers. His name is still used, wrongly, as a synonym for revolution and mass destruction for its own sake.[2]

Where did his passion for revolution and anarchism come from? As a child and young man Bakunin never felt the knout of the overseer or the fist of the foreman, never faced the uncertainty of crop failures and famine, never had to worry where his next meal or bed would come from. This has led critics to denounce his ideas precisely because of his noble status in the same way contemporary critics attack those who protest globalization as liberal elitists, idle rich kids, dilettantes, and professional troublemakers. This is of course ridiculous, for ideas must be judged on their merits, not the wealth of those who hold them. Other critics insist that the answer to Bakunin's politics lies in his childhood, despite the fact that many nobles of Bakunin's generation, each with very different upbringings, embraced revolution. Neither explanation is satisfactory, but Bakunin's family history and the history of Russia itself do hold some important clues.

The Russian nobility was a complicated tangle of wealth, status, service, and ancestry. Simply referring to Bakunin as a noble obscures more about the family's station than it reveals. The Russian word *dvorianstvo* may be translated as aristocracy, nobility, or gentry, but none is really sufficient. It was divided into six strata, including those who had been granted their status by patent, those who had earned it through service to the tsar, those with old titles such as prince or new ones such as count or baron, and the old aristocracy. Some ranks were comparable to the English peerage, while others were more like American planters on small plantations.[3] Nobles guarded the privileges of rank jealously and carefully calculated their own position as they plotted the rise and fall of their allies and rivals in the ranks.

This bewildering system reflected the diverse needs of the Russian empire. Ironically, while Russia's land mass was larger than that of any other nation, as early as the 1760s the regime was alarmed that it faced a land shortage. Agriculture was the principal source of wealth for Russia's preindustrial nobility, and farm production for profit required huge amounts of land and peasants to work it. Russia did not have a consistent system of primogeniture; more often, all the sons of hereditary nobles inherited equal shares of the estate and title. Over time, this meant that more and more nobles competed for increasingly scarce arable land. At the same time, much of Russia's land was not very productive. Famine was a constant threat, as the available land could not always sustain the population. The obvious solution was to keep expanding the empire. Trade, especially for Siberian furs, pushed the empire outward, and constant expansion was the key to preserving the integrity of Russia's borders from its host of enemies, even while enlarging its territory created new problems of security. As the empire spread, the new territories had to be settled, new subjects administered, and new lands made productive. Established nobles were reluctant to move to the distant, rough regions, and so new nobles were created and given charge of settling the new lands while indigenous landholders were incorporated into the Russian system.[4]

The complicated ranking system had political consequences as well. As nobles competed among themselves for status, favor, and promotion, their incessant squabbling kept them from pursuing their common interests. The Russian aristocracy could rarely act as a united class, for each group and member suspected any change as a potential threat to their own particular privilege. This meant that reform could rarely come from the nobles. It could rarely come from the tsar either, for even the most obvious and needed changes confronted stiff opposition. Even in times of emergency the tsar could not always act swiftly or firmly. When war broke out, as it did often as the empire expanded its designs on its weaker neighbors, the nobility expected to be appointed to the higher echelons of the officer corps, with appointments based on family connections, court favor, status, rank, and seniority. The civil service worked in much the same way, and this practically guaranteed the regime would flounder, for competence was far down on the list of qualifications for generals, ministers, and officials.

In an attempt to promote people by merit, Peter the Great created the Table of Ranks in 1722. It established corresponding hierarchies of fourteen ranks, or *chiny*, in the three state services of the armed services, the civil service, and the judiciary. The fifth *chin*, for example, was equivalent to the military rank of brigadier. Nobles entering state service began at the fourteenth, or lowest, rank and worked their way up. While promotion through service was not unknown before, and while the tsar could not ignore the claims of aristocrats, the reform codified and regulated promotion based on skill.

The Table of Ranks did two other things. First, while it did not abolish the importance of lineage—the same old noble families continued to dominate Russian society—it placed great emphasis on education. Kinship still provided tangible advantages and privileges, but credentials and education were necessary to win promotion. It followed that families would be less likely to expend money and influence on family members who seemed unlikely to fare well under the merit system. Second, Peter the Great opened the Table of Ranks to commoners, who could now compete with the hereditary nobility for positions and influence. Commoners who entered the military service and were commissioned as second lieutenants or ensigns obtained the lowest rank and the right to own land and serfs. Their sons were automatically entered in the fourteenth rank and could work their way up. At the eighth *chin*, the rank was hereditary and title passed on to children.[5]

The Bakunin family benefited from Peter's system. Sometime in the sixteenth century, Ivan Bakunin established the family as *pomeshchiki*, that is, landowners who held peasants as serfs, at Iaroslavl. The family entered the nobility, but Ivan's title was not hereditary. He could maintain his status, land, and serfs only at the pleasure of the tsar and in return for service to him. During Peter the Great's reign, the family secured its position in the aristocracy. Like all noble families, service to the tsar was still required of the Bakunins, usually in the form of military service and supplying serfs to the army, but now their noble title was a hereditary rank that did not have to be won anew by each generation.

In a culture that put great emphasis on ancestry and lineage, the Bakunin family sometimes claimed to be descended from Stephen Bathory, king of Poland from 1575 to 1586. Stephen, originally a Transylvanian prince, waged several successful military campaigns against the Russian tsar Ivan the Terrible for control of Livonia, roughly present-day Estonia and parts of Latvia on the Baltic Sea. The Bakunins were careful not to press the dubious family connection too hard. Stephen's niece, Elizabeth, died in prison in 1614, after being convicted of lycanthropy. During her career as werewolf, Elizabeth was alleged to have slaughtered more than six hundred virgins, bathing in their blood to preserve her youth. It is probably just as well for the history of anarchism that the connection to the Bathory family was slim. Otherwise his detractors would undoubtedly insist that Michael Bakunin's political views were the result of the werewolf gene. Instead they have had to rely on the less scientific theories of psychology and psychohistory.

Whatever the family's roots and appetites, it continued to prosper and rise through the ranks. Michael's paternal great-great-grandfather, also named Michael, was a military officer during the reign of Peter the Great and served in Tsaritsyn, later Stalingrad, now Volgograd, in the southeast corner of Russia on the Volga River. His son Vassily entered the civil service and served in the Foreign Affairs office. In the 1740s, under the reign of Empress Elizabeth, Vassily took up postings in the Persian embassies and made his way to the office of Active State Councillor, the fourth-highest *chin*. His three sons took up state service, two of them, both named Peter, in foreign affairs. The middle son, Michael, whose grandson would become the notorious anarchist, entered the court system and was appointed to the sixth *chin*, Collegiate Councillor, under Catherine the Great. Over the next sixteen years, he rose to the fourth rank, as his father had before him.[6]

He was virtually an archetypal Russian noble of his period, of the kind that inspired caricatures of Russians as vital and excessive, bear-like and overbearing. Large and physically powerful, he was given equally to feats of daring and fits of rage. Family lore credited him with single-handedly driving off a band of brigands with a hastily seized wooden board. Less creditably, he was noted for reacting badly to perceived insult and on one occasion jerked a rude coachman from his perch and tossed him into the river.[7]

He married Liubov Petrovna Myshetskaya, a princess from a very old Russian family. The family was an ancient one, much older than the Bakunins, but not as distinguished. It was, however, extremely wealthy, and the match combined status and wealth to the benefit of both families. Unlike most European countries, Russian noblewomen could own property and serfs, and Liubov inherited substantial holdings in Tver province. In 1779, she purchased a village called Priamukhino in Tver, and Michael retired from court life to manage the provincial estate.

They raised three sons and five daughters. Two of the daughters married, three remained single, and two of the sons followed the traditional paths of the male nobility, one to the civil service and the other to the military. The youngest son, Alexander, followed a different path. If his father was the archetypal Russian noble of old, Alexander would represent and help shape the modern Russian nobility of the late eighteenth and early nineteenth centuries. Unlike his father, Alexander was not physically powerful or impetuous. Believing him to be frail and unable to withstand the harsh Russian climate, his family sent him to Italy at the age of nine.[8]

As a young man, Alexander studied at the University of Padua. It was the same university his alleged ancestor Stephen Bathory attended, in itself not surprising as Padua was especially attractive to foreign students. If the Italian geography and climate differed greatly from that of Priamukhino, so too did the intellectual and political climate. In the Russia of the tsars, even if you were an ambassador to England or France, you were going to have to serve somebody. Bob Dylan made it scan, but Nicholas I said it first: "I consider the entire human life to be merely service, because everybody serves." Of course the tsar served only God, who did not resort to prison, the knout, or the gallows if his immediate servants didn't obey. Political freedom was virtually unknown in Russia. Even those of noble birth had few ways to make their voices heard or to influence public events, for the tsar was bound by no constitution or parliament. As Tsar Paul was alleged to have remarked to the Swedish ambassador, "the only important person in Russia is the one speaking to the emperor, and only while he is so speaking."[9]

By contrast, students, especially when they move from the countryside to the city and are far from family scrutiny, often find university a time of liberty, even license. This was especially the case at Padua. Created in 1222, the university was built as an expression of freedom when professors and students at Bologna left in protest over the usurpation of academic freedom there. Its motto, *Universa universes patavina libertas* (Paduan freedom is total, complete, general, for everyone), could not be more different from the orthodoxy, autocracy, and cultural poverty that Russia represented. Alexander did well there, ultimately receiving his doctorate in natural history for a three-volume thesis on worms. The topic was apparently good training for a career in diplomacy, for upon receiving his degree, he began a career in the Russian foreign office, serving as secretary in the legations in Florence and Turin. His postings allowed him to observe firsthand the most important event of the eighteenth century: the French Revolution. It would have a profound effect on him and his family.

Like much of our history, the reality of the revolution has been replaced with a jumble of images: an effete aristocracy, ragged peasants bearing pikes, Marie Antoinette suggesting the starving eat cake if they could not obtain bread, the tricolor, Napoleon. Behind all is the grim silhouette of the guillotine. The intensity of the images and the antirevolutionary propaganda that was thrown up in the English-speaking world—even the twentieth-century Hornblower novels of C. S. Forrester may be read as paeans to reaction—tend to make us forget the profound accomplishments of the French Revolution. "The people rising in its majesty" destroyed the absolutist monarchy and proclaimed the Rights of Man and an era of *liberte, egalite, fraternite*. By comparison, the American Revolution was little more than a change of management, albeit a hostile one. The events in France reverberated around the world and changed everything, from political power to the arts to the concepts of nation and nationalism to the way things were measured. Across Europe artists, philosophers, musicians, and poets applauded and supported the revolution, at least in its early years. This identification with the ideals of the revolution was taken to heart in the field as well as the salon and concert hall and lecture room, most directly and effectively in Haiti, where black slaves took the revolutionaries at their word and in August 1791 launched the world's first successful slave revolt against the French themselves.[10]

Alexander Bakunin too, a young man in his twenty-first year, was swept up in the upheavals. He may even have been present as an observer or a participant in the single most important event of the opening days of the revolution: the storming of the Bastille on 14 July 1789. The Paris prison, with its moat, thick walls, and menacing towers, was a hated icon of the old regime and Louis XVI, and the taking of the prison by insurrectionists became one of the crucial symbols of the French Revolution, for it heralded the end of absolutism and gave substance to the hopes of the oppressed.

If Alexander Bakunin was not in Paris on 14 July, he should have been. He sympathized with the revolution and was convinced that the old ways of his father were no longer sufficient. Upon his return to Russia, Alexander would bring with him new ideals of freedom, education, and justice. If these were to be largely restricted to his family and would remain dependent on the enserfment of peasants, they were no less dear to him.

His return came sooner than expected. His father's health faded, and Alexander's brothers had to remain in the tsar's service. The sexism of the period deemed his mother and sisters unable to manage the estate; that left Alexander. His parents petitioned to have him released from service on the grounds of family hardship and in 1790, barely in his twenties, fresh from duties in some of the most sophisticated cities in Europe, exposed to the turmoil and excitement of revolution, Alexander gave up a promising career in the glitter of diplomatic service and foreign postings for the rustic routines and pleasures of a provincial manor.[11]

Certainly the estate was beautiful enough. Priamukhino was on the Osuga River in Tver province, about sixty miles due east of the city of Tver, known as Kalinin from 1933 to 1990. The family estate, located one hundred and fifty miles northwest of Moscow and perhaps twice that southeast of the capital, St. Petersburg, was far removed from the intrigue and culture of the cities. It was made up of three villages, including Priamukhino itself, and spread over four thousand acres of birch, pine, and spruce forest, about 675 acres of farmland, and about 340 acres of pasture. By comparison, the standard nineteenth-century homestead allotment in the Canadian and American prairies, the quarter section, consisted of only 160 acres.

The wealth of Russian nobles, however, was customarily measured not by the size of land holdings but by the number of adult male serfs, or "souls," controlled by the lord. The Bakunins in this period owned about five hundred "souls" and probably as many women and children. Sixty-five serfs were used as domestic servants, about thirty-five for the Priamukhino household alone. The remainder worked the Bakunin land, cut timber, raised stock, fished, and produced clothing and other goods as family units. Combined with the service the family rendered the tsar and the pedigree supplied by Liubov Myshetskaya, the Bakunin family was somewhere in the middling ranks of the complex social order of the Russian aristocracy.[12]

Putting aside for the moment the plight of the serfs—something most Russian nobles did regularly—Priamukhino appeared a peaceful, harmonious setting. It disguised, however, a harsher reality. Alexander's father was foul-tempered and in ill health, and his mother was cold, inflexible, and sternly religious. The estate was deeply in debt, mortgaged to the tune of 53,000 roubles, roughly the entire worth of all the Bakunin holdings. Far from giving up the cares of the workaday life for life as a country squire, Alexander was summoned home to resuscitate the failing estate.[13]

Alexander took up his duties with a mixture of optimism and resignation. Managing the affairs of estate, however, was much more difficult than he had anticipated. After two years of work, despair replaced his initial optimism. In 1797, he left Priamukhino to take up service again, this time under

Tsar Paul I, the son of Catherine the Great, at the tsar's estate at Gatchina, thirty miles southwest of St. Petersburg.

Court life under Paul, however, was very different from that under Catherine the Great. Catherine was intelligent, ambitious, and at least in the early years of her reign, cultivated a taste for the Western European Enlightenment and intellectual life. She corresponded with Voltaire and designed sweeping reforms for Russia. While the reforms were rarely put into place and Catherine's commitment to the ideals of the Enlightenment was perhaps more of a fashion statement than a heartfelt conviction, her court was a hospitable and rewarding one for the nobility in general and bright young men such as Alexander Bakunin in particular.

Paul's court was not. He was a narrow, ferocious man of few ideas and much hate. His father, Peter III, reigned for but a year before Catherine forced him to abdicate so she could take his place; Peter was mysteriously murdered soon after. Catherine despised their son Paul and in an attempt to keep him off the throne, insisted that Peter III was not his real father. Despite her best efforts, Paul, aged forty-two, became tsar when she died in 1796. One of his first acts was to have his parents disinterred so his father's remains, from more than thirty years ago, and his mother's relatively fresh corpse could be crowned. The ghoulish ceremony was intended to underscore Paul's royal lineage, but it tended instead to underscore his dubious mental health.[14]

It was a dangerous time to have an idiot on the throne. The French Revolution had brought war in its wake as monarchs and reactionaries sought to crush the spread of radical ideas. When Austria and Prussia attacked France itself, the republic hastily organized popular mass armies that repulsed the invaders and swarmed over the Austrian Netherlands, seized Savoy and Nice, and invaded Germany. Panicked, by 1793 a hasty coalition of Austria, Prussia, Great Britain, Holland, and Spain arrayed itself against revolutionary France. Catherine too was edging toward the alliance against France at the time of her death. Paul, however, keeping to his policy of doing precisely the opposite of whatever his mother had, first remained neutral, then sided with the reactionary coalition. He then reversed himself, and in 1800 allied with France, in the belief that the ascension of Napoleon Bonaparte to the position of first consul—virtually dictator—would end revolution and restore stability to Europe. It also put Russia at war with its former ally, Great Britain.

By then Paul had alienated nearly everyone from peasants sick of war to nobles angry and fearful of the tsar's shifting policies and mercurial temper. Even his own son, Alexander, plotted against him. In March 1801, the conspirators seized the unhappy tsar from his bed to force him to abdicate. In the scuffle that followed, Paul was strangled with a scarf, his chaotic reign and sad life finally over and his son, Alexander I, firmly on the throne.

Ten months was all Alexander Bakunin could stomach in the service of the capricious, mad tsar, and he had returned to Priamukhino by 1799. Whatever the idiocies of rural life, they had nothing on the idiocies of the court, and Alexander resolved to abandon ideas of service and devote his energies to making the estate profitable. Even with his new resolve, life at Priamukhino was difficult. In a letter to his brother Michael, after nearly a decade on the estate, Alexander warned him off giving up service to return permanently to Priamukhino. Granting his brother that the blossoms of spring awakened nostalgia for the country life, he assured him that the reality of the bucolic retreat was considerably less pleasant. Education in the country was poor; as Alexander put it, moving there meant risking having the children grow up to be "bumpkins." The lack of proper medical attention was a serious concern, as was the lack of cultural life. Furthermore, Priamukhino could not support an extended family.[15]

Despite his gloomy, if realistic, appraisal, by 1801 Alexander's efforts were starting to pay off. His mother inherited several villages and the serfs who lived in them, almost doubling the number of "souls" the family controlled. The debt was reduced significantly, and Alexander made improvements to Priamukhino. A watermill used to grind grain was expanded, a lumber mill was erected, the family house was renovated and enlarged. With the death of his father, Michael, in 1803, Alexander reigned over the estate in name as well as in fact. His mother deeded him the bulk of the estate, much of which she had brought to the marriage, thereby giving him a real and permanent stake in Priamukhino.

It allowed Alexander to put into practice the ideas and ideals he had imbibed as a young man and to return to his plans to reshape Priamukhino. The garden was extended, trees planted, meadows cleared, copses and hedges arranged, and over twelve hundred nonnative species of plants introduced and carefully charted as he drew on his expertise and interest in natural science. Alexander's interests were as much cultural as horticultural. He saw himself as a bridge between two worlds, and consciously set about "grafting foreign shoots to native roots" as he adapted and applied European advances to Russian tradition in a pastoral climate of peaceful coexistence. There were, of course, limits to what was possible, but he turned the constraints to advantage, suggesting both practically and metaphorically, "Aren't huge apple trees better than imported peaches which cannot live outside a greenhouse?" Conspicuous consumption was neither possible nor desirable and Alexander would later take pleasure from that, writing that while the house was large, it was "without parquet flooring; we have no expensive rugs . . . no precious porcelain adorns my board but three or four simple dishes . . . The divan and carved chairs are upholstered in tapestry, and only on great holidays are the covers removed from them. But when, at the evening hour, the whole family is gathered together like a swarm of bees, then I am happier than a king."[16]

His project was a political and cultural one as well. Like many of his generation, Alexander was acutely aware of the problems Russia faced, at least as they applied to his own class. In discussions and writings he called for a reformed judicial system that would end corruption and arbitrary decisions, with laws that would clearly outline the mutual rights, obligations, and responsibilities of subjects and rulers. Property should be protected by law and not subject to seizure by the autocracy, he continued, and the rights of all should be protected from tyranny. The clergy in deeply religious Russia should be cleansed of superstition so that the arts and sciences would not be impeded by outmoded thought, while the economy, chiefly based on agriculture and the export of raw materials, should be modernized so trade and industry could flourish.

Perhaps most trenchant was Alexander's assessment of serfdom, the very basis of Russia and Priamukhino's economy. While he was not prepared to abandon serfdom, he deplored the terrible conditions in which peasants lived. Unlike many, then and now, who blame the poor for their poverty, Alexander understood that it was Russia's own underdevelopment, itself the result of economic and political repression, that was chiefly responsible. Hoping to create a model of enlightened serfdom, he drew up "An Agreement Between Landlord and Peasant" for his own serfs that outlined the mutual rights and responsibilities of each, and even proposed a scheme to give peasants land and hereditary title. That would give them a stake in improving their productivity and remaining loyal to the nation.

But Alexander was no revolutionary. His reforms were largely, if not exclusively, aimed at improving his own lot, and his views on enlightened serfdom did not extend to freeing his "souls" anytime soon. At best, he hoped to create a society in which all classes knew their place and were content to remain there, while contributing happily to the general prosperity. Economic, political, and moral independence were to be encouraged, but this independence would have strict limits. The end he desired was a society where all would cheerfully agree to do things his way and his proposed reforms sought to continue the exploitation of serfs while eliminating the conflict between landlord and peasant. If this seems at once self-serving and naive, undoubtedly it was, in much the same way employers today hope that calling people "associates" rather than "workers" will cause them to identify with the company even while they are paid minimum wage. But it did indicate Alexander's desire to make Priamukhino into a model of progress and tranquility.

Such a project bespoke a broad romantic streak in Alexander Bakunin, as he hoped to use modern ideas and techniques to return to a state of nature and harmony. In 1810, at the age of forty-two, Alexander was swept away with another romantic impulse. He fell in love with Varvara Muravieva, the eighteen-year-old stepdaughter of Pavel Poltoratsky, lord of the neighboring estate. Such a gap in ages was common among the European nobility. The Russian poet Alexander Pushkin was thirteen years older than his partner when they wed in 1831; Michael Bakunin's contemporary and friend Alexander Herzen was the love-child of a forty-two-year-old father and a sixteen-year-old mother. Indeed, it is not uncommon today among royalty. The spread between Prince Charles and Princess Diana was thirteen years, and among the more significant royalty of the entertainment world, larger gaps are common: Cary Grant was thirty-four years older than Dyan Cannon, Michael Douglas is twenty-five years older than Catherine Zeta-Jones, and Celine Dion twenty-seven years younger than her husband.

Alexander and Varvara produced eleven children over the next fourteen years. Large families were not just the result of insufficient birth control. They were common in preindustrial societies, where children were a potential source of wealth and status rather than a net cost. In peasant families, more children meant less work for everyone and a greater chance that someone might make good, while in the nobility they increased the chances for successful marriages and well rewarded service to the regime. Even in industrializing England, the average noble family had six children in this period. In Russia, a higher infant mortality rate due to the greater distances and worse medical care encouraged childbearing. Furthermore, the custom among Russian nobility was to employ wet nurses, which deprived mothers of breast-feeding as an unreliable but statistically significant form of birth control. Two daughters, Liubov and Varvara, were born to the Bakunins in 1811 and 1812; Michael was born in 1814. Then came Tatiana and Alexandra in 1815 and 1816, followed by five boys, Nicholas, Ilya, Paul, Alexander, and Alexei between 1818 and 1823. A year later, another daughter, Sophia, was born but died from dysentery before she was three.

Varvara paid a high price for such fecundity. Michael noted as an adult that while they all adored their father, none of her children loved her, believing her to be vain and selfish.[17] Varvara was often described as a martyr, and certainly she had cause to see herself as such. She was responsible for running the household and tending her mother-in-law. Both duties were tiring, often tiresome, and rarely appreciated. Married to a much older man, exhausted from continuous childbearing, it was hardly surprising that Varvara was thought by her children to be distant and remote. But this was less a personal attitude than the role imposed by society. Russian noblewomen were tightly circumscribed and their behavior was expected to fall within strict limits. While they could own property, it was usually given over to the husband or male children to manage. The household was her sphere, and if some found fulfillment in this, undoubtedly many did not. Their relationship with their children was expected to be restricted and formal. Mothers were rarely closely involved with bringing up the young sons; instead, they oversaw the nurses and governesses who were responsible for training and ensured that the proper values and lessons were learned. Cast as managers and disciplinarians, they sought respect rather than warmth and affection from their children.

This respect was based on the notion of the mother as the embodiment of virtue. Virtue in turn was derived from her sacrifice for the family, in particular the pain of childbirth. The particular status let mothers assert some authority using the tools of the powerless—shame and guilt. Their martyrdom had a deeper social significance as well. In addition to giving women some power in the family, indirect to be sure, it offered them some political status outside the home. Wealth and beauty bestowed status, but so too did virtue, measured in the public realm by devotion to duty and chastity. These in turn were measured by the degree of martyrdom women expressed. The martyrdom of nobles was also a sophisticated way to demonstrate that being rich carried its own burdens and that the nobility, like the peasantry, was making sacrifices for the good of the empire. That it was essentially a fraudulent exercise had no bearing on the intensity of feeling and belief. The melancholy and aloofness of Varvara Bakunin, then, were typical of her class and gender. They undoubtedly made up part of the allure she held for Alexander, for they were among the defining features of the perfect wife of the day.

Unable to exercise power directly in the home or society, even over their own children, manipulation was a fundamental survival tool for noblewomen. Undoubtedly this had an effect on the children, especially since even adult children often depended on their mothers to intercede on their behalf to obtain official favors and aid. In the complex world of Russian autocracy, status, and hierarchy, where harsh rules and the tsar's whim made it necessary to find exceptions and appeals, mothers were often crucial interlocutors who could plead on behalf of their children to win favors at court, ranging from positions in the civil service to release from military service. This combination of shame, guilt, manipulation, and necessity that characterized the relationships of sons and mothers practically guaranteed conflicted relationships. As Michael Bakunin's contemporary and sometimes friend Ivan Turgenev described his own mother, "It was so easy for her to force us to love her and take pity on her." Such a reaction was typical, and Michael was no exception in his conflicted feelings toward his mother. Her behavior also meant that open rebellion against her was difficult and conflicts were likely to be left unresolved. The point to be emphasized, however, is that Michael Bakunin's relationship with his mother was typical of his era and class, while her relative powerlessness was felt more profoundly by her than anyone else.[18]

In the meantime, Alexander determined to make the children part of the liberal experiment at Priamukhino. Inspired by Jean-Jacques Rousseau's *Emile,* Alexander earnestly tried to avoid the mistakes that had turned his own childhood into one of "boredom and captivity." In 1814, the year Michael was born, Alexander crafted his ideas for raising children. In place of his own mother's coldness and his father's rage, Alexander would be warm and kindly. Instead of insisting that his paternal authority be obeyed, he would encourage his children to disagree with him; when it was necessary to instruct or correct them, he would use reason, guidance, and suggestions. Perhaps most striking in Orthodox Russia, he would not insist that his children be religious, but would "only attempt to show them that religion is the only basis for all virtue and our entire good fortune."[19]

His efforts to provide a kind, warm environment for learning were largely successful. Writing near the end of his life in 1871, Michael recalled his father as "a man of much spirit, well educated, even scholarly, very liberal, very philanthropic, a deist not an atheist, a free thinker . . ."[20] The characteristics applied equally to Alexander's principles of pedagogy. The children were given a great deal of liberty, but not license; they were encouraged to express themselves and were treated gently. Tutors were engaged to teach the subjects Alexander could not, and the children had regular lessons in French, English, German, Italian, art, and religion. They read Western literature and philosophy, and took classes in music. Michael proved adept at the violin and had a talent for sketching. While their education was more liberal and progressive than the norm, it was not far different from that of their peers, except in one crucial aspect. Alexander educated his daughters as well as his sons, unlike most Russian nobles who generally restricted their daughters' education to domestic duties, etiquette, and the like.[21]

Michael's earliest writings suggest that he was a well-behaved son, mindful and respectful of his family and custom. He wrote birthday greetings and thank-you notes to family members in a careful, schoolboy's script that was as far from his cramped, illegible adult scrawl as his filial obedience was from his career as a revolutionary. The nine-year-old signed himself "your affectionate and respectful son" as he dutifully wished his father "much happiness" on his birthday. The following year he promised his maternal grandfather that he would always keep his word and would try always to improve himself. In other letters, the young Michael wished his mother well on her birthday, hoped for her speedy recovery from illness, and undertook to work harder at his Latin and arithmetic. Dutiful letters penned in squirming protest under the eye of a stern parent or schoolmaster should not be given too much weight, but little in Bakunin's early life pointed to a later career as a dangerous revolutionary. The family was comfortable, if not wealthy, and the children's upbringing was a model of liberalism.[22]

Yet there was less to this liberalism than met the eye. For despite his best efforts, Priamukhino would be shaped by far more powerful forces than Alexander Bakunin: war, revolution, and the all-pervading rot of serfdom.

2

WAR, SLAVERY, AND SERVICE

The British poet Philip Larkin nicely pointed out the effect that family life has on children. In his poem "This Be the Verse" he concluded, "They fuck you up, your mum and dad."[1] However true this may be—and likely it is self-evident to all adolescents—the ways in which parents warp their children take place within the limits and possibilities of society. Inevitably these are more important than the idiosyncrasies of individuals, for to a large degree they determine behavior and circumscribe choices. Parents and children react to the world they live in. They are formed by it, and their choices are not entirely free, while their virtues and faults both reflect the larger society and are defined by it. To Larkin's imprecation we need to add that of Karl Marx in "The Eighteenth Brumaire of Louis Bonaparte": "Men make their own history, but they do not make it just as they please; they do not make it under circumstances chosen by themselves, but under circumstances directly encountered, given, and transmitted from the past."[2]

One of the circumstances that profoundly affected Russia and Priamukhino was war. In one of those minor coincidences that later generations make into profound ironies, Michael Bakunin was born on 30 May 1814, the day the Treaty of Paris was signed. The treaty was to put an end to the more than ten years of war that pitted France against Russia, Britain, Austria, Prussia, and a host of other nations. Two years earlier, Napoleon's Grande Armee invaded Russia and smashed its way to Moscow, further than Hitler's panzers would make it 130 years later. It would be an exaggeration to argue, as one historian does ruefully, that if not for 1812, there would have been no Bakunin, no Lenin, no Bolshevik revolution.[3] Yet the war and its aftermath would have a greater effect on Michael Bakunin than the mysteries of his id or his relationship with his parents and siblings.

That year of 1812 should have been a good one for Priamukhino. Alexander and Varvara's first daughter, Liubov, was barely a year old, and a second was on the way. They had abandoned the formality and intrigue of court life in Tver and, like Voltaire's Candide, they decided to tend their gardens, as Varvara planted flowerbeds and Alexander transplanted violets. If the estate was not wildly profitable, it was comfortable and stable. More and more Priamukhino became the idyll Alexander hoped to create, a sanctuary from the outside world where peace and harmony could flourish and inspire others.

The outside world, however, was not content to let it be, and the horrors of war that convulsed Europe would soon affect Priamukhino. When the French army crossed into Russia, Alexander, along with other local nobles, was called to the provincial capital to organize evacuation plans and the conscription of peasants. Conscription, however, put lords on the horns of dilemma. Sending off serfs to fight could result in bankruptcy, for who would remain to work the land? Yet who else could be sent to stop the invader? Equally dangerous, a stingy commitment to the war effort was a quick way to lose the favor of the court. After some haggling, the nobles voted to send one male serf out of every twenty-five to the wars. Alexander used the opportunity to dispose of some of his more troublesome peasants, and tried to induce the unproductive household servants to enlist along with them, hoping thus to fulfill his imperial duty while preserving his labor force.[4]

The invasion quickly dimmed Alexander Bakunin's fondness for things French. It was one thing to admire French literature and cuisine, even to toy with the radical implications of French philosophers and revolutionaries and the cry of liberty, equality, and fraternity. But Napoleon represented none of these, and it was something else to face the French artillery, cavalry, and infantry.

For the revolution that had promised freedom and equality in 1789 had devoured its parents and its children by 1794. French moderates sought to crush the sweeping changes that radicals, workers, and peasants fought for, and they used Napoleon's reputation as a war hero and his cannon in their political war. They planned a coup d'etat to oust the radicals from the government, scrap the constitution, and install themselves as an oligarchy, but when the coup was finally launched, the little Corsican general turned on his backers to catapult himself into power and become emperor. Much of his ensuing program reflected the aims of the moderates. Elections were curtailed and the power of the legislature was curbed; strikes and unions were violently suppressed; women were deprived of the property rights and civil liberties they had won; democracy was first stopped and then rolled back. The middle class was now safely protected from the demands of the people and the revolution was stopped.

Russia's relationship with first revolutionary and then imperial France was as twisted and tortuous as events in France itself. Under Paul, Russia treated with France, then fought against her, then settled again. Tsar Alexander was no less torn. He made overtures to the British and strengthened his ties with

France's greatest foe; he also signed a treaty with France, for his primary foreign policy aim was to keep Russia out of war. When Britain and France signed the Treaty of Amiens in 1802, his hope for peace in Europe seemed attained. Then war broke out between the two the following year. Worried by France's advances in Italy and on the Adriatic coast, Russia cautiously sided with Britain; in 1805, Russia formally joined with Britain, Sweden, and Austria against Napoleon in the Third Coalition. Confident of victory, since the combined Austrian and Russian armies outnumbered the French forces, Alexander himself led his army against Napoleon at Austerlitz on 2 December 1805. In the most brilliant battle of his career, Napoleon defeated both armies, killing, wounding, or capturing nearly half of the troops arrayed against him and nearly capturing Alexander himself.

The catastrophic loss at Austerlitz forced Austria out of the war. When Napoleon went on to shatter the Prussian army at the battles of Jena and Auerstadt, Russia stood alone against the triumphant French army. Worse, encouraged by Russia's defeats, the Ottoman Empire declared war in 1806 and forced Alexander to fight on two fronts. He eked out a costly draw at Eylau, then at Friedland lost the second of the best of three falls match. By June Alexander was forced to sign a peace treaty with France.

The terms of the Treaty of Tilsit bound Russia to Napoleon's Continental System, his attempt to blockade and bankrupt Britain. By banning its ships from continental ports, the emperor hoped to cut off Britain's import of vital war supplies and its export of manufactured goods to Europe. Denied these much needed markets, English manufacturers would soon stop producing goods and would fire workers who were no longer needed. That in turn would lead to labor unrest and chaos and would divert attention and troops to the home front. Such a plan might seem far-fetched, especially to those who believe today's working class and trade unions are the last bastions of a blue-collar, hardhat patriotism. But by 1812, Britain deployed more troops pursuing labor radicals and Luddites at home than the Duke of Wellington had to fight Napoleon in Spain.[5]

If the plan seemed sound to Napoleon, it was less useful to his sullen allies. The Continental System meant that, officially at least, Russia could no longer sell wheat, minerals, timber, and hemp—these last two crucial in the age of wooden ships and rope rigging—to Britain. Nor could it purchase British manufactured goods. But France did not step in to buy Russian products; trade with France actually declined. Russian industry, still in its infancy, was unable to supply the country with the manufactured goods it had formerly purchased from Britain. As a result, Russia's imports and exports both fell drastically between 1808 and 1812. That meant that customs revenue, an important source of state income, plummeted and the rouble decreased in value by half. Britain was also the capital for finance, and Russian merchants found credit hard to secure. Even nobles found the system tiresome as the price of imported luxuries such as sugar and coffee shot up by over 500 percent.

As a result, the Continental System blockade leaked like a sieve as enterprising smugglers and neutral vessels happily took advantage of the creaking Russian economy, often with the tacit approval of local authorities and the tsar. This in turn angered Napoleon, who was already annoyed with Russia's limited participation in the war against Austria. Even on the personal level, the two emperors were increasingly hostile as Napoleon jilted Alexander's sister to marry Marie Louise of Austria. Finally, on 23 June 1812, five hundred thousand troops of Napoleon's Grande Armee crossed the Niemen River into Russia.

They had every reason to be confident of victory. Napoleon had defeated virtually every continental army in a series of lightning wars, and of the major powers, only Britain and Russia remained outside his grasp. His plan was to reprise the previous campaigns: a war of mobility and rapid maneuvering leading to an early, decisive battle that would quickly convince the tsar to sue for peace. Such a strategy had made Napoleon the master of Western Europe.

But Napoleon's blitzkriegs were largely forced upon him, for they were the only battles the French army could win. Surrounded by hostile states whose combined armies greatly outnumbered his own, Napoleon had to outmaneuver his opponents quickly. A war of long duration or attrition was impossible for the French to sustain, for they had neither sufficient troops nor adequate supplies. Feeding the army was largely a matter of letting troops forage the surrounding hostile countryside. That worked well enough in the short-term in areas where the land was rich and occupied by producing farmers. But it meant Napoleon had to win quickly and often to keep his opponents off balance, prevent them from coordinating their attacks, and keep the army fed. A fast, furious war was the only kind he could hope to win.

If Napoleon could win only a rapid war, the Russians could survive only by avoiding battle as long as possible. Russia's military was divided into two widely separated armies, each outnumbered by Napoleon's forces, each ready to be smashed in turn. The Russian general staff had no strategy other than to retreat and avoid catastrophe; indeed, it was less a strategy than the only means of survival. It worked, but only just.

As the Russian forces melted away to avoid his knockout punch, Napoleon was drawn farther and farther into Russia. His rapid advance looked like success, and concealed the growing problems. Hoping for a decisive battle at Smolensk, Napoleon pushed on. But the Russians continued their retreat, torching the city as they left, leaving the French army without food or shelter. Its soldiers, most of whom were not French, increasingly discovered that discretion was the better part of valor, and headed for home when they could.

Word of the retreat from Smolensk reached Priamukhino seven days later. Alexander began planning to move the family away to its holdings in Kazan. The next morning, however, Varvara went into labor and could not be evacuated. The family stayed at Priamukhino, though Liubov and her new sister, named after her mother, were soon sent away for safety. Alexander set about forming his serfs into a fighting force of irregulars. Similar bands of partisans harried and harassed the French invaders throughout Russia, cutting supply lines, creating confusion and panic, picking off stragglers, inflicting casualties while avoiding pitched battles, and demoralizing an increasingly dispirited army that could not find a foe to fight and yet could not protect itself.

Meanwhile, the regular Russian forces continued to withdraw and to force the enemy to overextend and overreach. In September, with the Grande Armee approaching Moscow, it was time to make a stand, if only to rally troops and populace alike who grew increasingly dispirited by the constant retreats and ceding of territory to the invader. General Michael Kutuzov engaged the French at Borodino, less than seventy-five miles from Moscow. He could not hope to win, but he turned Napoleon's triumph into a Pyrrhic victory, best described not in military accounts but by Leo Tolstoy in *War and Peace*. Fifty thousand Russians died; about forty thousand of Napoleon's soldiers were killed. The Russians withdrew again, and one week later, on 14 September 1812, the Grande Armee entered Moscow.

Still Alexander refused to treat with Napoleon. Instead, the city was set afire and Napoleon's soldiers found themselves with the fruits of victory literally turning into the ashes of defeat. Unable to obtain food, harassed at every step, their triumph was no nearer than it had been at the banks of the Niemen. On 19 October, Napoleon began the long march back to France, hoping to flee both the Russian army and the Russian winter. Meanwhile, Kutuzov planned his counteroffensive.

The horrors of the French retreat from Russia are well-known. Kutuzov's forces blocked the more fertile southern land and the tattered Grande Armee had to retreat over the earth it had already scoured and that the Russians had scorched. Of the six hundred thousand troops that had ultimately entered Russia, fewer than a hundred thousand straggled back across the Niemen. We might remember that a fighting force today is considered to be effectively unfit for action when its casualties reach 10 percent. By 14 December 1813 the Grande Armee had been pushed back across the Niemen, its orderly retreat collapsed into a rout.

At Priamukhino, the Bakunins rejoiced at the news of the retreat and again tended their gardens, this time in a spirit of celebration rather than contemplation. They planted a grove of linden trees to honor Kutuzov, whom Alexander had met at Tver in 1812, and in the spring put in lilacs and poplars "to remind us of this horrible epoch."[6]

As Napoleon retreated, erstwhile allies broke with him, new coalitions arrayed against him, and the French empire was rolled back on itself. On 31 March 1814, Alexander I, now hailed as the savior of Europe, led his triumphant troops into Paris. Two months later, the Treaty of Paris was signed, signaling the end of war, at least until Napoleon escaped from exile. In far-off Priamukhino, where news of the treaty would not arrive for some time, there was another reason to rejoice: Michael Bakunin, son of Alexander and Varvara, named after his legendary grandfather, was born.

The Bakunins were delighted to have a third child, and in the aftermath of the war, Michael's birth—the first male child, so important in those days— seemed especially cause for celebration. But if Priamukhino and the Bakunin family had avoided the ravages of the war, they would not be spared the repression of the peace.

At the beginning of his reign, Alexander I appeared to be a rational, progressive, humane improvement over his father. As a young man, he had remarked that Russia needed significant political reform, and he assured his subjects that he wished to follow the model of his grandmother, Catherine the Great, rather than his half-mad father, who had been persuaded to do the right thing only by having the oxygen supply to his brain choked off. Certainly the new tsar's early actions were cause for optimism for enlightened nobles such as Alexander Bakunin. The restrictions on foreign travel were relaxed and the censorship of books and journals slackened. There was even reason to hope cautiously that the autocratic rule of the tsar might be eased as Alexander I hinted at the possibility of a Russian constitution and something like the limited parliamentary democracy of France, the United States, and England that represented their bourgeoisie and aristocracy so well.

The sincerity of Alexander I's desire to loosen the strictures of autocratic rule and his ability to institute reforms in the face of the intransigence of the nobility, the bureaucracy, the military, and the peasantry are still debated by historians, but war with France put an end to any progressive ideas he might have had. Some reforms were undertaken during the peace of 1807, but when war with France broke out again in 1812, all the plans were shelved. With the signing of the Treaty of Paris, many hoped that the tsar would turn again to questions of reform, especially to the two pressing matters: greater access to a more open government and serfdom. In the event, Alexander I continued to float ideas, but never tried to implement them. If he was not the reactionary that his predecessor and successor to the throne were, neither was he the visionary the empire had hoped for.

Yet reform was desperately needed. Even in victory, the conflict with France had revealed Russia's relative weakness on the European front. While an optimist might conclude that the war showed Russia could defeat the mightiest army on earth, a pessimist could reasonably argue that Napoleon had made it to Moscow and had been defeated by the weather as much as by the Russian military. In the future, headlong retreat might not prove an effective strategy; at the very least, it was embarrassing. Furthermore, if the *war* with France had taught anything, it was that space was Russia's greatest defense. That meant expansion of the empire, and that increased the need for a larger and more efficient army. Pushing the boundaries of the empire outward for protection, however, brought conflict and competition with other powerful states. As Russia expanded in different directions, it alarmed Austria, Prussia, Persia, and Turkey. Any expansion alarmed Britain, which interpreted every move as a threat to the balance of power on the continent or as a threat to the jewel in the crown: India. The same expansion necessary for defense constantly risked war.

Expansion also meant policing an ever-increasing territory. When the victors finally divvied up the spoils of war, the good news was Russia received the largest share of Poland. The bad news was Russia received the largest share of Poland, a country constantly on the edge of revolt. So too were the other nations subordinated by the Russian empire. Thus the costs of empire expanded along with its territory. Modern armies cost money, and that could come only from the nobles, who in turn extracted it from their peasants. As taxes were raised to pay for defense, the nobility became increasingly alienated from the tsar and the peasantry became increasingly alienated from the nobility. The opposition of the peasants to taxes and conscription meant the army had to be strengthened to meet this internal threat. It was a vicious spiral: the security of the state depended on expansion, but expansion threatened the empire from without and within. Russia was difficult to defend, hard to rule, and nearly impossible to develop.

No one was more aware of the failures of the regime than the nobility. Like Alexander Bakunin, nobles discussed over and over what was to be done. Inspired by the early gestures of Alexander I himself, they understood that a constitutional monarchy would empower them. Thus they talked about the rule of law, made in public by representatives of the people. Their definition of "the people" often varied. Did the empire's peasants count? Others outside the nobility? Non-Russians? Jews? Rarely. So too did their solutions vary. Would petitions to the tsar be considered or would they simply lead to mass arrests? After 1812, the latter seemed more likely. How then would change come about? A coup d'etat? The officers' corps had put Alexander on the throne and presumably could remove him. But should it? Revolution? By whom? Could the officers and nobles link up with peasants? Should they? What did peasants want? Who knew? Who cared?

But talk of coups and revolution, however hypothetical or theoretical, was dangerous. Even barroom speculation on constitutions and limiting the power of the tsar was an invitation to prison. The recourse of many was to form secret societies to discuss reform. In particular, army officers from the nobility, well traveled in the course of chasing Napoleon back to Paris, educated, and dedicated to reform of some sort, began to organize. Bright, articulate, thoughtful, hungry for access to power and change, they drew up plans for constitutions, parliaments, even republics. By 1816 they created a clandestine organization; by 1821 it was large enough to be split into two groups, the Northern Society and the Southern Society. The Southern Society, headed by Colonel Paul Pestel, was more radical, calling for a republic on the American or French model and for the abolition of serfdom. The Northern Society was more moderate, arguing for a constitutional monarchy on the British model. It too called for the abolition of serfdom, but unlike the Southern Society expected peasants either to rent land or to work it as wage laborers.

How to make such changes? The officers had no clue. But when Alexander I died suddenly, far from the capital in 1825, probably from typhoid or malaria, it seemed as though fate had provided an ideal opportunity. Alexander I had no sons, so the next in line was his brother, the Grand Duke Constantine. Constantine, however, refused to take the throne; instead, a third brother, Nicholas, agreed to rule. The confusion emboldened the Northern Society and it decided to act. On 26 December, as guards units were to swear loyalty to Nicholas, the rebel officers hastily mobilized as best they could and soon about three thousand of them formed up in the Senate square of the capital. Once there, however, it was clear they had no idea how to proceed. As officers and nobles, they had little support among the peasants and other groups. Others agreed with their ideals but did not believe in revolution or violence to accomplish them and had no notion of what was going on. Isolated, naive, without effective leadership or plans, the rebels occupied the square and waited.

They were quickly surrounded by troops and officers who remained loyal to the tsar, or at least to their orders. Nicholas desperately wanted to avoid bloodshed on his first day in office, and the two sides faced each other uneasily for several hours. Finally, Nicholas ordered the artillery units drawn up around the square to load their cannons with canister, that is, metal balls or shot in a metal container, designed to spread out like a high powered shotgun blast and inflict maximum damage on human flesh. Twice Nicholas gave the order to fire, and twice he rescinded it. Finally, he gave the third order and the cannon belched smoke and fire and shot into the rebels massed together on the square. Some tried to rally on the frozen Neva River, but the artillery, now loaded with cannonballs, smashed through the ice and plunged many into the water. The rest fled as best they could.

The repercussions of their failure were swift and harsh. Hundreds of the Decembrists, as the rebels became known, were rounded up and interrogated, many by Nicholas himself. A court convicted them without a trial and ordered over one hundred officers exiled to Siberia. More were stripped of their rank and sent to the Caucasus; noncommissioned soldiers were caned, some to death. Five of the leaders were hanged, but such was the inefficiency of the regime even that grisly job was bungled. Three of the nooses slipped, and the victims had to be hanged twice. One broke his leg in the fall, and as he was hoisted up to be hanged again, he summed up the tragedy of his country perfectly. "Poor Russia!" he exclaimed. "Here we don't even know how to hang a man properly."[7]

The failed revolt and the bloody repercussions stunned Russia. Pushkin, who had known two of the hanged men, penned a bitter poem, "To the Emperor Nicholas I":

> *He was made emperor and right then*
> *Displayed his flair and drive:*
> *Sent to Siberia a hundred-twenty men*
> *And strung up five.*[8]

Nicholas I was not content with that. He created a secret police, the notorious Third Section, headed by the grim Count Alexander Benckendorff, who soon set up an extensive network of informers and surveillance, with a special detachment for opening mail. Benckendorff was aided by Admiral

Alexander Shishkov, who as the minister of public instruction insisted that the proper way to instruct the public was to censor reading material. Publishers could be held liable for books that had previously been cleared by the censors if the authorities suddenly changed their minds about what was permissible. Ambiguous passages were to be interpreted in the way most damaging to the regime and treated accordingly. Predating William Safire by more than one hundred years, political conservatism was accompanied by linguistic purity as censors insisted on excruciatingly correct grammar and syntax. Finally, the censor could make "minor" changes without informing the author. So widesweeping were the laws that one censor observed that "even the Lord's Prayer could be interpreted as a Jacobin speech."[9]

The rule of law was adjudicated firmly for subjects but largely ignored when it came to the tsar. Where Alexander I had considered constitutions and written legal codes, Nicholas believed that "the best theory of law is a well-intentioned morality, but it ought to exist in one's head, independent of abstractions, and have as its base religion." A lofty thought, perhaps, but of course in an autocratic state, it meant that law was arbitrary and fickle. Given his belief that no "system could be better than that by which Kings were delegated by Providence to govern the masses," reformers had little enough to hope for. Even travel abroad was restricted, for the tsar feared that "young people return from there with a special spirit of criticism which, perhaps with good reason, makes them find the institutions of their own country inadequate."[10]

If Nicholas was not a complete reactionary, he was close enough for most purposes. The chilly wind of his reaction blew across the empire, even to Priamukhino. The Bakunin family had special reason to be careful under the new regime. Alexander Bakunin was no radical, but he had traveled throughout Europe and had entertained moderate ideas that, in the shadow of the hanged Decembrists, could be misinterpreted. The Decembrists were closer to home than that, however. One of Varvara's childhood friends was a member of the secret society; so was one of Alexander's nephews. Most damning of all, Varvara's second cousin, Sergei Muraviev, was the unfortunate Decembrist who had his leg broken on the scaffold. Rumors dogged Alexander. It was known he had entertained friends and relatives who were connected to the Decembrists; how involved was he personally? In a fragment of his memoirs, Michael Bakunin wrote that his father was a member of the Society of the North and had been asked to become its president several times.[11] Given his age, his politics, and his retreat to the country, the story is unlikely. But perhaps Alexander enjoyed listening to the talk of the younger rebels, encouraging them here, restraining them there, warning them of their folly, enjoying the frisson of revolutionary talk in the comfort of Priamukhino. In any case, security now demanded that the Bakunin family sever its ties with the rebels. The education of his children, always chief among Alexander's concerns, now took a less liberal turn. His sons would be loyal subjects, while for his daughters the future would bring not emancipation, for as he put it in a poem,

> Life at home,
> For woman, as a peaceful angel,
> Keeps the hearth safe under her wings . . .
> [And] unites into a harmonious choir
> Many unanimous voices

Even more ominously, the Bakunins approached Admiral Shishkov for advice on educating their children, and while no record of the conversation has been kept, it is safe to assume he was no Dr. Spock.[12]

Michael himself noticed a radical change after the events of 26 December. "At first," he wrote, "our education was very liberal. But after the disastrous events of the December conspiracy, my father, frightened by the defeat of liberalism, changed his plan. Now he made it a point to make us into loyal subjects of the tsar."[13] It appeared to him as though his father had drawn down an "invisible barrier" and had become afraid of his efforts to educate his family.[14]

As significant an influence on Priamukhino as war and revolution was the economic base of the empire. How goods are produced, exchanged, and consumed, and how the labor of many becomes the profit of a few is crucial to understanding a society. Serfdom, like slavery in the U.S., underwrote the regime. All economic systems have rules that enable certain kinds of behavior and inhibit others. A capitalist business, for example, is always forced to innovate, for if it does not, other firms will. They will be able to produce their competing goods more cheaply and thus increase their sales at the expense of the firm that does not innovate. At the same time, all this innovation is tightly constrained, for its chief objective is not to make a better product or a more useful product or a longer-lasting product. The chief objective of capitalist innovation is to reduce labor costs, either by replacing people with machines or by making people work harder to produce more or by replacing high-paid skilled labor with lower-paid unskilled labor. Products may be better, though that does not happen as often as advertising implies. But simply making the product better for consumers does not give a company enough of a competitive edge. The real competition is in lowering costs, and since it is difficult to lower the costs of raw materials, for these are sold by other capitalists who also seek to make a profit, the company must go after the wages of its workers. Similarly, efficiency may be defined in many ways, but the only one that really counts for the employer is the one that increases profit rather than, say, giving employees shorter hours with more pay. This is the dynamic that makes capitalism so much more productive than other economic systems. At the same time, it means that unemployment and poverty are not, therefore, mistakes or unfortunate happenstances in capitalist societies. They are the logical consequences of the system itself as capitalists follow the rules for success. So too did serfdom have its own economic rules and logic, and these put strict limits on what was possible.

The needs of war and reform that so occupied the tsar, his officers, and the nobility, foundered on serfdom. The Napoleonic wars dramatically proved even to the most hidebound *boyar* that the modern world required modern weapons for a nation to survive. Yet the real problem was not technology. That could be developed or purchased abroad. The real problem was how to pay for the technology and the productive capacity that made it possible to compete with the most efficient economies. Modernization was not primarily about technology. It was about creating an economy that could sustain it and use it effectively. Certainly Russia lacked the armaments factories, transportation networks, and textile mills of Britain and France, but more fundamentally, it lacked the economic base to build them and the political superstructure to encourage and sustain them. In short, what Russia needed to compete with the most productive economies was capitalism and a corresponding political system that would enable capitalists to put all the powers of the state, from taxation to tariffs, from borrowing capacity to determining spending priorities, and from military defense to policing the population, at their disposal. This was the advantage France, Britain, and increasingly Prussia, had over Russia.

What was this capitalism then? Modern economists often cloud the issue. Their role, after all, is to defend capitalism, and that means denying its essential, exploitative nature. Capitalism is not the same as trade and markets. Markets have, after all, existed in virtually every society, and few of these can be historically described as capitalist. Nor is capitalism primarily about competition, for this too predates capitalism. It is not primarily about technology or invention, though these certainly accompany it. They are, however, effects, not causes. Nor is capitalism necessarily about manufacturing and heavy industry: Agriculture was the first sector to become capitalist in England and France.

The primary element of capitalism is wage labor. It is this that makes capitalism what it is. To create capitalism, it is not enough to have capital and capitalists. It is necessary to have workers, that is, a landless population that must go to work for the capitalist. In Russia, it meant turning peasants into wage laborers. Such a task, however, meant nothing less than destroying the very economic system that was the basis of Russian society. Therein lay the real challenge of reform: how to force the economy to evolve from one based on the exploitation of serfs to one based on the exploitation of workers without destroying the aristocracy, the tsar, and the social fabric along the way. For peasant-based economies could not compete effectively with capitalist ones based on wage labor. As a method for funneling wealth from peasants to lords, serfdom was effective enough for hundreds of years. When placed in competition with the new capitalist economies, however, it lagged behind.

Serfdom worked very differently than capitalism: the rules were different and so the conflicts and problems were very different. Profit in a capitalist system is easily explained. The employer owns and controls the coffee shop or factory where production takes place and determines who will be hired and fired and how things will be produced; that's what it means to be a "boss." Workers produce goods or services for their employer. Everything that they produce on the job belongs to the capitalist: workers have no more right to the coffee or cars they produce than someone off the street. Their employer, protected by law and by the apparatus of the state, owns all they produce. The employer then sells the goods that have been produced and gives the workers a portion of the value they have created. Capitalists and workers fight over the precise amounts of this portion, but the capitalist system is based on the notion that the capitalist owns everything that is produced and controls how everything is produced.

Under serfdom, exploitation was even more obvious and direct. Peasants produced an amount of goods and a percentage was handed over, either voluntarily or at the point of a sword, to the nobles and the church. Certainly some wealth trickled back down, in the form of churches and mills and so on, but the system existed to let nobles and clergy and state enrich themselves from the labor of the peasant. Intricate rationales were developed to "prove" the necessity and virtue of the arrangement, and peasants could sometimes exert countervailing pressure if the rate of exploitation was too high, but the basic fact of the system was the funneling of wealth from the mass of people at the bottom to an elite at the top.

Other classes did exist, including a middle class composed of artisans, professionals, and merchants, and there was a great deal of variation and even overlapping within each of the classes. But the relationship between lords and peasants was the important one, for peasants made up the largest segment of the population and produced most of the wealth, while the nobles, including the tsar, received most of that wealth.

A small number of Russian peasants were self-sufficient and independent, scratching out a subsistence living on their own land. The vast majority, however, lived on and farmed land owned by someone else. About 40 percent were state peasants who handed over their produce directly to the tsar. The majority, nearly 60 percent, were serfs, that is, humans owned privately by nobles such as the Bakunins. They were bound by law to a particular lord and plot of land; so too were their descendants. Some worked the fields, while others might work as shoemakers, blacksmiths, or domestic servants. Peasants paid rent to the owners, usually in *barshchina,* that is, direct labor for the owner, or in *obrok,* payments in kind from the produce of the farms.[15]

Owners had practically unlimited control over the lives of their serfs. Even a benevolent man such as Alexander Bakunin was, as Michael observed, "master of about two thousand slaves, male and female, with the right to sell them and beat them, to send them to Siberia or into the army, and above all, to exploit them without mercy, or, simply put, to plunder them and live off of their forced labor."[16]

However, this power over their lives and labor did not generally extend to authority over how the peasants worked. Peasants did not own the land, but they occupied it and farmed it with little interference. Rarely did the lord directly supervise the work in the fields; this was usually left to the peasants themselves, organized into the *mir,* or commune. This gave them a great deal of control over how work was done and how much was done. Absentee landlords were often happy, or forced, to leave the peasants to decide what was to be done and how. Decisions about which family would work which fields, or how the commune would meet its obligations to the lord were made not on the basis of what would be most profitable but what would be most fair for all. The *mir* took into account the individual circumstances that affected each household as work was assigned. Larger families, for example, might be given larger plots; families laid low by illness might have some of their work taken up by others. Most often, it meant regularly redistributing the land to ensure that no one was permanently stuck with poor fields or received an unfair advantage. Because they controlled and worked the land, peasants believed that it was theirs in a very real sense, even though formal ownership was acknowledged to reside with the lord. As a result, lords often viewed the peasant commune itself as an impediment to "modernization."[17]

Since surpluses were handed over to the lord, there was little incentive to produce more or to produce more efficiently; only a fool would knock himself out to benefit the Man. Nor were peasants inclined to adopt innovative farming techniques eagerly advocated by lords who hoped to increase productivity. While peasants were often chastised for their ignorance, stubbornness, clinging to hidebound traditions, and a general reluctance to "modernize," their refusal to change was a completely rational response. Untried techniques were risky; the lord, who did not know the land, might be inspired by the latest fad or book on agriculture, but had little practical knowledge. If the new, unproved farming methods failed, it would be the peasants, not the lord, who would starve. However inefficient the old techniques might be, their worth was obvious, for they had maintained the peasant family for generations. The same could not be said for the new notions of the lord.

Thus innovations by the lord were viewed with the same suspicion that time management and new managerial techniques are viewed with by workers today. Inevitably these aim to make employees work harder, longer, and faster, while the benefits of increased efficiency and productivity flow upward to management and shareholders. The most barbaric and humiliating techniques, ranging from the Wal-Mart cheer to the speed-up, are always introduced with smarmy promises that everyone will benefit from taking them up. Peasants, no less than workers today, were justifiably suspicious of the bright ideas and the enthusiastic exhortations of those who stood to gain from intensifying work without ever having to perform any of it.

Because peasants controlled how work was done, it was difficult for lords to squeeze more rent or work out of them. As a result, it was difficult to accumulate the surpluses needed to revamp production. Nor could payments in kind be used to invest in new equipment for farming or small industry: foreign manufacturers and suppliers demanded payment in cash, not chickens, however plentiful. Capitalism requires capital, and that generally meant selling something on the world market. Realistically, for Russia that meant selling grain, especially wheat. But again, production was difficult to control and boost. Peasants could not simply be directed to stop producing for their own subsistence to grow wheat instead, for without their own gardens, they would starve. If some lords cared little about this, most could see that killing off their serfs would soon result in their own starvation. Diverting peasant labor to cash crops then required first an agricultural revolution, either in technology or in technique or in turning serfs into farm wage laborers or all three, to produce more food with less labor, thus freeing serfs to work on the market crops. And that of course ran straight into the peasants' well-justified distrust of "modern" ideas that were too often divorced from reality and were obvious attempts to extract more labor.

Therefore, attempts to "westernize," "modernize," or "industrialize"— more accurately, to impose capitalist relations on the Russian peasantry—often foundered. A lord could strive to intensify the labor practices, and many tried. Using what one author has termed "repressive modernization," some forced peasants to adopt new methods. One of the foremost advocates of innovation and progress as practiced in England and Germany found especially creative ways to encourage his serfs to change their habits. Chief among his inducements were throwing them bound hand and foot into hot water and smearing them with blistering hot tar and feathers.[18] However useful such techniques might have been in the short term, there were practical limits to them. Physical coercion tended to make peasants work only hard enough to avoid punishment and to inspire them to find other ways to resist. Peasants could be very good at playing dumb. New tools might "accidentally" be left outside and ruined; "clumsy" and costly "mistakes" might be made. At the very least, increased supervision and control over the peasants was expensive and time-consuming, with no guarantee that these costs would actually be made up through increased production. Peasants believed they had the right to protest rates of exploitation that exceeded their sense of the moral economy, and they exercised that right even in the face of harsh punishment.

Their ultimate form of resistance was the specter of open revolt. Peasants vastly outnumbered lords and made up over 85 percent of the population. They were also concentrated. Most American slaveowners owned fewer than twenty slaves. In comparision, a Russian noble who owned twenty male souls was considered a small holder. Many Russian nobles had one thousand or more serfs; in 1860, only one American owned one thousand slaves. There was more than sheer numbers to worry about. Peasants had risen up in the past. Thousands joined the Don Cossack Stenka Razin in 1670-1671 to seize land and massacre lords and nobles. In the end, two hundred thousand peasants formed a rebel army that roamed the countryside, burning manors and crops and massacring lords and nobles. Eventually defeated and beheaded, Razin and his promise of freedom lived on in peasant folklore. Within living memory was the revolt led by Yemelian Pugachev between 1773 and 1775. Again peasants organized an army, sacked towns, and put the countryside to the torch along the Ural and Volga rivers, even threatening

WAR, SLAVERY, AND SERVICE **37**

Moscow itself at one point. They announced the abolition of serfdom and the expropriation of land for peasants, and called for peasants to execute nobles and government officials. Defeated because of the movement's lack of cohesion and discipline, the *Pugachevshchina* still stood as a powerful reminder of the limits of noble rule. Even a relatively benevolent noble such as Alexander Bakunin worried that his serfs would use Napoleon's invasion of Russia as an opportunity to rise up, and the tsar was forced to divert many of his troops to forestall a peasant revolt. Only when Napoleon refused to free peasants and seized their crops and animals did they discover their patriotism and form the backbone of the partisan resistance and the army itself.

No, the trick was to make peasants work harder by turning them into wage workers. As Karl Marx put it, the secret was to find a way for "great masses of men [to be] suddenly and forcibly torn from their means of subsistence, and hurled as free and 'unattached' proletarians on the labor market. The expropriation of the agricultural producer, of the peasant, from the soil, is the basis of the whole process."[19] The key to Britain's success was not in technology or innovation or scrimping and saving to raise capital. It was in forcing peasants off the land they possessed to work for wages for those few who owned the land. That allowed owners to direct production as they saw fit, using the methods and processes they decreed. It allowed them to force workers to produce not for their own subsistence but for the market. It allowed them to divert workers from the land to other forms of production, such as textiles, and it allowed for the efficient accumulation of capital for investment.

This process had begun in England in the fifteenth century as the notorious enclosures converted common property into the private property of the lords, who could then evict peasants and replace them with sheep whose wool was more profitable. By the time of the industrial revolution, roughly the 1780s, there was no English peasantry to speak of. Instead of peasants, England had free laborers—free, that is, in two senses. First, they were not slaves or serfs; they were no longer attached to the soil or to a particular lord, or bound by the rules of guilds that established limits to their labor. In this positive sense, they were now free agents. But more important, they were also "free" from the land, their traditional means of supporting themselves. Now they had to sell their labor to someone else if they were to survive. That someone else was the owner of the land or factory, and ownership meant he would determine how work would be done and at what rate. Furthermore, all the production of capitalist farms and factories belonged to the owner to do with as he pleased. All he owed his workers was a wage that represented only a fraction of the wealth the workers had produced.

Thus Russian nobles read Adam Smith carefully for suggestions and clues. But creating capitalism required sweeping changes that were not easily made. Nowhere had it evolved simply and easily. Peasants were expropriated, native people massacred, and populations enslaved to create capitalism. In Russia, it amounted to asking lords and serfs to abolish themselves, or more accurately, their way of life, with no real alternative in hand. Voluntary attempts most often failed. When Alexander I changed the laws to allow nobles to free serfs and provide them with land, few took him up on the offer. Whatever they thought about serfdom, and many nobles, including Alexander I, sincerely believed it was immoral, the law was roughly the equivalent of the U.S. president signing a bill to allow General Motors to transform itself into a worker-owned collective if it wants to. Even those nobles who were especially keen to abolish serfdom had no effective way to do it and maintain their way of life during the period of transition. One sincere but misguided reformer announced his bold new plan to his peasants: they would be set free and could rent half of his land for their own use while working the other half for wages. Not surprisingly, the peasants respectfully requested that things be left as they were.[20]

It was in this light that Alexander Bakunin wrote an "Agreement between Landlord and Peasant" that outlined his own vision of how a more harmonious—and profitable—relationship between the classes might work. It is striking in its naivete. Under this ideal arrangement, peasant families were to be given about forty acres of land for their own, with hereditary title. This sounded like incredible bounty at a time when the average "soul" was lucky to have eight acres to till for his own needs. It was not, however, a gift, and it was intended to reinforce rather than weaken noble privilege, for the lord would receive one-third of all that was produced on this land—a harsher toll than under serfdom. In theory, peasants would work harder and more productively on their own land, thus creating more wealth for the lord, and the land would be exempt from redistribution by the commune. Indeed, one of the purposes of such a policy was to destroy the peasants' attachment to the commune and replace it with an attachment to Russia, and presumably, the new property relationship. Bakunin believed that as independent tenant farmers, the former serfs would have a stake in Russia, for "without hereditary tenure there is no property, without property—no citizenship, and if a farmer is not a citizen, then he is a prisoner, and what then is the Fatherland?" That the basic exploitation of the peasant would continue seemed to have escaped Alexander in his attempt to create loyal, more profitable "citizens." His dream, one shared by many nobles of his day and many capitalists of ours, was to create happy, hardworking, peaceful people who joyfully and freely worked hard to create prosperity for their masters and employers. It was a plan to reduce conflict between the classes, to create, as Alexander Bakunin put it, a society where "all private wills should agree," without, however, removing the root cause of conflict: the exploitation of the peasant.[21]

Political questions no less than economic questions rested on serfdom. When nobles spoke of liberty, often they meant their liberty from the traditions, customs, and laws that protected serfs from the harshest exploitation. What lords wanted was the right to do as they wished with the land, regardless of the wishes of peasants. Some hoped to obtain all the property for themselves, to control as well as own; others thought it preferable to have peasants own their own plots, believing they would be more productive if working their own land while still allowing the lords to skim from the top. Both cases required legal changes, and that meant changes in the political order so the nobility might press its case more effectively. A state where lords made up the parliament or constituent assembly or duma was more likely to do what they wanted than a tsar who had to listen to competing interests, including his own.

The nobility also sought political change so state resources could be allocated differently. Capitalist industry requires a huge investment in infrastructure, and private enterprise always insists that the state tax the rest of the population so business may be spared the expense. But with 50 percent of its annual budget going to the military, Russia did not have sufficient resources to hand out largesse to capitalists and nobles eager to become capitalists. Given the strains of empire, this was impossible as long as the tsar spoke for himself and not for business. Even if the tsar wanted to make such changes, he could not simply impose his will on nobles and peasants. Many nobles were content with the system and saw no need for change, while the tsar could not afford to alienate one group at the expense of another; he had only to reflect on the murder of his own father to recall the danger of acting without support.

Round and round it went. Every way Russia turned, it was blocked and hampered. Everyone was for reform, but no two parties could agree on what exactly that meant. What peasants meant by abolishing serfdom was quite different from what lords meant, and any change risked upsetting a very wobbly applecart. With no consensus on how to proceed, even the tsar was hamstrung. If he tried to institute change from above, say by creating a modern bureaucracy that would ease Russia into abolishing serfdom, he would alienate the lords who relied on patronage and favor rather than merit. If he left reform to the nobles, it would be a patchwork affair that would weaken the central power and risk the collapse of the empire. Leaving the serfs to the tender mercies of the lords risked another *Pugachevshchina;* after all, even the most generous "soul" would stand for only so many tarrings on the way to modernity.

Priamukhino too faced such dilemmas. Alexander Bakunin understood that political and philosophical ideals paled beside economic realities. What use, after all, were "needles when there was nothing to sew?" he asked rhetorically.[22] Yet he was keen to offer prescriptions for Russia: the legal system needed to be revised and cleaned of corruption; in particular, it had to secure the right to property. The rights and responsibilities of tsar, nobles, and peasants should be carefully outlined, and tyranny banished. In practice, however, Alexander Bakunin was no more able to reform Priamukhino than Alexander I was able to reform Russia. The conundrum of reform proved too much for both, and both soon abandoned it. If Bakunin first tried to reconcile his ideals with reality by changing reality, he ended up by changing his ideals to conform with reality. There was no easy way out of serfdom for lord or peasant. Serfdom then had to be reinvented, at least on the intellectual plane, and Bakunin proved up to the task. In another poetic venture, he defended serfdom as the natural order:

> I don't know why our know-it-alls
> Call them slaves—
> By feasible daily labor
> They pay their regular rents
> And having their own plot in exchange,
> Fields, meadows, livestock, a house,
> They are just the same as their masters,
> The masters of their own daily lives.[23]

His son Michael made a more trenchant observation. In his memoirs he wrote, "My father was fully conscious of this immorality [of serfdom], but, being a practical man, he never spoke to us of it, and we were ignorant of it for a very long time." The evil of serfdom could not be so easily escaped through ignorance, however, and ran through Russia and Priamukhino like a syphilis spirochete, working its damage largely unnoticed for years while its victims treated only the most glaring manifestations with palliatives as they ignored the fundamental disease. As a result, Michael wrote, "my moral education was warped by the fact that my entire material, intellectual, and moral existence was based on the crying injustice, the absolute immorality, of the enslavement of our peasants who furnished our leisure."[24] Michael was writing about Priamukhino, but his observation applied equally to all of Russia.

There were more immediate effects as well. The peculiar institutions of the Russian empire meant there were few options for the men and women of Michael's generation. Given an excellent education at home, there was little opportunity to use it productively. For young men of Michael's age, there were really only three choices: managing the estate, entering the civil service of the tsar, or joining the military. His father decided Michael would enter the military, and at fourteen he was packed off to artillery officer school in St. Petersburg. He went willingly, to please his father and because there were few options. The decision would have large ramifications for Michael, his family, and Europe.

3

RULES, REBELLION, AND ROMANCE

If politics is the art of the possible, even the tsar had little to work with; bound by serfdom, Russia was a country of few options or choices. For all Alexander Bakunin's liberal ideas of education and idylls of Priamukhino, he had no thought of any career for his eldest son save service to the state. Court favors and military pay were essential to maintain the family's status and wealth. Tradition insisted that the eldest son go to the military, and Alexander arranged for Michael to go to St. Petersburg to prepare for the entrance examinations necessary for admittance to the Artillery Cadet School. He commemorated the event with a poem:

> *Misha [Michael] I sent away to [military] school.*
> *Young boys must become men*
> *And be sons of the Fatherland*
> *Fearing only of their consciences,*
> *And serving the Tsar faithfully.*
> *For them—the broad realm of service.*[1]

While one hopes this loses a little something in the translation, Alexander's intent was clear. After a tearful going-away party for the fourteen-year-old boy at the end of November 1828, Michael set out for the city. In an era before asphalt, rubber tires, shock absorbers, and Preparation H, the carriage trip from Priamukhino was an adventure in itself. Until the railway was built in the 1850s, it took the tsar himself, mustering all the resources of the Russian military and propelled by *raisons d'etat* as well as horses, about forty hours to cover the 460 miles between Moscow and St. Petersburg. While the Bakunins had less distance to travel and could take a more leisurely pace, it was not a journey to be taken lightly. Visits with relatives along the way made it less arduous as the young lad was fussed over and congratulated. He was looking forward to visiting the capital of the empire, and upon his arrival in St. Petersburg, he teased his sisters in a letter by allowing that the mighty Neva River that ran through the city was "a little different" from the quiet, meandering Osuga of home. They could take some comfort, however, in the knowledge that the gardens of Priamukhino were much more beautiful than those of the capital. Michael passed the entrance exams, and his mother was quick to announce that "Michel's future is decided: he is to serve in the artillery."[2]

While strictly accurate, her prophecy would not be fulfilled in quite the way she hoped. St. Petersburg was, and is, filled with art, culture, excitement, and intrigue. Little of this, however, was available to the young Bakunin. The intellectual action happened at the universities, not the military academies; the interesting possibilities of the city, at least those of interest to a young man from the country, happened in spite of bureaucracy, not because of it. As the capital of the empire, St. Petersburg tended to emphasize the regime's bureaucratic face, as capitals often do. No one, after all, has ever accused Washington, D.C., of being a "city that never sleeps" and the torpor of Bonn was legendary. Nicholas I was dull, rigid, and conservative, and had no patience with unorthodoxy or abstract thought or controversy. His ideology was orthodoxy, autocracy, and nationality, that is, obedience and loyalty to the church, the tsar, and a romanticized notion of "the people." Official St. Petersburg did its best to deliver these up, and officers' school was hardly the place to find a vibrant counterculture.

At the same time, St. Petersburg was a big, modern city, and the shock registered by country-raised nobles upon encountering it is a standard motif in Russian literature. Built on the banks and islands of the Neva River, the city is rightly known as the Venice of the north. But *neva* is the Finnish word for "swamp," and like all European cities of the day, it had little in the way of public sanitation. Animal and human waste was dumped into the streets and the alleys, where it froze during the winter. Spring thaw happens quickly in St. Petersburg, often overnight, and the new season was announced with an assault on the senses. Michael, fresh from the country and more than a little homesick, noted sarcastically that the "charms of the city in springtime" were mud and stench, so unlike the blossoms of Priamukhino.[3]

Education too suffered by comparison with home. Michael lived in St. Petersburg with his aunt and uncle Nilov before attending school, and their ideas on the education of young nobles differed considerably from those of Alexander Bakunin. He had stressed freedom and paid little attention to formal religion. Michael had received some religious instruction, but the chief benefit he took away from the lessons was a fondness for the sweets brought by the priest. The teaching itself had little impact, "neither positive nor negative, on my heart or my spirit," he wrote, and Bakunin remained indifferent at best and skeptical at worst—or perhaps the other way around—to the claims of religion even as a young man.[4]

Uncle Nilov, however, insisted that Michael be given an orthodox religious education to undo the damage caused by the freethinking Alexander. He assigned Michael to read the *Cheti Minei,* an eighteenth-century telling of the lives, exploits, and miracles of Russian saints. Worse, he expected his nephew to believe the ridiculous stories and legends. Not surprisingly, the effect on the young cadet was to kill off whatever religious sentiment he still had.[5]

Military school and life in the barracks freed Michael from his overbearing uncle and aunt, and exposed him to new subjects to study. Other than that, it was hardly an improvement. The army's ranks were filled with peasant conscripts who resented their twenty-five-year term of service and the officers who could turn a life sentence into a death sentence through whim, duty, or incompetence. Discipline was harsh and severe corporal punishment, often fatal, was administered for trivial offenses. Even in peacetime, men were paid poorly and were expected to scavenge and purchase much of their food themselves. Eighty-five years after Michael Bakunin joined up, life in the Russian army was still so frightful that a young man named Chomsky decided to flee his homeland rather than serve; as a result, his son Noam would be born in the United States.[6]

The resentment at the bottom flowed from the incompetence and inertia at the top. Little interested in the philosophy or grand strategy of warfare, Nicholas I was obsessed with the minutia of drill, parades, regulations, and uniforms. To be sure, drill was important for all European armies in this period. The standard military tactic was the concentrated musket volley, and that required moving large numbers of troops into precise position. Once there, they had to load, aim, and fire their weapons in the same direction at the same time, ideally with the first rank then crouching down to reload so the next could fire over their heads, and so on. The impact on the enemy was significantly lessened if the timing was off by a second or so and the deeper ranks blew the heads off their comrades in front. Yet even by the requirements of the day, the Russian army was noted for its intense, not to say neurotic, devotion to drill.

This reflected Nicholas's personality but it was also forced on the army by the economic strain of the empire. The military was necessary for the survival of the regime, but it was also bankrupting it. Russia's serf-bound economy meant the army had to rely on older technology; it could not innovate on the same scale as the English and French empires. As a result, the Russian military had to rely on masses of troops to outnumber and overwhelm the enemy. That required levies of serfs to fill the ranks, more weapons, and higher taxes to pay for it all. But taking labor and capital out of productive enterprise and putting it in the army crippled the economy. That made it impossible to modernize the army and so the problem continued to replicate itself.[7]

Officers fared better than enlisted men, but their life in the service held no guarantees of success or prosperity. Desperate to economize, the state expected its officers to supply much of their own food, even in combat. The job paid poorly: an ensign might have been paid 440 roubles a year at a time when tea sold for ten roubles a pound. A major-general in the cavalry might have pulled down eight thousand roubles a year, but had to pay for expensive dress uniforms, supply the officers' mess, and cover incidental job expenses, such as his horse, out of that sum. Promotion brought higher pay, but rising through the ranks was not easy, for a successful officer needed family connections and patrons as much as ability. Promotion also required new positions to be available, and so rapid career advancement for the unconnected officer depended on slaughter on the battlefield. Such job openings were a good bet once hostilities began, but even the least self-reflective graduate of Nicholas's mind-numbing schools could soon figure out that promotion was likely to be a good news/bad news story with the potential for a fairly nasty punch line.

The vastness of the empire that required such a large and expensive military meant that it was impossible to supply the army properly with arms, food, or medical supplies. Even victory came at a high price. The casualty rate of Russian soldiers during the eleven-hour battle at Borodino, for example, was not equaled until the battle of the Somme in 1916, where it took all the techniques of modern industry to set new records of death and destruction. The lack of food and medicine meant Russian soldiers were killed by disease at a rate double that of other European armies. A glorious death, or, even better, a glorious though not disfiguring wound acquired while leading valiant and snappily dressed troops in the service of the Tsar of All the Russias was one thing. Facing death doubled over a makeshift latrine while shitting your guts out with dysentery or typhoid or cholera was something else again.[8]

To create officers to serve in such an army, officer training schools used much the same brutal techniques to train the sons of the nobility as the military used to train peasant soldiers. The nature of military education is to remove observable differences from a large, disparate group of individuals—after all, they're called "uniforms" for a reason. Hierarchy, exaltation of the unit, the service, and the nation, and unquestioning obedience have long been deemed crucial to the making of an efficient, effective army. Idiosyncrasies, original thinking, and flouting of rules may be tolerated if they are confined to the battlefield and are successful, but expressions of individuality and creativity are generally knocked out of recruits and students. What is required is obedience and complete interchangeability among officers and troops. The emphasis on perfecting meaningless rituals from spit-shining shoes to saluting is designed to inculcate these characteristics. No one needs discipline to agree with a reasonable or useful suggestion, after all. Discipline is necessary to make people obey unreasonable, inhumane, and dangerous orders that benefit someone else. The irony in our modern, free nations is that soldiers are ordered to fight for democracy while being denied any experience of the concept. Such reflection, however, was no more welcome at the St. Petersburg artillery school than it is at West Point.

When Michael Bakunin attended, Russian military schools were entrusted to the direct control of Nicholas I's brothers, first Constantine and later Michael. The latter was considered "a petty and pedantic representative of the most narrow-minded military formalism," and the schools reflected this. Such formalism was more than the tsar's whim or military necessity; it was a calculated policy for political ends. Nicholas I was determined that future officers would not repeat the treason of the Decembrists. The best way to do that, he believed, was to stifle independent thinking and "infection" from the West. "Intellectual dressage," not creativity, was the goal. This goal was accomplished with unforgiving codes of discipline, unbending attention to tiny details of dress and drill, and stifling regimentation. The purpose was to drive out free thought and to train cadres of conservative, loyal, and conformist officers.[9]

Thus, minor infractions were met with harsh, arbitrary, and swift punishment designed to break the spirit and instill unquestioning subordination. Officer cadets could be confined to barracks, stuck on endless, meaningless guard duty, jailed, beaten, and lashed for breaking the smallest of regulations. Running the gauntlet may be a quaint schoolboy penalty today, but in Bakunin's time it could be fatal, for it meant receiving as many as five thousand kicks and punches from men who desired to appear highly motivated in front of their officers. So fearsome was the corporal punishment meted out for trivial offenses that it was not uncommon for erring students to attempt suicide rather than face the terrible penalty that awaited them. As the historian John Keep has observed, "it is hard to overestimate the psychological impact of the educational experience which young men went through" in the tsar's officer schools; his observation that induction to the military was a "traumatic experience" sounds almost charitable. Even Nicholas's own mother worried that military life would "coarsen" her little brute and make him a "brusque and crude" fellow. The cadet schools were one reason the

Russian nobility was increasingly disinclined to see military service as a fitting career choice. Believing themselves to be the carriers of civilized virtue and values, they saw the barbaric conditions in the schools and in the field as an assault on their dignity and privilege. Even Alexander Bakunin admitted privately that the military "schools were insufficient for the education of all noble children," but saw no alternative for his son.[10]

The system worked well enough on Michael in the beginning. As a young cadet, he thrilled to Pushkin's patriotic poem, "To the Slanderers of Russia." While Pushkin had written poetry radical enough to get himself exiled, this poem was a revanchist defense of Russia's brutal suppression of the Polish uprising in 1831. Suggesting that Western Europeans hated Russia because it had stood up to Napoleon and "did not acknowledge the insolent will / Of him under whom you quaked," the poet warned them that if they attempted to intervene and to send armies to defend the Poles, "There's room for them in Russia's fields / 'Mid graves that are not strange to them." The jingoistic verses appealed to the young Bakunin, who found them "delightful, full of fire and true patriotism." Noting that the original title had been "Verses on the Address of General Lafayette," Bakunin went on to denounce the hero of the American and French revolutions as an "old babbler" who tried to shake up the Russians with his nonsense. With what would prove to be delicious irony, he denounced Lafayette as a "destructive spirit."[11] Such sentiments from the pen of the man who would later pledge his life to the overthrow of all tsars and kings were testimony to the values his father had worked hard to instill and the commitment of the cadet school to drive out independent thought from the heads of its students.

Michael's letters home faithfully detail his studies, outline the workings of the school and its chain of command, and reproach his sisters and brothers for not writing more often. But the letters soon reveal his discontent. As time went on, he became more and more disillusioned with the school. Soon he was writing his sisters of how he envied his siblings at home who could play with each other under the warm gaze of their parents. About to turn seventeen, the boy who once eagerly looked forward to traveling to the capital now longed for home, eager to give up any dreams of travel to foreign cities "for the chance to spend my life with those dear to my heart."[12]

Yet we should not make too much of his claims or accept that his experience was as traumatic as he sometimes averred and his critics have insisted. It was a common enough experience, and the theme of the lost happy childhood later became a staple in Russian literature.[13] Even the letters in which he was most emphatic about his isolation at school were calculated attempts to wheedle sympathy and money from his family. The art of the money-from-home letter lies precisely in suggesting one is bearing up admirably under tremendous strain, oh, and by the way, a few roubles would let me ace the exams. Bakunin hardly invented the genre, but he was an able practitioner.

He even found some small ways to resist the authority and discipline of the school. In any institution that demands obedience and punishes those who don't obey or who cannot feign enthusiasm convincingly, passive-aggressive behavior is a common response. Indeed, the term was originally created by the U.S. War Department to categorize and stigmatize soldiers who responded to the banality and insanity of military life through performing at less-than-peak levels, procrastinating, sulking or arguing, doing inefficient work, complaining about demands superiors think reasonable, "forgetting" obligations, resenting useful suggestions, or criticizing authority figures. Anyone who has been a parent, boss, or teacher will immediately recognize these "symptoms" as the commonplace, if irritating, resistance employed regularly by their subordinates. At the same time, anyone who has been a child, employee, or student will recognize the categorizations as the inappropriate labeling of perfectly reasonable behaviors as pathology when they are simply a way of registering resistance to unreasonable, irritating, undemocratic, and arbitrary authorities who have considerable power to punish. It is a way of preserving some shred of autonomy in the face of tyranny, of mounting some small resistance that acknowledges the tyrant's ability to punish while rejecting his right to command. Restaurant workers spit in the soup and more; those who lack imagination may rent the movie *Fight Club* for details. Soldiers "soldier" on the job, and young men in military school take their opportunities where they find them.

In time-honored tradition, Michael and his fellow students complained about their teachers and officers, blew off exams, avoided studying until the last minute, and promoted vague physical symptoms to major disease status to avoid unpleasant duties. Michael pulled all-nighters to make up for slacking off during the year, only to fall back into sloth after passing the exams. "During the three years of my studies at school, I hardly did anything," he confessed. "I worked only during the last month of each year in order to pass the exams."[14]

There were more open acts of resistance, though none stand out as particularly strident. Early in 1830, Michael's second year at the school, one of the students was sent ten roubles. He set out to hand it over to the officer in charge of his division, according to the regulations, but was intercepted by the junior officer of the day, who took the money, claiming he would turn it over to the proper authority. The cadets were skeptical and started jeering. The day officer complained to his superior who called in the colonel-general, who demanded to know who had shouted. No one answered. Finally all the cadets in that section were confined to quarters over the holidays. Michael had not taken part in the shouting, but refused also to inform on his comrades and with them was confined to quarters. "I would rather be wrongly punished," he wrote, "than commit such a sordid act" as informing.[15]

The following year a number of the cadets were confined to quarters for protesting the injustices and the brusque, offensive manner of their officers by complaining loudly and boisterously. Michael's own response was more muted, at least as he told the story to his parents, but he was still confined to quarters for a day. Another weapon of self-defense for oppressed groups is of course to lie to the authorities. "A clever lie was not counted among our cadets as a vice, but was unanimously approved," Michael noted, and he was not above using the tactic himself. He may not have been very good at it, however. In 1832, he was confined to his quarters for two weeks for lying to his superior officer in order to avoid punishment for some other infraction.[16]

Three episodes over three years hardly mark the beginning of the proletarian revolution or stamp Bakunin as a rebel. They are, however, indicative of the rigid code of the school and of the spirit of muted protest that existed despite it. This early experience may well have impressed itself on the future revolutionary who would argue that the possibility for rebellion always existed, even among the most oppressed, and who would always support revolt even when he believed it was doomed to failure. Whatever the material conditions, he would argue, the spirit of revolt made resistance, if not success, always possible.

Another form of resistance was to play hard. The Russian military historian John Keep has, rather tactfully, noted that officers occupied themselves with "carousing, gambling, and pursuing the fair sex," and cadets did likewise. Michael sometimes claimed that he was above such pursuits, telling his parents that "I stayed away from most of the young folk, my comrades" because he was repulsed by their preoccupation with alcohol, cards, "and other pursuits that modesty keeps me from citing." Returning to the theme some years after leaving the school and the military, he claimed that while his "soul and imagination had been pure and innocent, unstained as yet by evil" when he left Priamukhino, military school had shown him some trajectories more interesting than the parabolas traced by artillery shells. There was revealed to him "the dark, filthy, nasty side of life." While his letters do not reveal just what these nasty pursuits were, it does not take too much

imagination to reflect on what young men in such a setting might have got-
ten into.[17]

As E. H. Carr pointed out, if Michael told his parents that he steadfastly
avoided such pursuits, we are not obliged to believe him. When he wrote of
the vices of his comrades he was deeply in debt. He owed nearly two thousand roubles by 1833—about four and a half years' pay for a junior officer.
No doubt aware that his father would be disinclined to cover the debts if they
were for "vice," his letters portrayed Michael as an upstanding young naif
led astray by a dishonest comrade and devious moneylenders who were quick
to accept his promissory notes. Perhaps; but it is hard to imagine that a young
man could get into so much debt while remaining alone and aloof with only
a good book for company.[18]

He did manage to find some time to read. He was keen on the historical
fiction of popular writers such as Faddey Bulgarin, Nicholas Grech, and
Michael Zagoskin. Virtually unknown and unstudied today, they might be
compared with G. A. Henty and Horatio Alger, for they wrote to instruct
the young in the peculiar values those in charge found useful. Their popularity had less to do with their skill than with their patronage by the tsar,
who rewarded them for their loyal service on the literary front. There they
helped prop up the regime with their romantic novels and combated progressive literary critics. Bulgarin, for example, argued in the journals with
Pushkin over the merits of censorship—he was in favor of it—and worked
closely with Benckendorff and the Third Section to ensure that Russian literature was safe, conservative, and devoid of any literary merit. More daring
was Bakunin's reading of Alexander Bestuzhev, an exiled Decembrist who
wrote romantic tales in the style of Byron under the pseudonym "Cossack
Marlinsky." Michael did have more serious tastes in literature, and he
enthused over Pushkin's *Boris Godunov* and Schiller's retellings of "William
Tell" and *Macbeth*. Finding a copy of *The Swiss Family Robinson* was like
coming across an old friend and later he would commend to his family James
Fenimore Cooper's sea story *The Red Rover* as "a very good novel," and
thought they would enjoy *The Bravo*.[19]

There was also time to enter the swirl of St. Petersburg parties and social
events, largely through the graces of relatives and friends, especially the Lvov
family, who had a daughter about Michael's age and who treated him like
kin. He enjoyed the time spent at country *dachas*, dinners, and concerts,
though he was not, like the latter-day anarchist Emma Goldman, keen on
dancing. Where Emma is alleged to have insisted "if I can't dance, I don't
want to be part of your revolution," Michael offered some hope for those

rebels unable to cut a mean rug, confessing in a letter to his sisters that he hated dancing. Still, there were trips to the country and quiet evenings spent in the homes of friends and relatives, where they would recite verse, read to each other, sing, make handicrafts, and do impersonations to while away the hours pleasantly. Michael's letters mentioned upcoming exams, visiting relatives, pleasant and agreeable Christmas and Easter holidays, and school work "so varied and numerous that we have no time to be bored." In short, his letters complain of the strictures and cruelties of military school even as they demonstrate how he made the best of it.[20]

His course of instruction ended in 1832, and at the end of that year he threw himself into studying for his examination. His cramming technique paid off yet again, and in January 1833 Bakunin was commissioned an ensign. He was now set to work studying fortifications, strategy, mathematics, physics, mechanics, Russian literature, and the German language. Allowed to live off campus, he returned to room with the Nilovs. No longer the frightened child from the country who could be set to reading hoary fairy stories and myths, but a strapping young man of nineteen years, successful, in a fashion, in his studies, accustomed to, if not appreciative of, the hardened life of military school, he "suddenly gained individual freedom" and took it on eagerly.[21]

Naturally, this meant falling in love. Now able to spend afternoons and evenings on his own, he spent more time with the Lvov family, and increasingly with Marie Voyekov, a distant cousin a few years his junior. Marie was pretty, charming, and shared—or reflected—his tastes in music, art, and discussion. It was not just a physical thing, he insisted to his sisters; he loved her charm, her even temper, her fine soul, her noble heart. The two discussed all the big themes that swelled romantic hearts in a romantic age: love, compassion, sentimentality, art, music, "and a thousand other things." He accompanied her to soirees, where he reacted to the hypocrisy of "society" with all the scorn, self-righteousness, and alienation only an adolescent could muster. He scoffed at the smarmy toffs who offered up "the same compliments and spouted the same twaddle to each young lady," and who despaired if they were not seen at the right affair in the right company. Worse, the same lounge lizards who made such a point of being seen with an important lady would later mock her when gossiping with their friends.[22]

They both had a passion for music, and while Mozart left him "enraptured" and "hardly able to breathe," his favorite composer was Beethoven. In retrospect, it is an appropriate choice. Beethoven stressed the expression of feeling and his music was designed to evoke strong, visceral reactions. His work burst through the strictures of the classical period as he broke all the rules of composition and wrote music with a political edge. His Third Symphony, the *Eroica,* meaning "heroic," for example, was written to celebrate the life of Napoleon Bonaparte, but when Bonaparte declared himself emperor, Beethoven denounced him as a tyrant and removed all references to him. The Ninth Symphony has a complicated political history, and the music has been claimed by revolutionaries and reactionaries, aristocrats and communists, Nazis and the European Union alike.[23]

Bakunin's passion for Beethoven has given rise to an oft-repeated story that shows how badly the anarchist has been served by some of his historians. According to several biographers, Bakunin was overcome by emotion while listening to the Ninth Symphony with Marie. So wracked was he that Marie was frightened by the expression on his face, which looked, numerous scholars have repeated, as if "I were ready to destroy the entire world." This statement has been used as an insight into the dark soul of the ferocious anarchist-to-be. As always, the intent is to imply or insist that his radical ideas stemmed neither from reality nor insight but from psychological torment and personal neurosis.

In fact, Bakunin does not use the French verb *detruire,* which is usually translated alternately as "to destroy," "to demolish," or "to raze." Instead he chooses the verb *devorer,* usually translated as "to devour," "to eat up," "to consume," even "to swallow or stifle." It may be translated as "to destroy," but this is very much a secondary meaning. To translate it as "to destroy" is an idiosyncratic and political choice. The entire story is from a long letter from Michael to his sister Varvara, and it takes up but a few lines in a section where he wrote about the effect Beethoven's music had on him. The music seemed to help his soul escape from the body that imprisoned it, he wrote; it elevated him to the celestial regions and made him very happy even while it made him pity those for whom ambition and the thirst for riches rendered them incapable of appreciating its heavenly sounds. It is even unlikely that they were listening to Beethoven's Ninth Symphony, for Bakunin explains that it was "the storm *[l'orage]* of Beethoven that had transported me." Of all of Beethoven's works, only the *Pastoral,* the Sixth Symphony, contains a section named "The Storm," and a powerful piece it is, coming right after the lilting "Merry Gathering of Country People" and announcing itself with a blast of horns and strings. This is a tiny matter, to be sure, but it does show how historians have been much too quick to read violence and destruction into Bakunin's most innocent remarks.[24]

Whatever he thought about Beethoven, Bakunin and Marie were doomed lovers. She had to leave for Moscow, and in best romantic style, the two promised never to forget each other as they parted tearfully. He asked her for a token to console him in her absence, and she gave him the bead bracelet she always wore. He kissed her hand—"for the first time in my life I kissed her hand! And I was truly happy!" "Adieux, Michel! Do not forget me!" she called to him from her carriage, and "her voice was lost in the air, her image disappeared from my eyes, and St. Petersburg was empty to me." He pined for a few weeks, pledging to make himself worthy of "She," hoping that she remembered him, but as far as can be judged from his letters, he recovered quickly enough. He was diverted by the need to study, particularly German, French, Russian, and literature, and "a very interesting book," Adam Smith's *The Wealth of Nations.*[25]

But it was increasingly clear to the young man that he did not fit the army and the army did not fit him. While the army was indifferent to this observation, Michael was not. The routines and drills of military life were boring. It was especially frustrating that one could not reason with one's superior officers but had to obey orders even when they were stupid, futile, or irrational. At first he was prepared to put up with this, on the grounds that it was the only honorable pursuit open to him and the only way he could be of use to his country and his family.[26] Yet it is easy to trace in his letters his growing discontent and his dawning awareness of the gap between the expectations of his family—and himself—and his real interests, passions, and abilities.

Even life with the Nilovs was becoming confining, and he chafed under their rules and regulations. Reproved by his aunt for what she believed was too much indecorous attention paid to "She," the young man bridled when she forbade him to leave the house without her permission. "I loved my good aunt," he later reflected, but her orders seemed to him "despotic." Conceding that the fight was childish, he still insisted that his need for liberty was natural, especially since he had so recently shed the shackles of the artillery school. She mistook his meditations for indolence and responded by scolding, sermonizing, and hectoring. When she accused him of stealing a book to get back at her for her reprimands, he was flabbergasted and outraged; it was exactly what he needed to make his first real proclamation of open rebellion, and he left the house, vowing to never to see her again.[27]

He at least had another place to stay, for his unit was being sent to Krasnoe Selo, some miles outside of St. Petersburg. Michael took with him the works of Dmitri Venevitinov, a Romantic poet and literary critic. It was a natural enough choice, given that his love affair with Marie had ended abruptly and tragically enough for a nineteen-year-old. But there was much more to it than that. Romanticism was a powerful intellectual current in Russia and would continue to be for several years.

The Russian interest in Romanticism has attracted a great deal of attention from historians, many of whom dismiss it as a sign of intellectual immaturity, political naivete, even psychological pathology. But Romanticism spread across Europe in roughly the same pattern as the economic and political revolutions of the eighteenth and nineteenth centuries.[28] To understand Romanticism, including its Russian variant, we need to understand the world that gave birth to it. It was a world of chaos, of rapid change, of struggles over power. The revolutions of 1776 and 1789 had turned it upside down, yet there was less order in that inversion than chaos and indeterminacy, for if old forms of oppression and power had lost their meaning, the new were still in flux and were on their way to creating new oppressions. The Industrial Revolution too wreaked havoc as it brought to power a new class of oppressors, the capitalists. It was a world of incredible wealth and astounding poverty. It was a world in which for a time everything seemed possible—at least to those who did not do the work that kept everything going, the peasants, workers, and native peoples. Caught between the possibilities opened up by the French Revolution and the terrible reality of the Terror, reaction, empire, and capitalism, it was clear the world could not—and should not—return to the old ways while the new ways offered up new forms of horror along with their promises.

Romanticism spoke to the chaos, promise, and betrayals of the age. In the English-speaking world, this was obvious in the work of Percy Bysshe Shelley, who celebrated the possibility for freedom as he deplored the harsh reality of wage labor in field and factory. William Blake wrote of the "dark, Satanic mills," while Byron's first speech in the House of Lords, delivered in 1812, was a vigorous defense of the Luddites, those highly skilled weavers who smashed the machinery brought in to lower their wages and throw them out of work. Other writers reacted against industrialization as they saw how it turned human beings into factors of production, pressed children into factory labor, took peasants from the countryside and smashed them into those dark Satanic mills and foul, diseased, dank city boroughs. They saw full well the dislocation and rot of the new world order. They noted how the promise of rational enlightenment was betrayed not by its thinkers but by the pragmatic men of politics and business, who used the potential of political and economic revolution not to free humanity but to imprison it with chains as hard and tight and short as any the aristocracy had ever forged. In a world where reason itself had been shackled to the loom, where art was now a mirror to reflect the fat faces of contented captains of industry, the Romantics shouted, "Stop!"

In Russia too, Romanticism was not a withdrawal into a dreamy, languid world of unrequited love, quixotic gesture, and heavy sighs. There, the failure of social change created much the same reaction among its educated young men and women as violent change had provoked in other parts of Europe. After all, what more graphic proof of the failure of the old regime could one ask for than the disaster of the French invasion? What regime in Europe offered less opportunity for its educated youth? Where had "the people" done so much to save the empire and received so little in return? Where were new ideas more fiercely burned out by secret police, imprisoned in dank dungeons, and suspended from the hangman's noose? The inability of the regime to change and its retreat to orthodoxy, autocracy, and nationality under Nicholas I pushed young Russian thinkers and artists to look to the West for inspiration. That meant Romanticism and its ideals, conflicted though they may have been.

Thus it was not odd that the foremost Russian poet, Alexander Pushkin, would take up Romantic themes, for everything in his experience confirmed the critique of the British Romantics. His work hearkened back to a mythic Russian past in *The Bronze Horseman* and praised the virtues and lamented the sufferings of the folk in *The History of the Pugachev Rebellion*. Though political thought was much less developed in Russia, Pushkin and other Russia Romantics such as Venevitinov, like Shelley and Byron, were deeply concerned with political questions. Pushkin's 1820 "Ode to Liberty" was judged sufficiently rebellious to get him exiled to Southern Russia. Venevitinov had been arrested in 1826 for his connections to the Decembrists and had created a small society or circle called the "Society of Wisdom Lovers" that read and debated literature, philosophy, and politics. As a literary taste, as a way to make some sense of a troubled world, as an available commodity, as a rebellious attitude, Romanticism was as prevalent in Russia as anywhere and for all the same reasons, and it signaled an engagement with the real world, not a retreat from it.

Michael Bakunin was not making much of a political or philosophical statement when he took the volume of Venevitinov with him. But he was beginning to ask important questions about his life and surroundings; he was beginning to evolve into a rebel. Trapped between wanting to do what his family thought was right and what he needed to do to be true to himself, there was no clear or obvious way out of his dilemma in a regime that provided so few options. For Bakunin, it meant that soon the personal would become the political.

4

SHOOTING BLANKS

Whatever misgivings about his career and his life Bakunin had were temporarily put aside, for he was finally entitled to go on leave and return to Priamukhino. In August 1833, the dashing young officer strode into his family's dining room unexpectedly, and everyone jumped up to greet him. There were tears of joy all around and much news to exchange; even seeing "little Michel" as an adult for the first time was something to marvel at.

But if Michael had changed dramatically since he left for school five years earlier, so too had his family. The happy reunion could not paper over the cracks in the Priamukhino idyll. If the restraints of the regime put Michael on the horns of a dilemma between duty and freedom, they affected his sisters Liubov, Varvara, Tatiana, and Alexandra even more profoundly. Their father had educated all the children well; they had bright, inquisitive minds and enjoyed reading literature and philosophy. Nonetheless, Michael's options were few, and only one existed for his sisters: the social whirl of society with the object of finding suitable spouses. Suitable did not mean spouses who evoked romantic love; it meant arrangements that would be useful maintaining and improving the family's position in the complicated ranking system of status and wealth. When the Bakunin women bumped into the limits of their world, it was a shock no less rude than the one Michael experienced at military school. Just as Michael was torn between being the dutiful son and becoming his own man, the sisters were torn between wishing to obey their parents and social norms and their own fulfillment.

The sisters had little patience for duller suitors, no matter how "suitable," and were quickly bored with the rounds of dances and balls and the stylized rituals of flirtation and courtship. They, like Michael, thought court and salon life was filled with hypocrisy and they resented having to play their shallow roles. Worse, "society" took time away from their studies, music, and art. Even earlier than Michael, they had determined that the life they were expected to live offered them nothing. The structured roles that had been so important for the nobility in the past were now empty forms, especially for smart women who wanted to put their education and talent to use. And if Priamukhino appeared to Michael as a sanctuary, to his sisters it loomed as a prison. Life on the country estate offered them no challenges or inspiration. Women were assumed to be the repositories of virtue and purity, but as Liubov noted, at Priamukhino, "we are deprived of the means to do wrong" and thus were never put to the test, never able to exert any real virtue or demonstrate real purity. Because there was nothing to resist, the sisters never experienced the "delicious sentiment one feels when one comes to surmount some bad instinct when one does one's duties despite all the temptations." Their untested virtue was as formulaic and empty as their social life.[1]

It was increasingly clear to them that fulfillment was unlikely to be found in society, in marriage, or on the estate. With much of the external world denied the sisters and that which was open boring and oppressive, they increasingly turned to Christianity for solace, meaning, and intellectual challenge. While religion provided an outlet for powerful feelings, it also offered a creative and compelling way for the sisters to grow intellectually. Together with their friends Alexandra and Natalie Beyer, they debated philosophical and religious doctrine, read deeply, and sought philosophical and religious truths in their lives.[2]

It was a serious, scholastic undertaking and the Bakunin and Beyer sisters came to be crucial to the development of philosophy in Russia in this period. The universities had been greatly expanded as successive tsars sought to attain the technological benefits of the West without adopting its values or its economic and social changes. However, students like Michael Bakunin in the military and his sisters at Priamukhino were not merely interested in the official curriculum and in learning what the authorities deemed appropriate for them to learn. Physics might be important to the military; philosophy held the key to life and liberty.

But philosophy was forbidden in Russian universities, precisely because it insisted that no received wisdom should go unchallenged. Implicitly and explicitly, it challenged the myths of the regime and called into question its corrupt, exploitative, and crumbling pillars. For that reason, students interested in thinking outside the boundaries of state-sponsored orthodoxy formed their own study groups, or circles, that met outside of class to read and discuss the ideas and issues that mattered to them. The two most important circles were one headed by and named after Nicholas Stankevich and another jointly by Alexander Herzen and Nicholas Ogarev. Almost exclusively male, the Stankevich circle and the Herzen-Ogarev circle became centers for avant-garde thought in literature, philosophy, and politics.

According to Herzen and the many historians who have accepted his memoirs uncritically, the circles sprang up spontaneously. More careful historians, however, have noted that they owed much to the sophisticated discussion groups of the Bakunin and Beyer sisters. One reason Bakunin loved his sisters was the intellectual equality they shared, and they proved able sparring partners as he thought and rethought his own philosophy. The sisters did not restrict their philosophical inquiries to letters. They transformed their social life into something between the society salon and the philosophical circle, creating the first spaces for provocative discussion. Here Stankevich would first explore the metaphysics that defined his worldview; through debate with the Bakunins and Beyers on the nature of religion and art, he would be challenged to rethink his own ideas; here he would meet still others, including Michael Bakunin, who shared his quest for knowledge.[3]

By the time Michael returned to Priamukhino, his older sisters were more conscious rebels than he. He was sick of army life, but they had been aware of their own dilemmas much longer and had less to look forward to. He quickly discovered how deeply frustrated they were with Priamukhino. Women were expected to know of the new worlds of knowledge but to refrain from participating; they were expected to defer to and marry men who had none of their education or abilities. The Bakunin and Beyer sisters created new opportunities for themselves, but these were deeply divided by gendered realities. Young men were not expected to embody virtue and purity. That meant they could stay out unescorted; they could meet in pubs. They could seek employment or start irregularly published journals that paid them a pittance; they could, in a word, act. Women had no such choices, and they used philosophy and religion to try to convince themselves that if there was happiness to be found on earth, it was not an external happiness dependent on circumstance, but an internal happiness.

In the meantime, however, reality was intruding on them all. The problem was a social as well as personal one. Russia was a state in transition. The old ways, rituals, and arrangements were backward and ineffective compared to the new freedoms offered, at least in theory, in the rest of Europe. The French Revolution and the war with Napoleon had shown that the nobility was effete and irrelevant; at best, it could exert its power only to delay the inevitable. What was the percentage in sticking with that? Yet while Western ideas had made it across the borders of the empire, the economic and political and social changes that gave them a basis in the real world traveled much more slowly. Put more concretely, it made little sense for a military officer to study the most modern strategy and tactics knowing full well he would never have the trained men or equipment to implement them. Russian universities offered an excellent curriculum in the sciences. But when eager students turned their inquisitive, trained, skeptical minds on Russian history, literature, economics, or politics, they found the doors to those subjects welded shut. To open them was to risk expulsion, exile, even execution. This generation was caught between the promise of the sweeping changes they observed just over the border and the reality of Russia's creaking stasis.

The first response of these young men and women was rarely rebellion. More often it was an evolving desire to live lives that made sense and that were fulfilling and interesting. That this simple desire threw them into opposition with the tsar says more about the repressive regime than about the young, inadvertent rebels themselves. Simply trying to live the lives they had been educated to live put them in immediate moral dilemmas with family, friends, and authorities. What did one owe one's family? Where did true duty lie? Was duty even a virtue? When it clashed with freedom how was one to decide? Since these were bright, highly literate young men and women, they turned to books for help. These themes were not unique to the Bakunins or Russia. They were tossed up in every nation that was exposed to the political and economic upheavals of the age.

For the Bakunins, philosophy and reality collided when Liubov, the oldest of the children, agreed to marry Konstantin Renne, a cavalry officer and noble with an estate near Priamukhino. Michael had learned of the engagement in a letter some months before he returned home and applauded his sister's choice.[4] Now that he was home, however, his sisters could tell him what they feared to put in their letters. Liubov did not love Renne and had agreed to marry him only because it was what their parents wished. The choice between duty and freedom, to marry or not, was still hers, but it was an agonizing one. She loved her parents and did not want to hurt them or dismay them by open revolt. Yet to marry Renne would be an act of sacrifice, not love, and even the dubious promises of unearthly salvation could not make that choice more palatable. In the real world of nineteenth-century Russia, she had no other meaningful choices. She could not go to university, could not work, could not run away to Haight-Ashbury or the circus. Liubov herself put the dilemma plainly in a letter to the Beyer sisters, long before Michael learned of her crisis: "I know that I am completely free in my choice, but this thought never leaves my head: I must entrust myself blindly to my parents and believe that they desire only my happiness."[5] Undoubtedly they did desire her happiness, but it was impossible for them to conceive of her being happy outside of the social norms of their generation and experience.

When his sisters told him of Liubov's plight, Michael sided with them and together with them pleaded her case to their parents. While several historians playing on the rebel without a cause theme have cast Michael as the "outside agitator" who led his unwitting sisters to rebel, more recent work by John Wyatt Randolph and Marshall Shatz has shown he was far from being the instigator. Instead, his sisters appointed Michael champion of the oppressed in the hope that his status as eldest male child would be an important strategic asset. After the initial arguments, however, his first reaction was to try to restore peace to the family. When his leave ended and he had to return to St. Petersburg, he sent a quick letter to his sisters, asking them to listen to their parents, to stop causing them pain, and to put aside their "small actions, small words, and very small thoughts" in the interest of the family. He reminded them of the sacrifices their parents had made, that their parents were essentially good, that this conflict could be healed if the children took the lead in seeking peace and resolution, and that no irreparable rift existed.

Once in St. Petersburg, however, he reread Liubov's letters and realized the depth of her dilemma and despair. Michael now delivered the help he had been asked to give. He sent Liubov's letters to their father, in the hope that they would convince him that she loved her parents and was not acting simply to spite them. Making amends for his earlier lack of solidarity, he wrote to Liubov to strengthen her resolve and to forestall her from sacrificing herself on the marriage altar for the presumed good of the family. Any thoughts she had of happiness with Renne, even the dulled happiness of self-sacrifice, were an illusion, he agreed. It meant subjecting her will and her ideas to Renne, and he was clearly her inferior. Her marriage would be a lie to herself and to God, for she would have to swear love and obedience to a man she did not love. Worse, it would be a futile sacrifice that would not accomplish what she hoped it would, that is, to make her parents happy. For her parents desired her happiness, and if she were to marry Renne, they would know she was miserable and would thus be unhappy themselves. There was no way Renne could truly love her, for he knew how little she cared for him. Worse, he was a Courlander, that is, an Estonian, and of course, Bakunin continued, all the Baltic people hated Russia for sucking them into the empire. Renne's parents would despise Liubov, yet she would have to be pleasant to them and do their bidding. Now on a roll, Michael hearkened back to the Romantic literature they had enjoyed to suggest that her marriage would separate the dear Liubov from her loving family. This separation would so fill them with melancholy, he assured her, that they would pine away even unto death. Is that what she wanted? he asked. Would that make everyone happy?

On the other hand, he pointed out, refusing Renne would not, as Liubov feared, bring dishonor on her family. There was no dishonor in their father letting his daughter out of a marriage she did not want, and not even their mother wanted Liubov to sacrifice herself. His arguments, Michael concluded, were not insubstantial but were the result of much reflection. If she could answer them, then, and only then, would he go along quietly with the marriage plans.[7]

His letter, with all its rhetorical excesses, had its intended effect. As Michael had predicted, once their father understood how strongly Liubov felt, he relented and the marriage was called off. The consequences of the episode were as profound as the event itself. It confirmed to the Bakunin sisters that they could try to seek happiness outside the narrow roles prescribed for them, though it would not be easy. It confirmed their turn to religion and philosophy and encouraged them to continue to seek truth there. It was also a formative experience in Michael's political development. He had been raised to believe his sisters were his equals. The conflict with their parents reaffirmed this and pushed him to think about women's emancipation early on. Admittedly this was on a private, not a political, level, but it continued to inform his ideas all his life.[8]

The fight for Liubov encouraged Michael to consider the question of his own emancipation more carefully now that he was back at school. Inspired by his sisters and his earlier dabbling with the works of Venevitinov, he continued to read far outside the military curriculum and to discuss philosophy in his letters to his sisters. He sought out people in St. Petersburg with similar interests, including Nicholas Muraviev, yet another famous cousin of Michael's mother. Recently retired from state service, his children, especially three of his daughters and his son Sergei, were about Michael's age. The older man welcomed Michael to his home and encouraged him to read and talk about politics and philosophy with him and his children. The sisters shared the same education with the Bakunin and Beyer sisters and they too "have no patience for society," Michael wrote. While they played the game well, their real life began when they excused themselves to "discuss literature, history, the sciences, philosophy."[9] Continuing to extend his reading, Bakunin worked his way through Christophe-Guillaume Koch's *History of the Revolutions in Europe*, a classic multivolume work that stressed technology, trade, the role of the church, and political developments and would likely serve well enough in first-year Western Civ courses taught today.[10]

By January of 1834, he was writing to his sisters of his "intellectual revolution." He had examined his life carefully and reiterated that, like his sisters, he was bored with high society and the "pleasures of the ball and the dance." While he felt awkward and out of place there, the real problem was he found it deadly dull. To be fully human, one had to use one's mind on ideas and issues that mattered. Where he had previously lived an "external" life, aimed at maintaining appearances and pleasing others, now he proposed to throw himself into his studies. These would decidedly not be military studies. He was finished with studying just to master the material and please others, he noted. Now he set out to study for himself, to seek happiness in intellectual work. Unlike his sisters, his understanding could not come through religion but through knowledge of the real world. "Knock and it shall be opened, the Gospel says," he wrote his sisters, but he added that religion too often meant knocking one's head on the floor. Those who sought happiness through prayer and acts of grace were misled. After all, even a hungry dog could beg, he went on, and if that were all humans were meant to do, why then were they given consciousness? No, if they had brains, they were meant to use them, and that meant trying to understand the mysteries of the world.

Naturally that left little time to attend to the routine of the classroom. Now completely uninterested in the military or in military school, Michael wore his duties lightly. He apparently wore his uniform lightly as well. When the commander of the school caught him inappropriately attired—a venial or even possibly a mortal sin in this tsar's army—and gave him a dressing-down, Michael's response was not to the general's liking. Unlike his earlier incidents of dumb insolence and sullen rebellion, this one was met with severe consequences. The commander expelled Michael from school, officially charging him with poor grades and "lack of attention through the entire course of studies," and transferred him to active duty on the Polish border.[11]

"Active duty" was perhaps an exaggeration: Michael's letters from the field complain that he was bored and alone. The only amusements were the officers' balls that he had never much enjoyed, while his intellectual work was more difficult and less satisfying for there was no one to talk to.[12] He told the Beyer sisters that his posting was a "hole" in which he was interred, surrounded by fellow officers most of whom walked on four paws, and that he was entirely isolated and alone. Even nature seemed to turn against him: as he approached his new station, he noted, literally in flowery language, that the luxurious birch trees were giving way to thick stands of somber pine and the scented orchids were disappearing, their place taken by dried out, boring daisies that could survive anywhere. In French, the word for "daisy" is *immortelle,* and he punned off that to call them "dried out and inanimate immortals." But surely the charming orchid was a thousand times more dear than drab, prosaic, and insensible life eternal?[13] Driven to ennui by the activities of his comrades—"cards and vodka," he complained to his parents—he discovered that Rousseau was wrong to preach about the charms of solitude. Instead, Michael wrote, "Man is made for society," and this observation would continue to mark his politics. Never an individualist anarchist in his later political career, he understood early on that humans needed family and friends to share the joys and pains of life. "Voluntary solitude," he continued, was virtually the same as egoism; could, he asked, the egoist be happy? For him, the answer was a resounding no, and he looked forward to rejoining his family, for only among others could he pursue all his "hopes, desires, projects, and dreams." In keeping with his view that intellectual needs were founded upon physical ones, he also asked his parents for money, since he was essentially penniless. As a serving officer, he had to pay for his own uniforms and food, and Michael was, he claimed, subsisting on black bread and water, without money even for tobacco and tea.

Yet he was still unable to break with the military. He wrote to his parents about the dilemma of wishing to fulfill his duty even as he threw himself into studying philosophy, history, mathematics, languages, and grammar, anything but the official curriculum. He transcribed and notated his readings, hoping that in this work he might find himself, or at least stave off the "sad state of insensibility and disillusionment." Later he found a few people to talk with, in particular a doctor who was in touch with one of Russia's foremost Romantic and idealist thinkers, Danylo Vellansky, who in turn had studied with Schelling in Germany. But Michael's future was still unclear; he was unable to properly devote himself to studying philosophy and increasingly worried that his father would not be able to arrange a longed-for transfer to Tver. Worse, his expulsion from military school curtailed any chance for promotion or early release.[14]

Finally he decided to take matters into his own hands. He had written to Sergei Muraviev in late January 1835 that he was trying to "free myself from the military yoke." The answer lay, as it so often does, in the proper application of history. Bakunin had been studying Russian history, and of course, he was a military officer who studied strategy and tactics. His plan was conceived in the finest tradition of the Russian general staff: when faced with an untenable situation, run.[15]

Priamukhino was eight hundred miles away but the opportunity to adopt his strategy was given to him when he was ordered to Tver to secure horses for his unit. He simply spontaneously demobilized himself and went home, applying for the first time the anarchist tactic of direct action, that is, resolv-

ing the issue through his own actions, not those of politicians or others acting on his behalf.

His parents, of course, were appalled. Their son was absent without leave,
possibly even a deserter depending on the whim of the military courts, and
Alexander Bakunin scrambled to secure a relatively honorable discharge for
his son on the grounds of illness.[16] While few officers took the drastic action
Michael did, it was common for young noblemen to leave the service as soon
as practicably possible, for it offered them nothing. Unfortunately, Russia
offered little else for them, either. At Priamukhino, Michael hoped, well fed,
surrounded by bright, literate people who shared his concerns, with nothing
particularly pressing to do, he could devote himself to philosophy.

But family responsibilities and battles made it impossible for him to study.
His father kept going on about getting a job, and had secured a civil service
post in Tver for his wayward son. Michael rejected this out of hand, writing
a friend that it was impossible to take up his studies while holding down a
job as a functionary. Nor could he give up his studies, for they were "the
essential foundation, the religion, of my life." To abandon them would vio-
late his "human dignity."[17] The solution came to him when Michael Bakunin
met Nicholas Stankevich at the Beyers's Moscow home in March 1835. Their
similar backgrounds and interests practically guaranteed the two young men
would hit it off. "Meeting Stankevich saved me," Michael wrote his sister
Varvara. "It marks an epoch, a turning point in my life. I was influenced not
just by his profound intelligence and noble goals, but also by the beautiful
spontaneity and total clarity of all his being." In January 1836, he headed
for Moscow to join Stankevich and the other members of his circle.[18]

Stankevich was one of the most influential young Russian intellectuals of
the day, and the two quickly became close friends, though they made an
unlikely pair at first glance. Bakunin was physically imposing, boisterous in
company, and assertive, even aggressive in his debating style. Quick-witted,
he synthesized vast amounts of material and was drawn to the bold insight
and the dramatic overstatement. He borrowed and spent money freely and
was often incautious in his philosophy and his friendships. Stankevich was,
at least outwardly, the sober yin to Bakunin's raging yang. Quiet, pale, physically frail, he too was the son of a landowning noble, but his family was
wealthier than Bakunin's and so Stankevich had not been pressed into the
military. Born in 1813, he was educated in a school attended largely by children outside the nobility, and this democratic upbringing influenced him
greatly. He later attended the University of Moscow, where he formally studied literature and history and was introduced to German idealist philosophy

through one of his teachers, a Professor Pavlov. Living at the professor's home, Stankevich took part in discussions with academics who were determined to study philosophy informally despite the official ban. While Pavlov taught natural sciences, not philosophy, the moment one stops to ask, "What is science?" or "What is nature?" philosophy becomes part of the subject matter. Even in physics and agronomy, idealist philosophers found their way into the Russian academy.

Upon graduating in 1834, Stankevich was made a school inspector, a job that gave him some official status and an income but did not divert much time from his vocation of philosophy and literary criticism. While he wrote little during his short life—he died of tuberculosis at the age of twenty-seven—Stankevich insisted upon clear, critical thought and inspired a generation of thinkers. One of his admirers, Konstantin Aksakov, recalled him as "an absolutely simple man, devoid of any pretensions; a man of unusual and deep intelligence . . . [who] argued so coherently, logically, and clearly in debates that the most refined dialecticians . . . had to capitulate." Another contemporary, Paul Annenkov, noted that those who worked with Stankevich "were morally elevated by him and were—if only for a moment—superior beings." Another central member of the Stankevich circle, Vissarion Belinsky, wrote of his "divine personality" and described him as "holy, lofty . . . harmonious, sweet, blessed."[19]

Moscow and the Stankevich circle provided Bakunin with the time and comrades to take up serious study in exciting surroundings, combining scholarship with friendship in ways familiar to contemporary university students and their professors. In an oft-quoted passage from his novel *Rudin*, the novelist Ivan Turgenev has one character describe the life:

> I was completely reborn. I curbed my conceit, began asking questions, learned, rejoiced, worshipped—in short, it was like entering some kind of church. . . . Imagine a gathering of half a dozen boys, our only light one tallow candle, tea like slops and dry biscuits as old as Adam—but if only you'd heard our speeches and looked at our faces! Excitement in everyone's eyes, cheeks on fire, our hearts beating fast, and we'd talk about God, about truth, about the future of humanity, about poetry, sometimes talking nonsense, carried away by empty words, but what did that matter! . . . Oh, it was a marvelous time then![20]

Priamukhino continued to figure heavily in their intellectual development. As the historian Marshall Shatz has pointed out, it would be reasonable to speak of the "Priamukhino circle" as well as the Stankevich and Herzen-Ogarev circles, for over the next few years, members of the Stankevich circle would often visit Priamukhino while the Bakunin and Beyer sisters would continue to be important intellectual figures.[21]

The pleasant bohemian existence was not without tensions and problems. The members of the circle were young, passionate, strong-willed, and fierce in their polemics. Bakunin's dynamism sometimes angered others who surrendered to his arguments not because of the strength of his logic but because of the force of his personality. Belinsky, who would become Russia's most important literary critic of this era, was nicknamed "Furious Vissarion" by his comrades, and it was a descriptive, not an ironic, nickname. In such an atmosphere, jealousy was not uncommon as each member of the circle vied for the respect of others and for primacy. The old class distinctions of the regime made life complicated, no matter how much the circle may have deplored them. Belinsky was the son of a doctor and thus not of the nobility. If that didn't matter to Bakunin, it mattered a great deal to Belinsky, who was quick to take offense at actions and comments he perceived as insults. Belinsky had been snubbed by Pushkin, who regarded him as an oddball, and the young critic often felt psychologically and physically overshadowed by Bakunin. Even Bakunin's sisters frustrated him, as their aristocratic education prepared them to read Schelling and Fichte in the original German, which Belinsky could not. As one of his colleagues, Turgenev, put it, "Belinsky knew how to hate—he was a good hater."[22]

Belinsky did have important street cred, though, and he made the most of it. He had been expelled from university for writing a play that was critical of serfdom and was a strong fan of Fichte. He worked on a literary journal, the *Telescope,* which was published in Moscow from 1831 to 1836, when it was shut down for publishing the first of Peter Chaadaev's "Philosophical Letters," a critical note on Russia's backwardness. Foreshadowing the use of psychiatric hospitals as prisons by the Soviet Union, the regime declared Chaadaev insane and kept him under house arrest. But Belinsky continued to attack conservative, orthodox Russian literature and his articles won the young critic some acclaim and notoriety. His visits to Priamukhino both elated and angered Belinsky, for the idyllic country estate left him isolated and at odds with the family, which had its own customs and practices. He did not make matters better when he remarked to Alexander Bakunin, now a frail, aged man whose passion for the French Revolution had long since burned out, that the violence of the Terror was completely justified and added meaningfully that there were "heads that still await the guillotine."

Whatever his own views on revolution, Michael regarded this as an unnecessary provocation of an old man and an abuse of his hospitality, especially inopportune as Michael needed his father to fund his travels.[23]

The circle was also riven by romance, for the intense intellectual work was accompanied with strong, complex emotions. It is not uncommon for romance to break out whenever like-minded people of a certain age spend a great deal of time together in intense intellectual discussions. Matches and mismatches continued over three years: Natalie Beyer fell in love with Stankevich, who was not interested; Natalie and her sister Alexandra in turn developed strong feelings for Michael, who observed that while he loved the Beyer sisters, he was not in love with them. Stankevich and Liubov Bakunin became secretly engaged, though Stankevich soon discovered that he did not love her and left Russia to avoid further entanglement and to find a healthier climate; he was soon joined by Varvara, who left her husband to be with Stankevich and was at his side when he died in Italy in 1840. Belinsky fell for Tatiana Bakunin, but it was Alexandra Bakunin who fell for Belinsky; later, she became engaged to yet another circle member, Vassily Botkin, to the horror of her parents, who could not conceive of their daughter marrying the son of a merchant, even though his income greatly exceeded theirs. Finally, in 1840, the novelist Ivan Turgenev fell for Tatiana, but ultimately decided that he did not love her romantically. Such entanglements of course were hardly restricted to nineteenth-century students, but they remind us that these Russian intellectuals were living, breathing people with complicated lives that they handled as well, or as poorly, as any of us. They were not rarefied, ethereal beings who dealt only with spirituality or epistemology; they were human, and the interplay between their lives and their ideas was dynamic, complex, and profound.

The complicated relationships also let us dismiss once and for all the notion that Michael Bakunin somehow exerted a Svengalian influence over his sisters. He was not the ringleader who got them all worked up in frenzies of rebellion. They gave as good as they got, and were active participants in their battle for liberation, the study of philosophy, and the relationships that marked the development of the circle. A measure of their influence was the attacks Varvara, Tatiana, and Alexandra suffered from the pen of "Furious Vissarion." The sisters, two of whom had rejected Belinksy, had been ruined by their brother, he insisted. Women could only fulfill themselves, Belinsky thundered, by becoming wives and mothers. Philosophy was beyond them and would ruin them. Singling out Varvara as an example of his point, he continued, that Bakunin's "thoughts did not give her strength;

she was intimidated by them . . . She is a mother, and has contemplated many things, about which our trite philosophy has not even dreamed." For women, "marriage is the only reasonable way to experience life and the only reality . . . Society regards her freedom as willfulness, which, if reprehensible in a man, is even more so in a girl . . . Marriage for her is an emancipation, the beginning of her individuality."[24] In response, Bakunin fired off a twenty-one-page letter to set Belinsky straight on philosophy and sexism; unfortunately, the letter has not survived. The entire episode reinforces the argument of the literary theorist Lydia Ginzburg, who understood that as part of defining himself, Belinsky created a caricature of Bakunin, a straw man to embody the ideas Belinsky himself was working out.[25]

Belinsky's hostility toward Michael and his sisters matters because generations of historians have relied on Belinsky to support two connected arguments about Bakunin. The first is that Bakunin was caught up in a mystical world of idealism, separated from reality, and unable to connect with the world around him. Belinsky, they insist, moved quickly through idealism to realism, and so was better grounded, more connected with reality, and less alienated. Therefore Bakunin, his critics conclude, was later drawn to anarchism precisely because it was fantastic and Utopian, unreal and irrelevant. But the route to Bakunin's anarchism was much more complicated and cannot be reduced to a philosophical position and a psychological state. More importantly, such a categorization is simply incorrect. It is largely based on Belinsky's interpretation of the feud between the two men, and so must be considered carefully. Belinsky accused Bakunin of stifling his feelings and having cut himself off from reality to pursue a fruitless life among books and abstract ideas. Instead, Belinsky insisted, the correct task for their generation was to take up jobs in the civil service to serve society by becoming functioning parts of it. Unlike Bakunin, Belinsky insisted he was a man of feeling, not of intellect, and so was superior. "My strength, my power, is in my direct feeling," Belinsky insisted, while Bakunin was "a man with a marvelous head but decidedly without heart, and, moreover, with the blood of a rotten salt cod."[26] This appeal to feeling rather than reason hardly suggests that Belinsky was the rational realist of the two. Bakunin, he continued, knew nothing of the real world, only the dream world of Priamukhino and the abstract world of philosophical thought, while Belinsky, on the other hand, was now dedicated to becoming part of "reality." His immersion into the real world, signified by his getting a job, gave him, Belinsky maintained, much greater insight and a monopoly on truth. What was important was to become a useful member of society, he reproved. Happy to use any weapon to hand, he even suggested that Bakunin's father, whom Belinsky had earlier hinted might deserve beheading, was now the best model for Michael himself, for at least his father had buckled down to do what had to be done.[27]

Bakunin himself regarded Belinsky's "reconciliation with reality" as less of a revelation and more of a sellout. Belinsky, he wrote to Stankevich, "has gone to the extreme of turning any ordinary, commonplace, existing being into his ideal." Far from anchoring himself in the real world, Belinsky had simply surrendered to it. For himself, Bakunin agreed that one could not escape reality, but he insisted that reality could be changed through action. This idea was soon put to the test as he worked once again to help liberate one of his sisters from an unhappy reality.[28]

Of the Bakunin sisters, Varvara was the most interested in and consumed by religion. As a teenager, she had had an intense religious experience that led her to consider becoming a nun. Her parents were horrified at the prospect, and she quietly dropped the idea for the sake of family harmony. Thus she, no less than Michael, understood well the frustration and depression caused by having ambitions and talents thwarted for the sake of others. In 1835, she had married a noble military officer, Nicholas Diakov. Michael and his sisters, including Varvara, regarded him variously as good but rather dull, an amiable idiot, and a potential tyrant. Varvara agreed to marry him for the good of the family and as part of the religious mission she had assumed. In her mind, the marriage was a sacrifice that gave her life a purpose. Through having a purpose, perhaps happiness could be found. She made it clear to her family that this was a sacrifice: during the marriage ceremony she turned from the altar to face her family and said, "Now sisters, be firm: I have redeemed all of you with myself." Her sacrifice, however, did not lead to happiness. Whatever Diakov's good points, Varvara deeply resented his control over her. "He has even now," she wrote, "every right to kiss me, to caress me—he can enter my room at any time, say to me whatever he pleases—and I must be silent and cannot forbid it."[29] Diakov had little patience for her philosophical work. He wanted her to be a "good," traditional wife. But prompted by her religious studies, she came to believe that living with a man she did not love was a sin rather than an empowering sacrifice. This wracked her with guilt and made life with Diakov intolerable.

Michael, unlike many of his peers, such as Belinsky, understood that it was "horrible" for a woman to "marry a man whom you do not love, to marry out of calculation, even if you do not feel revulsion for him, even when he has merited your respect." Foreshadowing Emma Goldman's writings on marriage, he insisted that "marriage out of calculation is prostitution."[30] Nor was it possible to argue that in suffering one might find salvation, he warned. "Humanity's calling is not to suffer here on earth with folded arms in order to win a mythological paradise. It is instead to move that heaven, that God that is in oneself, to the earth, to raise practical life, to raise the earth to heaven."[31] Far from retreating to idealistic speculation on the immaterial nature of reality, Bakunin used philosophy to understand and confront practical concerns. In turn, the family disputes and the liberation of Varvara had an impact on his philosophy, for these struggles helped convince him external conditions did indeed matter. He had become keenly aware that happiness was not something that could be found only within oneself or in heaven. Happiness could be found only in the real world; it had to be created by humanity through grappling with and resolving personal and social problems.[32]

Thus it is a little silly for historians to assert, as many have, that Bakunin's interest in German romanticism and idealism was a retreat from reality. In fact, the issues he took up were immediately bound up with real-life questions. The struggle for Varvara's liberation would meet with some success. She would soon leave Russia, and her husband, for Europe, and would begin an affair with Stankevich that ended only with his death. The notion that when duty and freedom conflicted, freedom was the higher virtue continued to echo throughout Bakunin's life.

Historians have also relied on Belinsky to make a second argument about Bakunin: that he was sexually impotent and his quest for sexual wholeness drew him to German idealism and then to anarchism as a form of sexual sublimation. Put this plainly, it sounds ridiculous enough, but speculation about Bakunin's sexual abilities has long tainted the debates over his ideas.

The high road to debunking this line is to argue that Bakunin's sexuality is absolutely irrelevant. Whatever thinkers do with their private parts has nothing to do with the content or validity of their ideas. It has no bearing on their ideas if they are promiscuous or celibate, straight or gay or bisexual, indifferent to or obsessed with sex. Ironically, other anarchists, such as Emma Goldman, have been attacked because they had too much sex. If you're an anarchist, it seems you are damned if you do and damned if you can't.

For those of us more accustomed to the gutter or the median strip than the high road—and the relative popularity of *People* magazine to *The American Historical Review* suggests we make up the vast majority—such a principled argument has the whiff of evasion. "Ah, so he *was* impotent," we wink, confident that the refusal to get down and dirty is a tacit admission. The problem is, of course, that no one can plausibly explain how sexual dysfunction leads to anarchism or revolution. If there were anything to this argument, the sales of Viagra would prove that millions of North American men are ready to smash the state any day now. More importantly, Marshall Shatz has laid the impotence argument to rest in an excellent piece of historical detective work. Only two pieces of evidence have ever been put forward to support the claim that Bakunin was impotent. The first is that he did not have an affair with either of the Beyer sisters, both of whom had indicated that an advance made by him would be welcome. Bakunin made it clear that he loved the sisters for their "beautiful souls" but did not feel "fervent, stormy passion" for either.[33] His reaction to the Beyers, who were by all accounts brilliant and lovely, may disappoint present-day matchmakers, but as evidence of sexual dysfunction it is ridiculous.

The second piece of evidence also falls short of the standard of evidence usually acceptable for medical diagnosis, even by the standards of the nineteenth century. In 1840, Bakunin walked in on Michael Katkov and Maria Ogarev, the wife of Nicholas Ogarev, and found them in what is usually described as "a compromising position." Katkov apologized to Maria's husband, and the three remained friends. Some months later, however, Katkov cornered Bakunin and accused him of maliciously spreading the story among their friends and colleagues. Bakunin, nonplussed by the sudden attack, demanded to know what Katkov was talking about. The enraged Katkov called Bakunin a scoundrel and Bakunin responded in kind. Katkov then called Bakunin a eunuch and pushed him. Bakunin grabbed his cane and whacked Katkov with it; according to different accounts, Katkov either slapped Bakunin or spat in his face. Either way, this could only be resolved by a duel, and the appropriate challenge and acceptance were made. Cooler heads, however, eventually prevailed, and both parties retreated.[34]

That is the second piece of evidence: the name-calling in the middle of a quarrel between two young men. From this insult has issued an entire school of explanation of Bakunin's personality, family relations, and political thought. For readers of the "where there's smoke, there's fire" school, there is even less to the Bakunin story than first appears, for the only account of this incident comes to us from Belinsky, who, as we have seen, had his own reasons for implying that Bakunin was bloodless and ineffectual.

The myth of Bakunin's impotence has lasted in large part because it fits in nicely with the psychological theories advanced by liberals to explain the radicalism of his generation. Thus Isaiah Berlin devoted his scholastic life to defending liberalism, that is, capitalism and the limited democratic rights established by the parliaments of Western Europe and North America in the eighteenth and nineteenth centuries. Paramount for him is the notion that there should be a rigid division between the political and economic spheres. Democracy is something that happens in the voting booth, and it ends at the door of the workplace, where the economic right of the employer to control property and labor—that is, human beings—trumps any notions of democracy. Bakunin and others of his generation went far beyond that cramped view of democracy to insist that liberty had to extend equally to every facet of life. That meant destroying serfdom and capitalism as well as repressive states, for these economic systems restricted human liberty as effectively as any political regime. To denounce this radical critique of capitalism, Berlin argues that Bakunin, Herzen, and others were wracked with guilt over Russia's terrible poverty, backwardness, and drabness. Under the repressive reign of the tsar, these nobles could do nothing. They were isolated and unable to influence their world; they were, in a word, impotent. Frustrated politically, and, allegedly in Bakunin's case, sexually, they retreated into a neurotic fantasy world of impossible ideals, Utopian programs, and mystical philosophy. For Berlin, their radical vision demonstrated the failure of Bakunin's generation to understand the real world, by which Berlin means the world of pragmatic politics, of deals, compromise, and surrender. In short, Berlin's project was to defend the status quo and to denounce other philosophies by any means that came to hand. That the psychological interpretations were based on no evidence made them better, for as untestable hypotheses, they could not be proved false.

Martin Malia brought Berlin's seminal arguments to term. What attracted Bakunin and others to German idealism, Malia argued, was the promise thinkers such as Schiller, Schelling, and Fichte held out: that freedom was essentially a mental state that could be achieved regardless of social and political reality. When this illusion became impossible to sustain, Malia continues, the frustrated Russians turned to politics. But they were unable to transcend their early idealism, unable to take up the pragmatic, practical politics of accommodation that Malia deems appropriate. They remained committed to the ideal and the Utopian, precisely because these were unrealizable. For them, politics was the art of the impossible; their vision was religious in its blind faith, intensity, and the quest for perfection. Unable and unwilling to act effectively, Herzen, Turgenev, Bakunin, and the others became, in their own phrase, "superfluous men." Malia expands on this to insist that the generation was "alienated" from the regime and everyday life. Used loosely, alienation, in the sense of standing apart from or turning away from the Russian regime, is an accurate enough description. But Malia goes further to imply that Bakunin's generation was also "alienated" in the psychological sense, that is, powerless to make sense of their lives, unable to make meaningful connections with other people, completely separated from their culture, their fellow humans, and themselves. Following both Berlin and Malia, Aileen Kelly applies the concept of alienated social psychology specifically to Bakunin. In the same way that the meaning of "alienation" was subtly twisted to cast aspersions on political theory, so too did "impotence" morph from a metaphor of the nobility to political description to psychological explanation too salacious and easy for biographers to resist.

Yet as we have seen earlier, there is no evidence that Bakunin was impotent or that his colleagues were alienated in the psychological sense. The classical, contemporary alienated being ends up in a high school or a bell tower with a rifle; the closest these young Russians came to that was to found a journal titled *Kolokol,* or *The Bell.* They quarreled, they debated, they loved, and they hated; they drank and smoked and threw themselves into their culture and their studies. Taken together, these psychological arguments are a textbook example of the fallacy of begging the question, that is, basing a conclusion on an assumption that itself needs proving. To recap, the fallacious argument goes like this: political ideas the historian finds distasteful are offered as proof of mental imbalance. It is then argued that since people who hold those views are unbalanced, we can reject their political ideas without bothering to examine them.[35]

Bakunin and Herzen were alienated, that is, separated from, the regime in the sense that Russia had no place for them, no reasonable career they could take up. There is some truth to this, but it is easy to forget that both men rejected the regime before it rejected them. That is, it was their criticism of Russia that made them unemployable, not the lack of jobs that made them critics. The first source of their disenchantment was their social role as intellectuals. The regime had devoted considerable resources to educating young men as it tried to modernize and renew. The problem with education, however, is that once you encourage people to think, it becomes increasingly difficult to restrict what they will think about. Even engineers must be taught to think critically, to go beyond the surface appearance of structure and materials, to follow ideas where they lead, to insist that claims about truth be proved, not merely asserted by authority. Indeed, the first duty of the intellectual is to criticize, for only by stripping away false ideas can they begin to discover the truth. Roping off areas of inquiry only inspires intellectuals to trespass. That is why it is often argued that there is no such thing as a conservative intellectual. Conservative journalists, writers, academics, pundits there may be in plenty, but not intellectuals, for in accepting and supporting the status quo, they have given up meaningful criticism. Thus for a generation of Europeans, mostly men from a certain class and stratum, their first duty was, as Marx put it, to ruthlessly criticize everything. When they ran into orthodoxy and authority, they turned their criticism on the regime itself and launched themselves into politics. Bakunin and his generation did not retreat into fantasy worlds or strike out blindly. Romanticism was not a refuge: It was the first step in their critical, active response to the strictures of the regime. The next step was as obvious to them, and they turned eagerly to German idealism, especially the work of Fichte and Hegel, to change reality, not to praise it.

5

THE MAIN ILLNESS OF OUR GENERATION

German idealism is often denounced as ethereal and unconnected and as an inherently conservative reaction. In fact, it closely echoed political and economic developments, just as Romanticism reflected the Industrial Revolution, and it had both conservative and revolutionary incarnations and implications. Some groups believed they would prosper in the newly developing world of industrial capitalism while others feared they could only lose, and so some embraced change while others rejected it. The conflicts of class, status, and power were obvious, but the coalitions needed for competing sides to win were not so clear and the proffered solutions reflected this chaos.[1]

In Russia, it was clear one had to reject the autocracy as repressive, inefficient, and boorish. But it was not so evident what one could or should put in its place, so it was natural enough for Russian intellectuals to dip into the new wave of European philosophers, the German idealists ranging from Schiller to Fichte and ultimately to Hegel, for answers. Far from being an odd, irrational escape and leap of faith, it was a reasoned progression from familiar novels such as *The Swiss Family Robinson* and James Fenimore Cooper's Leatherstocking tales to Schiller's "William Tell," eased by Beethoven's use of Schiller's "Ode to Joy" in his Ninth Symphony. From Romantic literature and music, it was rational and obvious to turn to the philosophy that underlay them.

There Bakunin and his colleagues discovered writers who spoke to the very issues of duty and freedom they faced in their daily lives. In the chaotic Europe of clashing classes, politics, and ethics, the moral ambiguity explored in works such as Schiller's play *Die Räuber (The Robbers)* resonated powerfully among young intellectuals. In the play, the bad son deceives his elderly father into disowning his good son, then schemes to murder them both. Discovering there is no justice in society, the good son seeks liberty and passion in the life of an outlaw. Unlike Robin Hood, however, his band of scary men is not a force for justice and retribution, but for destruction and immorality, and the good son creates more harm and evil in the name of liberty than the bad son does in the name of greed. Indeed, the good son is ultimately responsible for the death of his father and his brother, ironically committing the same acts his evil brother had only planned. Thus Schiller illuminated the hopes and disillusionment of the French Revolution and suggested that the consequences of one's actions might well be unpredictable but were nonetheless as important as one's intentions. Such ethical uncertainty reflected the tumultuous world of the early nineteenth century, where it was not clear how to rid the world of evil without falling prey to evil oneself. The relevance of such insights was obvious and compelling in tsarist Russia as Bakunin and his generation sought real-world answers to real-world problems in German philosophy. So too was the observation that human existence was as much about conflict and change as it was harmony and stability.

The German idealists that Bakunin turned to were not obsessed with asserting that the idea, or the mind, constructed the real world. Nor were they pursing metaphysical questions of the "How many Hegels can dance on the head of a pin?" variety. They were asking important questions about the nature of reality and the mind, of the nature of political and ethical dilemmas. In fact, they took up practical questions as well as larger ones about the nature of reality. Above all they tried to create a coherent philosophy of progressive change. The rulers of German states and principalities, like Russian tsars, insisted that political change was evil. They had, after all, no reason to love the political ideas of France, with its revolution that had removed, quite literally, the head of state. German idealist philosophers, on the other hand, understood that change was inevitable and necessary for humanity to flourish, but were less convinced than Enlightenment philosophers that it could be easily and effectively implemented. Thinkers from Hegel to Alexander Bakunin had welcomed the French Revolution and the end of regal despotism, but quailed at the aftermath of brutal repression and war. If capitalism brought untold riches, it also created untold poverty, urban blight, and suffering. Like the Romantics before them, they sought to understand how a world that promised so much could deliver such betrayal.

Bakunin was particularly interested in the ideas of Johann Fichte. One of Fichte's primary tasks was to attempt to reconcile the experience of free will with the observation that the world seemed to be determined. In his language, he sought to reconcile freedom with necessity, to understand how humans who believed themselves to be free agents able to make meaningful moral choices could also be part of a material world in which laws of nature determined cause and effect. Contrary to popular belief, he did not maintain that human existence took place only in the mind or as a kind of spiritual existence, or that the "I," the ego, the mind, created the objects that it observed.

His starting point—"posit the I"—did not mean that only the mind existed but rather that one starts by asserting one's self and that one should start by assuming one had freedom.

This assumption was not based on wishful thinking. There were two possible starting points for the philosopher: either pure freedom, sometimes called "selfhood," or pure necessity, or "thinghood." Either we could make choices as free beings or we were merely objects, completely subject to the laws of physics, chemistry, and the like. Idealism started with freedom; fatalism, or determinism, or, as Fichte called it, dogmatism, started with necessity. Neither position could effectively refute the other, but Fichte believed it was more useful to start by assuming freedom, for dogmatism could not explain consciousness or the belief that humans had real choice. A strict determinism, he argued, would have to make an unsupported leap from the world of things to the world of thought. Idealism, however, could explain our experience of the material world without making a similar jump of faith, and thus provided a firmer starting point.

So assume freedom. Whatever freedom might mean to the "I," to the world of the mind, in fact, nothing happened in isolation. In practical terms—and Fichte insisted that practicality was crucial—humans existed in a real, physical, material, and limited world, not one of mind or spirit in which all things were possible. Thus there were limits to freedom. But humans could push those limits and could exercise agency within those limits to expand the boundaries. This was not done by mental gymnastics such as imagining oneself to be free or ignoring external reality. As he emphasized, "It is not possible purely by means of the will alone to modify things in accordance with our necessary concepts of how they should be." It required action in the real world.

For Fichte, idealism was the operation of the intellect within certain laws in the real world, rather than fantasy or complete freedom, and he assumed that humans acted in the real world. We did not, however, have to accept the real world just as it was. That is, we could say, "This is how the world works at present, but it is not how it should work," or, "This is how things are, but we can imagine a better world and should work to achieve it." As Fichte put it, "Reality must be judged in accordance with ideals and must be modified by those who feel themselves able to do so." The point of philosophy was not to escape the world but to "Act! Act! That is what we are here for." One had to act responsibly and ethically, and the philosopher and the scholar, having benefited from society's investment in their learning, owed a debt that could only be repaid by applying their education "for the benefit of society."[2]

What did a better world look like? For Fichte, it was a world of freedom and equality. The two were not, in his vision, antithetical; each implied the other. For the desire to master others—inequality—was a sign of immaturity in both individuals and societies. Once one had "developed his own sense of freedom and spontaneity . . . he would necessarily have to wish to be surrounded by other free beings like himself."

Much of Fichte's work dealt with ethics, which obviously assumes both a "real" existence and one in which one is in society, that is, with other humans. It is true that his attempt to base ethics on first principles sounds odd to many of us today. Yet it is apparent, even in a cynical, non-metaphysical world, that we do make some fundamental assumptions about reality and causation. It makes no sense, for example, to punish criminals unless we believe that they have some measure of free will. If their actions were determined, either by fate or God or by circumstance, punishing them is both irrational and unjust. If they could not have acted otherwise, if they had no choice, we are punishing them for something for which they are not responsible. The job of the philosopher, Fichte insisted, was to find the first principles upon which humans could make ethical decisions.

The effect of this philosophy on Bakunin's generation is hard to overestimate. It did not turn them into navel-gazers but gave them a sophisticated framework to resolve both philosophical and practical questions. "Assume freedom"—what does that mean in the face of duty to family and state? German idealism gave these Russian thinkers the tools to think beyond the narrow boundaries defined by the tsar to consider how to give their lives meaning. It enabled them to contemplate a life, a society, a world, in which people could make free choices unbound by selfish authority. Fichte was right: there was no irrefutable starting point, one simply chose either freedom or necessity, and "the kind of philosophy one chooses depends on the kind of person one is." Fine: Let the tsar choose his, and let us choose ours! One path led to repression, to narrowing the scope of human activity, the other to the expansion of freedom, and ultimately happiness. What sort of a mope would choose the former? Fichte had an answer for that, as well: the less developed, the immature, the fearful. Well, who wanted to be that?

Fichte held that the ideal was a world where "reason, rather than strength or cunning, will be universally recognized as the highest court of appeal," where justice, not force, was the principle upon which decisions were made. It would be a world of freedom and equality, for while "man may employ mindless things as means for his ends," it was wrong to "employ rational beings [even] as a means for their own ends." This ideal pushed the boundaries of the tsar's restrictions and those of Priamukhino, for it was wrong to use others. Indeed, the one "who considers himself to be a master of others is himself a slave," or at least has a "slavish soul . . . and will grovel on his knees before the first strong man who subjugates him." Fichte had a point still applicable today; according to folklore, and to a dominatrix who once was a neighbor of mine, most of the customers of her profession are powerful men in business and politics who pay handsomely to be dominated.

Fichte penned some important political lessons as well, and if Bakunin was not particularly interested in them at first, their influence on his later thought is clear. Fichte asked why men were unequal, and found the answer in the inequality of classes. To be sure, he did not mean economic classes in the way Marx and Bakunin would later use the term, but in a more general sense, to mean something like the skills or vocation one followed. He insisted that class inequality was not natural, and could not be justified, whatever advantages this inequality provided to society. Every class was necessary and thus deserved respect; moreover, nearly everyone could learn from nearly anyone. Therefore all people should be educated equally and left free to choose their class, based on their abilities, skills, and preferences, rather than have their class position fixed by birth, tradition, or law. It was wrong for another to place one into a class, first because no one could know another's talents well enough to make an intelligent choice, and second because "a member of society who is assigned to the wrong place in this manner is often totally lost for society." But more importantly, it was wrong because it treated one as a means and not an end, as an object, rather than a human. As Fichte wrote, forcing one into a class meant that "we desired a member of society, and we produce a tool of society. We desired a free fellow worker on our great project, and we produce a coerced, passive instrument of the same . . . we have killed the man within the person . . . we have wronged him and we have wronged society." By society, Fichte meant something rather different than did conservative philosophers. Society was not the same as the state or government. The state, he argued, was "only a means for establishing a perfect society. . . . The goal of all government is to make government superfluous." As a nice statement of the anarchist vision, this is fairly succinct. Fichte insisted that humans should work toward and for a society in which reason, not force, mediated human interaction, where freedom and equality made possible the increased cultivation and development of humanity, to free humanity from the bonds of nature and greed and stupidity.

To his detractors who thought this was "muddled enthusiasm" or "romantic nonsense," Fichte replied that such criticism showed only their complacency and lack of imagination. "Since you are unable to imagine a better state of affairs," he pointed out, "everything really is good enough for you." He had little patience for those who only carped; it was not sufficient simply to "stand there and complain about human corruption without lifting a finger to diminish it." Fichte sided with those who were not blinded by their pursuit of wealth and favor, who instead felt pain when they saw "the imperfection, the corruption, and the misery of our fellow men." The role of the scholar was not to order the impoverished and oppressed into freedom, as the French Revolution had done, but to foster "that strength to help themselves which men possess within themselves."

Fichte's popular lectures, which Bakunin translated and published in *The Telescope,* were hardly injunctions to contemplate one's navel. They were a call to thoughtful, reasoned action, aimed not at selfish, narrow ends but at broader social improvement. In this way, Fichte sought to expand the vision of freedom and equality expounded by the Enlightenment but overshadowed by the Terror and empire and war and capitalism. And the message was of immediate practicality as well to those in the Russian empire who sought their own liberty and that of their compatriots.

From Fichte, Bakunin turned to Hegel. Georg Wilhelm Friedrich Hegel has the dubious honor of being even less understood than Bakunin. As Terry Pinkard notes in his biography, anyone who knows anything about Hegel knows that he believed that reality was spiritual, not material; that reality existed only in the mind and not as an exterior reality; that he celebrated a mystical notion of the "Absolute"; that change over time was based on the "dialectic" of thesis-antithesis-synthesis; and that he held up the authoritarian Prussian state as the desired and desirable end point of human history. Sadly for the storehouse of human knowledge, every one of these statements about Hegel is flat-out wrong, even though they have been repeated to generations of students from Hegel's day to the present.[3] Considered an essential thinker by those trained in the Western European tradition, Hegel has often been ignored by Anglo-American philosophers. The sides of the modern debate are nicely characterized by the title of an article in the journal *Historical Materialism:* "Hegel: Mystic Dunce or Important Predecessor?"[4]

Hegel deserves some of the blame for the misinterpretations. His prose is ponderous and dank in the worst German tradition. By comparison, the contemporary Marxist theorist Fredric Jameson, who regularly wins well-deserved prizes for the worst writing in the academy, reads like John Grisham. Much of Hegel's work has survived only in the form of his lecture notes and those taken by his students, and anyone who has ever sat through or given a lecture will be suspicious of their accuracy. Worse, Hegel had a speech impediment and a distinct Swabian regional accent, in Germany then roughly the equivalent of sounding like Jed Clampett, that made his lectures less intelligible. Reading him in translation puts another barrier between his thought and his audience. More importantly, Hegel was dealing with the large philosophical questions of the day as a professional philosopher and so was speaking in code to those who understood the jargon and the history of the debates and were highly motivated to pick their way through his work.

It is not, of course, necessary to be a Hegelian to be an anarchist. Bakunin later denied that his political ideas were influenced by Hegel, and indeed attacked Marx on the grounds that he had not moved far enough from Hegel. The anarchist Peter Kropotkin, who picked up where Bakunin left off, had no use for Hegel, and preferred to argue for anarchism on the basis of science, not philosophy. Others have held that liberalism itself, taken to its logical conclusions, leads to anarchism; still other anarchists have insisted that historical materialism, existentialism, mysticism, or postmodernism provide sufficient justification. It may be that all roads, or none, lead to anarchism, or that political theory and practice may be rooted in human experience in which formal philosophy plays but a small role. In any case, it is useful to examine Hegel briefly to see what Bakunin found interesting and useful in his work.

Born in Stuttgart in 1770, Hegel studied theology at the University of Tübingen with the plan of becoming a Lutheran pastor and was a contemporary and friend of Schelling's. When the French Revolution broke out, he endorsed it enthusiastically and celebrated Bastille Day throughout his life. The successes of the Revolution and Napoleon were obvious enough: only after Napoleon's invasions was serfdom done away with in parts of Europe, and the French legal code was a distinct improvement over the more personal and arbitrary tyranny of the lord. But Hegel denounced the Terror as grotesque excess, an example of freedom asserted as an abstract principle without regard to civil society and real people. Like many thinkers of the day, he was keenly aware of the possibility and need for sweeping reform and just as keenly aware that human intentions were rarely realized perfectly.

After graduation from university, he worked as a private tutor, a job for which he was not well suited, and soon took up the study of political economy, especially Adam Smith, and philosophy, especially Immanuel Kant. He moved to the university at Jena in 1801, where Fichte taught until his death in 1814, and where Schelling was making his reputation. The two friends soon feuded, in part because Schelling, five years Hegel's junior, was a more popular teacher and writer. When the university was shut down in the aftermath of Napoleon's Western European tour, Hegel taught high school in Nuremberg. In 1811, aged forty-one, he married a much younger woman, and in 1816, Hegel was made a professor of philosophy at Heidelberg; two years later, he signed with the University of Berlin, where he taught and wrote until his death, officially from cholera, but more likely from a chronic gastrointestinal ailment.[5]

In a "Germany" that consisted of over three hundred independent and often quarreling cities and principalities, the notion of a larger nation that could draw on the resources of an expanded area and population to resist the waves of invasion, war, and foreign occupation and get on with the business of business and civilization was as appealing to Hegel as it was to the Russian nobility. Like other romantic and idealist philosophers, Hegel sought meaning and harmony in the chaos of the period. Unlike Kant, Hegel disliked the notion that humans were always torn between reason and desire, and believed it was possible to reconcile the two. Unlike Schiller, who tried to resolve the dilemma through art, Hegel insisted that the way to avoid the dilemma was through philosophy. Again unlike Kant, Hegel believed that human nature was not fixed or static and that humanity changed and developed over time. So too did human societies, and Hegel believed that there was meaning and direction to this evolving history.

The idea that there could be, and could be shown to be, a path of historical development was not in itself new to Hegel, and has not vanished today. Many religions hold that life on earth is merely the preparation for life in the hereafter or rebirth and that humans should work toward this higher end. Writers such as Francis Fukuyama have concluded that the end purpose of human history is present-day capitalism. With better logic and rather more evidence, Calvin of the comic strip *Calvin and Hobbes* holds that "History is a force . . . Everything and everyone serves history's single purpose . . . to produce me, of course!"[6] More seriously, if with less clarity, Hegel held that history—change over time—was not random or accidental. Through studying the past, it was possible to understand its direction. History was not determined by strict "laws" of development the way the orbits of the planets were, but neither was human history haphazard or purposeless.

What was the direction, the purpose, the end, of history? For Hegel, "world history is the progress of the consciousness of freedom."[7] Freedom, in turn, could be formal freedom, that is, freedom from restrictions, the ability to do what one wanted to do, but for Hegel, this was more complicated than it appeared. Such a definition rested on the concept of the free individual, but he pointed out that we made our choices from a limited number of options. Our freedom of choice was, to be sure, based on our will, but our very will, including the notion of free choice, was itself based on our society. Our choices were restricted by what was possible and permitted within that society. This freedom from restrictions, this freedom to choose, for Hegel, ultimately meant little more than the freedom to be swept along by current political and social forces. And these forces were hardly neutral or objective, for politics served interest groups, not "the people."

Instead, he continued, real freedom was that the individual be free to judge and freely choose truth and morality. It was the development and expansion of this idea of individual freedom, based on reason, not on secular or religious authority, custom, tradition, legal codes, or social orthodoxy, that Hegel saw developing throughout human history. This idea, or spirit, of freedom was not a ghost or metaphysical construct, as many have claimed. It was, for Hegel, the expression of different peoples and cultures and could be shown to have developed and refined and expanded over time.

Turning to history to provide examples, Hegel argued that in societies such as China and India, only the ruler was free. One person had the power, the authority, and the right, to determine what people should do and what was moral. The ruler's will mattered, and it was all that mattered. Ancient Persia saw the consciousness of freedom expand slightly, for while there was an emperor as in China and India, the emperor was expected to be bound not by his own will or desires, but by religious principles.

Ancient Greece extended the consciousness of freedom and actual freedom substantially, but even in the city-states such as Athens it was limited. First, whatever liberty citizens may have enjoyed rested on the labor of slaves. This was, according to Hegel, a matter of necessity, for the idea of freedom developed over time and was tied to the level of material, economic development. In societies of scarce resources, only some could be free, for others had to produce the means of existence that gave them the leisure time to contemplate and engage in civic society. In this way, Hegel argued that the development of the "spirit of freedom" was more than an exercise in logic; it was connected to the development of the real world, and the two influenced each other.

The freedom of the ancient Greeks was limited in another way. Freedom, for Hegel, required critical thought and free inquiry. Much of what appeared to be free activity in ancient Greece, such as the notion of duty to the city-state, was in fact custom, habit, and tradition. That is to say, it was accepted practice, based not on critical analysis and free choice, but on being taught and accepting ideas without question. Orthodoxy and community standards were, in Hegel's view, a step beyond simply obeying the emperor, but fell far short of complete, real freedom.

Rome pushed the boundaries of freedom further. Unlike the Greek city-states, Rome was an empire. Empire by definition meant organizing different groups, polities, and cultures that are pushed by centrifugal force away from the center. To survive, the empire needed to impose discipline and rules based on principles—a legal code—rather than arbitrary rule. By limiting and codifying the power of the rulers, Rome developed further the idea of the individual and provided for formal recognition of the individual under the law. The individual, however, was in conflict with the needs of the state for conformity and obedience. This need for conformity saw philosophies such as stoicism develop, for they taught that the individual could observe outward conformity but look inward in resignation for development and fulfillment. This was rational when confronted with the power of Rome, but it did not resolve the tension between the needs of the individual and the needs of society.

Christianity was an attempt to resolve this tension by emphasizing the spiritual aspect of human beings. In Hegel's view, humans were both material and spiritual beings, and only by developing both sides could humanity progress. Christianity, in stressing that Jesus Christ was both man and God, contained the empowering notion that humans were made in the image of God and thus had intrinsic value as individuals. Furthermore, Christianity developed the idea that the task of humanity was not just to achieve inward peace but to act in and on the world to change it. Finally, Christianity based morality on principles, especially the idea of love, and these principles were more than habit or custom, for they were developed through critical thought.

But Christianity was flawed and could only take the search for freedom so far. The Middle Ages saw the Catholic Church dominate individuals as the Church put itself between God and humanity. It demanded not critical acceptance of principles, but uncritical devotion to the teachings of the Church. The spiritual world that Christianity had opened was largely replaced by blind devotion to relics, icons, and ceremonies, to devotion to the forms but not the essence of the Christian message. The Reformation heralded the new dawn and Protestantism created a direct connection between the individual and God. It reinforced the original message of Christianity and reestablished the principle of conscious, rational, human activity in both the spiritual and the material worlds. With the Reformation, the chief human task became the reformation of the world in accordance with the principle of freedom, and thus Hegel insisted that it was not enough to understand the world; it was also necessary to act in it.

But how could individuals agree on what was to be done? How could anyone know what actions were in tune with the progressive expansion of freedom? According to Hegel, the answer lay in rational thought. States, governments, and economies should be based upon rational principles on which all could agree. But rationality itself was not enough, any more than was the simple consciousness of freedom. The French Revolution was an example of humans changing the world based on rational principles, but the subsequent terror was the result of the attempt to apply these principles from above on a people who were not yet ready for them. The principles of the French Revolution, however, remained, and could be built upon; thus Hegel's celebration of Bastille Day every year. Furthermore, some formal principles of freedom remained in the French legal code and constitutions, and this again showed that humanity built on what went before, discarding those aspects that contradicted freedom and were no longer necessary. Just as slavery had been abolished when and where other productive relations had evolved, so too were political forms abandoned when they no longer expanded human freedom.

What was the next step in historical development? Hegel argued it was time to resolve the conflicts between the state and the individual and between self-interest and duty. Kant had argued that real freedom was to be free from natural impulse, instinct, and desire; one had to think to choose, and one should choose rationally and morally. For Kant, moral choices—for morality is above all about choices—meant to act according to the "categorical imperative": roughly, to make those choices that could be extended to and made by all. In his words, "I am never to act otherwise than so that I could also will that my maxim should become a universal law." Put another way, moral choices were those made without individual, narrow, particular interests or desires; with these out of the way, the moral choice could be made.

Fair enough, Hegel agreed, but Kant gave us only the principle, not concrete examples. Kant assumed that all humans started at the same spot, that their ideas, desires, and logical processes were essentially the same, but Hegel argued that this was not the case. It is entirely possible to imagine, and to observe, cases where people have very different ideas about right and wrong, and it may be impossible to say who is correct. You might say that everyone has a right to property, and therefore theft is immoral. I respond that property itself is theft and thus no one has a right to it. For you, property is a moral principle; for me, it is wrong.[8] How can we possibly know what should be extended to a universal law, given that humans often disagree on fundamental issues?

Furthermore, Kant's argument, stripped down, said that you were supposed to choose in accordance with the law of universal reason. So you didn't really have a choice: you were supposed to do your duty because you were supposed to do your duty. So freedom meant doing your duty. Put more crudely, freedom meant doing what you were told to do. More subtly, it meant following your conscience, which was supposed to have the notion of duty built into it, but again, that meant ultimately doing your duty as defined by your society, which had educated you and shaped that conscience and thus could hardly be seen as universal. If Kant skated around this by insisting that conscience was more than a conditioned reflex, that it was the rational choice to accept the categorical imperative as the guide to our actions, this was an argument made with little reference to real people and real societies.

Finally, Hegel insisted that Kant left us with the premise that humans were inherently torn between desire and reason, between the individual and society, between satisfying the self and contributing to the collective. That meant humanity would always be in conflict. Kant's solution, that we do our duty, Hegel argued, amounted to saying that we could be moral only if we suppressed our desires, which was hardly the way to develop freedom. If the concept of duty had been a step forward because it recognized a relationship between the individual and the community, the question now was how to incorporate human desire to increase human freedom while adopting principles for behavior without turning them into reflexes of habit and conformity.

History held some clues. Each generation benefited from the efforts of the previous, and though it was always possible to stumble and slide—the Middle Ages and the Terror were proof of that—even these mistakes helped humanity learn and advance. Rationality too progressed and spread throughout cultures, and these two tendencies combined with real changes in economies and politics to help ensure humanity moved forward over time. Thus slavery, though it still existed in Hegel's day, as in ours, was no longer the preeminent economic relationship in the world, partly because humanity understood that it was wrong and partly because in an age of wage labor and industrialization, it was no longer necessary. Peter Singer gives a clear, contemporary example of the development of humanity in the Hegelian model. Imagine a small community, say a European town. The town develops slowly, without conscious planning, and so the streets are crooked and narrow, following creeks and paths, avoiding obstacles, essentially following nature. There is no need for sewers or garbage collection—the backyard and the vacant property are sufficient. As the town grows, the streets are crowded, inefficient, even dangerous, and waste disposal can no longer be a matter of dumping the chamber pot out the window. The community is too complicated to work effectively without planning and conscious development. Old buildings are torn down, wide, straight streets are laid out, ordinances replace customs, and mercifully, someone creates a sewer system.

But this new rational city presents new problems. The destruction of old neighborhoods robs areas of their vitality and their sense of community; people are now surrounded not by friends and family but by strangers. The new wide streets are nothing more than thoroughfares; no one stops for lunch and conversation and civic life alongside a major traffic intersection. The solutions to the old problems, imposed from above, have solved some problems but have created new ones. The new city doesn't work as its planners hoped. But the way forward was obvious. Planners and city officials had to work with citizens to develop new ideas more sensitive to the needs of people rather than simple efficiency as viewed from the top. Much of the old city had worked well; the key to progress was to integrate the old and the new.[9]

If this sounds rather like a Civics 101 lecture on modern government, the ideas that governments were accountable to the people, that change was necessary and progressive, and that history could be propelled from below as well as from the top, were radical enough in Hegel's time of absolutist rulers. We might also ask ourselves how accurately the civics lecture reflects the reality of politics today before we congratulate ourselves on reaching Hegel's final stage of human development.

Since he was a historian, not a prophet, Hegel was sketchy on the details of humanity's next step. He spoke of "organic communities," for he understood that human needs and wants were shaped by the community; the key was to create communities that could think clearly and rise above narrow self-interest or class interest. Suspicious of parliamentary democracy, for it represented blocs of votes and interest groups rather than individuals, he suggested that a constitutional monarchy in which the monarch was subservient to the legislature might provide the right combination of access and efficiency. This argument put him in the vanguard of progressive reformers of the day. No anarchist, Hegel's comments on the state sometimes strike us as totalitarian, especially when he writes about the "divine nature" of the state, an idea that taken literally opens the door to all kinds of state repression.

But a more sensitive reading of Hegel shows that he understood clearly that any state was a creation of humans and thus was prone to errors, mistakes, and misinterpretations. He understood full well that "supreme executive power" could be misused. Furthermore, by the state, he meant not just the government with its legislature, police, and bureaucracy, but the community and culture that created such structures as were necessary to pursue an ethical life. He believed not in the rule of a dictator—rational or not—but in the rule of law, understood and agreed to by members of the community, not imposed upon them from above.

In Hegel's view, the task of philosophy was not to teach what one ought to do in a specific circumstance or to divine what ought to happen. History, not a philosopher, would determine that. But philosophers could, Hegel believed, use rational thought to determine what was reasonable and necessary and to demonstrate what was in line with the historical development of freedom. This was summed up in his famous, and utterly confusing, statement, "What is rational is real, and what is real is rational." Subsequent scholars have interpreted Hegel's remark in contradictory ways. Some suggested it means that it is irrational to oppose whatever exists. Cast that way, Hegel could be used to support the most tyrannical state or economic system. All one could, and should, do was become reconciled with existing reality, for since it existed, it was real and therefore rational and in tune with the march of history. Others turned his phrase around to see it as a call for action, for whatever existed and could be shown to be irrational, such as serfdom, was not "real," because it hindered historical development and should be torn down. Thus conservatives and reformers, reactionaries and revolutionaries, could all appeal to Hegel. His followers split into two camps, the Right Hegelians and the Left Hegelians, depending on their political views. In Russia, Belinsky temporarily moved to the right to adjust to his new job with the regime. Herzen, on the other hand, concluded that Hegel had discovered the "algebra of revolution."

Bakunin has often been interpreted as taking a Right Hegelian position in 1838. This is based on the preface to Hegel's *Gymnasium Lectures* that Bakunin published in the March 1838 issue of the *Moscow Observer*. The lectures were originally given by Hegel while he was head of the Nuremburg high school, laying out his ideas on education. For Hegel, education was the way to resolve the separation of the individual from the community, for it served both to critique and to develop a common culture and ethic. Bakunin and others had purged the editor of the *Observer* and put Belinsky in charge. In the first issue under the new editor, Bakunin called explicitly for a "reconciliation with reality," and insisted that it was folly to "rebel against reality." This appeared to be a call for his generation to get with the tsar's program and support orthodoxy and conservatism. In fact, it signaled an end to the romantic engagement with ideas and art and represented his generation's turn to realism, practical action, and resistance. As Bakunin put it in a letter to the Beyer sisters, "It is time to speak up."[10] And so he did:

> Who nowadays does not fancy himself a philosopher, who does not speak today with conviction on what truth is and on what truth constitutes? Everyone wants to have his own, personal, particular system; he who does not think in his own original way, in accordance with his own arbitrary feelings, does not possess an independent spirit, he is considered a colorless, insipid man; he who has not thought up his own little ideas, well then, he is not a genius, there is no profundity in him, and nowadays no matter where one turns, one encounters geniuses everywhere. And what have these so-called geniuses thought up, what have been the fruits of their profound little ideas and views, what have they advanced, what have they accomplished of real significance?[11]

Bakunin's answer: "Noise, empty chatter—this is the only result of the awful, senseless anarchy of minds which constitutes the main illness of our new generation—a generation that is abstract, illusory, and foreign to any reality." In an attack that could have been aimed at his earlier views as much as those he critiqued, he complained that until now—that is, until Russia took up Hegel—philosophy was synonymous with "abstraction, illusion, and the absence of any reality." Thus the philosopher was alienated from the "natural and spiritual world." This separation from the real world led the philosopher to falsely believe that only the individual mattered, that the philosopher was the judge of truth, and that therefore his ideas, not objective reality, were true. These beliefs, Bakunin continued, alienated the individual from reality and caused him to waste energy railing against a reality he could not, in fact, alter by an act of will. This sounds conservative, but the article was written in the double code familiar to Bakunin's colleagues and comrades. Bakunin first encoded the article in Hegelian language and definitions and then recoded its controversial ideas in Aesopian language that used the rhetoric of patriotism, indirect metaphors, irony, and sarcasm to disguise the real message from the tsar's censors. The real meaning, however, was plain to those in the know. A clever example of this is Bakunin's critique of education in Russia. On the face of it, he critiqued the Russian education system because it "does not form a strong and real Russian man, devoted to the tsar and to his fatherland, but rather something mediocre, colorless, and without character." Yet as Bakunin knew full well from his own experience, and as his friends and readers knew from theirs, the education system did indeed create loyal subjects; the real point of his text was that criticism, not slavish devotion, was true loyalty to the organic community. A state that did not cultivate the virtues of criticism and reason—and Russia patently did not— was not an organic, whole community but a divided one that cherished the wrong values. In Hegelian terms, the present Russian state was thus irrational and unreal. It was something to be criticized and prodded, not reconciled with.

For Bakunin had long attempted to reconcile himself with Russian reality, from his school days in St. Petersburg to his failed military career to his relations with his family. By 1838, however, he had concluded that Russian reality was awful and not worth reconciling with. His article represented a rupture with, not a reconciliation with, Russian reality. It was the first concrete step in his radical political thought, and may be viewed as a critical transition.

The article established Bakunin as the most important Russian Hegelian of the period and put him in the ranks of young Hegelians anywhere; according to Belinsky, it also helped put the *Observer* out of business, for it was hardly accessible to the general reader. For his part, Bakunin blamed Belinsky for the decline of the journal, but it may be that both were right. Nonetheless, to be the most important Hegelian meant much, for Hegel was now the fashion, and Bakunin would continue his exploration of the philosopher.

6

CONTRADICTION IS THE SOURCE OF MOVEMENT

Bakunin followed up his promising start as a philosopher with a two-part article entitled "On Philosophy." The first was published in 1840 in the journal *Notes of the Fatherland,* edited by Andrei Kraevsky. The article expanded on some of the issues Bakunin had raised in the preface to his translation of Hegel, and made even clearer his growing commitment to philosophy as a practical means aimed at the end of action and change. He set out to ask and answer three questions: What is philosophy? Is philosophy useful? Is philosophy possible? He distinguished "philosophy" from its literal translation as "love of wisdom," for as he pointed out, "it would be a great pity if wisdom and love of it were the exclusive property of only a small number of people who studied philosophy, and remained inaccessible to the rest. These others constitute the majority of the human race, and mankind, no matter at what level of development it is, thirsts for wisdom and cannot exist without it."[1] Philosophy was more than practical knowledge and experience of life, though that was often called "wisdom," and it was not an attitude of taking adversity well by being "philosophical" about it. Philosophy went beyond logical analysis of "the questions of the day" and the "ratiocinations" of the French *philosophes* of the eighteenth century. In fact, Bakunin argued, their work was dangerous for philosophy, for it tore them away from "essential and important interests in life" and subjected them to the "pernicious rule of rash and senseless arbitrariness." In this, of course, he was following Hegel, who believed the excesses and horrors of the aftermath of the French Revolution resulted from the attempt of a radical elite to impose its ideas on the people: while their ideas may have been logically consistent and correct, the attempt to impose them from above was artificial, arbitrary, and doomed to failure. No, he declared, in what would become a nice irony, real philosophy "will never be atheistic and anarchistic." Philosophy was, he declared, the unity of "the real truth and true reality," the absolute "knowledge of the truth."

This truth went beyond the obvious acceptance of external reality, such as the existence of a table in one's room. While it may be correct to point out that there was a table there, it was no more than contingency or accident, and as such was of little interest to the philosopher. For the philosopher, what was true and real in the nontrivial sense was that which was historically necessary. This argument was Bakunin's attack on those thinkers who insisted that all that could be known and all that mattered were empirical facts as determined by objective observation and experiment. For them, there was no necessity in history, "only the empty play of contingency," or what we might call the Joe Friday school of history: just the facts, ma'am, without interpretation or the suggestion that there is a purpose or meaning to history. While these empiricists claimed that their approach was scientific, because they insisted that the observer was neutral and outside the events under study, and thus objective, Bakunin pointed out that it was logically inconsistent to claim that history was both just one damn thing after another and a science. In his words, "If universal history is, in effect, nothing more than a senseless succession of accidents, then it cannot be of interest to man, it cannot be an object of his knowledge, and it cannot be useful to him." History as accident could, by definition, have turned out very differently, and was thus meaningless, for it taught no lessons and led nowhere. Pursued in this way, human history "is reduced to the dead work of memory, the duty of which is contained only in the preservation of the accidental existence of contingent, singular facts." His point was not that objective facts did not exist, or that only ideas were real, or that nothing existed but thought. It was the much more subtle observation that facts alone did not give understanding or truth. We might illustrate this by referring to the way much history is still taught in schools today, that is, as the memorization of names and dates. Knowing the date of the War of 1812 is a bit of trivia of little interest and absolutely no use in itself, apart from being a way to bludgeon students into submission and identify those who will sit up straight and become cheerful cannon fodder, dutiful workers, and frantic consumers. That, of course, is the purpose of much education, in Bakunin's time and ours, and much of his critique of Russia and contemporary thought focused on education.

Furthermore, the empiricist could not be considered objective and impartial. Borrowing from Hegel, Bakunin noted that while the "ordinary consciousness," that is, the untrained philosophical mind, tried to understand the "real world" through "observation, comparison, abstraction, and analogy," these were insufficient. They were inadequate because "all men are formed under the influence of that society in which they were born. But each nation, each state, has its particular moral sphere, its popular beliefs, its prejudices, its particular limitations, depending in part on its individual character, on its historical development, and on its relationship to the history of all mankind." Furthermore, each state was itself divided into different social strata, and each stratum had "its individual character." In short, different cultures produced different ways of seeing the world, and passed these on to their members. As a result, no observer was neutral or objective. All attempts to understand the world, even those of the empiricists, were subjective and therefore were "always limited and one-sided" and "incapable of embracing the absolute truth."

Bakunin acknowledged that empiricism as a scientific method freed the "natural consciousness from its individual limitations, from its prejudices"; it tore away the "fetters of determined space and determined time, enriching its experience with its experiments carried out in different spaces and times. As much as possible, it expands the spiritual sphere of ordinary consciousness." But still it had limits. It divided the world into distinct, separate subjects and divided these subjects even further into arbitrary subdivisions for dissection and study. That encouraged the belief, false in Bakunin's view, that the world was in fact divided and unconnected, and scattered understanding of the whole into knowledge of fragments and discrete bits. True knowledge, he insisted, "searches for the universal unity." Real knowledge, "the essence of any knowledge," he maintained, lay not in compiling dead facts but in "finding the internal, necessary link within facts." This could not be accomplished only by theory, however. If empiricism "does not satisfy the principal criterion of knowledge, which requires thought, but not dry facts," then theories alone "do not accomplish anything and are nothing more than fantastic flashes, not based on anything and proving nothing." The problem with theory, he explained, was that the theorists started from the same point as the empiricists, that is, with "experimental observation, diversity of facts, and particular laws," but then went "running to hypotheses, to presuppositions: the theorist takes some thought or other . . . as a principle and attempts to explain and deduce all facts . . . from it."

In contrast, true knowledge required bringing together theory, or explanation, with empirical research, to avoid on the one hand mere collecting of trivia and on the other hand, abstract separation from the real world. Either approach, taken alone, was unable to discover real, existing, necessary truth and was therefore doomed to irrelevancy and sterility. What he called for, in short, was praxis, the unity of theory and practice, each informing the other. In truth, he admitted, there was no real contradiction between theory and empiricism, for in the real world, "there is no theorist who is not an empiricist, just as there is no empiricist who is not a theorist." The battle between the two sides was really a struggle of contradictions, of two poles of thought that together pointed the way to real knowledge. In the heat of the struggle for knowledge, "abstraction and extremism" on both sides often resulted, and both sides could forget how necessary each was to the other. When the struggle was creative and energetic, "the arid collectors of facts prepare the materials for the theorists; the theorists elaborate and work them in all directions, elevate them to relative-universal thoughts, and hand over the great deed of human knowledge to philosophy, which crowns it, producing out of all these fractions a united, organic, and absolutely transparent whole."

Through this chain of argument, Bakunin arrived at short answers to the three questions he had initially posed. Philosophy is the pursuit of real knowledge, of reality. It was useful because humanity could only advance when it had real knowledge. Finally, it was possible, but only if its students brought together empirical studies—practical action—and theory, in the best Hegelian tradition.

If this argument seems obscure or dated, we might remember that similar debates, though expressed in the language suited to our culture, still go on today within philosophy journals, and more importantly, in everyday life. Should children be taught history as facts to memorize or as explanations of process? Should history be taught as myth and propaganda or as critical inquiry? Is science value-free or blinded by the values of its culture? Should we pursue "pure science" or applied, practical science? Can the two be separated? Is there value to a liberal arts education or should it be abandoned for "practical" studies, by which is meant something that will lead to a specific job deemed useful by employers?

Bakunin's article, while framed as a broad inquiry into the nature of philosophy, had practical implications for Russia. Philosophy as a subject was banned in Russian universities because the authorities understood that free, critical thought would undermine the regime. Yet Bakunin was insisting that without such thought, no knowledge was possible. His argument against the dry, dusty preservation of simple facts was a critique of tradition and conservatism. His suggestion that contingent, accidental occurrences were of no use in understanding the world strongly implied that the Russia of the tsar was temporary, or, in Hegelian terms, was irrational and thus unreal. If the official censor could not connect the dots, Bakunin's enthusiastic readers certainly did. For anyone who might have missed the picture, he spelled it out, writing that Russia was stuck at the phase of "ordinary consciousness," that is, empiricism, since it had "hardly followed the development of contemporary philosophical thought."

"On Philosophy" outlined a dialectical approach to study, with the apparent opposites of theory and empiricism mutually reinforcing each other and reconciling their opposition with the creation of new knowledge. This too had political overtones. For Bakunin was declaring that the nature of the world was change, not stability or stasis. That which appeared real might not actually be real or remain real. That which was necessary today might not be necessary tomorrow, and could be done away with. History, not the pronouncements of the minister of the interior or the noose of the tsar's hangman, would be the ultimate judge.

The article was greeted with much praise and excitement, even from Bakunin's critics. Belinsky declared it "wonderful, so wonderful, as it is wickedly observant: I do not know any praise higher than this. This man can and must write—he will do much for the advancement of thought in his country." Kraevsky, the editor of the journal in which it was published, thanked Bakunin for an article that was "simply the model for philosophical articles in the Russian language" and urged him to send in the second part.[2] Bakunin did, but the piece was never published. It is of some interest here, however, because in it Bakunin outlined two other Hegelian ideas: those of "negation" and "contradiction."

The reader may by now be sharing Herzen's opinion of German philosophy, that its chief defect was its "artificial, heavy, scholastic language of its own," in which "very sensible and very simple things" were dressed up in a "strange jargon."[3] But these two ideas, so central to Hegel, are worth some attention, for they make intelligible one of Bakunin's most quoted remarks and established once and for all the revolutionary potential of Hegelian thought for young intellectuals of the 1840s.

Today "negation" is generally considered, well, negative. We're told to overcome adversity with the power of positive thinking; the song encourages us to "accentuate the positive, eliminate the negative," and no one wants to be a nattering nabob of negativism, as Richard Nixon's critics were once denounced. Nearly as bizarre as Nixon is the confounding world of negative numbers, and no one wants a negative balance in a bank account. It will come as no surprise by now, however, that Hegel and Bakunin used "negation" in a very different sense. While Herbert Marcuse is not recommended as a model of concision and clarity, in a preface to *Reason and Revolution: Hegel and the Rise of Social Theory* he did outline nicely what Hegel meant by negation. "Philosophical thought," Marcuse wrote, "begins with the recognition that the facts do not correspond to the concepts imposed by common sense and scientific reason—in short, with the refusal to accept them."[4]

The positive, for Hegel and Bakunin, was that which already existed. The negation was the critique of what existed, the realization that much of what we accept as true is in fact taught to us by those who profit from us believing it. For Hegel, "thinking is, indeed, essentially the negation of that which is immediately before us."[5] From this criticism comes new thought, new ideas, and the determination of what is real and rational. Thus negation was the first step in resolving contradictions, a word that had many meanings for Hegel. It applied to the potential disjuncture between appearance and reality, to the conflict between what one is told to believe and what one experiences, and to concepts such as the struggle between freedom and oppression, where opposites clash.

Again, Marcuse helps make sense of the concept with an overtly political example. If we concede that freedom is desirable for humanity, then the "realities" of the status quo that "perpetuates itself through the constant threat of atomic destruction, through the unprecedented waste of resources, through mental impoverishment, and—last but not least—through brute force" are the "unresolved contradictions" we face. To confront these grim realities, we have the power of negation and refusal.[6]

Bakunin, less firmly anchored in politics in 1840, nonetheless stressed negation and contradiction—struggle, in other words—as the way in which humanity moved forward to discover truth and reality as it progressed toward freedom. Human "potentiality" was "infinite truth," but it was contradicted by its "limited actuality." As a result of this tension between potential and actuality, "man" was driven "forward toward the realization of the internal, potential truth," and in that way elevated "above his external, temporary limitation." He traced the development of human consciousness, from individual perception of physical objects, such as "the knowledge of this birch tree, standing before me," through the development of generalized knowledge gained from experimental observation, "of birches in general, of the species or the type of birch . . . independent of individual perception," through the highest stages of reason and finally "absolute, true knowledge." How this might be applied to birch trees was not made clear, but the more important point Bakunin made was that human thought developed through negation, contradiction, and struggle. Human life was not static or fixed, as the tsar might wish, and did not develop in a controlled, gradual, straightforward way, as the tsar might hope. Instead, existing ideas and institutions, however necessary and progressive they may once have been, became inadequate for the continued progress of humanity, were challenged, struggled with, and left behind, as the best elements were incorporated into the new forms and ideas. Again Bakunin insisted that human action and change were driven by the "contradiction between the infinity of [humanity's] internal ideal essence and the limitation of his external existence; contradiction is the source of movement, of development, striving only toward its resolution." As with Hegel, the resolution, the goal of this dialectical struggle, was human freedom.

His articles established Bakunin as Russia's most influential Hegelian thinker. If this seems rather a dubious honor, it put Bakunin in the vanguard of progressive Russian thinkers and on par with some of the most interesting intellectuals in Europe. Even Herzen, who would later assail Hegelianism in his memoirs, stole some of Bakunin's thoughts for his own article on Hegel five years later. Yet whatever personal satisfaction his writing may have brought Bakunin, it indicated only that he was bright, articulate, and in tune with the times. It did not amount to a vocation or a career, and could become neither in Russia. His interest was philosophy, not journalism, and his writing would never be popular enough to sustain a career. Nor was it possible to create a career as a philosopher. Philosophy was still banned as a university subject in Russia; in any case, an academic post required university degrees. Clearly Bakunin knew the material, but in the Russia of the 1830s, as in much of the world today, credentials mattered more. Despite his publications, there was little left for him to do in Russia as a writer or thinker.

The jobs that were open to him, managing the estate and service to the regime, were equally unpalatable. Worse, family life at Priamukhino, despite detente with his parents, meant wasting one's energies on squabbles, quarrels, and crushed expectations all around. As he confessed in a letter to Stankevich, "the vile pettiness of everyday family and . . . vain internecine dissension among family members and friends" was wearing.[7]

Worse, intellectual life in Russia was fissuring and collapsing. The circles were falling apart as people took up careers, married, or found other interests. Belinsky moved explicitly to a Right Hegelian position and tried to reconcile himself with the reality of a mind-numbing job. If everyone remained critical of the regime, now each was critical for different reasons. Some, like Bakunin and Herzen, looked to Western Europe for ideas and inspiration. Just as Bakunin insisted that Russia had no real, that is, original and modern, philosophy, so too did other "westernizers" such as Belinksy, Chaadaev, and Kireevsky hold that Russia had no genuinely national art or literature. By this they did not mean that no Russians produced art or even that were no Russian motifs. They meant that Russian art was in its essence borrowed and copied. More importantly, it was not progressive. It did not challenge the official ideas of orthodoxy, autocracy, and nationality; on the contrary, they held, sanctioned culture was pressed into the service of conformity. Other Russian intellectuals, known as the Slavophiles, felt differently. They saw much that was good in traditional Russia and did not abandon religious faith as a way to understand and know the world; the Russia they sought drew on what they believed was unique to "the people." Personal problems too split the circles as everyone fell in and out of love. Old friends were gone: Bakunin's sister Liubov had died of tuberculosis in 1838, while Stankevich, stricken by the same bacillus, had left for Europe; Varvara soon followed him. Bakunin had pursued his dream of studying philosophy and become accomplished at it, only to find that Russia had no place for men with such skills. If he had freed himself from the army, from service, from convention, he was not free to do what Fichte and Hegel insisted had to be done: to act in the service of freedom.

Rather than retreat into despair and clinical alienation, he planned to leave Russia and seek in Europe what was denied him at home. By the beginning of 1840, even before his articles were published, he wrote to Alexandra Beyer that his efforts now were dedicated to finding a way to get to Berlin; otherwise, his life would stagnate. It was necessary "to tear myself away from the narrow limits of our reality," and to throw himself into "the life-giving atmosphere of Europe," where all could "breath in the divine idea: science, religion, art, nature, people."[8]

The problem was money. While the Bakunin family had impressive holdings, all were heavily mortgaged and could not provide ready cash. From his early days at military school, Bakunin had become accustomed to borrowing and spending freely, accumulating debts when necessary and living well when possible. When his father balked, he turned to his friends to stake him in his adventures. Belinsky, who had to count every penny, noted acerbically that "for you to ask someone, 'Do you have any money?' is the same thing as asking, 'Do you have any woodchips?'" He added, rather more kindly, "You also share and distribute it as if it were woodchips. I can't ever remember that, having ten roubles in your pocket, you were not immediately prepared to give me five, and if I had expressed an extreme need, to give me the rest also, except for a few kopecks for tobacco and coach fare . . . And you gave me that which you had borrowed from others or which you had earned from your lessons."[9]

Many, including Belinsky, attributed Bakunin's casual attitude toward money to his noble upbringing. After all, the definition of a gentleman is one who consumes without producing. If this also seems a useful definition of a tapeworm, a gentleman may conclude sadly that bourgeois ideology and the Puritan ethic have spread their baleful influences everywhere. They have spread especially among Bakunin's critics, Marxist, liberal, and conservative alike, who have often used his casual attitude toward money to suggest that he was not entitled to speak on behalf of peasants and workers and was sufficiently detached from base reality as to be hopelessly Utopian. But of course Bakunin's attitude was scarcely typical of a class. His father, for example, kept exceedingly careful records and did not, to his son's constant dismay, freely hand out cash. That Marxists use this to attack Bakunin's character and ideas is hypocritical, for Karl Marx lived off his father, his wife's unpaid household labor, her work as editor on his writing, his wife's family, the unpaid work of their maid, and of course, the largess of Friedrich Engels, who supported Marx from his own dividends and salary as a manager of his father's textile works. Hundreds had to labor each day for Marx to research and write. The liberal and conservative pundits are usually in a worse moral position. The friends of Bakunin and Marx freely chose to support them. The tenured don, the syndicated columnist, the public relations flack, have their salaries paid from the taxes and prices exacted from workers and consumers who have no say in how the monies are collected or spent. The blunt fact is that all intellectual work is paid for by someone else, either retail or wholesale.

In any case, Bakunin turned to his list of usual suspects in the hopes of making his way to Berlin. He penned another lengthy confessional letter to his parents in March of 1840, apologizing for his misdeeds but remaining firm in his conviction that philosophy, not running the estate or service, could be his only pursuit. In words calculated to win over his skeptical father, he acknowledged that he had made mistakes and blunders, though a number of his disappointments and unfortunate circumstances were caused by events outside his control. Nonetheless, he had learned from all this. Especially he had learned that it was impossible to live only an "interior life." He understood that humans had to live and work in the real world. He went further: it was necessary for all citizens to be "useful to their country," and in conformity with the "forms and means dictated to him by the direction and spirit of the state to which he belongs." More specifically, he went on, he had at last come to terms with the need to find a vocation that would enable him to earn his bread and take up a useful place in society. Deftly combining his alleged new leaf with Fichte and Hegel, Bakunin now understood that "real external activity" was the only way to be happy. But what occupation, what profession, what vocation, would be suitable? Teaching was out—it didn't pay enough, and was not snooty enough for someone of his station, family, and education. The military was right out, as was service and managing the estate. All that remained was to become a professor. That would let him combine his studies and his career, and would confer on him a suitable rank and position in society.

This required more education, he pointed out, and that could not be obtained in Russia. While the University of Moscow looked good, his formal education was limited, and he would have to start at the beginning. That was unseemly for someone his age—he was now twenty-six—especially as he would be behind his younger brothers. Furthermore, he would be required to take a number of courses he was manifestly uninterested in to meet the requirements for the degree, and could not take up his real subject of study. All told, it would mean losing four years at a time when he wanted to get on with his life. Only the University of Berlin would give him the training he needed as quickly as possible and equip him to sit the exams to take up a position at a Russian university, in either law, history, or, with luck, philosophy. He had now, he affirmed, the talent, drive, and perseverance to succeed; he was interested only in studying and would not waste his time abroad on "debauchery" and "orgies." Having lived without money, he had learned its value, and was watching each kopek, living on cabbage soup and gruel. In short, he told his parents, their money would not be wasted, and after only three years, he could return to Russia to take up a post at a university and never have to ask for money again. He formally requested that his parents forgive his previous ways and fund his studies. One of his colleagues had assured him that he could live frugally in Berlin on two thousand roubles a year. If that were too rich, perhaps fifteen hundred roubles would do, and he could make some money writing articles and doing translations. In any case, he concluded, despite the troubles of the last few years and the injustices of his parents toward his sisters and himself, he loved his parents deeply. Nothing they had done justified his own disloyal actions, and he repented, sincerely and totally.[10]

Was he sincere? The letter was an admixture of earnest declaration, calculated rhetoric, wishful thinking, and hope, and perhaps Bakunin himself would be hard pressed to know which was which. Undoubtedly he very much wanted to go to Berlin and study, to take part in "real external activity" and perhaps even open the door to a career. Probably he was happy enough living in poverty if he could read and write, but if he had learned to take care of his money, the lesson was lost soon after; for the rest of his life he wracked up debt and borrowed from friends, family, and strangers alike.

It is likely that he did regret the family controversies and the hard feelings, not just because it made borrowing money awkward but also because he loved his parents and siblings deeply. Perhaps it is enough to conclude that he was as capable of sincerity and self-deception, straight talk and duplicity, as any of us.

His father, still dubious enough to dub his son "Don Quixote," was suitably impressed by his plans to agree to fund him to the tune of fifteen hundred roubles, contingent on the income of the estate and its new paper mill, and in any case not until the fall of 1840. Desperate to leave, Bakunin turned to a new friend, Alexander Herzen. The two met in early 1840, when Herzen, just returned from five years of exile, was keen to become involved again in the life of the circles. He and Bakunin shared a similar background, though Herzen's family was much wealthier, and both were strident westernizers. Herzen was keen to learn about Hegel, and the two soon became fast friends. During the spat with Katkov, Herzen alone of the group sided with Bakunin. Of course, to be a friend of Bakunin's was to be hit up for money, and Herzen agreed to lend him five thousand roubles for the passage to Berlin and his studies.

All was falling into place. Bakunin returned to Priamukhino in May to say his good-byes. He wrote enthusiastically to Stankevich, asking him for advice on studying, promising to write, looking forward to seeing him and his sister, delighted that the two were together. Tragically, Stankevich would be dead before the letter arrived, with Varvara Bakunin and their friend Efremov at his side at Novi, near Lake Como in Italy.

It would be some time before Bakunin would learn of Stankevich's death. In the meantime, he was busy preparing for his trip. On 25 June, he arrived in St. Petersburg. He had come to peace with his family, but not with his friends. Katkov and he fought; Belinsky remained cold. He spent the three days before his ship left with Herzen and his wife, Natalie, and Herzen saw him off. He would not return to Russia for eleven years, and when he did, it would be in chains and under sentence of death.

7

THE PASSION FOR DESTRUCTION IS A CREATIVE PASSION

After several days at sea—"the first time I had seen the real sea, without shore"—and bone-jarring carriage trips, Michael Bakunin arrived in Berlin, the capital of the kingdom of Prussia, on 25 July 1840. His first impressions of Germany were generally positive. "Here I will attain my goal," he wrote the Beyer sisters. "It will give me what I need." The Germans were "charming," he reported, but they did have an obsequious habit of exclaiming "Jawohl!" at every turn.[1]

The sense of excitement and purpose, however, was tempered by the news of Stankevich's death. This was devastating, not just for Bakunin but for his generation of scholars, rebels, and friends. But at least Michael and Varvara were reunited and could offer each other some consolation. Varvara's decision to stay in Berlin with her young son eased Michael's adjustment to the new city.

He soon found other comrades. There was a significant colony of Russian students and emigres in Berlin, and they gathered in the cafes, especially Spargniapani's on Unter den Linden to discuss literature, history, and politics, to read newspapers and journals from around the world, and to argue. Bakunin quickly found another large, imposing Russian, the novelist Ivan Turgenev, and the two became fast friends, even living across the hall from each other for a time. Turgenev, four years younger than Bakunin and the beneficiary of a university education at St. Petersburg, was deeply affected by their friendship. He looked forward to learning from Bakunin, who after all was the acknowledged Russian expert on Hegel. "Stankevich brought us together," Turgenev exclaimed, "and death shall not part us." In his copy of Hegel's *Encyclopedia of the Philosophical Sciences*, he wrote, "Stankevich died June 24, 1840. I met Bakunin July 20, 1840. I want to keep no other memories from my previous life." For his part, Bakunin noted that Turgenev was "the one person with whom I have really hit it off."[2]

Turgenev would later turn their friendship into material for his novel *Rudin*. Published in 1856, while Bakunin was entombed in the tsar's prison and long after Turgenev had abandoned radical politics, the book's title character superficially resembled Bakunin. The book was set in the 1840s, and Rudin was "tall, somewhat round-shouldered, curly-haired, swarthy of complexion, with an irregular but expressive and clever face, with a faint gleam in the quick, dark blue eyes, a straight, broad nose, and finely chiseled lips." Like Bakunin, Rudin was a retired military officer from "T[ver] province," who depended on the kindness of strangers and friends for financial support. The character was a clever debater who insisted that greatness sprang from man, not heaven. However, the overall characterization of Rudin is of an ineffectual, cold, intellectually smug, and petty blowhard, unable to love or to act decisively. While several historians have seized upon this as a useful portrait of Bakunin and his politics, we must be more careful in drawing any conclusions from the novel.

It is true that Turgenev claimed several years after the novel's appearance that Rudin was "rather an accurate portrayal" of Bakunin. Alexander Herzen, however, sniffed that in fact "Turgenev, carried away by the biblical custom of God, created Rudin in his own image."[3] Turgenev's Rudin, like the characters in his later, more famous novel, *Fathers and Sons,* was less an accurate portrayal of an individual than a caricature of a philosophical and political position for which the author had little taste. Furthermore, Turgenev had carried on a romance with Bakunin's sister Tatiana that ended badly, and later was interrogated by the Russian authorities about his connection with Bakunin. To the degree that the author intended Rudin to resemble the young Bakunin, it is a highly personal and colored sketch, and one largely based on Belinsky's distorted version at that. Whatever the art of Turgenev, the thoughtful historian must agree with Marshall Shatz that while Turgenev borrowed some physical attributes and habits from Bakunin, his Rudin is "by no means a reliable picture of Mikhail Bakunin, and it should not be regarded by historians as a key that helps to unlock the mysteries of Bakunin's character."[4]

But Rudin was fifteen years in the future. In 1840, Bakunin and Turgenev were inseparable as they took classes at the university, studied, dined, attended concerts, and entered the world of the Berlin salon. Both were keen to hear the lectures of Karl Werder, a Hegelian and colleague of Stankevich's, but Bakunin soon found his other classes shallow and stultifying. The great Schelling was now a dull conservative, brought to Berlin to block the radical trail blazed by Hegel. History too must have been a disappointment. Bakunin had looked forward to the lectures of the celebrated historian Leopold von Ranke. But von Ranke, still today a staple in courses on historiography, declaimed that historians should only present history *wie es eigentlich gewe-*

sen, "as it actually happened." His motto may sound straightforward and sensible, but it was highly misleading. No historian has ever advocated presenting the past as it actually wasn't, and von Ranke's belief that historians should not judge the past or instruct the present was camouflage for his own ideological use of history. For all his alleged objectivity and historical neutrality, von Ranke was extremely conservative in his politics. He would become an energetic supporter of Bismarck, and for all his protestations that history had no ultimate purpose, his writings supported the monarchy and strongly implied that existing institutions were essentially following God's divine plan. For these reasons, von Ranke, like Schelling, had been brought to Berlin not as an objective seeker of fact but to deliver a counterattack to Hegel's progressive thought. Bakunin of course had already delivered a sophisticated attack on history as the collection of dry facts pressed into the service of reaction, and presumably had little interest in von Ranke's approach. More to his taste were the radical works of the Catholic humanist Felicite Robert de Lamennais and the German economist Lorenz von Stein. Stein's *Socialism and Communism in Contemporary France* presented readers with a radical reinterpretation of history and politics and introduced the ideas of Fourier, Saint-Simon, and Proudhon to a receptive audience with an impact similar to that of Howard Zinn's *A People's History of the United States* today.

The circles in which Bakunin traveled included students, bohemians, artists, and increasingly political thinkers and activists. Soren Kierkegaard and Friedrich Engels attended some of Werder's lectures, and Engels recalled years later that he had sat a few seats behind Bakunin and his group of fellow Russians. The two even lived on the same street, Dorotheenstrasse, at the same time. Among Bakunin's acquaintances was Bettina von Arnim, friend of Beethoven and Goethe, whose Romantic works Bakunin had read in Russia. By the 1840s, she was keenly involved in political issues. She took up her pen to defend Silesian linen weavers in the northeast of Prussia who rioted as their handicraft industry was destroyed by mechanization, and lobbied the king, Friedrich Wilhelm IV, to install the Grimm brothers at the University of Berlin when they were dismissed from their posts at Göttingen. Another member of this diverse group was the poet Georg Herwegh, the "Iron Lark," who called upon poets to decide to "be a man: for or against? And your slogan: slave or free?" His radical poetry savaged the Prussian state and eventually led to his expulsion, but it captured the mood of many in Germany.

In particular, Herwegh's cry to "Tear the crosses out of the earth! / Turn them all into swords!" echoed the evolution of the Left Hegelians and

Bakunin himself. While Hegel himself remained a Christian of some sort, the Left Hegelians ruthlessly applied his methodology to religion itself, concluding that the only rational position on the nature of God was an unyielding atheism. In 1835, David Strauss's book *The Life of Jesus* insisted that Jesus had to be understood as a historical—that is, human—figure, not a divine one. It was a radical, revolutionary argument, just as it is today, and others soon joined in. Ludwig Feuerbach, writing in 1839, argued that all religion had to be seen in its historical context, rather than as divine truth, for "what yesterday was still religion is no longer such today; and what today is atheism, tomorrow will be religion." Bruno Bauer, who almost alone among the Left Hegelians had studied with Hegel himself, proclaimed that the "core," the "center point" of Hegelian philosophy was the "destruction of religion."[5]

This was as alarming in the Prussia of the 1840s as it would be in the United States of the twenty-first century. As it did in Russia, as it does in the U.S. today, religion functioned as one of the pillars of German autocracy. Since there was no question of a mandate from the masses, divine right was left as the only grounds on which the rule of kings could be justified. If Jesus were human, if religion were little more than a folktale, autocracy could not be defended on any rational grounds; it would have to rely solely on force to compel obedience. But the ruler who must constantly use force has an unwieldy, treacherous, and expensive reign. It is far better over the long run to create founding myths and to wrap the population in shrouds of false beliefs. Questioning something as fundamental as the nature and existence of God put everything up for grabs, and rulers everywhere understood that the critique of religion was simultaneously a critique of politics, for its fundamental question, asked implicitly and explicitly, was this: Who should rule? It was an argument Bakunin anticipated in his 1838 preface to Hegel, where he observed that "Where there is no religion, there can be no state . . . religion is the substance, the essence of the life of any state." Religion bound people together; that is the original meaning of the world. If religion was displaced, what could take its place? What would bind humanity and give it common cause? For the Left Hegelians, the answer was obvious: politics. Bakunin expressed it pithily in a note to his sister Varvara and brother Paul: "Politics is religion and religion is politics."[6]

Politics, however, took thinkers from the realm of mysticism and theory to the practical world. That of course was the intention of the Left Hegelians, who were not content merely to philosophize. Hegel's "theory is praxis," thundered Bauer, "it is the revolution itself." While he framed his article as a nearly hysterical rant by an anti-Hegelian, one did not need the secret decoder ring to understand that Bauer was not engaging in parody or irony when he insisted that "philosophy must be active in politics" and that "servitude, tutelage, is unbearable to the free spirit." It was left to another Left Hegelian, Arnold Ruge, to sum up their position clearly and without cumbersome rhetorical device in 1842, in his newspaper, the *Deutsche Jahrbücher:* "Our times are political, and our politics intend the freedom of this world. No longer do we lay the ground for the ecclesiastical state, but for the secular state, and the interest in the public issue of freedom in the state grows with every breath that humans take."[7]

While Engels and other writers have suggested that Bakunin was influenced by another Hegelian, the fiercely individualist Max Stirner, there is no evidence of this. Stirner denounced the state in language that seemed to foreshadow anarchism, but his polemics on individuality failed to comprehend that humans were social beings who only developed and progressed in community. Where Stirner insisted that freedom meant having no responsibility to or for others, Bakunin had long understood that humanity could be free only in society. Stirner boldly proclaimed that there was no good or evil, only the ego, and rejected any constraints on human behavior. It followed that he rejected political action, for it was by definition collective action concerned with society rather than the individual. For all his fiery pronouncements, Stirner was rather colorless and boring in person; his real name, Johann Kaspar Schmidt, more accurately reflected his personality and importance. Bakunin mentions Stirner precisely once in his collected works, and then only in passing. Stirner's exaggerated individualism, expressed most passionately in his book *The Ego and Its Own,* had little appeal for Bakunin or his fellow Hegelians. Indeed, it was Marx and Engels who devoted considerable space to Stirner, albeit very critical space, in *The German Ideology* and *The Holy Family;* as far as can be determined, Bakunin had no interest, even a negative one, in Stirner's ideas. The individualist was out of step with his times and with his fellow Hegelians who saw political action as the necessary expression of their era.[8]

For if the particular ideas of the Left Hegelians were not widespread, the call for freedom and justice and change resounded throughout the German states, principalities, kingdoms, and duchies. While there was little unanimity about what was to be done, people pressed for political reform ranging from constitutions that would abolish or limit the monarchy to representative legislatures to German unification.

Different groups turned to politics—the state—for different reasons. Industrialists wanted a stronger, unified state to protect their claim to property rights, to shelter their fledgling industries from competitive goods from other nations, to build modern infrastructures, and to expand their markets. Workers wanted an interventionist state that would protect them from the depredations of employers and regulate terms of trade and employment. A growing class of educated professionals, from scientists to doctors to lawyers to journalists, and of course students, wanted their freedom to inquire into the nature of the physical world and the intellectual world protected, and believed that their expertise entitled them to participate more fully in the affairs of state. An expanding bureaucracy, now necessary to run an efficient regime, preferred the rule of parliamentary law and written regulation to the whim of the sovereign, and sought to harness those elites who believed themselves exempt from directives and equal treatment. Independent farmers needed protection from and compensation for cheap competition and bad harvests. Peasants who were transformed by fiat overnight from serfs to agricultural laborers were forced to compensate landowners with either money or property, and often lost both; they sought protection, redress, and land. Nearly everyone would benefit from legally constituted freedom of speech and trial by jury. If appeals to the ruler were unsuccessful—and with so many competing interests, including especially his own, even the most enlightened ruler could never decide any issue in a manner that would make everyone happy—then "the people," however they might be defined for the immediate purpose, understood that "they" would have to become the state if they were to be free or were to use the state for their own purposes. If the ruler would agree to stand down, fine; if not, well, everyone now understood that history was about change made by the people. Petitions, protests, and pikes could all be pressed into service. The issues were particularly grating in Prussia, where many had hoped for liberal reforms when Friedrich Wilhelm IV took the throne in 1840. His subsequent reaction did not quell the call for change. Instead, it intensified it and caused it to reverberate throughout Prussia.

Bakunin thrived in this swirl of philosophy, politics, and protest. Events in Germany paralleled his own evolution over the past several years: the rejection of official ideology whether of state or parent, the transition from Romantic themes of individual discontent to social analysis, the realization that theory alone was insufficient, and finally the connecting of criticism with action and theory with practice, to go beyond understanding the world to changing it. In 1842, now living in Dresden to escape the repressive atmosphere of Prussia, Bakunin pulled these personal and political themes together in an essay for Ruge's October issue of the *Deutsche Jahrbücher*. The essay's sophisticated analysis put his own ideas in the context of the turmoil of the 1840s and roughly outlined the political ideas that he would develop throughout his life. Here Bakunin voiced his most famous, and least understood, adage: "The passion for destruction is at the same time a creative passion."

Sadly, for those of us who might wish return to the chemistry sets of our youth to find a creative spark, and for those who wish to turn Bakunin into the fifth rider of the apocalypse, he did not mean that the political was pyrotechnical. No one accused the poet E. E. Cummings of advocating a holocaust when he wrote, "To destroy is always the first step in any creation," or suspected the economist Joseph Schumpeter of pyromania when he observed approvingly that capitalism is a "process of creative destruction."[9] So too must Bakunin's phrase be understood not as a simple desire for destruction but as an analysis of the power and necessity of revolutionary change.

The article, entitled "The Reaction in Germany: A Fragment from a Frenchman," was published under the pseudonym Jules Elysard. The *nom de guerre* both protected Bakunin from unwanted attention from the authorities and highlighted his interest in French political philosophy. Unlike German and Russian thought, French theory was more concerned with practical politics and economics than speculative philosophy. Even French Utopians such as Saint-Simon, Fourier, and Proudhon grappled with concrete issues and questions rather than metaphysics and discussions of spirit and species-being and *Zeitgeist*. In adopting a French pen name, Bakunin demonstrated his own conviction, one that was at once personal and political, that it was time for action. Even the writing style made this clear. No one would mistake it for Hemingway, but the writing was tighter and more concrete than the baroque and abstract language Bakunin had polished in Russia. So too were the ideas more practical and forceful, even if they did not form an electoral platform or manifesto.

The first sentence flatly declared his politics. Who could deny, he asked, that freedom "today stands at the head of the agenda of history?" Even those who worked to destroy it had to cover their politics with the rhetoric of freedom to be taken seriously. But, Bakunin pointed out, language was not reality, and the fact remained that many rulers would use any means to crush the popular movements for democracy and liberty. The first job of the democrat then was to blow away the fog of language and understand the different groups who wished to obstruct the progress of humanity.

The first group was made up of a type satirized eighty years later by Sin-clair Lewis in his novel *Babbitt*. Bakunin characterized them as those "high-placed, aged" people who in their youth had been "dilettantes in political freedom." Never truly committed to the movement, they had taken a "piquant pleasure in speaking about freedom and equality," largely because it had made them "twice as interesting in business." Now that they were older, they claimed also to be wiser, hiding behind "that much abused word, experience," to justify their conservative politics. The species Bakunin described may be recognized today by its mating call, "a person who is not a socialist before thirty has no heart, and a person who is a socialist after thirty has no head." Variously ascribed to Francois Guizot, Georges Clemenceau, Winston Churchill, assorted kings, and the U.S. 1936 Republican presidential candidate Alf Landon, it is the motto of those Bakunin identified as the "prudent and aged" who were "never serious about freedom" and with whom "there is no profit in speaking."

More depressing than the tired old conservatives were the "many young people" in business, commerce, aristocracy, and the military "who share the same convictions or, rather, lack of any conviction." "Completely involved in their paltry, vain, or monetary interests, and completely occupied by their commonplace concerns," oblivious to the wider world and the momentous struggle that surrounded them, they were "colorless, ghostly beings," and they too could be safely ignored.

The real threats to freedom and democracy were the active "reactionaries." They were "everywhere the ruling party," and through the media, education systems, the church and other avenues, they exerted a more subtle power that today would be called "hegemony." In politics, Bakunin observed, their ideology was "conservatism"; in jurisprudence, the "historical school"; and in philosophy, in a jab at Schelling, "positive philosophy." Their success, Bakunin cautioned, was not due to accident, contingency, or chance. If revolutionaries had history on their side, reaction too had been the result of historical necessity, and it was important to calculate accurately its present strengths and weaknesses. Otherwise, "we must either wholly lose our courage, depressed by the dreary picture of daily drudgery, or—and this is perhaps still worse—since a vital human being cannot long tolerate despair, there comes upon us a groundless, boyish, and fruitless exuberance." "Pessimism of the intellect, optimism of the will," the Italian communist Antonio Gramsci put it nearly a century later; for both thinkers, realistic analysis made it possible to steer between resignation and recklessness.

It was also necessary to assess realistically the side that fought for freedom. Bakunin acknowledged that the chief strength of the "Democratic party" was that its founding principle—"the equality of man realizing itself in freedom"—was in harmony with the most fundamental desires of humanity. It had, however, to remake itself if it were to succeed in negating the positive and overcoming reaction. It had to step "out of the uncertainty of fantasy and into the reality," for the "fullness and totality of human nature" could never be understood only through "abstract theoretical propositions." Its principles had to be implemented "not only in thought and reasoning" but "also in real life down to life's smallest manifestations." In other words, the movement had to move beyond theory into action.

The key to effective action was understanding that the democratic movement was not a reformist movement, but a revolutionary one. It "not only stands in opposition to the government and is not only a particular constitutional or politicoeconomic change, but a total transformation of that world condition and a herald of an original new life which has not yet existed in history." Real democracy meant much more than regime change or new elections or legal frameworks that restricted the power of the monarch.

The revolution he called for would not seek a "synthesis" of the old with the new. Instead, Bakunin argued, "the whole significance and the irrepressible power of the negative is the annihilation of the positive." But since democracy did not yet exist independently, but only as "the denial of the positive . . . it too must be destroyed along with the positive, so that from its free ground it may spring forth again in a newborn state, as its own living fullness."

While the reader may be forgiven for thinking that as rallying cries go, this is not as compelling as "Workers of the world unite," "I like Ike," or "God is great," Bakunin made two important advances here. First he demonstrated that Hegel, the dominant philosopher of the period, could be interpreted to support not just progressive historical change but revolutionary change. Historical change could happen abruptly and radically. We might compare this with Stephen Jay Gould's theory of punctuated equilibrium. Gould suggests that while evolution usually takes eons, a meteor striking the earth or other catastrophic events could introduce a period of rapid change, such as the extinction of the dinosaurs and the subsequent flourishing of mammals.[10] Bakunin's argument lent the power and authority of Hegel to radical, revolutionary politics.

Second, Bakunin introduced a new idea into Hegel's dialectical model of historical change. If Hegel's process view was essentially triadic, or three-part, simply put as "thesis-antithesis-synthesis," Bakunin proposed a dyadic, or two-part dialectic, where the negative did not merge with the positive but destroyed it and created a new positive that owed nothing to the old. This too was of interest to more than speculative philosophers, for it was a political argument against reformism. Because the "positive and the negative are once and for all incompatible," it was pointless to conceive of the role of the Democratic party as "an eternal mediation with the positive." Its purpose was not to reform or improve the positive, but to replace it.

For all the talk of the "annihilation" and "destruction" of the positive, it is clear this was about overturning and overcoming the old world order, not the apocalyptic obliteration that Bakunin is usually accused of desiring. In "The Reaction in Germany," he firmly rejected the argument that the revolution was justified in using any and all means to its end. While reactionaries believed "every means is permitted" to maintain their rule, revolutionaries could not "repay them with the same coin," for that "would be unworthy of us and of the great cause whose agents we are." Indeed, the greatest advantage the revolutionaries possessed was that their principle allowed them to be "just and impartial, without, by so being, harming our cause." Certainly in their fight against reaction, "all evil passions are awakened also in us . . . we are also very often partial and unjust." But this was a temptation to overcome, not embrace. Unlike the reactionaries, revolutionaries had "to remain true, even contrary to our self-preservation, to our principle as the only ground of our power and of our life." For revolutionaries were "justified only through our principle," the principle of "freedom of which the one true expression is justice and love." Ironically, this meant that it was the revolutionaries, accused by their enemies of atheism, and not the reactionaries who claimed God was on their side, who had "really to exercise love, this highest commandment of Christ and this only way of true Christianity."

Having established the broad principles necessary for the democratic movement to develop its strategy and tactics, Bakunin returned to the Reactionary party. It was, he held, divided into two camps: the consistent reactionaries and the compromising reactionaries. The first, like Bakunin, understood that the positive could only be "maintained through a complete suppression of the negative"; there could be no negotiation or conciliation. Determined and ruthless, they employed every weapon at their disposal. Their positions in institutions of church and state let them use language to label freedom and progress as "heresy" and thus cut off real discussion and debate. They did not hesitate to use all the violence of the state, and "if it were possible they would perhaps even call out of the arsenal of history the subterranean power of the Inquisition in order to use it against us."

For all their ferocity, the consistent reactionaries were morally superior to the compromising reactionaries, for they were at least sincere. The compromisers were "the clever men, the theorists *par excellence,*" and they, not the consistent reactionaries, were "the chief representatives of the present time." Their chief characteristic was "theoretical dishonesty," for unlike the consistent reactionaries, they held no solid convictions or moral principles, and their slipperiness of language and tactics made them more difficult to pin down. They did not reject democracy and the negative out of hand. Unlike the consistent reactionaries, they often agreed that the Democratic party raised important questions and identified real abuses. But the compromisers refused to accept its radical solutions and instead claimed that truth lay somewhere between the left and the right. Bakunin acknowledged that their approach had some appeal. After all, everyone sought to "reconcile the positive and the negative," and this seemed a workable approach. But this apparent reasonableness was an illusion, Bakunin insisted. If the negative and the positive were truly in opposition, compromise could not resolve the struggle.

The obvious retort to this argument against reform, Bakunin admitted, sounded plausible enough. Surely the compromisers further progress "far more than you do yourself, for they go to work prudently and not excessively as do the democrats who want to blast the whole world to pieces." But the soothing words of the compromisers disguised their real agenda, for they played a complicated game. They had to open the door for reform to topple the old order of the consistent reactionaries, then slam the door shut to prevent the masses from creating real democracy and equality. Bakunin pointed out that the constant refrain of the compromiser, "To a certain extent you are right, but, yet . . ." was a tactic calculated to let them play left against right for their own benefit. A path midway between right and left was not neutral or objective. The middle way too represented a particular, narrow political interest, not the interests of the overwhelming mass of humanity.

And while everyone could agree, in principle, that peace was preferable to conflict and struggle, the peace sought by the compromisers was the peace imposed by the conqueror on the conquered, the peace of the slave owner imposed on the slave. Such a peace could not end conflict. It could only suppress it for a time. That time, Bakunin suggested, was now running out. Signs of revolt were everywhere, as orthodox ideas and politics were being challenged. Putting a more radical spin on his 1838 observation on the connection between state and religion, he observed that "the state is currently in the throes of the deepest internal conflict, for without religion, without a powerful universal conviction, the state is impossible." "Visible appearances are stirring around us," he continued, "indicating that the spirit, this old mole, has brought its underground work to completion and that it will soon come again to pass judgment."[11]

Though the spirit may have been that of the "old mole," it had a new agent. The revolt now was led not by intellectuals or nobles or industrialists, but by "the people, the poor class, which without doubt constitutes the greatest part of humanity." The rights of the poor had been acknowledged in theory, of course. The Declaration of Rights of Man, after all, did not contain fine print indicating the offer was void where prohibited by insufficient income. In practice, however, the working class was "still condemned by its birth, by its ties with poverty and ignorance, as well, indeed, as with actual slavery." But now, "this class, which constitutes the true people, is everywhere assuming a threatening attitude" and was demanding "the actualization of the rights already conceded" in theory. Germany and France were obvious examples of proletarian revolt; so too was England, where workers were organizing and fighting for political and economic freedom under the radical banners of the Chartist movement. "Even in Russia," Bakunin prophesied, "dark clouds are gathering, heralding storms."

The old road was rapidly fading. It was confronted not only by philosophers but by proletarians, and it was time for all to choose sides. Bakunin made it clear which side he was on. "Let us therefore trust the eternal spirit which destroys and annihilates only because it is the unfathomable and eternally creative source of all life," he concluded. "The passion for destruction is a creative passion, too."[12]

The article was hot. Bakunin urged a political platform of no compromise and no reform. Hegel was acknowledged as the springboard for revolt, but he was interpreted in a forceful, dynamic way. The people, now defined more closely as the poor, the working class, and those in bondage, rather than as a broad, vaguely mythical force, were identified as the new revolutionary force. These were the ideas Bakunin threw into the political mix. If none of them was strictly original, the synthesis was bold and energizing and both summed up the leading work of the age and indicated the way forward. As a result, "The Reaction in Germany" was circulated throughout revolutionary and avant-garde circles throughout Europe. In Russia, Herzen, Belinksy, and Botkin all forgave Bakunin his trespasses and debts both intellectual and monetary.

The authorities could be expected to express an equally fervent but rather different interest. The climate throughout Germany was becoming less hospitable. The *Deutsche Jahrbücher* was shut down by the government, and Ruge beat feet for Paris to start another newspaper, the *Deutsche-Französische Jahrbücher,* with another exiled German editor, Karl Marx. When Georg Herwegh was expelled from Berlin, Bakunin, probably overestimating his own notoriety, assumed he might be next and decided to join the poet in Zürich. He quickly found himself at home with Switzerland's radical and literary circle. It included the theologian Karl Vogt and his sons, Karl Jr., who would be an activist in the revolutions of 1848, and Adolf, who would remain close to Bakunin until the anarchist's death. It also included Louis Agassiz, who later held a professorship in zoology and geology at Harvard; the chair in zoology Stephen Jay Gould held until his death in 2002 was named after his son.

This intellectual and social life, however pleasant, did little to develop Bakunin's political thought. "The Reaction in Germany" called for revolt and for the proletariat to play the leading role. But Bakunin was short on practical suggestions. His radical connections were far removed from the working class; indeed, in some of his first uses of the word "proletariat," it is obviously a condition he hoped to avoid, not experience.[13] Nonetheless, while Bakunin's foes and contemporary conservatives are quick to accuse leftist intellectuals of studying the working class to avoid being part of it, it is not clear what their accusation amounts to. If anything, it is an acknowledgment that class exists and is a system that often leaves workers exhausted and unable to pursue intellectual work at the same level as the academic. Intellectual work does not require genius; it requires time and training, and workers in capitalist societies are denied both. It makes more sense to attack the sons and daughters of privilege who seek to maintain such a world than those who struggle to fix it.

In any case, Bakunin soon had his lofty view of struggle and justice tempered by the earthy realism of the proletariat. As he left for Zürich, he obtained an exciting new book of radical social commentary, Wilhelm Weitling's *Guarantees of Harmony and Freedom.*[14] Unlike Bakunin, Marx, and many other left-wing writers of the day, Weitling was a son of toil. His father was a French military officer garrisoned in the German city of Magdeburg, his mother a maid. The two lived together without benefit of clergy, and in 1808 produced their son. Four years later, however, the father received orders to march with Napoleon into Russia and became another victim of the ill-fated campaign. Mother and son lived in extreme poverty, made worse by the ravages of war as French, Prussian, and Russian troops alternately besieged and held the city. Yet Wilhelm was a gifted child. Though he received only a very elementary formal education, he read voraciously and taught himself several languages. He was apprenticed to a tailor and became a journeyman at eighteen.

While tailoring was a skilled trade, by the late 1820s it was no longer a lucrative one. The Industrial Revolution began in the textile industries with the express aim of reducing the cost of goods, which primarily meant reducing the wages paid to labor. Machines replaced humans; mass-produced clothing replaced the handmade garment and the bespoke suit. Weitling possessed a skill that was rarely able to fetch a price much above that of unskilled labor and offered him only jobs for which many others competed. He walked across much of Europe seeking regular employment and living the desperate life the poets, philosophers, and politicians of the day described in such dire terms.

If there was any benefit to his trade, it was that tailoring, unlike factory work, was quiet. Tailors and other workers such as cobblers and cigarmakers arranged to have newspapers, books, and journals read aloud as they labored and thus were well versed in the politics and news of the day. Weitling was particularly drawn to economics and politics, and despite his twelve-hour workday read Strauss's *Life of Jesus* and the work of Lamennais. Unlike the Young Hegelians, he had no difficulty in combining theory with action. Skilled workers drew on the traditions and their common experience of the craft to form educational, recreational, and self-help societies, cooperatives, and secret societies for mutual protection. Weitling took part in these throughout the continent. In Paris, he joined the Society of Exiles, an underground organization of German emigre workers, then, in 1837, the League of the Just, a more radical offshoot. When the League joined other Parisian workers and took to the streets in angry protest and fighting in 1839, Weitling was already well-known as a working-class activist, speaker, and writer, his pamphlets and books financed by his fellow workers, printed by volunteer labor and distributed by wandering journeymen. His first book, *Mankind As It Is and As It Should Be,* was a powerful critique of capitalism, drawn from his experience and his interpretation of Christian values. His Christ, however, was not the Jesus who turned the other cheek, but he who scourged the money changers from the temple. The new money changers, the capitalists and industrialists, were to be driven out by revolution in Weitling's recasting of biblical myth. For him, revolution was not a dialectical construction or a rhetorical device. It was to be a violent uprising that would unleash the fury of the oppressed as they tore down private property and privilege. In the new world workers would create, all would be equally educated and rewarded. Work too would be shared without the rigid division of labor that misshaped bodies and starved intellects.

Tailor that he was, Weitling laid out intricate patterns for what he called communism in *Guarantees of Harmony and Freedom,* down to the shape of buildings, the styles of clothing, and the sounds of a universal language. It was a plan that spoke to the deepest aspirations of a bright man denied opportunity for the crime of being born into poverty, who saw his trade devalued and his labor exploited. An industrial army composed of youths trained in different trades and skills would be set to work building infrastructure and colonizing other lands. Goods and services would be valued and exchanged according to the labor time it took to create them, and production and consumption would be carefully monitored, with resources shifted according to need and demand. The system required able administrators and overseers. These could not be selected through elections, Weitling believed, for elections tended to reward those with oratorical skills. Instead he devised a complicated scheme that would ensure those with technical skills and abilities were selected impartially by those deemed best able to judge.

It was far from a democratic system, and many suspected Weitling had penciled himself in for the top job, but it was a sincere attempt to provide an alternative to capitalism that insisted on equality and justice over poverty and on freedom and harmony over exploitation. The book impressed workers and radicals and philosophers alike. It was widely reviewed in journals and newspapers across Europe, including the imperious London *Times.* Ludwig Feuerbach thought the work established Weitling as the "prophet of his class," and Bruno Bauer commented favorably. Even Karl Marx praised the "unbounded brilliance of the literary debut of the German worker."[15]

Weitling's solid prose was the broom needed to clear out abstract Hegelian cobwebs. Bakunin found *Guarantees of Harmony and Freedom* "truly remarkable" for its "just and profound . . . concrete consciousness of the present epoch." He was particularly struck by Weitling's ability to develop revolutionary ideas not from "idle theory" but as an "expression of a new practice" springing from his life as a proletarian.[16] Here Bakunin's own thoughts on the necessity of revolution were reinforced by a worker with real revolutionary experience. Their common aim, he realized, was "to free the people . . . the majority, the masses of the poor and the oppressed . . . from the tutelage of the rich and powerful." Intellectuals had a crucial role to play. The chief obstacle workers faced was not their "weakness," for they made up the vast majority of society. It was their "intellectual enslavement" engineered by state and church. Philosophers had torn down religion and the false beliefs in god and king and had restored to the people their "sense of their own value, the consciousness of their dignity and their inalienable and sacred rights." Nonetheless, it was not from theory but from the people that sprang "all the great acts of history, all liberating revolutions." What this proved was the necessity for the practical proletarians and the far-sighted philosophers to join forces. Each was stumbling toward the same goal of a free society, and each needed to learn from the other. "Thought and action; truth and morality; theory and practice": these needed to be united to forward humanity's progress. And they were agreed on what that progress should be. Weitling had poetically summed up the broad principle on which the new world would be based. "In the perfect society," Bakunin quoted enthusiastically, "there is no government, only administration; no laws, only obligations; no punishments, only remedies."[17]

Weitling's intricate plans for the future society, however, were cause for concern. In language that foreshadowed his criticism of Marx, Bakunin warned that Weitling's communism was both "a very important and an extremely dangerous phenomenon." It spoke vibrantly to the plight of workers and was drawn from their dire needs, but, Bakunin declared, "we are not communists . . . we could not live in a society organized according to Weitling's design." Such a society was not a "genuine, living community of free men," but an "oppressive regime" comparable to a "herd of animals brought together by coercion," concerned only with "material satisfaction" and ignorant of humanity's deeper needs.[18]

Despite this, the two found much to admire in each other when they met in Zürich in May 1843. Bakunin later recalled Weitling as possessing "much natural keenwittedness, a quick mind, much energy, and especially much wild fanaticism, noble pride, and faith in the liberation and future of the enslaved majority"—a man, one might conclude, much like himself, despite the vast differences in class, education, and experience.[19]

Through Weitling, Bakunin received a thorough introduction to practical politics, though in an unexpected fashion. In his new book, *The Gospel of a Poor Sinner*, Weitling built on Strauss's theme of Christ as human, all too human, emphasized his bastard birth into poverty, and claimed him as the first insurgent communist. This would remain a popular theme for rebels of all sorts; the Wobblies of the twentieth century would often refer to Christ as that carpenter, Jerusalem Slim, but it allowed the Swiss authorities to charge Weitling with sedition and heresy. He was arrested, jailed, and expelled from the country. From his papers and correspondence, the Swiss police learned of his association with Bakunin. They had already investigated the young Russian soon after his arrival, and upon their request, Count Benckendorff and the Third Section opened a file and dispatched agents to investigate the family.[20] When the Swiss authorities made public the connection between

Bakunin and Weitling, the Russians took action. In February 1844, they requested Bakunin to present himself to the Russian Legation in Berne, where he in turn was presented with an order to return to Russia. What little desire he had to return home was killed by the thought that whatever the authorities had planned would not be pleasant.

Instead of home, Bakunin headed first to Brussels and then to Paris. Evading Russian justice, however, was not so easy. For the crime of refusing the order to return, he was stripped of his noble rank. His property, such as it was, was forfeited, and he sentenced to an indefinite period of hard labor in exile in Siberia. Practical politics came with a high price indeed.

8

GAY PARIS

Could there have been a better time to be young and in Paris? Workers and intellectuals from all of Europe spilled out from the workshops, factories, cafes, and universities to discuss the most important political and social questions humanity has ever raised. But they were not content to debate. They met across the lines of ethnicity, status, and class to plan protests, strikes, and revolution. Posters, printed by volunteers who learned the rudiments of the craft on the run from police, were blazoned with slogans that combined the sophistication of the seminar with the heartfelt passion of the sweatshop. The tyrant trembled in his palace and the world watched with rapt attention and anticipation. Yes, Paris in 1968 was the place to be.

It paled, however, beside the Paris Bakunin entered in 1844. He brought with him only a trunk of clothing, a field cot, a washbasin, and a strong desire to join in the revolutionary movement. He would stay nearly four years in this city where emigre thinkers and political exiles met with migrant artisans, peasants, domestic servants, and factory hands who were beginning to understand themselves as a working class. The intellectual climate was headier even than that created by Simone de Beauvoir and Jean-Paul Sartre as Bakunin met authors and activists he had been reading from and about for years, including George Sand and Lamennais. Old friends and foes such as Ruge, Herzen, Belinsky, Turgenev, and Herwegh came. He encountered representatives from the spectrum of left-wing thought, from the Saint-Simonist Pierre Leroux to the Fourierist Victor Considerant, from the Utopian colonist Etienne Cabet to Karl Marx and Louis Blanc, who penned in 1839 perhaps the best short description of socialism ever: "From each according to his abilities, to each according to his needs."

But the most important influence on Bakunin's political thought in this period was the controversial and contrarian Pierre-Joseph Proudhon. The first to use the words "anarchy" and "anarchist" not as equivalents for "chaos" and "bogeyman" but as positive descriptions of his politics, he nonetheless ran for and was elected to a seat in the French National Assembly. Once there he reverted to his anarchist principles and voted against the adoption of a new constitution "not because it contains things of which I disapprove and does not contain things of which I approve. I vote against the constitution because it is a constitution."[1] An advocate for the working class, he deplored strikes. His passion for liberty did not prevent him from defending capital punishment or torture, and his definition of humanity did not always include women. An avowed revolutionary, he remained aloof from much of the political struggle of his day and was a reluctant participant in the revolts of 1848; a fierce atheist, he loved to quote the Bible and to draw upon religious motifs and ethics in his writings and speeches.

His apparently contradictory ideas reflected the peculiarities of his class position. Proudhon's family was poor and he wore to school the peasant's wooden clogs, or *sabots,* whence the word "sabotage" may be derived, rather than leather shoes. But his family were independent peasants and self-employed artisans rather than wage workers. His father was unsuccessful at several small businesses, most notably a brewery, but still, he was a businessman. Proudhon himself worked as a printer and journalist, usually self-employed or in partnerships. His politics were consistent with this position somewhere between capital and labor. He regarded the state with animosity and despised big capital, and while he was sympathetic to workers, he was wary that unions would make it difficult for small employers such as himself to manage their workshops. His views were simultaneously progressive and reactionary as he hoped the world could go back to the future of an economy of small independent producers and a rough equality of all who toiled. His vision of the new society was one that retained the moral values and politics of an age that industrial capitalism was destroying and that dispensed with the new state apparatus that taxed and regulated and meddled. It was an ideology that reflected the vanishing world of the independent commodity producer, now increasingly squeezed between the capitalist class and the working class.

Yet it is too easy to dismiss his views as the narrow outcome of an ambiguous class position. He was, unquestionably, sometimes contradictory. Largely self-educated, his analysis often lacked rigor. He glossed over gaping holes and inconsistencies in his arguments that were immediately apparent to those well versed in philosophy and political economy. Still, if Proudhon was not a member of the industrial working class, his ideals of justice and equality spoke powerfully to artisans and laborers alike. He drew less on systematic analysis than upon older, ingrained traditions of liberty, of a moral economy, of a just price, and of rights, all expressed in language that was grasped immediately and intuitively by his audience. His arguments were less science than art, as they were intended to evoke an emotional response and to reflect back in more articulate form the aspirations and hopes of working people. He spoke of justice, not ratios of fixed and variable capital; neither he nor his audience needed intricate complex mathematic formulae or complex distinctions between labor and labor power to understand that capitalism robbed them of their land, their labor, and their dignity. The opening sentences of his most important book, *What Is Property?*, demonstrate the power of his ideas and passion:

> If I were asked to answer the following question: *What is slavery?* and I should answer in one word, *It is murder,* my meaning would be understood at once. No extended argument would be required to show that the power to take from a man his thought, his will, his personality, is a power of life and death; and that to enslave a man is to kill him. Why, then, to this other question: *What is property?* may I not likewise answer, *It is theft.*[2]

Those who fear that Proudhon's call to abolish private property means they would have to share their underpants may relax. He, like other socialists, distinguished between simple possessions and property that was used to exploit others. Proudhon believed that people were entitled only to that property, including land and machinery, that they could use employing only their own labor. Landlords and capitalists were parasites who used property to profit not from their own work but from that of others. It was, after all, the farm worker, not the landlord, who made the land productive. It was the factory worker, not the employer, who produced the goods. The landlord did not create the land; the capitalist did not build the factory or the machinery. They may have purchased land and machinery, but their money represented nothing more than the expropriated labor of others. Capitalists and landlords had no moral claim to property, for property was a legal fiction maintained by a state they had created of themselves, by themselves, and for themselves.

From property Proudhon turned to examine that state. His experience in the National Assembly reaffirmed his anarchist convictions; as he put it, "As soon as I set foot in the parliamentary Sinai, I ceased to be in touch with the masses; because I was absorbed by my legislative work, I entirely lost sight of the current of events . . . The men who are most completely ignorant of the state of a country are almost always those who represent it . . . Fear of the people is the sickness of all those who belong to authority; the people, for those in power, are the enemy."[3] His observations on government may speak to readers today, when states that proclaim themselves to be freedom-loving democracies regularly erect surveillance cameras on public streets and send in masked, armored troops against their citizens, all in the name of liberty. "To be governed," Proudhon wrote,

> is to be kept in sight, inspected, spied upon, directed, law driven, numbered, enrolled, indoctrinated, preached at, controlled, estimated, valued, censured, commanded by creatures who have neither the right, nor the wisdom, nor the virtue, to do so . . . To be governed is to be at every operation, at every transaction, noted, registered, enrolled, taxed, stamped, measured, numbered, assessed, licensed, authorized, admonished, forbidden, reformed, corrected, punished. It is, under pretext of public utility, and in the name of the general interest, to be placed under contribution, trained, ransomed, exploited, monopolized, extorted, squeezed, mystified, robbed; then, at the slightest resistance, the first word of complaint, to be repressed, fined, despised, harassed, tracked, abused, clubbed, disarmed, choked, imprisoned, judged, condemned, shot, deported, sacrificed, sold, betrayed; and, to crown all, mocked, ridiculed, outraged, dishonored. That is government; that is its justice; that is its morality.[4]

Bakunin saw both the strengths and the weaknesses of Proudhon's ideas. Unlike Bakunin and Marx, Proudhon was never a materialist or a realist. Instead, as Bakunin observed, Proudhon "remained all of his life an incorrigible idealist, drawing his inspiration sometimes from the Bible, sometimes from Roman law, and always from metaphysics. His great misfortune was that he had never studied the natural sciences, or taken up their methods." Proudhon remained a "perpetual contradiction: a vigorous genius and revolutionary thinker who struggled against the phantoms of idealism yet was never able to overcome them." What saved him were the "instincts of a genius that let him catch a glimpse of the right path." He "understood and felt liberty" and "when he was not creating metaphysical doctrines," Proudhon had "the true instinct of the revolutionary—he loved Satan and proclaimed anarchy."[5] This instinct for revolt made Proudhon distinct from his fellow socialists. Cabet, Blanc, the Fourierists, the Saint-Simonians—and Bakunin might have added Weitling—all shared a "passion for regulation." They sought to "indoctrinate and organize the future according to their ideas; they were, more or less, authoritarians." But this "son of a peasant" was "in fact and in instinct a hundred times more revolutionary than all these authoritarian and doctrinaire socialists. He armed himself with a profound, penetrating, unrelenting critique in order to destroy all their systems. Opposing liberty to authority, he boldly proclaimed himself an anarchist." For Proudhon, and later Bakunin, socialism had to be founded on "individual as well as collective freedom" and on the "voluntary action of free associations," without government regulation or sanction of the state, "subordinating politics to the economic, intellectual, and moral interests of the society."[6]

Proudhon both shaped and echoed Bakunin's own developing ideas on revolution. Socialism, or democracy, or communism—the words had less definite meanings at this time—had to ensure the rights of the community without sacrificing those of the individual. Capitalism, based on private property and exploitation, made a mockery of equality, while the state made a mockery of liberty. Taken together, the two institutions reinforced each other. The revolution had to make an end to both. What would replace them? It would be ridiculous to design the future in detail. Certainly it could be done; many earlier socialists were full of ambitious, intricate schemes, right down to the clothing people would wear. But such plans were repugnant to Proudhon and Bakunin. What mattered was that people should be free to design their own future, free from the compulsion of the state, free from the demands of capital, free from the manipulation of religion, and free even from the schematic designs of well-meaning socialists.

At the same time, by the fall of 1844, Bakunin, unlike Proudhon, and contrary to his critique of Weitling made the previous year, was now convinced that he was "a communist with all my heart."[7] Despite this political difference, Bakunin genuinely liked Proudhon and they remained friends until the printer's death in 1865. But while Proudhon usually did not to want to belong to any political club that would accept him, Bakunin understood the necessity of organizing and working with others, and in 1844, he took up the fight for Slavic independence from Russia. To strike at Nicholas I was to strike at the heart of reaction. The tsar repressed his own people as well as those nations under the yoke of empire, and through treaties and alliances, propped up autocrats across Europe. At the same time, the regime was creaking under its own weight; if one nation could be freed, would not others, conceivably even Russia itself, follow?

Poland provided the impetus. It had been contested terrain for centuries as its native inhabitants tried to carve out an independent existence from the competing empires of Russia, Austria, and Prussia while extending their own hegemony over Lithuania, Ukraine, and Sweden. Constantly invaded, it was divided up between its powerful neighbors three times between 1772 and 1795. The final partition wiped independent Poland off the map, placing the bulk of the country under the benighted tutelage of the tsar. Still the Poles fought on. No less than the rest of Europe, Poland was swept up by the waves of nationalism and Romanticism, and in November 1830 it launched an insurrection to free itself from Russia. At first an ill-planned attempt at a coup d'etat by Warsaw officer cadets, similar to the Decembrist revolt of 1825, it turned into a full-fledged revolt when workers and rank-and-file soldiers drawn from the peasantry broke into the arsenal and passed out weapons to the people. Suddenly the handful of conspirators found themselves at the head of a spontaneous militia of thirty thousand. Soon after, Poland declared itself independent.

The reaction of the tsar was fierce and resolute. Nicholas I sent in the Russian army with orders to crush the revolt decisively. But plagued metaphorically by incompetent officers, uninspired troops, and a resourceful Polish resistance, and literally by cholera that claimed among its victims the tsar's brother Konstantin, the army took nine months to put down the insurrection. The brutal aftermath shocked much of Europe and confirmed Nicholas I as the leader of reaction and destroyer of nationalities, roughly analogous, some argue, to George W. Bush at the beginning of the twenty-first century.

By the 1840s, Poland had a symbolic importance to democrats, republicans, nationalists, and revolutionaries, just as Spain would have in the 1930s and Poland would again in 1939 and 1980. Its failed revolutionaries made their way to Paris to continue to agitate and work for the liberation of their homeland, and in 1844 Bakunin threw himself into the struggle. He was, after all, no stranger to the iron hand of the tsar, who had sentenced him to Siberia and forced him out of Switzerland. He had some firsthand experience of the Russian repression of Poland as well, from his military exile to the frontiers. At the time, he had shown no sympathy to the Polish cause. He wrote to his cousin Sergei Muraviev that the company of the "good and simple Russian peasant" was infinitely preferable to that of the "noisy, silly chatter of the stupid Polish nobles," and argued that the cruelty of the Russian government that had so outraged them while comfortably settled in St. Petersburg was absolutely necessary.[8] A decade later, the petulant, disgruntled young officer was now the thoughtful critic whose earlier experience gave him sympathetic insight into "the Polish question."

His first act of solidarity was a short letter attacking the tsar, published in Louis Blanc's radical newspaper *La Reforme*. Bakunin outlined the repressive nature of the regime. He pointed out that, contrary to popular belief, even nobles in Russia had no rights before the tsar. His own case, where he was sentenced without trial for relatively minor offenses on foreign soil, was evidence of that. While there was a senate of nobles, it was powerless against the tsar, who often intervened and overruled its decisions. In Russia, he thundered, "the law is nothing but the whim of the tsar." As a result, the nobility was demoralized and apathetic, reduced to meaningless court intrigues and gossiping. While the rest of Europe engaged with the grand social questions of the epoch, the Russian nobility was occupied with wringing meaning out of every gesture made by a member of the royal family and laughing at the puns of the Grand Duke Michael. In truth, he observed, "there were no aristocrats, only servants, in St. Petersburg."

Despite the ennui of the nobility, Bakunin held that there was hope for Russia. Democracy was possible; indeed, it was the only solution for both Russia and Poland. Certain members of the nobility, especially the younger generation, increasingly sought each other out to make sense of politics and work to end the repressive regime. More importantly, "the Russian people," despite the terrible slavery and the policeman's club, were "in [their] instincts and ways entirely democratic." If the masses were uncivilized, they had an abundance of spirit and passion that proved they had "some great mission to realize in the world." The hope of Russia lay in "that innumerable and imposing mass of humanity" that was advancing despite the efforts of the tsar. The insurrections of serfs against their lords were ill-formed and incomplete, it was true, but they were serious and growing. If the revolts could be organized and coordinated, it was not too much to hope that Russia would see either a great revolution or significant reforms.[9]

His observations were largely correct. New circles among the intellectuals had sprung up in Russia. The founder of the Petrashevsky circle in St. Petersburg was explicitly interested in Fourier and Proudhon, and there Fyodor Dostoevsky learned about politics. He learned too about repression: in 1849, the young novelist and other members of the circle were arrested and sentenced to death. Dressed in the white execution shirt and tied to the post against which he was to be shot, he was pardoned at the last moment. Another writer, Nikolai Chernyshevsky, traveled on the fringes of the Petrashevsky circle. Unlike Dostoevsky, he became more committed to the revolutionary ideal over time, writing his most famous work, the revolutionary, if exceedingly dull, novel *What Is To Be Done?* in the tsar's prison. Bakunin was correct too about the volatility of the peasantry. By 1834, the secret police was forced to report that "every year, the idea of freedom spreads and grows stronger among the peasants owned by the nobles." Acts of insubordination were on the rise, and most alarming, these increasingly stemmed not from "ill-treatment or abuses, but purely from the idea of obtaining the right to freedom." The uprisings were localized and ill-planned, but Benckendorff, the head of the Third Section, warned that a crisis, such as famine, war, or the ever-popular outside agitator, could "easily provoke grave disturbances." Admittedly, spies are noted for overcounting dissenters, for the spy who reports "all quiet" is soon out of a job. But the reported acts of insubordination more than doubled from 1834 to 1844, and peasants increasingly turned to violence: more than four hundred were deported to Siberia for the crime of attempted murder over the same period. Bakunin understood that this unrest was not a unified, conscious revolution, but it was cause for hope that all the tsar's horses and all the tsar's men could not completely extinguish the spark of rebellion.[10]

The following year, the Poles again raised the flags of revolt, national independence, and democracy in Cracow against the Austrian empire and in Poznan against the Prussian. Peasants attacked landlords and seized land while urban workers and miners set their sights on nobles and capitalists. But the revolt was not well coordinated and counterattacks by the armies of Prussia, Austria, and Russia put it down by early March.

The events in Poland galvanized Paris, not least because it was home to many refugees from the 1831 revolt. Bakunin recalled that "for two or three days the whole population lived on the streets; stranger spoke with stranger, everyone asked for news, and all awaited reports from Poland with anxious impatience." The "common movement of passions and minds," as he called it, "also seized me with its wave." In a letter in the Paris newspaper *Le Constitutionnel*, he labeled the oppression of Poland a "disgrace," and hoped that the insurrection would both liberate the Poles and point the way forward for Russia. Pointing out that the tsar had long been dedicated to destroying Poland as a country and as a nation, he assured readers that the stories of atrocities that were surfacing were completely in keeping with the tsar's aims and past practices.[11]

While he volunteered his services to the exiled Polish community in Versailles and supported the local agitation, the defeat of the uprising threw the movement into chaos and recriminations. It was difficult enough for Poles to trust each other, let alone a Russian noble. Bakunin's revolutionary democracy was of less interest to emigre Polish nobles, many of whom saw in revolution only their opportunity to replace the Russian nobility. Furthermore, national liberation was, for Bakunin, about liberation, not nationalism, but the Poles were "narrow, limited, exclusive. They saw nothing but Poland."[12]

Despite his misgivings, when asked to speak at a banquet to commemorate the 1831 uprising, he responded enthusiastically. This was more than an opportunity to give an amusing after-dinner talk on the rubber chicken circuit. Banquets had long been a customary forum for revolutionary organizing where other forms of political activity were banned. They bridged the gap between secret meetings and open-air rallies and provided an admirable pretext for assembling hundreds of people without alarming the authorities. They performed a valuable cultural function as well. Solidarity is about more than agreeing on common ideas. It is about building trust and support between people, and sharing food is one way humans begin that process.

Bakunin's prepared talk ran to ten pages and he delivered it with power and conviction. He started by reminding his audience that their very presence at the banquet, some fifteen hundred strong, was itself an act of defiance "thrown into the face of all the oppressors of Poland." He understood, as they did, that Russia was one of the "principal causes of all their misfortunes," yet he stood before them as a Russian, and one who proclaimed his pride in being Russian. He explained this apparent paradox by making the important distinction between the Russian government and the Russian people. The government was rightly condemned as "an ever-growing danger to the liberty of peoples," a virtual synonym for "brutal oppression" and "shameful oppression." But the Russian people were no less victims than the Poles and other repressed nationalities. For that reason, the struggle for Poland was also a struggle for Russia. For that reason, Russians too could honor the memory of the struggle of 1831 and celebrate the spirit of freedom that it represented, just as all could revere the Decembrists who met their death in the cause of liberty.

He was a Russian repentant of the crimes of his government, but one who dared to proclaim his love and respect for Poland and who dared to urge the Poles to ally themselves with the people of Russia against the government that oppressed them all. It was precisely because the Poles were the enemy of the tsar that they were the friends of the Russian people. The people, he continued, were oppressed but not corrupted. Despite their suffering, they remained vigorous, powerful, and vibrant. Peasants, progressives from all classes, the generation of nobility that was coming of age, even soldiers in the tsar's army, were alive to the need for reform and change. Despite its apparent strength, the regime was hollow. It had no popular support and depended instead on lies and brutality to preserve the myth of omnipotence and control. Its most powerful weapon was the disarray among the Russian people and the lack of unity between Russians and Poles. If that unity could be forged, with Russian and Pole "united by the same ideas, fighting for the same cause against a common enemy," it would mean "the emancipation of sixty million people, the liberation of all the Slav people who groan under a foreign yoke, finally, the fall, the ultimate fall, of despotism in Europe."[13]

The crowd went wild as the fifteen hundred rebels, exiles, and radicals jumped to their feet to cheer and applaud. The enthusiastic response showed Bakunin that the cause of Slavic liberation was a window of opportunity. But his speech also opened a door. The Russian authorities soon learned of Bakunin's remarks and their overwhelming reception. Indeed, since they undoubtedly had spies in the audience, the Third Section probably knew about it before the banquet plates were cleared away. When the Russian ambassador pressured the French government to expel Bakunin, the minister of the interior showed him the exit within a fortnight. Bakunin headed to Brussels. It was a revolutionary backwater compared to Paris. The Polish community was riven and squabbling, and Bakunin soon sought out other political groups. Chief among these was the Democratic Federation, a loose organization of workers and intellectuals bound not by nationality or craft but by left-wing ideas. The leading figure in the Federation was Karl Marx, who, like Bakunin, had recently been thrown out of France. They had the potential to be a dream team of the left. The one synthesized complex arguments and delivered them with power to crowds of workers and peasants; the other sat in undershorts of iron to produce voluminous research and turn dry debates and facts into revolutionary ideas. Bakunin's writings were always dashed off, often left unfinished, always left unedited, yet still had the power to move the reader; Marx polished and edited and elaborated, making brilliant deductions and beautiful analyses that took years to craft. Every political movement, like any other collective endeavor, requires different skills and abilities. It needs educators, popularizers, theorists, organizers, dreamers, pragmatists, logicians, rebels, lovers, and fighters. Though each of us may have some of these qualities at different stages in our lives, no one has all of them, and it is impossible to know the correct configuration and balance needed at any particular moment. Too often rebels think pragmatists to be cowards while the pragmatists see the rebels as crazy adventurists who will wreck the movement with their hormone-laced politics; the popularizers get bored by the academic theorists, the theorists are embarrassed by the simplistic formulations of the popularizers, and so on. With luck, different individuals with different attributes come together and find a healthy, dynamic tension. If the strengths of Bakunin and Marx could have been combined, they would have made the hottest duo until Jimi Hendrix met Leo Fender.

They had much in common, including a physical resemblance, though

Bakunin towered over Marx. Both came from privilege. Marx's father was a prosperous Trier lawyer who sent his son to the best schools and universities. Marx himself would marry into the German aristocracy; his brother-in-law would become the Prussian minister of the interior in charge of the police. Like Bakunin, Marx drove his father mad with his insistence on studying philosophy rather than something practical, his reckless spending and borrowing, and his refusal to take up an orthodox career. Marx studied under some of the same instructors at the University of Berlin, though unlike Bakunin he would receive his doctorate, from the University of Jena, notable for being a bit of a diploma mill. The two made similar treks through German idealism, Hegel, and Europe, propelled across the continent by the police. They published in the same journals, had many of the same friends, acquaintances, enemies, and intellectual interests, and even used similar metaphors and tropes in their writing. Their politics, until 1848, were roughly similar, as both could be classified as radical democrats who looked to workers and elements of the middle class to lead revolutions to secure political gains such as suffrage and constitutions and to redress economic grievances. While both spoke of the importance of the developing working class, neither had much acquaintance with it, for both traveled in the circles of artisans and intellectuals and emigres rather than the proletariat. Their politics were more alike than not, though some important differences would develop over time; both remained dedicated revolutionaries who grappled creatively with some of the most important questions humanity has faced. Each shaped the ideas of the other, yet over a relationship that spanned thirty years they went from nodding acquaintance to grudging respect to academic disagreement to personal and political loathing.[14]

Bakunin respected Marx's intellectual abilities and frequently found himself in agreement with him. In particular, he quickly understood that Marx's development of historical materialism as a way of understanding history and revolutionary change was essentially correct. While Marx rarely acknowledged intellectual debts, his mature ideas owed much to his engagement with anarchism and anarchists, from Stirner to Proudhon to Bakunin, for Marx usually developed his ideas through criticizing others, in the best dialectical fashion. But he and Bakunin never really liked each other, and it is hard to separate their personal animosity from their political differences. Some of their hostility was undoubtedly due to their very different personalities. Bakunin summed it up frankly, admitting that while in Paris in the 1840s, "we were friendly enough . . . we were never really close. Our temperaments did not allow it. He called me a sentimental idealist, and he was right. I called him vain, treacherous, and cunning, and I too was right."[15] Where Bakunin was expansive and personable, Marx tended to be confrontational and belligerent. Bakunin preferred the bold, insightful overstatement to the precise, diligent layered arguments Marx crafted; quickly grasping and sketching the essence of an idea, Bakunin had little patience for the extended, detailed research and careful elaboration that occupied much of Marx's life.

Each liked to argue, each liked to be right, and each had a competitive nature, though they competed on different fields. Bakunin was on good terms with leading activists such as Weitling and Proudhon, while Marx was not. Marx's work as a writer and editor had brought him some attention, but none of it had had the impact of Bakunin's "Reaction in Germany." Even Marx's most famous work, the Communist Manifesto, first published in 1848, was virtually ignored outside of small circles of German artisans and intellectuals until the 1870s. It was Bakunin, not Marx, who brought the crowd to its feet. Marx, with his high, nasal, academic delivery might impress with his logic, but rarely with his sheer presence. Bakunin fashioned an effective speaking style aimed at convincing people through the forceful expression of his ideas rather than careful exposition. Nonetheless, he realized and graciously conceded Marx's talent and ability. Nearly thirty years later, in the middle of a foul confrontation with Marx, Bakunin recalled that when they first met in 1844, Marx "was much more advanced than I was, as he remains more advanced and incomparably more learned than I today. I knew nothing then about political economy, I had not given up metaphysical abstractions, and my socialism was only instinctive." In contrast, Marx, four years younger, was already a "well-informed materialist and a reflective socialist." Bakunin respected Marx for his "learning and for his passionate and serious devotion . . . to the cause of the proletariat," and enjoyed their "instructive and lively" conversations. Nonetheless, he was aware of the "vanity, spitefulness, and gossip" that characterized Marx's work with the Democratic Federation in the 1840s.[16]

Their prejudices too played a role in their quarrels. Marx was quick to denounce Slavs as a backward, reactionary people; unlike "civilized Germany," Russia had "nonsensical prophets and nonsensical followers," and he often included Bakunin in that characterization. But both men had an ample share of the racial ideas and racism of their age, and these escaped from their leaky ids in the heat of polemics with each other. They were also quick to indulge in class prejudices when they fought. Marx was dismissive of Bakunin's aristocratic roots and Bakunin was sardonic about Marx's bourgeois behavior and hypocrisy. Engels and Marx—especially Marx, Bakunin complained—labeled everyone who disagreed with them "bourgeois," though the two remained "more bourgeois than anyone in a provincial city." Worse, their engagement with the Democratic Alliance amounted to little more than a "disgusting flirtation" with workers.[17]

This last criticism of Marx and Engels, however, had some substance to it. Stripped of its class prejudice, it reflected a fundamental political difference centered on the role of intellectuals in workers' movements. The question surfaced in the practical political questions of the 1840s and would continue to frame the conflict between Bakunin and Marx, anarchists and communists, for decades.

Intellectuals and workers formed an uneasy alliance in the 1840s, and important differences divided the left and labor movements. Intellectuals, including Bakunin, Marx, and Engels, were not from the working class, however much they pledged to serve the working class. This prompted an important question: how could non-workers understand and speak for workers? Certainly they could empathize with the plight of workers; they could offer useful analyses, and they could put their skills at the service of working-class organizations. But they did not share the same experiences of work, culture, and class. This was not a problem for earlier socialist theorists such as Robert Owen or Saint-Simon who believed that workers were unable to understand the real nature of political and economic problems and so would have to have the solutions imposed upon them. But thinkers such as Bakunin and Marx believed that ideas were not created in a vacuum and were not just the product of speculation and contemplation: they stemmed from specific economic and political conditions, and they in large part reflected the material interests of the people who held them. That monarchs believed in the divine right of kings told you nothing about God or rights, but did tell you something important about the self-interest of kings. That capitalists insisted on the rights of property told you nothing about natural justice but did indicate fairly clearly how they profited from the system. That workers organized around principles of justice and liberty that they defined differently than kings and employers did suggested that they too knew on which side their bread was buttered and that class experience and class interests influenced ideas as much as pure thought.

Marx and Engels emphatically set out the argument that ideas came from the material, economic, and real world in "The German Ideology." Written in 1846, but not published until 1932, the manuscript summed up their powerful critique of idealism. To those who believed that ideas had an independent existence or were the result of independent cogitation, they responded fiercely:

The social structure and the state are continually evolving out of the life-process of definite individuals, but of individuals, not as they may appear in their own or other people's imagination, but as they really are, i.e., as they operate, produce materially, and hence as they work under definite material limits, presuppositions, and conditions independent of their will.

The production of ideas, of conceptions, of consciousness, is at first directly interwoven with the material activity and the material intercourse of men, the language of real life. Conceiving, thinking, the mental intercourse of men, appear at this stage as the direct efflux of their material behavior. The same applies to mental production as expressed in the language of politics, laws, morality, religion, metaphysics, etc. of a people. Men are the producers of their conceptions, ideas, etc.—real, active men, as they are conditioned by a definite development of their productive forces and of the intercourse corresponding to these . . .

In direct contrast to German philosophy which descends from heaven to earth, here we ascend from earth to heaven. That is to say, we do not set out from what men say, imagine, conceive, nor from men as narrated, thought of, imagined, conceived, in order to arrive at men in the flesh. We set out from real, active men, and on the basis of their real life-process we demonstrate the development of the ideological reflexes and echoes of this life-process . . . Morality, religion, metaphysics, all the rest of ideology and their corresponding forms of consciousness thus no longer retain the semblance of independence. They have no history, no development; but men, developing their material production and their material intercourse, alter, along with this their real existence, their thinking and the products of their thinking. *Life is not determined by consciousness, but consciousness by life.*[18]

"Life is not determined by consciousness, but consciousness by life." This was the crucial insight developed by Marx and Engels, and it was one that Bakunin enthusiastically shared. Indeed, it expressed more forcefully and concretely ideas he had been developing in his writings of the 1830s and early 1840s. "Life is not determined by consciousness, but consciousness by life." This was the lever needed to pry off centuries of mystification and ideology; it was the tool Weitling and Proudhon reached for but could not quite take hold of as they struggled to understand and change the world.

It was, however, a tool that could bark the knuckles of those who applied it. If consciousness—ideas—were determined by life, how could intellectuals speak for workers? Weren't the ideas of intellectuals formed by their material existence, which was different from that of workers? After all, Marx was quick to label Feuerbach's ideas as "bourgeois," Proudhon's as "petit bourgeois sentimentality," and Proudhon himself as "from head to foot . . . the philosopher and economist of the lower middle class." For his part, Proudhon was content to reply that "Marx is the tapeworm of socialism," but the question still arose: by the logic of his own argument, how could Marx's political program transcend his own class interest? After all, kings and capitalists and politicians all insisted that they were really acting in the interests of everyone, even when it was pretty obvious that they weren't. Why should workers regard Marx differently? What made him immune from his materialist explanation? [19]

Marx's answer was not altogether convincing. While workers learned only from their own experience, Marx held that the "communist consciousness . . . may, of course, arise among the other classes too through the contemplation of the situation" of the working class. As the proletarian revolution approached, "a portion of the bourgeois ideologists, who have raised themselves to the level of comprehending theoretically the historical movement as a whole," would go "over to the proletariat." That is to say, intellectuals could form the correct consciousness not from their own class experience but from contemplation and understanding, theoretically, the movement of history. [20]

This was, however, not an answer that would satisfy the artisans and workers. To many of them, it appeared to be merely a way of exempting intellectuals such as Marx and Engels from their own theory of materialist history. This was pointed out rather firmly by thinkers such as Weitling and Proudhon who noted that it was certainly an interesting coincidence that Herr Doktor Marx was willing to grant a special dispensation to people like himself. In contrast, they insisted that the job of liberating workers had to fall to the workers themselves, and that included developing social and political theory. Where Marx insisted that theoretical knowledge was the key, they argued instead that political will was more important, and workers, not intellectuals, had that by virtue of their oppression.

Nonetheless, Marx's argument that other groups could comprehend the movement of history was an important insight, for it suggested that ideology could not simply be reduced to class experience. One could not know someone's ideas merely by calculating their class position; ideas could not be simply reduced to class. Nor did Marx insist they could. Historical materialism was not a precise mathematical equation but rather a method of analysis that introduced material interests into the realm of ideas. But this was an insight that cut both ways. If bourgeois thinkers and ideologists such as he and Engels could make the leap to understand the ideas necessary for other classes, why couldn't artisans such as Weitling and Proudhon? They were, after all, much closer to the experience of workers than Marx and Engels. What prevented former aristocrats such as Bakunin from understanding the path of history? For that matter, why couldn't peasants extrapolate from their experience and thought to contribute to the debate over freedom and equality? Why should intellectuals assume the role of spokesperson for the working class? On what grounds could they claim to lead workers, either politically or theoretically? One of course could argue that time would tell who was correct and that many of the issues could be resolved empirically. But this was not a scientific experiment that could be run and run again to duplicate results; it was a social movement that had to proceed very differently. And as a social movement, it was also comprised of human beings who jostled and competed to be heard. Undoubtedly some too wished to be followed. Each side used their best arguments to make their case. Marx claimed theoretical rigor and precision. Workers and worker-intellectuals such as Proudhon and Weitling explicitly denied that academic intellectuals should be privileged. They argued instead that experience and firsthand knowledge justified their positions as the leaders and theoreticians of working-class movements, and the debate continues to this day.

Marx responded to their challenge in two ways. First, he took on Weitling and Proudhon directly. Marx had little contact with workers' organizations but in 1845 he helped create a new body that would become the Communist League. Engels, Marx's wife, Jenny, one of her brothers, and Weitling were the most significant members of the tiny, clandestine group. In Brussels on 30 March 1846, at a meeting called, chaired, and stacked by Marx, Weitling was subjected to a verbal assault by the good doctor. "Tell us, Weitling," he thundered, "you people who have made such a rumpus in Germany with your communist preachings and have won over so many workers, causing them to lose their jobs and their crust of bread, with what fundamental principles do you justify your revolutionary and social activity and on what basis do you intend affirming it in the future?" He then demanded that Weitling tell the group "what are the arguments with which you defend your social-revolutionary agitation and on what do you intend to base it in the future?"

Weitling was visibly taken aback by the unprovoked attack. His interrogator was, after all, the same man who had earlier praised his work as a writer and a leader and who had sought him out to take part in the new organization. He started to answer, pointing out that his aim was not to devise new socioeconomic theories but to "open the workers' eyes" to the horrors and injustices and to teach them to trust not in governments or messiahs but in themselves. Marx cut him off and blistered him with sarcasm. What workers needed, Marx interjected, was not fantastic hopes but "a rigorous scientific idea" and a "positive doctrine." Anything else was merely an "empty and dishonest game," appropriate perhaps for barbaric Russia but not for a "civilized country like Germany." Weitling responded by pointing out that he had mobilized thousands of workers, that he had inspired and educated them, not through preaching theories but by making sense of their experience. This work was, he suggested, more use than the philosophy and theory generated in ivory towers. He pointed to his own relative success as an author. Weitling had, after all, published three books, while Marx had produced little more than some newspaper articles. At that moment, Marx pounded the table and shouted, "Ignorance has never yet helped anybody," and the meeting broke up. Marx and Engels followed up on this ritual humiliation by slandering Weitling among other groups, intimating that someone else had written his books, denouncing his ideas to anyone who would listen, and attacking his supporters. Soon after, Weitling left Europe for the United States.[21]

Proudhon avoided a direct confrontation with Marx, largely because he declined Marx's offer to join with him in the Communist League. He had some intimation of what was up and may well have heard of Weitling's humiliating experience. In answer to Marx's invitation, Proudhon professed "an almost total anti-dogmatism in economics . . . For God's sake . . . do not let us think of indoctrinating the people in our turn." He was concerned that socialist thinkers should avoid "your compatriot Martin Luther's inconsistency," that is, of smashing Catholicism only to institute the "shambles" of Protestantism. "Let us set the world an example of wise and farsighted tolerance, but simply because we are leaders of a movement let us not instigate a new intolerance. Let us not set ourselves up as the apostles of a new religion, even if it be the religion of logic or of reason. Let us welcome and encourage all protests, let us get rid of all exclusiveness and all mysticism . . . On this condition I will join your association with pleasure, otherwise I will not."[22]

The letter went unanswered. Instead, Marx devoted himself to a lengthy critique of Proudhon's new book, *System of Economic Contradictions, or the Philosophy of Poverty.* Entitled *The Poverty of Philosophy,* Marx's review ran to over 160 pages. A brilliant polemic in which Marx developed further his ideas of historical materialism, it was nonetheless widely interpreted as a sneak attack on a thinker who had contributed much to the left-wing movement and to Marx's own ideas. For many, it reinforced the suspicion that Marx privileged academic intellectuals over workers, and they could point to some of his earlier work to buttress their argument. In 1844, for example, in a critique of Weitling and others, he had written that "we do not then set ourselves opposite the world with a doctrinaire principle, saying: 'Here is the truth, kneel down here!' It is out of the world's own principles that we develop for it new principles. We do not say to her, 'Stop your battles, they are stupid stuff. We want to preach the true slogans of battle to you.' We merely show it what it is actually fighting about, and this realization is a thing that it must make its own even though it may not wish to." This passage may sound liberating, but the skeptic may interpret this to mean that while Marx insists he is not laying down doctrine, he is saying that intellectuals divine the real nature of struggle and history.[23] In the same year, he wrote, "As philosophy finds in the proletariat its material weapons, so the proletariat finds in philosophy its intellectual weapons, and as soon as the lightning of thought has struck deep into the virgin soil of the people, the emancipation of the Germans into men will be completed." However much one might agree with the idea that philosophers and workers should unite, one does not have to be Freud, Fellini, or a psychohistorian to raise an eyebrow at that metaphor. But if there was any doubt about who was going to get their virginity electrocuted by whom, Marx removed it when he concluded that "The head of this emancipation is philosophy, its heart is the proletariat." Naturally, the head is to rule the heart, or so many workers and others believed Marx intended.[24]

Marx's second response was less violent and less sectarian. Politics was one thing, and he had jousted successfully with the best the workers' movement could throw at him. However, the real proof of his ideas lay not in political squabbles but in research. He would soon abandon active politics for the archives. He would continue to write philosophy, history, and political economy, but would largely curtail political activism for several years, working instead, as one writer has suggested, as a consultant to the labor and left movements, though often an ill-tempered and prickly one.[25]

Bakunin resolved the issue of the relationship of workers and intellectuals differently. Certainly he believed in education and criticism; he did not believe that experience alone yielded all the answers, and he was often critical of Proudhon and Weitling. Aware of their very real limits as thinkers and theorists, still Bakunin understood that their experience both limited and enhanced their insights, and he preferred not to savage them but to appreciate their strengths. For him, the answer to the revolutionary question "What is to be done?" lay in the blending of experience and theory, of action and ideas. Following Fichte's insight, Bakunin continued to believe that everyone, including intellectuals who learned life's lessons in the academy, could learn from everyone. Furthermore, Bakunin held that it was less important to get one's metaphysics together than to act. Unlike Marx, Bakunin was inclined to believe it was more valuable to reach thousands with a message that was a little less clear than to reach scores with the tightly argued results of years of research. Furthermore, he believed that actions spoke louder than words in the revolutionary Europe of 1845-1848. Where Marx was busy trying to "make workers into logicians," Bakunin threw himself into the tumult of 1848.[26] What mattered as much as theory was actively supporting movements of liberation. Marx too understood the necessity of uniting theory and action. After all, in 1845, he had proclaimed in his "Theses on Feuerbach," that "philosophers have only *interpreted* the world, in various ways; the point, however, is to *change* it." While both might agree on the answer, each was drawn, through personality, experience, and analysis, to assign a different value to each of the factors.[27]

Even at the level of theory, however, the two differed in a substantial and meaningful way by 1848. Bakunin had, in "The Reaction in Germany," argued for a two-part dialectic, in which revolution would smash the existing social relations and replace them with a new, if vaguely sketched, political and economic structure. Such an argument reflected the Russian experience, where any attempts at progressive discussion, let alone political reform, resulted in sudden and severe repression. There could be no hope of gradual change and progress; the Third Section saw to that. In the tsar's empire, it could be only revolution or nothing; a middle path was an invitation to suicide. In the 1840s, Marx, reflecting the greater possibility for reform in the West, tended to argue in a more traditional Hegelian mode that social change would build on existing structures and move in stages through the triadic formula. In particular, it would evolve in response to the expansion of society's "productive forces," that is, the development of humanity's ability to create more goods, from foodstuffs to luxury goods. The revolution could not be accomplished until an appropriate level of production had been reached. Ironically, this meant that Marx, later respected and reviled as the archrevolutionary, came under fire in the 1840s for not being revolutionary enough. After all, it was Marx who told "the workers and petit bourgeois" in 1849 that "it is better to suffer in the contemporary bourgeois society, whose industry creates the means for the foundation of a new society that will liberate you, than to revert to a bygone society, which, on the pretext of saving your classes, thrusts the entire nation back into medieval barbarism." This was hardly Marx's last word on revolution. In the previous sentence, he had been careful to assure his readers that "we are certainly the last people to desire the rule of the bourgeoisie." But coming at the end of the revolutionary upheavals of 1848, neither was it a clear call to action. As a result, Marx's article was widely interpreted as a rejection of proletarian revolution until certain economic and political conditions had developed sufficiently.[28]

This may seem a rather esoteric point on which even unreasonable minds might cheerfully agree to differ. Yet it had some very practical and immediate consequences. It meant that Bakunin supported open revolt wherever it appeared, believing that successful revolution did not depend solely on society reaching an appropriate stage of development. Tyranny had to be opposed and rebellion supported, if only to maintain the habit of resistance so later generations had precedents to point to and draw upon. It was easy to sit back and preach that socialism could only be reached after capitalism had developed the means of production to a sufficient level, but how could one tell when that level had been reached? In the meantime, what did one tell starving workers? For that matter, if socialism had to build on capitalism, did that mean peasants, indigenous people, and slaves were supposed to . . . to what? Fight to create capitalism so they could be exploited as workers? Was the revolutionary supposed to fight only for the next stage of Marx's dialectic? How was that supposed to motivate anyone? Workers might not grasp the intricacies of economic theory, but they understood where the shoe pinched and when the stomach grumbled. Revolt was a response to existing conditions, not a meta-historical process known only to professors and aimed at fulfilling their predictions. If Marx could afford to wait for the appropriate level of material production, starving workers and those under the lash of empire could not, and Bakunin believed his place was with them, even if it was clear that mass revolution was unlikely or impossible.

Of course, Marx did not simply advocate that workers should wait passively for the productive relations to develop. He made many different arguments at different times on the nature of revolution. Historians still debate which was the "real" Marx, and in the volumes of his work one can find evidence to support nearly every political position. In 1850, for exam-

ple, he theorized on the possibility of "permanent revolution," an idea
Bakunin developed independently later. Marx suggested that it was possible
for workers to fight alongside the middle class against the aristocracy to
establish capitalism, then, once that battle was won, immediately take up the
struggle for socialism against their erstwhile allies. Even here, however, he
was careful to insist this was a strategy applicable only in Germany, where
the productive forces were well developed. His idea of permanent revolution
was not a prescription for workers to go beyond stages of economic development so much as an acknowledgment that one nation might already be
sufficiently developed. In any case, he would quickly reject the permanent
revolution even for Germany.[29]

More consistently, Marx argued against Weitling, Proudhon, Bakunin, and
others that while revolution was inevitable it required the development of productive forces, the transition from earlier forms of production to capitalism,
and the development of capitalism to the point where the proletariat and the
bourgeoisie were the two significant classes. Thus in 1842, when Bakunin was
calling for revolution, Marx warned of the "crisis of conscience caused by the
rebellion of man's subjective desires against the objective insights of his own
reason . . . Ideas that have overcome our intellect and conquered our conviction, ideas to which reason has riveted our conscience, are chains from which
one cannot break loose without breaking one's heart." It was theoretical error
he sought to eradicate even then.[30] Two years later Marx warned that "revolutionary energy and intellectual self-confidence alone are not enough to gain
this position of self-emancipation. Revolutions need a passive element, a material base . . . It is not enough that thought should tend toward reality, reality
must also tend toward thought." What did that material base consist of? In
Germany, it meant that for "one class [to] appear as the class of liberation,
another class must inversely be the manifest class of oppression." The class
of liberation was to be the proletariat, but as Marx admitted, the proletariat
was just beginning to form in Germany. Sixty-five percent of the population
still lived on the land and faced poverty in near-feudal conditions. Marx's prescription in the Communist Manifesto in 1848 was for workers to join with
the bourgeoisie to secure the bourgeois revolution.[31] True, he hoped that
immediately after that revolution workers would move straight on to a proletarian one, but the crucial message was one of fighting for the development
of capitalism. Marx's logic was clear enough: Socialism required the full development of capitalism and classes before it could succeed.

It is an argument he would continue to develop throughout his life. In
1859, it was summed up nicely: "No social order is ever destroyed before all

the productive forces for which it is sufficient have been developed, and new superior relations of production never replace older ones before the material conditions for their existence have matured within the framework of the old society." In *Capital,* first published in 1867, he insisted that it was not until "the monopoly of capital becomes a fetter upon the mode of production," not until "centralization of the means of production and socialization of labor at last reach a point where they become incompatible with their capitalist integument" that "the knell of capitalist private property sounds."[32]

Again his critics asked, what precisely did this mean for displaced artisans and proletarians? How long was one supposed to wait? One Marxist cheerfully would argue 156 years after the Communist Manifesto that capitalism still had a long life ahead of it and that Marx would still be cautioning us to hold off on that socialist project a little longer.[33] What, for that matter, did it mean to Eastern Europe, which was just beginning to industrialize and where the vast majority of the population were peasants? Were they supposed to give up being exploited peasants to become exploited proletarians, buoyed by the appreciation that this new form of oppression was another example of the universe unfolding as it should? Marx gave a hint in the Communist Manifesto, where he declared that one of the great virtues of capitalism was that it had "rescued a considerable part of the population from the idiocy of rural life." As capitalism spread, it would make "barbarian and semi-barbarian countries dependent on the civilized ones, nations of peasants on nations of bourgeois, the East on the West."[34] Marx's thinking in the 1840s was less an appreciation of the plight of serfs than a wordy elaboration of King Arthur's dismissal of Dennis—"Bloody peasant!"—in *Monty Python and the Holy Grail.*

Bakunin, on the other hand, argued that peasants and workers had much to teach intellectuals. He believed that the peasants of Russia were further advanced than Marx held, for they understood that the formal, political freedom represented by the bourgeois revolutions in the West meant little without economic freedom. For the peasant, that meant possession and ownership of the land, not as private property but on the basis of the peasant commune. "The peasants reason very clearly on this subject," he wrote in 1849. "They do not say 'the land of our master,' but 'our land.' The social character of the Russian revolution is already set out, already bound up in the nature of the people and their communal organization." That suggested that they did not need to go through the same historical stages of capitalism to create socialism. Furthermore, the peasants had the revolutionary tradition and memory of Pugachev. Folklore and memory reminded them how the peasantry had torched the castles and piled high the corpses of nobles and functionaries, how even Catherine the Great had "trembled on her throne" until Pugachev had been captured. "The memory of these popular heroes continues to live," he reminded his readers," and still "the people speak with pride of the era of the Pugachev uprising." Peasants, far from being an immovable object, had reason to revolt and traditions of social, collective production and resistance that were as empowering as the full development of the productive forces. They need not wait until Russia became capitalist before embarking on revolution. In 1848, he believed that it was time for workers and peasants to take revolutionary action on their own behalf. His evidence for this was the fact that they were taking such action.[35]

The point is not that Bakunin was right and Marx was wrong, or vice versa. Bakunin admitted later that he had been "carried away by the intoxication of the revolutionary movement" of 1848 and had been "much more concerned with the negative than the positive side of the revolution." Marx, he conceded, had largely been right in arguing that the time was not appropriate.[36] For his part, Marx would fundamentally rethink his positions on revolution, Russia, and peasants. Furthermore, it is easy to overstate their differences. Those who argue, for example, that Marx was essentially a liberal democrat in this period are surely mistaken. Those who insist that he was a technological determinist, that is, someone who believed that history was essentially a process of technological change in which human activity mattered little, depend on a reading that is too narrow and selective to be persuasive. At the same time, Bakunin's position has often been parodied as an idealist belief in willpower, that one could make the revolution no matter what the objective reality. This was a position he emphatically denied repeatedly throughout his life. Nor is it fair to conclude that Bakunin was the man of action while Marx was the man of theory, or as has been recently suggested, that Bakunin was the "heart," Marx the "head" of the revolution. Such a conclusion underestimates the contributions each made to theory and practice and simultaneously undercuts the fact that social struggles are about collective action, not individual effort.

What is apparent is that the two had taken on different, if overlapping, revolutionary projects. Marx's primary concern was to analyze the structural causes of revolution and historical change. The Communist Manifesto is a brilliant example of this, as relevant today as in 1848. Bakunin, on the other hand, was chiefly concerned with revolutionary methods and tactics. He would support revolt wherever it broke out, believing that the example of rebellion would inspire others, that workers and peasants understood from the conditions of their lives that freedom meant struggle, that resistance might be doomed but it was never futile. The two projects were not necessarily antithetical. Ideally, each could have contributed creatively to the other. In practice, they more often led to misinterpretation and suspicion that lasted until Bakunin's death in 1876 and continues between anarchists and Marxists to the present day.[37]

In 1848, their differences of theory, personality, and philosophy took them in very different directions. As Europe roiled, Bakunin threw himself on the barricades of Paris and Dresden while Marx would begin his long trek through the British Museum.

9

BARRICADES PILED UP LIKE MOUNTAINS

The differences between Bakunin and Marx soon transcended theory and personality to manifest themselves in political action. The tensions in Europe had been evident for years; Bakunin had pointed them out in 1842, and other observers could not fail to notice that something was happening there, even if it wasn't exactly clear. Crop failures, notably of potatoes in Ireland, the Netherlands, and Germany, and of wheat in other areas led to food shortages and riots. Attracted by the higher rate of profit offered by manufacture, landowners shifted capital from agriculture to industry. This neutral-sounding, rational business decision masked a brutal reality. Peasants and tenant farmers were thrown off the land and forced to move to cities where they could choose between unemployment and overwork at starvation wages. The new industries and factories forced household and small-scale producers to the wall, and inflation and financial crises wracked even the well off. If these problems appeared in different forms in different nations and empires, the solutions were increasingly seen as political. The bourgeoisie and the proletariat alike understood that the necessary changes could not take place under king, tsar, prince, or empire. The first of the dual revolutions, capitalism, spread almost by accident, but the second, parliamentary democracy, required will and action and could be defeated much more easily. Nor did workers and peasants understand revolution the same way political reformers and employers did. Some hoped revolution would dethrone kings and emperors and replace them with elected assemblies. Others had equally passionate but less articulate hopes to empower the people economically and politically. Still others simply sought bread and work, but these too were radical demands. What was different about 1848 was that so many different social groups across the continent turned to revolution, despite very different social conditions and very different political alignments. They were united less by specific grievances and solutions than by a general demand for liberty common enough that peasants in Galicia, farm laborers in Sicily, workers in Germany and France, and many others rose within days of each other to topple governments, expel kings and ministers, and change the face

of Europe forever. Even in Switzerland, where four hundred years of broth-
erly love, democracy, and peace combined to produce the cuckoo clock, civil
war raged briefly in a prelude to 1848.

But it was in France that real revolution first erupted. The monarchy had
been restored in 1814. Though the July Revolution of 1830 forced Charles
X, the last of the Bourbons, to abdicate, his replacement, Louis-Philippe, and
his chief minister, Francois Guizot, ruled firmly if warily. When public disturbances broke out in Palermo against Ferdinand II, king of Naples and
Sicily, in early January 1848, they refused to heed the sign. Others were not
so sanguine. Alexis de Tocqueville spoke in the French Chamber of Deputies
of "the working classes . . . forming opinions and ideas which are destined
not only to upset this or that law, ministry, or even form of government but
society itself," and cautioned "that we are at this moment sleeping on a volcano."[1] He was treated as a Cassandra, gloomily warning of disaster that
never came. But Cassandra's curse was not that she was a doomsayer. The
ancient Greeks were much more sophisticated than that. Her curse was to
be a true prophet who was never believed.

De Tocqueville's volcano soon erupted as French workers and intellectuals stepped up a campaign of leaflets and revolutionary banquets. When they
announced a Paris march and banquet for 22 February 1848, Guizot and the
king decided that a show of strength was needed, and forbade the public gatherings. When the organizers declared they would hold the banquet regardless
of the government's order, people gathered in the streets to support them. Support turned to active protest as the police clashed with the demonstrators.
They had dispersed similar crowds before with little consequence, but this
time was different. Workers throughout Paris rushed into the streets, overturning carts and stalls to create makeshift barricades and prying up paving
stones to use as projectiles. Police and protestors fought in the streets for two
days. At the end, the regime's last best hope, the National Guard, comprised
largely of "respectable" citizens of the middle class, refused to fire on protestors or even to cheer for the king when called out on parade, and Paris
belonged to the people. Louis-Philippe dismissed Guizot, hoping this sacrifice
would satisfy the protestors. It did not. With no hope of restoring his control,
the king exercised his royal prerogative and handed the throne over to his
grandson, then caught the next carriage out of town. On 24 February, workers, artisans, middle-class republicans, democrats, and radicals declared the
end of the monarchy and proclaimed the Second Republic. They organized a
people's militia, headed by Marc Caussidiere, to replace the police and defend
the revolution, abolished capital punishment, held elections under universal

male suffrage, and declared work for all an essential right that the government had to uphold.

News of the success of the February Revolution flashed across Europe.
Within days popular uprisings broke out across Germany. By the middle of
March, revolution had spread to Vienna and Austria's Prince Metternich,
chief architect of forty-five years of intrigue and reaction, was on the lam to
England. By the end of the month, constituent assemblies had been created
in Vienna and Berlin, Frankfurt had called for a parliament, and Milan and
Venice were in revolt. That revolution could spread so quickly, at a time
when it took news a week to travel from Paris to Berlin, is perhaps the most
convincing evidence of the widespread unrest and anger on the continent.

For Bakunin, it was the best of times, it was the . . . no, it was the best of
times, full stop. Or rather, full speed ahead, as he threw himself into the
tumult. He could take little credit for predicting or fomenting the February
Revolution but it surely proved he was in tune with the spirit of the age. Revolution was no longer an idealistic or metaphysical concept. It was a living,
breathing reality, just as he had insisted. Securing a false passport, he headed
back to France, only to find that passports were now irrelevant: the new
Republic had no use for such artifacts from the old regime. Instead, he found
his passage stalled not by the police but by the workers themselves, who had
cut the railway lines. Despite the difficulties, he arrived in Paris on 26 February, where he discovered that the city, the "center of European
enlightenment, had suddenly been turned into the wild Caucasus: On every
street, almost everywhere, barricades had been piled up like mountains,
reaching the roofs, and on them, among rocks and broken furniture . . .
workers in their colorful blouses, blackened from powder and armed from
head to foot." He described the revolution in words reminiscent of George
Orwell's description of anarchist Barcelona during the Spanish Civil War,
noting that "all the hated social lions with their walking sticks and lorgnettes
had disappeared and in their place my noble workers in rejoicing, exulting
crowds, with red banners and patriotic songs, reveling in their victory!" The
workers were "forgiving, sympathetic, loving of their fellow man—upright,
modest, courteous, amiable, witty," in short, all he knew they could be once
their chains were cast off.

He took his place among Caussidiere's militia for several days and found
much that would shape his future anarchism. "These simple, uneducated people," he exclaimed, "always will be a thousand times better than all their
leaders!" The world was turned upside down, yet with no laws and no compulsion, the people developed their own discipline and selflessly took on the

work of defending and building the revolution. The streets were filled with "meetings, gatherings, clubs, processions, outings, demonstrations," and Bakunin took part in all of it. The slogan of Paris '68 was "Be realistic: demand the impossible!" In the Paris of '48, Bakunin saw that "the practical men of the old regime have today become the utopians and the utopia of yesterday is now the only possible, reasonable, practical thing . . . The inconceivable had become the usual, the impossible possible, and the possible and the usual unthinkable."[2]

If the revolution were to survive, however, it had to spread. "Unless royalty completely vanishes from the surface of Europe," he warned, "the revolution will perish." The urgent task now was for the peoples of the empires to overthrow their Prussian, Austrian, and Russian masters, for these governments were poised to crush the revolution. Of these, Russia was the most formidable bulwark of reaction. That had been its historic role since Napoleon, and the tsars proudly wore the title of "gendarme of Europe." Napoleon was right, Bakunin concluded: "Europe will be republican or Cossack."[3] Russia's soft underbelly was Poland, and Bakunin decided to leave Paris for Poznan, a Polish city under the control of Prussia. Caussidiere supplied him with two different passports: if France was no longer concerned with such bureaucratic measures, other governments now intensified the scrutiny at the border as they desperately sought to hold the revolution at bay. Bakunin secured some two thousand francs from the provisional government that now included his old comrades Louis Blanc and Ferdinand Flocon, editor of *La Reforme,* and headed off.

He made his way to Frankfurt by early April in time to observe its Pre-Parliament, called by democrats and rebels to try to coordinate a German national assembly. Here he had his first doubts about the fate of the revolution. The Pre-Parliament quickly moved from the sublime to the ridiculous, ending up as little more than a talking society dominated by moderates who failed to understand that the real threat to the revolution came no longer from the kings and princes, but from the bourgeoisie. For the bourgeoisie was preparing to cut off the revolution once its own ascendancy had been secured. Now the social revolution and "the triumph of democracy" were at risk as the "philistines" played with elections and readied themselves to take "all measures possible against the people." Worst of all, the German liberals and bourgeoisie were prepared to ally with the hated Friedrich Wilhelm IV of Prussia to retake Schleswig-Holstein from Denmark by force of arms and to carve up Polish Poznan, all in the name of German nationalism. If Bakunin needed further instruction in the relationship of class and ideology, the German liberals provided a doctorate. The machinations of the German bourgeoisie reinforced his understanding that nationalism could be used in the service of reaction as well as revolution unless it was firmly and irrevocably linked to the masses and the social revolution. This insight would guide his politics for the rest of his life.

Despite the efforts of the moderates and liberals to choke off the revolution, Bakunin believed, or perhaps, more accurately, hoped that it would continue. His old acquaintance Herwegh organized a legion of some eight hundred German workers in Paris to invade from the west and aid the revolution; there were encouraging signs that the German proletariat and peasantry were mobilizing. But the farce of the Frankfurt assembly made it even more imperative to expand the revolution to Russia to prevent the "gendarme" from quelling popular revolt in Europe, and, increasingly important, to forestall a united, bourgeois Germany from launching an imperialist adventure against the Slavic nations and people. The only hope of the revolution, Bakunin believed, now lay in a pan-Slavic revolution that would break up the Russian and Austrian empires and simultaneously stave off any attempt by Germany to take their places.[4]

He left Frankfurt, hoping to get to Poznan by way of Cologne and Berlin. In Berlin, he was mistaken for Herwegh and arrested; his two passports raised the eyebrows of the German police and he spent a day in jail. He was released after promising to stay out of Poznan and headed instead for Breslau, arriving in the Polish city in May. Along the way, he tutored his old friend Arnold Ruge on parliamentary democracy. The two met up in Leipzig, where the former Left Hegelian was campaigning for a seat in the Frankfurt assembly. Bakunin convinced him to invest his time in a more suitable enterprise: drinks at the Hotel de Pologne. The two talked the evening away until Ruge was informed that he had lost the election. All to the good, Bakunin cheerily consoled his friend, for nothing useful could come from the assembly anyway.[5]

Little useful came from Breslau either, and the news from other parts of Europe was disheartening. The German bourgeoisie had succeeded in curtailing the revolution and channeling its energy into parliamentary debates. Herwegh's legion had failed miserably at Baden. Poznan was, as Bakunin had feared, betrayed by Prussia; even in Paris, the revolution was barely holding its own. In Breslau itself, the lack of arms and the lack of unity disabled the rebels. When a Czech professor at the University of Breslau told him of a pan-Slavic congress assembling at Prague, Bakunin decided to attend, hoping to find there "an Archimedean fulcrum for action."[6] The Slav congress, however, needed more than a simple machine to lever it into action. There is an old joke about left-wing sectarianism. Question: How many Marxists does it take to go fishing? Answer: Fifty—one to hold the pole and forty-nine to find the correct line.

The difficulty was compounded among the Slavs. While to a ruler in St. Petersburg or Vienna or Berlin a Slav is a Slav is a pain in the ass, they were divided by language, history, and class. Bakunin listed some of the attending groups: Poles, Ruthenes, Silesians, Czechs, Moravians, Slovaks, Serbs, Croats, Slovenes, and Dalmatians. The Russian Slavs, by far the biggest population, had only two representatives, and one, Bakunin, had not been in Russia for the better part of a decade. The Slavs were also divided by empire. Those under the rule of Turkey looked to the tsar for aid; Polish Slavs had no such illusions about his imperial majesty's beneficence. Czech Slavs looked to Austria for protection from Germany and Russia, while Magyars chafed under its rule and Austrian Slavs remained indifferent to Russian imperialism. Though the chief Magyar spokesman, Lajos Kossuth, fought for national independence, he had little interest in sharing power with the Ukrainians, Romanians, Croats, Serbs, and Slovaks who lived in Hungary. To further complicate things, each empire skillfully played the different nationalities against each other, encouraging rebellion in other empires when useful and smashing revolts in their own territories.

As the congress debated and argued, workers and students took matters into their own hands. Following the pattern of Paris, Berlin, and the other cities of '48, they filled the public squares, established barricades, and demanded a provisional government. They were answered not with abdications and constitutions, but with cannon and grapeshot. While most of the congress delegates scurried for cover as the Austrian army rained shot and shell into the city, Bakunin fought on the hastily improvised fortifications and urged the insurrectionists to seize the town hall to prevent the politicians from treating with the Austrians. But the ill-planned uprising was doomed and as the flag of surrender was raised, Bakunin slipped out of the city before he could be arrested.

The events of 1848 reinforced his belief that revolution was as much an "instinct as a thought," as much an emotional, immediate response as an intellectual, deliberative one. Certainly it broke out and spread as an expression of anger and despair and hope rather than a calculated rational exercise. The events of that year also confirmed his suspicions of politicians and the gut feeling that liberals and industrialists were part of the problem, not part of the solution. In a letter to Herwegh, Bakunin declared that he had little interest in "parliamentary debates; the time of parliamentary life, constituent assemblies, national assemblies, and so on, is finished . . . I believe neither in constitutions nor laws. Even the best constitutions will not satisfy me. We need something else: spirit and vitality, a new world without laws and thus free."[7]

Chased from city to city by the authorities, with the Russians demanding he be turned over to them, he found a temporary refuge in the German city of Koethen. There he developed his ideas more carefully in a thirty-five-page article entitled "Appeal to the Slavs by a Russian Patriot." Contrary to those historians who argue that the failure of 1848 represents the victory of patriotism over class, Bakunin thought that nationalism and socialism could be linked in struggle. The article also demonstrated his awareness that nationalism had to be part of a larger social revolution, else it would serve reaction. A simple choice faced the Slavs: "an old world in ruins," or "the new world," with its "penetrating light" that belonged to the "generations and periods to come." For the world was now split in two: revolution and counterrevolution. Returning to one of the themes of "The Reaction in Germany," he insisted there was no middle road, no way to negotiate or compromise: it was impossible to remain neutral and impossible to "grant some small concession to each of the great parties in this struggle to appease them and thus prevent the explosion of the necessary, inevitable conflict." Unity now was crucial, and it was imperative that the Slavs not treat with the same diplomats and politicians who had betrayed Poland and who now used all the arts of their trade to carry on the old tactic of "divide and rule." It was too much to expect the enemy "to work for the birth of a new world that would mean its condemnation and death." It was necessary to seek real allies, determined by class, not nationality. "Extend your hand to the German people," he implored, "but not to the German pedants or the professors at Frankfurt or the sinister men of letters," not to the "petit bourgeois Germans who rejoice at each misfortune that befalls the Slavs. But extend your hand to the German people," especially those who are "pursued and oppressed as we are," and they would respond in kind. Nationalism could not be ignored, but it had to be harnessed to revolution and class.

There was ample proof for his argument. Europe had already seen how the pent-up "hatred against the old politics of the oppressors" was released "at the first sign of life from the revolution," followed by a "cry of sympathy and love for all the oppressed nationalities." The revolution demonstrated that "the enchanted seal was broken and the dragon that guarded the painful lethargy of so many of the living dead lay there, struck fatally and in its death throes." The people understood, if only viscerally, that they were subjected, but they had not lost the desire to fight. They required only the inspiration and hope that revolution brought.

Like de Tocqueville, Bakunin used the metaphor of the volcano to illustrate his meaning: even when there was no observable fire, resistance raged under the ground, ever ready to erupt. Such an eruption might appear spontaneous to those who paid no attention to the rumblings, but of course it was nothing of the sort. The revolt of Galician peasants in 1846 was a concrete example, and if the subjugated people of Russia were to explode, "the resplendent star of revolution would rise to the heavens from an ocean of blood and fire and become the polestar for the good of all free humanity."[8]

Stripped of its flourishes and rhetorical excess, the "Appeal" came to a plain and logical conclusion. The revolution had to be more than a political revolution that exchanged one set of rulers for another and continued the exploitation of workers and peasants by new means. It had to be a social revolution that would destroy private property as well as states and empires. These were the "two grand questions spontaneously posed in the first days of the spring . . . the social emancipation of the masses and the liberation of the oppressed nations." And it was the "admirable instinct of the masses" that raised these two questions above all others, insisting that they be resolved immediately. Clearly, "the social revolution presents itself as a natural, inevitable consequence of the political revolution," for "liberty was only an illusion when the vast majority of the population is reduced to leading a miserable existence, when it is deprived of education, of leisure, and bread, when it is fated to serve as a stepping-stone for the powerful and rich." No textbook solution, no insulated system could resolve these questions, for it was necessary to "overturn the material and moral conditions of our present existence, to completely overthrow this decrepit society that has become impotent and sterile and can neither restrain nor allow such freedom . . . The social question is primarily the question of the overthrow of society."[9]

It was this insistence on what Herzen and others would call the "permanent revolution" that led Marc Caussidiere to help Bakunin leave Paris for Poland and to exclaim of him, "What a man! What a man! On the first day of the revolution he is simply a treasure, but on the day after he ought to be shot!" For his part, Herzen replied dryly that the difference between the two splendid fellows was that Caussidiere should be shot the day before the revolution. Such were the political divisions on the barricades.[10]

Bakunin understood all too well that when the permanent revolution turned on property, it would draw the harshest measures from those who owned property. Usually completely indifferent to the rest of humanity, they had "no opinion, no religion, no conviction, no preference: monarchy or republic, freedom or slavery, native land, national independence or the yoke of the foreigner: all to them is exactly the same, provided they are left in tranquility." But threaten their "property or money, their sole passion," and these gentle souls "become as fierce as tigers," and were easily capable of "sacrificing the lives of ten men to save a few francs." Even the liberals among the bourgeois democrats would quickly go over to the side of reaction if their material interests were threatened by the social revolution.[11]

He was right. There were few representatives of the middle class among the dead on the barricades of Europe in 1848. Like most wars, it was overwhelmingly the peasantry and the working class who fought and died for the cause the respectable, the educated, and the privileged had bawled so loudly for. When the barricades went up, the middle classes quickly sought compromise and alliance with the old order in order to protect their privileges. For its part, the aristocracy was delighted to learn that the parliamentary democracy sought by the bourgeoisie was less of a threat than it had seemed and could be turned nicely against peasants and proletarians.

While the sound of marching, charging feet had turned Bakunin into a street fighter, Marx and Engels headed for Cologne to edit another newspaper, the *Neue Rheinische Zeitung*. Some of the most insightful analysis of the revolutionary period 1848 appeared in their paper. They also used their editorial desks to take up a polemic against Bakunin. In July, they printed an unsubstantiated rumor passed on from their Paris correspondent and fellow Communist League member, Herman Ewerbeck, that George Sand had documents proving Bakunin was a Russian spy and was responsible for the arrest of several Polish radicals. There could be no more serious charge leveled against an activist, then or now. When Caussidiere had discovered a spy in Paris, he handed the wretch a pistol so he could do the honorable thing and blow his own brains out. When he refused, Caussidiere solicitously offered him a choice of poisonous libations to send him on the path of righteousness. No spy could expect better. The unfounded accusation against Bakunin, made as he was on the run from police and still under the tsar's sentence of exile and hard labor, left him dumbfounded. It was not the first such accusation made against him. Real police agents often dropped such charges and countercharges to sow discord within the movement. Too often revolutionaries themselves falsely accused their rivals to eliminate and silence them. To publish such a story without a shred of evidence, however, was irresponsible and had potentially fatal consequences. Bakunin fired off letters to newspapers and to George Sand, urging her to refute the lie. She did so, writing Marx that the communiqué from Ewerbeck was "totally false" and had not the slightest appearance of truth to it. Furthermore, she had not the "slightest doubt" regarding Bakunin's loyalty and the "sincerity of his convictions," and she hoped Marx's "honor and conscience" would lead him to publish her letter immediately. He did so, claiming the newspaper had discharged both its duty to scrutinize public figures and its duty to give Bakunin a chance to set the record straight. This was disingenuous at best, for the decision to print the unsubstantiated rumor was little more than irresponsible character assassination that could easily have led to a real assassination.[12]

With the publication of his "Appeal to the Slavs," Marx and Engels renewed their political and theoretical attacks against Bakunin. The "Appeal" was first published in Germany, then quickly reprinted in a Czech newspaper. *La Reforme* serialized it, and Proudhon's newspaper, *Le Peuple,* reviewed it favorably. Polish émigrés in Paris applauded the article, and it impressed General Dubbelt of the Third Section, who considered having his secret agents kidnap Bakunin and return him to Russia.[13] But Bakunin's draft was heavily edited by the publisher. The version that saw print omitted all references to the "social question." Stripped of its crucial arguments on class, the abolition of property, and revolution, it was relatively easy for Engels to criticize the pamphlet along lines Bakunin himself would agree with. Nor did Engels seem to appreciate that the "Appeal" was not an effort to answer large questions about the meaning and movement of history. That was an exercise best left for the pages of the *Neue Rheinische Zeitung.* Instead, the "Appeal" was a call to action, written to revitalize the revolution and move it forward in the face of repression. The attack in the *Neue Rheinische Zeitung* was inappropriate; it was as if someone responded to Martin Luther King's "I have a dream" speech by insisting recent neurological research had proven that dreams were merely the random firings of synapses.

"Bakunin is our friend," Engels began, apparently unaware that friends don't call friends spies without a little evidence. From there, he attacked Bakunin's use of abstract words such as "freedom," "justice," "equality," "liberation." If they "sound very fine," such words "prove absolutely nothing in historical and political questions." What was needed was an analysis of the "actually existing obstacles" and the understanding that "all pious wishes and beautiful dreams are of no avail against the iron reality." "If the thing is impossible," he continued, "it does not take place and in spite of everything remains an empty figment of a dream." The key to determining iron reality from empty dreams was to understand that history was a succession of stages and that one had to back the winner. The invasion of Mexico by the United States, Engels elaborated, should not be deplored as "a war of conquest," for it was "waged wholly and solely in the interest of civilization." It was romantic sentimentalism to complain that it was "unfortunate that splendid California has been taken away from the lazy Mexicans, who could not do anything with it." No, the revolutionary had to support the U.S., for "the energetic Yankees by rapid exploitation of the California gold mines will increase the means of circulation, in a few years will concentrate a dense population and extensive trade at the most suitable places on the coast of the Pacific Ocean, create large cities, open up communications by steamship, construct a railway from New York to San Francisco, for the first time really open the Pacific Ocean to civilization, and for the third time in history give the world trade a new direction." True, "the 'independence' of a few Spanish Californians and Texans may suffer because of it, in some places 'justice' and other moral principles may be violated; but what does that matter to such facts of world-historic significance?" History moved in progressive stages of economic development and it was folly to oppose even war and empire if they were on the side of the new economic order.

The implication of this for Slavic independence was obvious, at least to Engels. With the notable exception of the Poles, the Slavs "all belong to people which are . . . necessarily counterrevolutionary owning to the whole of their historical position, or, like the Russians, are still a long way from revolution and therefore, at least for the time being, are still counterrevolutionary." They had no "future," for they lacked "the primary historical, geographical, political, and industrial conditions for independence and viability." The Slavs had no history, either, he continued, and empire was the best thing that could have happened to them. Either they had come "under foreign sway" after they had achieved only "the first, most elementary stage of civilization," or they had been "*forced* to attain the first stage of civilization only by means of a foreign yoke," and thus were "not viable and will never be able to achieve any kind of independence." Furthermore, even if the Slovenes and Croats could carve out independent states, "Germany and Hungary cannot allow themselves to be cut off from the Adriatic Sea." Nor could Austria be cut off from the Adriatic or the Mediterranean, for then "the eastern part of Germany would be torn to pieces like a loaf of bread that has been gnawed by rats! And all that by way of thanks for the Germans having given themselves the trouble of civilizing the stubborn Czechs and Slovenes, and introducing among them trade, industry, a tolerable degree of agriculture, and culture!" No, the German conquest from the Elbe to the Warthe "was to the advantage of civilization." And, he noted, if eight million Slavs had suffered "the yoke imposed on them by the four million Magyars, that alone sufficiently proves which was the more viable and vigorous, the many Slavs or the few Magyars!" "Big monarchies had become a historical necessity," he intoned, and in uniting "all these small, stunted, and impotent little nations into a single big state," the empires had "enabled them to take part in a historical development from which, left to themselves, they would have remained completely aloof." Nor was that process over, for now, "as a result of the powerful progress of industry, trade, and communications, political centralization has become a much more urgent need than it was then in the fifteenth and sixteenth centuries. What still has to be centralized is being centralized." It is difficult to know what historical crime could not be justified by such logic. For Engels, "these 'crimes' of the Germans and Magyars against the said Slavs are among the best and most praiseworthy deeds which our and the Magyar people can boast in their history."[14]

It got worse. The Slavs were doomed by history and the development of civilization, he continued; they were doomed also by their own actions. If they, like the intellectuals who could divine the course of history, had ever embarked on "a new revolutionary history," that would have redeemed them. But with the sole exception of the Poles, the Slavs "were always the main instruments of the counterrevolutionaries" and thus were "the oppressors of all revolutionary nations." For that reason, "hatred of Russians was and still is the primary revolutionary passion among Germans." True, he admitted, the Germans had also aided reaction, though Engels did not clearly distinguish between those who served reaction because they had been drafted into the tsar's army and those who consciously set out to create a German empire for themselves. But the Germans had rehabilitated themselves in 1848, he suggested, for "a single courageous attempt at a democratic revolution, even if it were crushed, extinguishes in the memory of the peoples whole centuries of infamy and cowardice." The Slavs lacked even that. Their recent insurrections did not count, for with the Slavs, "nationality takes precedence over revolution." Therefore, he concluded, the Slavs deserved "the most determined use of terror" against them.

All in all, it was a foul little screed and its argument could be used to justify virtually any conquest and any conqueror. It was a particularly raw version of the ideas Engels and Marx had already advanced about the nature of history; at times it was little more than the argument that might made right. It was less sophisticated than Bakunin's "Appeal," for unlike Engels he had carefully distinguished between people and governments and avoided labeling any ethnic group as inherently reactionary. Bakunin agreed with

Engels on several points, as was obvious even in the bowdlerized version that made it to print. He too insisted that the choice before Europe was revolution or reaction and Bakunin sided unequivocally with revolution. Like Engels, he saw nothing positive in the constituent assemblies and congresses, though he understood that the Prague convention had rhetorical value. Sadly, the deleted portions of his draft outlined his position on the social revolution; with those gone, it was understandable enough that Engels would go after the tepid arguments that remained. Still, his attack on Bakunin was an example of spiteful academic arrogance and of historical materialism at its absolute, most vulgar worst.

Their disagreement was much more than a narrow debate about the nature of Slavic society. It reflected differences over issues in philosophy, the nature of history, political strategy, and personal experience. Bakunin held that history could move rapidly in times of revolution and that humanity did not have to move through specific economic stages in proper order. The development of the economy was connected to, but not synonymous with, freedom. Where Marx and Engels saw the expansion of economic production as the essential ingredient in human freedom and thus supported the U.S. over Mexico and Germany over the Slavs, Bakunin argued that it was possible to create freer societies regardless of the level of the economy. It was possible for less developed societies to take up the social revolution and remove those obstacles, those social systems and structures of empire, state, church, lord, and capitalist, that prevented the people from controlling their own lives. Peasants did not need to replace the lord with the capitalist and exchange serfdom for a wage, Bakunin held; workers did not have to remain exploited until the productive capacity had reached a certain level. They could reorganize society, "from top to bottom . . . on the basis of complete economic and social equality," in the here and now. Might, even economic might, was not the same as right. To argue otherwise was to doom humanity to the yoke and to insist that the intellectual, not the people themselves, should lead the revolution.

It was an argument both sides would pursue over nearly thirty years and that their followers would carry on. Each tended to present the other's argument in the harshest, most exaggerated form, then debate the absurd conclusions no one had ever advanced. One sees similar exchanges in academic journals and publications such as *The Times Literary Supplement* and *The New York Review of Books,* where "my esteemed colleague" and "my learned friend" are genteel and formal declarations of war to the death. New ideas are often kindled through overstatement and rebuttal, though the bemused spectator may be forgiven for thinking more heat than light is given off. While Bakunin and Marx and Engels did have substantive and important disagreements on many topics, it is easy to exaggerate them. Bakunin had declared early on that the two were essentially right in their theory of historical materialism, while Marx and Engels would refine and make more subtle their original ideas. The year after Bakunin's death in 1876, Marx explicitly warned against interpreting his ideas as a "historico-philosophical theory of the general path of development prescribed by fate to all nations." Indeed, he came around to Bakunin's position and argued that Russia itself had a chance to bypass capitalist development and thus avoid "all the fatal vicissitudes of the capitalist regime." When Russian revolutionaries asked him in 1881 to amplify this statement, and in particular to address the question of whether the peasant commune rather than capitalist property could lead to socialism, he concluded that it could well be the "mainspring of Russia's social regeneration."[15] For his part, Engels would rethink his crude verdict in the *Neue Rheinische Zeitung* forty years later, writing that "according to the materialist conception of history the *ultimately* determining factor in history is the production and reproduction of real life. Neither Marx nor I have ever asserted more than this." This was not strictly true, as his exchange with Bakunin indicates, but he did confess that "Marx and I are ourselves partly to blame for the fact that the younger people sometimes lay more stress on the economic side than is due to it." The fault lay in the need "to emphasize the main principle vis-a-vis our adversaries, who denied it, and we had not always the time, the place, or the opportunity to give their due to the other factors." The excesses of later Marxists who applied the theory without understanding its nuances and subtleties had led to "the most amazing stuff" that needed to be criticized and corrected.[16]

In the meantime, there was work to be done. Bakunin wrote several newspaper articles for the radical press on subjects ranging from the need to organize revolution in the face of Russian and Austrian reaction, to answering the outrageous charge that he was a spy, to conditions in Russia, to the need to forestall war between Germany and Russia. Still dodging the authorities, he was constantly on the move throughout central Europe as the barricades were torn down by troops, constituent assemblies waffled and compromised, and time, always the best weapon of the old order, ground away. In March, the Frankfurt parliament, frightened by its audacity and now desperately seeking a conciliatory compromise to avoid further conflict, voted in favor of a constitution that outlined a united Germany, an elected legislature, provisions for public education and universal suffrage, and a restricted role for the monarchy. It then voted to beseech the king of Prussia to take the throne. Friedrich Wilhelm IV understood the offer for what it was: a sign of weakness. He rebuffed the offer, dismissing it as a "crown picked up from the gutter," and waited, confident he could win on his own terms.

By May 1849 Bakunin was in Dresden, in the German kingdom of Saxony. Its makeshift parliament had voted to accept the Frankfurt constitution, only to have their own king veto the resolution, dismiss the parliament, and request the Prussians to send in troops to help him put an end to all the talk about reform and change. In what was about the last replay of Paris '48, the people of the city threw up the barricades, raided the arsenal, and destroyed the railway lines. The people took the streets, the king took a powder, and another provisional government was hastily and nervously declared. But the rebellion was ill-prepared and the provisional government was made up of the same liberals who had sold out the proletariat on virtually every other occasion. Convinced they would soon abandon the barricades, Bakunin contented himself with leisurely inspections of the defenses, rating them in his professional opinion as inefficient, slovenly, and naive, according to his Dresden acquaintance and fellow activist, the composer Richard Wagner. He swallowed his misgivings, however, when it was clear that the people would fight, and drew up strategies and helped strengthen the ramparts. He urged the provisional government not to trust to negotiations and parleys, for these were calculated to lull them while fresh troops were brought up. It was no time for retreat, for the regimes, "having once successfully started a reactionary movement, would not stop halfway and would not rest until the old order, destroyed by the revolution of 1848, was completely restored."[17]

Even Engels would comment that Bakunin was "an able and cool-headed commander" at Dresden. He appeared all over the city, giving advice and orders, shouting encouragement, organizing troops, and preparing for counterattacks. "I did all I could to save the ruined and obviously dying revolution," he recalled. "I did not sleep, I did not eat, I did not drink, I did not even smoke." With the arrival of the Prussian troops, however, the position was hopeless. In five days of street fighting, their muskets and cannon did their foul work, killing about 250 of the rebels in a frenzy that appalled even the hardened Bakunin. He organized a careful retreat to forestall the rout that would leave even more dead, and made his own way out of the city at the end of the last day of fighting.[18]

He headed for Chemnitz, rejoining Wagner along the way, on the strength of rumors that the city was about to rebel. The rumors were ill-founded, and instead of rebellion, Bakunin found a posse made up of the mayor and several other good citizens of Chemnitz who arrested him. "Exhausted, drained not only physically but even more so morally," Bakunin was "completely indifferent to what happened to me" after he had destroyed the incriminating notes and papers in his possession.[19] His captors, however, were not indifferent to his fate. He was handed over to the army and taken back to Dresden; there he and the other captured leaders were put in chains and taken to the same Königstein castle in which the Saxon king had holed up during the uprising. Bakunin, still shackled, was kept in solitary confinement for eight months awaiting trial. Although one cannot commit treason against a country other than one's own, such a legal nicety escaped the Saxon court, which convicted the Russian of treason and sentenced him to death. The sentence was commuted, for unlike those governors and presidents and Mafia chieftains who insist on the death penalty, some nineteenth-century rulers understood that the occasional show of mercy was a far more subtle demonstration of their power.

But Bakunin's tribulations were not over, and neither were his trials, for the Austrian authorities demanded that he be turned over to them for judgment. In June 1850, Bakunin was bundled up and sent to Prague under heavy guard. The Austrians charged him under the code of martial law, not civil law, which meant he had no access to legal counsel and could neither receive nor send mail. He was again thrown into solitary confinement, again shackled constantly in his tiny cell for nine months as the police put together the case against him. In March 1851, he was taken to another prison, this time in Olmutz, where his captors found it convenient to keep him chained to the wall. Finally, two years almost to the day after he had been captured, he was found guilty of treason by another country that had no such jurisdiction and again sentenced to death.

Now the Russians insisted on their turn, and the Austrian authorities duly passed Bakunin over. One of the nice things about being an autocrat is one doesn't have to bother with boring, costly trials. Since Bakunin had years earlier been sentenced without trial to hard labor in Siberia, it took only the stroke of a pen to change that to indefinite imprisonment in St. Petersburg's Peter and Paul fortress, the same dank, foul prison where Peter the Great had tortured and killed his own son, where the Decembrists had been entombed, where Dostoevsky had undergone his mock execution, and where revolutionaries such as Chernyshevsky and Kropotkin would be thrown in later years. "From the times of Peter I," Kropotkin would write, "for a hundred and seventy years, the annals of this mass of stone which rises from the

Neva in front of the Winter Palace, were annals of murder and torture, of men buried alive, condemned to a slow death, or driven to insanity in the loneliness of the dark and damp dungeon."[20]

Bakunin would spend the next three years there. It is only in the context of his two years of solitary confinement and his sentence in the Peter and Paul fortress that we can evaluate a piece of writing that has puzzled and dismayed Bakunin's allies, and to their discredit delighted his foes: the confession he wrote to Nicholas I.

Two months after his internment in the fortress, Count Orlov, now the head of the Third Section, came to visit the prisoner. Unlike previous interrogations made under the threat of torture and worse, this new inquisitor made no demands for information, no menaces, no half-promises of aid in return for names of accomplices. He simply offered Bakunin the chance to unburden himself, to "write to the sovereign as though you were speaking with your spiritual father." Bakunin agreed with an unseemly alacrity and over the next month, he wrote out a detailed account of his life and activities from his arrival in Germany in 1840 to his meeting with Orlov. He filled ninety-six pages with his cramped handwriting, demonstrating his acute memory and considerable insight into politics and his own personality.

Why would he do it? Revolutionaries are supposed to hurl defiance at their oppressors, not spill their guts in a missive that started, "Your Imperial Majesty, Most Gracious Sovereign!" Had prison broken him? Was he bored? Did he want to repent? Did he hope a sincere confession would convince the tsar to reduce his sentence? Did he calculate that an insincere confession would fool the tsar into freeing him? Was he seeking the approval of the tsar to replace that of his father? Buried in prison, facing an indefinite sentence, did he seek to leave some trace of his existence for posterity? Historians have argued for each of these positions and for every possible combination of them, including "all of the above." His supporters have stressed the very real horrors of the prison, while his detractors have accused him of cowardice and hypocrisy.

That he would write to the tsar is less startling than it might appear, even without the spur of jail. Bakunin, though stripped of his rank, still saw himself as a noble with a traditional right to appeal to the tsar and likely saw nothing contradictory or hypocritical in availing himself of this right. We might also recall his comments in "The Reaction in Germany." While all reactionaries had to be struggled against, the revolutionary could respect the "consistent" reactionary as someone who genuinely desired the good but was simply unable to understand it. That is to say, the consistent reactionaries, unlike the mediating ones, could be seen as worthy opponents to whom notions of chivalry could be extended; they could be respected. Certainly there was no more consistent reactionary than Nicholas I.

Later generations of Russian revolutionaries came from other classes and ranks, and so their code of honor and silence evolved later and in very different circumstances. The precedent that Bakunin had before him was that of the Decembrists. They had used their interrogation as an opportunity to outline all of the critical problems that Russia faced, not with defiance or insolence but with sincerity and the hope that their sacrifice would at least impress upon the tsar the need for reform and change. It had some effect. Their confessions were compiled into a digest and given to Nicholas I, who read it carefully and kept it close to hand ever after. In following their lead, Bakunin wrote not so much a "confession" as an avowal. It was not a confession of the sort one sees on TV crime dramas where the victim turns over Mr. Big in return for a deal from Jerry Orbach. Bakunin revealed no conspirators, turned over no accomplices, ratted out no one; he made it clear to the tsar that he would not "confess to you the sins of others." The tsar himself noted dourly that Bakunin's refusal to name names cast doubt on the sincerity of the confession, for it "destroys all confidence: if he feels all the weight of his sins, then only a pure, complete confession, and not a conditional one, can be considered a confession."[21]

Bakunin revealed nothing about himself that was not already well-known or insignificant. Instead he used the confession to clarify his political ideas and to criticize the regime. While he often couched his criticisms in flowery homages to the tsar and Russia, he explained clearly and forcefully why he wanted revolution:

> When you travel about the world you find everywhere much evil, oppression, and injustice, in Russia perhaps more than in other states. It is not that people in Russia are worse than in Western Europe; on the contrary, I think the Russian is better, kinder, and has greater breadth of soul than the westerner. But in the West there is a specific against evil: publicity, public opinion, and finally freedom, which ennobles and elevates every man. This remedy does not exist in Russia.

This freedom often made the West seem worse, for every evil, every injustice, every grievance was exposed. But in reality, such openness was healthier for the body politic, for

> in Russia all illnesses turn inward and eat away the innermost structure of the social organism . . . Russian social life is a chain of

mutual oppressions: the higher oppresses the lower, the latter suffers, does not dare complain, but he in turn squeezes the one who is still lower, who also suffers and also takes revenge on the one subordinate to him. Worst of all is it for the common people, the poor Russian *muzhik* [peasant], who, at the very bottom of the social ladder, has no one to oppress and must suffer oppression from all; as the Russian proverb says, "Only the lazy man does not beat us."

In such an oppressive society, he continued, "the prime mover is fear; and fear kills all life, all intelligence, all noble movement of the soul." But fear was not enough to maintain a society. Fear led to silence, and silence to complicity in widespread corruption. From top to bottom, "thievery and injustice and oppression live and grow in Russia like a thousand-armed polyp that, slash and cut it as you will, never dies." Instead, the problem had to be attacked at its very base. Russia needed

nobility of feeling, independence of thought, the proud fearlessness of a clear conscience, respect for human worth in oneself and in others, and finally, public contempt for all dishonorable, inhuman people, social shame, a social conscience! But these qualities, these forces, bloom only where there is free scope for the soul, not where slavery and fear prevail. These virtues are feared in Russia not because people might admire them but out of fear that free thoughts might come with them.

He then addressed the two most profound social evils in Russia: serfdom and empire. He declared his sympathy for "the good Russian *muzhik* who is oppressed by everyone," and asked pointedly,

What might these people be if they were given freedom and property, if they were taught to read and write! And I asked: Why does the present government—autocratic, armed with boundless power, not limited by statute or in fact by any outside law or any competing power—why does it not use its omnipotence for the liberation, elevation, and enlightenment of the Russian people?

Bakunin then answered his own question, employing a clever rhetorical device to press home his point without openly courting further punishment. First he suggested that what he should have answered was that affairs of state were none of his business, or perhaps that politics was a difficult craft and he could not see all sides to a question and thus could not determine the correct answers. He then reminded the tsar of what he had actually said:

The government does not free the Russian people, first, because with all its omnipotent power, not limited by law, it is in fact limited by a multitude of circumstances, it is bound in invisible ways, it is bound by its corrupt administration, and finally it is bound by the egotism of the nobility. And even more, because it actually does not want freedom for or the enlightenment or elevation of the Russian people, seeing in them merely a soulless machine for its conquests in Europe!

That led him directly to a critique of empire, again posing it as questions he had asked and answered himself:

What benefit is there for Russia in her conquests? . . . What is the final goal of its expansion? What will the Russian tsardom give to the enslaved peoples in place of the independence of which they have been robbed? There is no point in even speaking of freedom, enlightenment, and national prosperity; perhaps it will give them its total national character, oppressed by slavery!

The result would be that Russia would become "abhorrent to all other Slavs as she is now abhorrent to the Poles. She will not be a liberator but an oppressor of her own Slav family."

Following this train of thought, Bakunin had "assured myself that Russia—in order to save her honor and her future—must carry out a revolution, overthrow your tsarist authority, destroy monarchical rule, and, having thus liberated herself from internal slavery, take her place at the head of the Slav movement." At that point, Russia could lead the revolt against the empires of Austria, Prussia, and Turkey and create a free Slav society.

What should replace the autocracy? Bakunin acknowledged bluntly that the revolutionaries had been "called to destroy and not to build; others better, more intelligent, and fresher than we will build." He had no schematic for the future. Nor could there be one at the present, because Russia's "tongue and all her movements are constrained. Let her but arise and speak and then we will learn both what she is thinking and what she wants; she herself will show us what forms and what institutions she needs."

Bakunin did know that he wanted a democratic form of government and not a parliamentary or representative system. He had already seen how such constitutional governments paid lip service to "the people" while looking after the interests of a few. Such a system in Russia might represent the gentry and the merchants, but "the huge mass of the people, the real people . . . would remain without representatives and would be oppressed and humiliated by that very same gentry which now humiliates them."

A socialist but not yet an anarchist, Bakunin believed that the state would still be necessary once the monarchy was abolished. Perhaps, he mused, Russia would require a "strong dictatorial government" for a time. Bakunin's detractors have pounced on this statement with glee to insist that he was the father of fascism and Stalinism. Even some Bolsheviks have argued that Bakunin was the prophet of the vanguard party. All of them have excited themselves unnecessarily. This was Bakunin's first attempt to resolve the questions of revolutionary tactics, strategy, and organization, not his last. Yet even here it is obvious that his idea of a "dictatorship" bore no resemblance to fascism or vanguardism. In 1851 "dictatorship" meant something rather different than it does now. It referred to the Roman practice of giving a magistrate limited, extraordinary powers in an emergency. This was the sense in which Bakunin used the term, for in his view, such a government "must strive to make its existence unnecessary as soon as possible, having in view only the freedom, independence, and gradual maturing of the people." That distinguished it from the monarchy, which, "on the contrary, must endeavor to prevent its existence from ever becoming unnecessary, and therefore must maintain its subjects in unalterable childhood." Later he would move even further from the notion of a benevolent dictatorship as his thinking became more sophisticated and subtle and as he understood that no one could be trusted to give up power once it had been placed in their hands and that paternalism created infants, not adults. Freedom was not a reward for responsible behavior; instead, freedom was necessary to develop responsibility.

Was he not worried that a Russian revolution would unleash "the drunken fury of the unbridled mob"? Would not an uprising of the peasants revisit the terrors of the Pugachev Rebellion? Indeed it might, he noted, but he justified such violence on the grounds that "sometimes even a terrible evil is necessary." Such thoughts, he admitted, were "criminal," even "stupid"; no doubt they deserved "the most severe punishment," but there they were.[22] Bakunin had placed his critique of the regime under the eyes of the tsar himself. He had not forsaken his comrades nor, despite the flowery language and stock phrases of deference, his ideas. He made that plain in a letter to his sister Tatiana three years later, confirming that he had not wavered in his convictions; rather, the enforced period of reflection had reinforced them, though he would perhaps temper his radical activities with forethought if he ever again had the chance to act. Later, in a letter to Alexander Herzen, Bakunin scoffed at the memory of the tsar's fond hope that he would register repentance.[23] The confession does show that Bakunin, like all of the radicals and revolutionaries of 1848, had no foolproof plan for revolution.

It reveals that his political ideas were developing as he struggled with the questions of how to make not a putsch or a coup d'etat but a social revolution and of how to represent the interests of the people in the face of counterrevolution and erstwhile allies who would abandon them as soon as their own narrow interests were obtained.

Despite his optimistic note to Tatiana, prison had its calculated effect on Bakunin. Isolated from other prisoners, allowed only three visits from his family over three years, he was deeply affected by desperation and depression that threatened to overwhelm him. Even the prisoner's traditional solace—tobacco and tea, the nineteenth-century Russian equivalent of cigarettes and coffee, the pleasures of which should not be underestimated by the contemporary smug health fanatic—was difficult to obtain. By the time of his transfer to Schlusselburg prison in 1854, after five years in German, Austrian, and Russian prisons, his physical health was broken. He was plagued with hemorrhoids—another point of commonality with Marx, though Marx could at least avail himself of a hot bath for occasional relief. Bakunin suffered from fever, severe headaches, and tinnitus, a roaring in his ears that he compared to the sound of boiling water; he had difficulty in breathing, likely the result of heart disease brought on by the lack of exercise and a diet that provided calories but little else.[24]

The prison diet resulted in another disease as well: scurvy. As anyone who has read a seafaring novel knows, and as medical science knew as early as 1750, a small portion of citrus fruit prevents scurvy. As a result, today one hears the word usually in pseudo-pirate patois, that is to say, in growled expressions like, "Avast there, ye scurvy dogs!" It is, however, a serious disease with terrible symptoms and effects. Without vitamin C, collagen, the protein that connects cells together, breaks down. The walls of the small blood vessels, or capillaries, collapse and blood leaks into cells throughout the body, causing open sores on the skin and mucous membranes. Hemorrhaging into the joints, muscles, and bone tissue causes excruciating pain; as the gums hemorrhage and the dentin of the teeth breaks down, the teeth themselves loosen and fall out, leaving only bloody sockets. The victim may suffer from rapid breathing, diarrhea, and anemia. Untreated, the disease is fatal.

By July 1854, the disease had ravaged Bakunin. Now forty years old, his teeth were gone, and the world passed him by.[25] His father died that same year, nearly ninety years old, without having seen his eldest son in fifteen years. By then 1848 was a distant memory, and if the revolution had not succeeded, Europe nonetheless looked significantly different than it had when Bakunin left it. Even the geography of cities changed, as working-class districts were broken up and subjected to "urban renewal," with the streets widened to prevent barricades and to make it easier for troops to form and attack protestors. Yet serfdom was abolished throughout the Austrian empire; most of Germany had representative governments complete with the constitutions Bakunin had railed against. Taken together, all these changes throughout Europe did not make the social revolution, and revolutionaries from Bakunin to Marx to Herzen to Proudhon reflected bitterly on how far from their mark they had fallen. History might be kinder to them than they were to themselves, however, for they drastically changed the nature of politics and protest. No one, not even kings, could ignore the people any longer. Politicians now had to court workers and peasants. If the bourgeoisie and aristocracy would soon learn how to manipulate the political process to channel protest from the streets to the back rooms and hallways of legislatures, the people too would learn how to use parliaments and legislatures and votes. The clearest example of this was France, where Louis Napoleon, nephew of Napoleon Bonaparte, was elected president of the Republic after capturing the votes of peasants and workers with a campaign that promised them protection from the rich, hinted at radicalism, and appealed to nationalism. His election demonstrated that those who had made the revolution in 1848 would have to be taken into account in ways unheard of before. That he would soon proclaim himself emperor showed clearly how the revolution had failed and that Bakunin was right to argue that constitutions and elections did not empower the masses. But 1848 had changed Europe forever, and whatever progress was made over the next century owed much to that revolutionary year.

In 1854, the Crimean War broke out, as Russia moved into territories the decaying Ottoman Empire was unable to defend and France and England set out to check the tsar. The Charge of the Light Brigade was only the most famous of the blunders and catastrophes of that war. Not even Florence Nightingale could mop up all the gore as more than six hundred thousand died, most of disease, over two years of fighting. All of the old problems, from inadequate weapons to incompetent commanders to insufficient supplies, ensured that Russia had the worst of it despite its numerical superiority in the field. The tsar himself was a casualty: Nicholas I died from disease at St. Petersburg in 1855, only fifty-nine years old.

His death brought as much rejoicing as mourning. Far away in London, Alexander Herzen popped open champagne and hired street children to chant "Emperor Nicholas is dead!" The emperor's son took the throne as Alexander II, and Bakunin's family used the occasion to ask the new tsar for clemency. Bakunin's most eloquent advocate was his mother, and she stepped into the traditional role of Russian noblewomen to exert what influence she could on behalf of her son. Bakunin himself, left by disease and "melancholy" with "only one prayer: liberty or death," petitioned the tsar himself in the hope that he could breathe the air of freedom once more.[26] Early in 1857, the tsar relented and commuted the sentence to permanent exile in Siberia. He even granted Bakunin's request that he be allowed to visit Priamukhino to say good-bye to his family. The reunion was brief and painful: The tsar's mercy extended to a single day and Bakunin remained under heavy guard. It was a measure of the horrors of prison that the once vital, brash, and energetic man now stood before his family moody and mute, unable to find any joy at Priamukhino or with his family, or even the effort to feign it. The next day, his guards escorted him to the horse-drawn sleigh and they began the three-week journey to Siberia.

10

WITHOUT ORGANIZATION, WE WILL NEVER GAIN VICTORY

At roughly the same latitude as Sitka, Alaska, present-day Tomsk is an energetic city of nearly five hundred thousand people. Its industrial base ranges from mining to farming to pharmaceuticals to power generation. Founded as a military outpost by Boris Godunov in 1604, it is now a hub city well served by a road network, railways, an airport, and a river port. It is the oldest city in Siberia, and with its universities and technical schools, a medical school and a pedagogical institute, it has the highest ratio of students per capita of any city in Russia and bills itself as the "Siberian Athens."

They called it another A-word when Bakunin began his life sentence there in 1857. The town's outer buildings formed a rough square reminiscent of the original walls of the fort, and the winters were cold enough to freeze solid the meat, poultry, and fish offered for sale in the outdoor markets. Its inhabitants picked their way carefully along unpaved streets to their small wooden houses and huts. But it was a major trading center, at least by the standards of Siberia, which meant there was a steady trickle of visitors that made it possible to get news and amenities and keep the samovar full. Traders, government officials, and political exiles, in roughly equal numbers, along with their families made up a population of about twenty thousand people. The status, ranks, and public identities that would have kept them separated socially and physically in Moscow or St. Petersburg were of less importance compared to the shared reality of Siberia, and they coexisted peacefully in a rough solidarity as they tried to maintain some of their Russian culture and customs. Compared to the Peter and Paul Fortress, the freezing temperature was invigorating, the social interaction almost overwhelming, the taste of freedom rejuvenating.

Still, political exiles had to fend for themselves. They had to support themselves, and Bakunin's resume—former occupation: revolutionary; hobbies: extracting teeth, killing lice; future plans: destruction of civilization as you know it—was unlikely to secure a suitable position, even in Tomsk. Bakunin had few skills and his money-management abilities had not improved. He received some funds from home, but these were insufficient to set up house-

keeping, even for someone more accustomed to the meager comforts provided to long-term guests of his imperial majesty. He began tutoring French,
a pleasant enough occupation that pushed his mind to work again and
brought him into regular contact with others. In particular, it brought him in
contact with Antonia Kwiatkowski, the elder daughter of a Polish businessman in the gold industry. It is hard to believe that Bakunin, now forty-four
years old, swept the seventeen-year old Antonia off her feet, but the two were
wed in October 1858. The difference in their ages was about that of
Bakunin's own parents, and there seem to have been no objections to the
marriage from Antonia's family or the church in which they were married.
This has scandalized later generations of historians, and no doubt one of
Bakunin's reasons for marrying was to confound the sexual dysfunction theorists. In a letter to Alexander Herzen, Bakunin expressed another reason.
"I fell passionately in love with her, and she with me, and so we married," he
explained. "It is good to live not for oneself but for another, especially when
the other is a dear woman. I gave myself to her entirely, and, for her part,
she shares in heart and spirit all my aspirations." In letters throughout his
life, Bakunin wrote of his love and affection for Antonia, and clearly she felt
strongly for him. She would leave her family to join him in Western Europe,
with no prospect of a comfortable or easy life, and would stay with the
errant anarchist until his death.[1]

The two moved to Irkutsk near the Mongolian border, about forty miles
from the shores of Lake Baikal. About the size of Tomsk, it was the capital
of Eastern Siberia and thus more of a cultural center. Its streets were paved,
the climate was better, and it was even possible, though not without some
difficulty, to get copies of Herzen's radical newspaper, *Kolokol,* or *The Bell.*
There were other political exiles there, including Petrashevsky himself, along
with other members of his circle, though Bakunin kept himself apart, regarding them as "only a sort of transition from the Decembrists to the real
youth—they were doctrinaire, bookish socialists, Fourierists, and peda-
gogues."[2] The move was made possible by the intervention of yet another of
Bakunin's well-connected relatives, this time his mother's cousin, Nicholas
Muraviev, the governor of Eastern Siberia. Muraviev met Bakunin in Tomsk
late in 1858, and the two became friends. Later, the governor gave Bakunin
and Antonia permission to leave Tomsk and helped secure Bakunin a position in a trading company. Muraviev also occasioned Bakunin's return to
political life.

The governor was an imperialist and a Russian patriot. He had been
largely responsible for the annexation of large parts of China north of the

Amur River, and for his efforts was known as Muraviev-Amur sky, roughly, "Muraviev of the Amur." He extended Russian trading networks along and beyond the river and colonized new territories for the tsar. At the same time, he regarded himself as a liberal, and in the context of nineteenth-century Russia, he was. He appreciated American democratic institutions and deplored serfdom, and if his professed political beliefs were often contradicted by his actions, he at least talked the talk, and Bakunin saw in him the potential for revolution, or at least reform, from the top down. This echoed the argument he had made in his confession for a powerful leadership cadre that could act for the people when they were unable to act for themselves. In theory, such a leadership could cut through the waffling and compromise of parliaments and directly represent the masses. It was precisely this notion that led many on the left, including some anarchists, to initially endorse Italian fascism in the 1920s, when the failure of representative democracy seemed clear to all. It was a hideous error in the 1920s and the 1860s, but in both cases, the idea was not to create a totalitarian state but to represent the people directly and so counter the power of the middle classes and bourgeoisie. Muraviev seemed to have both the ideas and the power to radically change Russia at a time when it seemed to Bakunin, long cut off from political circles, that there was little other hope for change.

Thus when Herzen's newspaper attacked Muraviev for his imperialist ventures and colonial schemes, Bakunin sprang to his defense. In a series of letters to Herzen, he claimed that Muraviev represented the best, not the worst, that Russia had to offer, that Muraviev was in fact one of them. He had the energy, the commitment, and the desire to carry the nation into the future. Muraviev advocated, Bakunin insisted, the freeing of the serfs with title to land, jury trials, public education, freedom of the press, and the "administration of the people by themselves," meaning by that the "abolition of the bureaucracy and the eventual decentralization" of government. Others shared Bakunin's view. The anarchist Peter Kropotkin recorded years later that due to Muraviev's efforts, Eastern Siberia's administration "was far more enlightened and far better all round than that of any province of Russia proper." Muraviev held "advanced views," he continued, and was "very intelligent, very active, extremely amiable, and desirous to work for the good of the country." However, he was also, "like all men of action of the governmental school, a despot at the bottom of his heart." Bakunin himself was not yet an anarchist, and he favorably contrasted Muraviev with those who mouthed "grand words and beautiful phrases," including those exiled in faraway London. Unlike the "parliament of babbling aristocrats,"

Muraviev acted decisively. He could create a "provisional dictatorship of iron" in order to abolish the futile government in St. Petersburg and set the people free.[3]

Bakunin was right to see some possibilities of reform from the top. Soon after his article appeared, nearly four years before the United States would pass the Thirteenth Amendment forbidding slavery, Tsar Alexander II announced the emancipation of the serfs of Russia. This proclamation of March 1861 was widely anticipated, not as an act of charity, of course, but of necessity. Russia's staggering losses in the Crimean War had shown yet again how the country lagged behind Europe, and it was obvious to all that the labor of serfs could not compete with that of wage workers or create and attract sufficient capital for rapid development. Many among the nobility belatedly concluded that not only was serfdom unprofitable, it was also immoral. Their spiritual awakening was hastened by the actions of the serfs themselves, whose increasing militancy convinced the tsar that if serfdom were not abolished from above, it would be dismantled from below. It is usually better to jump than to be pushed, and if the tsar acted, the pace and extent of the emancipation could be controlled.

Serfs were granted formal freedom, but they remained tied to their commune and forced to pay a head tax. While they could now legally claim for their own about half of the land they had tilled, roughly that portion they had worked for themselves, in practice they received about one-fifth less than they were entitled to. Nor were they given the land they had formerly used for themselves. It had to be purchased from the lords, who kept the most productive acres for themselves. Since few peasants had cash to purchase the land outright, they took out loans from the government. But loans come with interest, and freed serfs paid half again what their land was worth by the time the accounts were squared. Finally, freeing the serfs meant "freeing" them from the land, that is, taking from them their means of production and subsistence. As the lands they actually worked for themselves shrank with emancipation, as labor now became a commodity that was bought and sold, and as the traditions of the commune were uprooted, the freed serfs encountered a new problem: unemployment.

Nonetheless, emancipation suggested the possibility of reform from the top, though Bakunin's appraisal of his cousin was, at best, woefully optimistic and hopelessly idealistic. While he fancied himself a liberal, in keeping with current sentiment, Muraviev was little inclined, and far from powerful enough, to do much for the people. Bakunin's defense of his relative reflected his own isolation from contemporary Russian politics and thought; he was largely unaware of the struggles of a new generation of thinkers such as Chernyshevsky. It also represented not the first stage of Bakunin's anarchism, but the last stage of his belief that radical change could come from the top. Perhaps it seemed plausible enough after the failures of 1848, at least to one so isolated and out of touch, but soon he would abandon this naive belief.

He would also abandon Siberia. When Muraviev was recalled to St. Petersburg, Bakunin hatched a fantastic plan to escape. His position with the trading company and the governor's good graces gave him considerable freedom to travel in Siberia. In January 1861, he decided to make a break for it. It was a little more complicated than tunneling under a wall or climbing a fence, for it was impossible to leave on the roads that had brought him to Irkutsk and the ocean was two thousand miles away. His escape required all his charm, audacity, and presence of mind, as well as great dollops of luck and some useful turns of history.

The first bit of luck was the appointment of Michael Korsakov as the replacement for Muraviev. Korsakov, like Bakunin, was a cousin of Muraviev's and had served under him. Even more fortunate, Bakunin's brother Paul had just married yet another of Korsakov's cousins. While such genealogical connections may strike contemporary readers as shaky or insubstantial, in Russia in the 1860s they counted rather more. Equally important, Korsakov was, if anything, more liberal than Muraviev.

The first step in Bakunin's escape was to make it down the two thousand miles of the Amur River from Irkutsk to Nikolaevsk, just across the Okhotsk Sea from Sakhalin Island. This required permission, and Korsakov granted it when Bakunin, in his role as merchant, asked to travel for his company, promising to return before winter made the river impassable. He set out on 5 June 1861, and after four weeks on a steamboat, arrived at the port. So far, so good. Technically, he had not escaped or broken his promise. Getting out of Nikolaevsk, however, was trickier. The moment he set foot on a ship, he was violating the terms outlined in his traveling papers and was subject to arrest. Furthermore, Nikolaevsk was a small port and he had to wait a week for a suitable ship to take him further south. Worse, though Bakunin did not know it, word of his escape had leaked out and the Russian officials were trying frantically to apprehend him. Minutes before the port was sealed, however, Bakunin hopped aboard the departing Russian ship *Strelok*.

He may have been aided by an acquaintance from the days of the Moscow and St. Petersburg circles, Vassily Bodisco. Bodisco had been a member of Herzen's circle, and stayed in contact with him over the years, at some risk to himself. Likely he knew Bakunin from the 1840s. In 1861, he was with the government service and stationed in Nikolaevsk. He was close to the governor's chief of staff in the port, and may well have prevailed upon him to issue Bakunin the papers he needed to extend his "business trip" and managed to delay the plans to nab him.

Bakunin got another break. The *Strelok,* a steamship, came to the aid of a becalmed U.S. sailing vessel and took it in tow. Bakunin used the chance encounter to hitch a ride on the American ship and when it cast off from the *Strelok,* he stayed with it until it berthed at Olga. From there, he caught a ship to the Japanese port of Hakodate, where he was invited to dinner with the ship's captain. To his great shock, another of the hospitable captain's guests was the newly appointed Russian consul. Go big or go home is sometimes a useful strategy, and Bakunin went big. He introduced himself, announced that he was on a sightseeing tour, with, he assured the consul, all the necessary permissions, and would be returning to Siberia via China after he had toured Japan. He won him over, and they parted friends as Bakunin prudently hopped the next ship to Yokohama. Another chance encounter was much more pleasant than his narrow escape from the consul, for he met Wilhelm Heine, an old comrade from the Dresden barricades. On 17 September, Bakunin left Japan on the SS *Carrington* for San Francisco and freedom.

As the historian Philip Billingsley has observed, Bakunin had more to thank than his talents and connections for his escape. Japan had only been opened to foreigners, thanks to Admiral Perry's cannon, fewer than ten years before Bakunin's escape; before then, no foreign ship could have landed him there. Ten years after his escape, the telegraph connected Russia and Japan, and he could not have outrun electricity. As it was, the consul in Hakodate was not alerted until seventeen days after Bakunin had left for Yokohama and San Francisco.[4]

Just before he left Japan he mailed a letter to Korsakov, writing that he understood he was unlikely ever to return to Russia but that he left "full of love for my country." He expressed his pleasure that the tsar had loosened the reins he held over the serfs of Russia, but regretted that his majesty did not have the courage to go further. At the same time, he expressed his "contempt and hate" for the tsar's "malfeasant, stupid government" that kept Russia backward and in the abyss. These were the beliefs that had guided "all that I have said, written, and done," he added, and he hoped that the years that remained to him would not slip away in vain. It was hardly an apology for escaping, but it was an attempt to have Korsakov understand that Bakunin was motivated by an ideal to accomplish some great work, not merely to escape from exile. In that sense, it was a gesture of respect for the governor-general and an assumption that good men could understand and respect each other, despite their political opposition and their positions of jailer and prisoner. It was a characteristic attitude of Bakunin's, and one he would keep even in his most heated battles with Marx in the years to come. Thus what may appear audacious to the observer seemed only reasonable to Bakunin: he next asked Korsakov not to prevent his wife from leaving Siberia and to look after her family. Bakunin appealed to him in his official capacity as governor to be sure, but more importantly, as a man "good and noble" who understood that Bakunin must "listen to his convictions." With that, he bid the governor of Siberia "adieu."[5]

Bakunin had accomplished the hardest part of his journey. It only remained to cross the Pacific Ocean to reach San Francisco, then travel either across land by coach—the railway would not span the continent until 1869—or continue by sea to the Panama isthmus, cross overland there to the Atlantic and take another ship up to the U.S., where he could then sail across the Atlantic to England . . . Compared to the escape to Japan, these legs were more of a vacation. He struck up a shipboard friendship with an English clergyman about fifteen years his junior, Frederick Pemberton Koe, who was escorting a young charge on a voyage around the world. Koe had been packed off on the errand by friends and family who sought to prevent the Anglican from committing a most grievous crime: courting and marrying a Catholic woman. Koe's diary has only a few pages devoted to Bakunin, but it reinforces the often expressed opinion of Bakunin as a kind, open man, keen and able to strike up meaningful friendships quickly, and with a talent for drawing out others and nudging their political sensibilities without alarming them unduly. Koe jotted down a serviceable, short biography of Bakunin, sketching the broad outlines of his life in the military and his becoming a "strong revolutionary." He noted in particular Bakunin's two-week hunger strike while in Konigstein. The two spent much of the voyage in conversation, and Koe found Bakunin "a man of mind [who] interests me very much" and with whom he shared a general agreement on the "second or inner self-world or life" in which "friendships are made." Not surprisingly, they talked often of religion, and Bakunin chided him softly about his dilemma of whether to marry a Catholic. The Russian observed that his own wife was a Catholic, but advised that "under gentle treatment she begins to think she is becoming Protestant." Bakunin pushed the point further, gently suggesting that Koe would find a visit with Herzen in London instructive, even though, or perhaps precisely because, Herzen was "a rabid atheist." Koe enjoyed

Bakunin's singing of Russian songs, and by the end of the trip was "sorry to part with him. He has been more like a friend than any one I have met for a long time." Koe even was "glad" to lend Bakunin three hundred dollars, though he must have suspected his chances for repayment were exceedingly slim, and he was pleased when the two met up again in New York. There Bakunin reminded him of their discussions on interfaith marriages, suggesting gently that Koe's ambivalence "proceeds from pride." It was a brief encounter, but clearly one that touched Koe deeply, and it demonstrates a side to Bakunin that is often neglected in narratives about the fiery anarchist and fierce polemicist. Bakunin extended friendship and solidarity to a man he had very little in common with and tried to educate him in a kindly and helpful fashion.[6]

Upon his arrival in San Francisco, Bakunin fired off a letter to Herzen announcing that he had escaped Siberia and was keenly anticipating returning to active duty as a revolutionary. He asked Herzen to inform his family that he was safe and sound, and to make some housing arrangements for himself and Antonia, who, he believed, would be arriving in London shortly. He also made a request for money, as the journey had left him broke and the trip to the East Coast was expensive. He had decided to go via the Panama isthmus, as the prospect of another wintry voyage across a vast barren land five months after the U.S. Civil War had broken out was not appealing. For his part, Herzen announced to the world, on the front page of *The Bell*, "Michael Alexandrovich Bakunin is in San Francisco. He is FREE!"[7] Bakunin made his way to the isthmus and booked passage to New York. On the first day out of Panama, one of his fellow passengers, Union general Edwin Vose Sumner, arrested three Confederate sympathizers, but the ship continued the voyage without further incident and Bakunin arrived at New York on 15 November 1861, five months almost to the day after he had left Irkutsk.

There he met up with two other veterans of 1848, Reinhold Solger and Friedrich Kapp. Solger had marched with Herwegh's ill-fated legion, and he and Kapp knew Bakunin and Herzen from the Paris days. They had immigrated to the United States in the aftermath of the revolution and were now successful writers and radical republicans, active in the campaign to abolish slavery. From New York, Bakunin prepared to take Boston by storm, armed not with bombs or bullets, but with letters of introduction from his two old comrades. The letters granted him access to other veterans of '48 and to progressives and liberals of Solger's acquaintance, including the governor of Massachusetts, senators, and business leaders. One was Martin Kennard, who left his impressions of Bakunin in an essay written some years later. This "stormy petrel of the troubled waters of European politics," Kennard wrote, was "in bearing noble, in personage genial and attractive . . ." Bakunin had a "free and easy manner," and a "cosmopolitan complaisance that bespoke an intelligent and affable gentleman and energetic man of affairs." The two spoke of 1848 at length, and Kennard was impressed that Bakunin's "courage was still undaunted and his ardour in no wise abated." The Boston jeweler was surprised that Bakunin spoke English "with a fair facility," and had read a great deal of American literature, including James Fennimore Cooper. Even more surprising, given that his guest had been in prison and exile, Bakunin was very well informed about American politics, with a knowledge that "seemed intuitive."

Kennard also told a story of a coincidence of the sort that now seemed to be commonplace in Bakunin's life. His business partner asked a visiting Austro-Hungarian military officer if he had ever heard of Michael Bakunin. He had indeed, the officer replied, and wondered why his host had asked. When told that Bakunin was in the next room, the officer replied that it was impossible, for Bakunin had been exiled and had long been reported dead. Anyone claiming to be the famous prisoner must be an impostor. When the officer was invited to see for himself, he strolled casually past the door and was astonished to recognize Bakunin. He then revealed that he had been one of the guards who had escorted Bakunin, then under sentence of death, from the Prague courthouse to prison.[8] Less cosmic, but undoubtedly more congenial, was Bakunin's reacquaintance with an old friend from Switzerland, Louis Agassiz, who had been at Harvard since 1848, where he established its Museum of Comparative Zoology. Bakunin's next visit was with Henry Wadsworth Longfellow. The poet, grief-struck by the tragic death of his wife just four months earlier, nonetheless pronounced Bakunin "an interesting man . . . of education and ability . . . with a most ardent, seething temperament." Longfellow's youngest daughter, Annie, the "Laughing Allegra" of his poem "The Children's Hour," recorded a rather different impression. As the six-year-old came down for dinner, she saw at her usual place at the table "this big creature with a big head, wild bushy hair, big eyes, big mouth, a big voice and still bigger laugh." She recognized the creature instantly from her close appreciation of the Brothers Grimm fairy tales. It could only be, she realized, an "ogre . . . I had no doubts. Some things you don't have to be told, you just know. No entreaties or persuasion could induce me to cross the threshold of that door. I stood petrified and while I resented his having my place at dinner, what was dinner to me as long as he didn't make his dinner off me? So I vanished dinnerless." No doubt the encounter scarred both for life. But Bakunin and Annie pressed on, and as far as can be determined, only Bakunin was driven to anarchism as a result of the trauma. In the meantime, anxious to continue his journey, eager to see Antonia and start a new life, Bakunin left for England on 14 December, taking with him his few belongings and an autograph of George Washington given to him by Kennard.[9]

Thirteen days later, he arrived at Herzen's house in London. His escape had left him heavily in debt, as he outlined in a letter to his family. The travels from Irkutsk to London had cost about two thousand roubles, which came to about seventy-six hundred francs, or roughly fifteen hundred dollars, perhaps three years' pay for a U.S. carpenter or printer, most of which he had borrowed. His short stay in Yokohama, "where life is fabulously expensive," had drained his funds; he had exchanged francs into "Mexican dollars" for some unknown reason at a most disadvantageous rate; he had less than thirty dollars in hand when he arrived in San Francisco. But Bakunin's return from Siberia in 1861 rekindled the flames of youthful nostalgia and revolutionary solidarity among his old friends. Herzen and Botkin were independently wealthy, Turgenev was now a successful and well-off writer, and they were pleased to lend Bakunin money, though they were mistaken if they thought prison and exile had reformed his casual attitude toward debt. As a result, he was constantly changing residences: his longest stay in London was at 10 Paddington Green and lasted less than a year. Herzen noted with an admixture of fondness and alarm that Bakunin was still "despising money, scattering it on all sides when he had it," still "prepared to give to anyone his last penny, reserving for himself only what was necessary for cigarettes and tea." Attention to personal detail was never his strong suit, and poverty meant all his suits were in disrepair. A favorite red flannel shirt soon became so dirty that one acquaintance attempted one night to kidnap it for cleaning, only to discover that the revolutionary slept in it, too. Hopes that Bakunin would write his memoirs soon vanished, though there was considerable interest in his adventures and likely he would have found a ready publisher and market. Herzen had assured him he could likely make twenty or thirty thousand francs from them; he was never good, however, at writing about himself and while he attempted to put the story of his life on paper a few times over the next ten years, little came of it. His comrades talked of establishing a permanent trust for him, and though it probably would have been cheaper in the long run, nothing came of it, in part because Bakunin's politics soon alienated them. Turgenev in particular had abandoned politics altogether and was disconcerted to find that renewed contact with the revolutionary drew the attention of the Russian secret police to him. Bakunin's promise to his wife, Antonia, that if she could escape Russia and join him that they would live "neither in opulence nor poverty," proved only half right. His hope, that when she joined him he would be "freer, more peaceful, and stronger," too proved illusory. Even finding the funds to secure her passage proved difficult, and certainly he had found no peace; by the time Antonia managed to make her way out of Russia in 1863, she had to follow in his revolutionary wake not to peaceful London but to Stockholm where he had again taken up the revolution.[10]

While his family had taken Antonia in for a time at Priamukhino and helped her secure passage to Europe, it could offer Bakunin little assistance. The estate secured a living but little spare cash, and the family had other problems to deal with. Two of Bakunin's brothers had metaphorically followed in his footsteps and taken up politics. Protesting that the tsar's emancipation of the serfs did not go nearly far enough, Nicholas and Alexis signed a petition calling for better terms for the peasants. That led them to follow literally in their older brother's footsteps, straight to the Peter and Paul fortress, where they spent several months in prison. Another brother, Alexander, came to visit in London on the rebound from a spectacularly unsuccessful love affair that had led him to attempt suicide, and Bakunin wrote that their reunion "touched me profoundly." But he made little attempt to follow up on this contact with his family as he threw himself into politics. Undoubtedly he feared that communication would subject them to investigation by the Third Section; at the same time, after so many years of estrangement, he preferred to look ahead rather than back. Nearly fifty by the time he escaped Siberia, Bakunin determined to make up for lost time, and it was politics, not family, that concerned him.[11]

In London, Bakunin took up political work with a passion that approached frenzy. He fired off letters and notes, met incessantly with Polish and Russian émigrés and Italian nationalists such as Giuseppe Mazzini, and argued politics long into the night. Many of the arguments were with Herzen, as Bakunin insisted that *The Bell* was not radical enough. Herzen, for his part, complained that Bakunin had come out from prison "as though out of a faint," picking up where he had left off in 1849. "The European reaction did not exist for Bakunin," Herzen wrote; "the bitter years from 1848 to 1858 did not exist for him either."[12] There was some truth to this, but it was equally true that Herzen had been greatly disillusioned by the aftermath of the revolution. Personal tragedy too had left him cautious and restrained: his wife had long been ill and died shortly after giving birth to a son; the baby lived only a few days, and disease carried away two other children. He was in any case less interested in political action than political journalism. He believed in the power of the pen and printing press, and his hope was *The Bell* would reach into the Winter Palace itself to influence the tsar as much as it did young radicals, intellectuals, and émigrés.

Even when he and Bakunin shared the same goals, they often differed drastically over means and expression. Herzen was quick to pontificate on what should be done, quick to judge the tactics and strategies of others. Bakunin had a rather different view. Revolutionaries cannot be "doctrinaires," he wrote in early 1862. "We do not compose in advance constitutions or pose as the legislators of the people. We understand that our mission is quite different. We are not the teachers of the people, only their precursors; it is our job to mark out a path, and our destination is not one of theory but of practice."[13] He and Herzen differed on another issue as well. One of Bakunin's "strong qualities," Herzen ruefully admitted, was "as soon as he had grasped two or three features of his surroundings, he singled out the revolutionary current and at once set to work to carry it farther, to expand it, making of it the burning question of life." This was, surely, he concluded, "a sign of greatness." If it meant that Bakunin "looked only toward the ultimate goal, and took the second month of pregnancy for the ninth," Herzen was in danger of missing the blessed event entirely.[14]

Such was the case in 1862, when radicals in Russia published a manifesto entitled "Young Russia." It was the work of a small group of students, and while they had read and respected Herzen, Blanc, and Proudhon, they were convinced that propaganda was not enough. Herzen was a man of the 1840s, and those days were long gone. "Russia is entering the revolutionary state of its existence," they proclaimed in the manifesto, but Herzen's "revolutionary fire" had been extinguished by the failure of a few revolts. Having "lost all faith in violent upheavals," he was, in their view, content "to run a review of liberal tendencies and nothing more."[15] Young Russia was tired of talk and had no hope that the tsar could be convinced by an editorial to give the peasants land and liberty. These young Jacobins were prepared to lead peasants into action, and urged "revolution, a bloody and pitiless revolution, a revolution which must change everything down to the very roots, utterly overthrowing all the foundations of the present society and bringing about the ruin of all who support the present order." If that included Herzen, so much the worse for him.[16]

The manifesto brought to a head a very real problem that many social movements continue to face: how to combine the experience, wisdom, and resources of older radicals with the rebel energy of the younger generation.

Must every generation repeat the mistakes of the previous one? Must experience lead to reformism and paternalism? When does caution become cowardice? Herzen and Young Russia weighed each of these and came to very different conclusions.

Herzen had already been dueling in the press with the new generation of radicals—soon to become known as the "men of the '60s," just as Herzen was a "man of the '40s." The new generation believed he was out of touch and fooled by the cautious reforms of Alexander II. Herzen replied that

> we differ from you not in ideas but in methods; not in principles but in ways of acting. You are only the extreme expression of our own position . . . Our indignation is as young as yours, and our love for the Russian people is as alive now as it was in the years of our youth. But we will not call for the axe [the traditional weapon of the peasant], for that oppressive *ultima ration* [final argument] so long as there remains one reasonable hope of a solution without the axe.[17]

While Herzen was largely correct in pointing out that the differences between the two sides were less than the polemics suggested, the paternalism of his reply did nothing to build unity. Instead, it emphasized their political differences, their very different generational experiences, and their different class origins. Herzen was from the aristocracy, from "society"; he was cultured, comfortable, rich, and respectable. The new generation was largely made up of the children of a very different stratum, the *raznochintsy*, "those of other ranks." They were the sons and daughters of merchants, of low-level civil servants, of poor landowners, of professionals such as doctors and advocates, and, in the case of two of the most prominent radicals, Nikolai Chernyshevsky and Nikolai Dobroliubov, of priests. They had a very different outlook than the Herzens and Ogarevs, one at once less refined and more practical and more antagonistic to the old regime at a very personal level. The conflict had been foreshadowed in the 1840s with the tumultuous relationship between Belinsky, who, it will be remembered, was the son of a doctor, and Botkin, the son of a merchant, and the aristocratic Bakunin. In the 1860s, Herzen would decry Chernyshevsky as uncultured and crude; for his part, Chernyshevsky would find Herzen pretentious and irrelevant.

Bakunin made a more measured appraisal that saw value and mistakes on both sides. He agreed with Herzen that the two generations were not as far apart as they seemed, but insisted that it was important to acknowledge the revolutionary situation as it actually existed in Russia. To do otherwise was to risk irrelevance. At the same time, the experience he and Herzen possessed was not valueless. In his lengthy article, "The People's Cause: Romanov, Pugachev, or Pestel?" Bakunin outlined three different models for change in Russia. Hearkening back to his confession and his defense of Muraviev, he suggested it could come from the top. It could also erupt from below, as a peasant uprising similar to that of the Pugachev rebellion during the reign of Catherine the Great. Finally, it could come from a movement of the elite, typified by Pestel and the Decembrists. It was an important article, for in it he elaborated his conception of the relationship of the revolutionary to the masses in ways that began to move more decisively toward anarchism.

His article was given some urgency by events in Russia. During the spring of 1862, a series of mysterious fires broke out in several Russian cities. Coming just after the "Young Russia" manifesto, these events gave the government a pretext to crack down on radicals. Their newspapers and journals were shut down, and leading writers and activists were arrested. Among them was Chernyshevsky, who was condemned to exile, first in Siberia and then in Astrakhan, until 1889. He died four months after he was allowed to return to his home, aged sixty-one. His most famous work, the novel *What Is To Be Done?* was written while he was in prison, and like Bakunin until his anarchist period, he was equally famous as a revolutionary prisoner and as an activist.

Even at the time, many thought the fires were set by the tsar's agents-provocateur or other reactionaries. Several of the arsons turned out to be "copycat" crimes conveniently blamed on radicals but actually committed to settle old scores or to collect the insurance. Bakunin insisted that the revolutionaries were not responsible, and pointed out that the tsar had used the ensuing panic to his own advantage. By blaming the fires on the radicals, he had won considerable public opinion to his side. That did not, however, mean that revolution was impossible or that the masses were inherently reactionary, Bakunin argued. In fact, he suggested, it might be possible to use this popular support for the tsar to pressure him to make widespread and fundamental changes. Specifically, this meant land and liberty: land to the peasants and liberty for all. The slogan "Land and Liberty" was taken from Herzen and used by Russian radicals who in 1861 launched a political party under that name, and it was this popular call that Bakunin echoed in his article. The people demanded no less. The only question was whether the revolution would be peaceful or violent. If, Bakunin held, the tsar moved quickly and gave land to the peasants and created a grassroots, popular assembly—the *zemstvo*—it would be possible to prevent an "insurrection of all the people" that would have the "character of a pitiless slaughter." Half measures would not suffice. The tsar would have to give the people real autonomy and self-administration. Bureaucratic rule could no longer hold the regime together, for "the functionary is odious to the people," and "bureaucratic centralization, with its violence, can only destroy unity." "Real integrity and freedom will only return to Russia," he continued, "when the administration of functionaries is replaced by the self-administration of the people."

At the present moment, Bakunin continued, only the tsar had the trust of the people. They distrusted the bureaucracy and the nobility and so there was no chance that a Pestel could mobilize them. After all, in their daily lives, it was the priest and the clerk and the government official and the landlord who directly oppressed them, not the tsar himself. Furthermore, there was nothing to be gained from dissing the tsar, for most people still believed that he genuinely wanted to protect them from the bureaucrats and lords, that he sincerely wished to grant them freedom and land but was held in check by others. This moral authority was the key to the tsar's rule. So powerful was it that it had even been used successfully to whip up support for war, always under the pretext of "Holy Russia" and saving the Russian way of life. That was obviously a lie, but the point was that war remained the regime's ultimate safety valve. All the opposition to the regime could be swept away in the face of an external threat, even a bogus threat.

At the same time, Bakunin calculated, such loyalty meant that the tsar could use his moral authority to create the *zemstvo* against the protest of the bureaucracy and the nobility. If he did that he could rely on widespread, popular support from the people. But such moral authority, Bakunin warned, would not last forever. While the people's attachment to the tsar had the character of "faith" and "religion," this faith was "not celestial but terrestrial" and sought rewards on earth, not heaven. If the tsar did not act quickly, firmly, and radically, the faith would evaporate. Would he act? Bakunin had strong doubts. For the tsar "feared the people" and did not trust them. In part this was because the tsar believed that they were under the influence of the "young avant-garde," the "young revolutionary." Oh that it were so! Bakunin exclaimed. In fact, he pointed out, the tsar had nothing to worry about on that score. It was time to admit openly that radical propaganda, and here he included himself along with Herzen, had not reached the people and had not shaken their faith in the tsar. In reality, a "huge gulf" separated the radicals from the people. Thus while the radicals were ready to work with the people, the people would, at the moment, march with the tsar against the revolutionaries. If the tsar were smart, he could take advantage of this and undermine the radicals with a program of land and liberty. That would be preferable to bloodshed and ruin, and Bakunin hoped it were possible.

To this point, his article was a plea for caution and reform that largely echoed Herzen's. But unlike Herzen, Bakunin declared his support for the youth movement. While it was important to make every effort to avoid violence, he believed that it was unlikely the tsar would act decisively. If he did not, if he were only half smart and applied half measures, then "our young avant-garde, our hope and our strength, will undoubtedly finish beating a path to the people and extend their hand across the gulf." That alliance would drown the tsar and the nobility in blood, for the "young people" were essentially correct in their critique of the regime and the liberal wing of the radical movement symbolized by Herzen. If the young radicals lacked experience, it did not follow that they were therefore "mistaken in their ideas." The "expression of their ideas" might be overblown and impetuous, but in their fundamental beliefs and idealism "they are rarely mistaken." They were on the "side of life and truth," and had proven with their deeds that they were ready "to sacrifice all for the people." To those who insisted that the young radicals were carried away by "abstract revolutionary ideas," Bakunin conceded that this had a

degree of truth to it, but that it was a "superficial explanation" at best. More to the point, "doctrinaires of all types," and he seems to have included Herzen here, were angry because the youth movement fled from them and their "odor of pedantic self-righteousness." Its lack of experience might alarm some, but it was also a huge asset, for "youth ignores insurmountable obstacles," and "the people, themselves young and passionate, will recognize this sooner or later" and would seek alliance with those who had gone before.

The pressing task of the youth movement was to understand its own role in the revolution and the nature of the people. It was, Bakunin argued, crucial to understand that the new Russian movement was more than a revitalized Decembrist one of the "educated and privileged." Such people were useful and had something to offer. They could point out the "bitter experience of the West" and help avoid repeating its mistakes. Education provided a person with the ability to determine facts accurately and to generalize from them, to go beyond anecdote and local familiarity, and this was all to the good. But the contemporary movement was principally a mass movement of peasants and workers who did not live by "abstract principles" and who were not moved by impractical theory. They had, after all, survived a very long time in the harshest of conditions and had a wealth of experience, traditions, and customs that they would not abandon just because someone, either tsar or revolutionary, told them to. If the peasants seemed "coarse, illiterate," they had learned much from their historical development and had much to teach. Radicals had to abandon the "odious and ridiculous role of the schoolmaster," and needed to see the people not as a "means, but an end; we must not treat them as the raw material for a revolution made according to our ideas." On the contrary, the revolutionary was to be the "servant" of the cause—if the people consented.

Bakunin acknowledged that this role was not an easy one. It required sincerity, openness, and a complete absence of duplicity. Young Russia had some distance to go in that direction; to date, it had shown too much of the pedantry and condescension toward the people that it so rightly despised in Herzen. It was too given to abstraction, and that led to misjudgment, for in "the world of theory, anything is possible." In the real world, theory had to give way to practical politics, since "without discipline, without organization, without humility in the face of the grandeur of the goal, we will only amuse our enemies and we will never gain victory.

Instead of abstract ideas, Bakunin outlined a political program that reflected the goals of the people and the aspirations of Young Russia. In essence, it was a program of Land and Liberty. All land was to be given to the Russian people, held collectively so no one was deprived of it or could profit from the labor of others. Centralized government was to be replaced with "popular self-administration," starting at the level of the local commune then in expanding free associations of the district, region, and nation. Russia's empire was to be dissolved, with Poland, Lithuania, Ukraine, Finland, and other nations given the right of self-determination. Russia would seek a "fraternal alliance" with these new nations to protect each and all from the encroaching empires of Prussia, Austria, and Turkey, and to work to free the Slavic people already under their yoke; it would seek alliances with the Italian principalities and the Magyar people to win their self-determination as well.

He then returned to the theme of his title. Would such a program come about from the tsar, from a social revolution, or a putsch? As he had indicated earlier, it was possible that the tsar would come to understand that his only salvation lay in leading the revolution. If he did, Bakunin claimed, he himself would gladly follow Alexander II. For revolutions caused great suffering, both to their thousands of victims and to the cause itself. The French Revolution gave ample proof of that. At the same time, he insisted that revolutions became "absolutely necessary thanks to human stupidity." If the tsar acted stupidly, the blood would be on his hands. For the moment, however, "we are not his friends and we are not his enemies; we are the friends of the popular cause of Russia and the Slavs." For his part, Bakunin promised he would follow the cause wherever it led.

If the tsar betrayed Russia, there remained two other ways to conceive of the revolution: Pugachev or Pestel, social revolution or Jacobin coup. It was impossible to predict which would follow, and each had its strengths and weaknesses. In either case, however, the present need was obvious: Young Russia had to organize and make itself worthy of joining the people.[18]

The essay brought together several themes and ideas that Bakunin had considered throughout his life. From Fichte came the importance of action. Unlike Herzen, Bakunin made it plain that he would always side with the revolutionaries and the people, even if they appeared to be wrong. To do otherwise might be prudent, might be reasonable, but his place would always be with the people and the revolution, even if he disagreed with their tactics and their calculation of the chances of success. From Hegel came the understanding of the need for change and the progression of history with all its excesses and extremes. His own insistence, dating from "The Reaction in Germany," on complete and radical change remained, but it was tempered by his experience of the misery of actual revolution and the price paid by the defeated. No one in Young Russia had yet paid the price he had, and Bakunin's hope that revolution might be instigated from above reflected his bitter experience of counterrevolution and repression. It reflected too his experience of the betrayal of the revolution by parliamentary institutions and the reformers who filled them. At the same time, he understood that it was likely an exercise in wishful thinking to hope that the tsar would act progressively. Bakunin had moved some distance from his position, outlined in the confession and his defense of Muraviev, that the best hope for change was from above. Clearly, the tsar only acted when pressured from below, and if he would now do the right thing, it would not be because of principle or ideals. Furthermore, no matter how enlightened, the self-interest of tsar, noble, and capitalist was not the same as that of the student, peasant, and worker, and the demands of the people were what ultimately mattered. And their demands did not require interpretation or implementation by others. Bakunin had learned that from Weitling and Proudhon, and, more recently from Peter Martyanov, a freed Russian serf who had made his way to London where he worked with Herzen and Bakunin before returning to face arrest, imprisonment, and exile. The revolutionary was to learn from the masses, not teach them; the revolutionary had skills to put at the service of the cause, not divine revelations with which to lead it.

The essay also signaled Bakunin's break with Herzen. Herzen refused to publish it in *The Bell,* and refused to offer Land and Liberty the same support Bakunin did, believing the movement was much too weak and reckless. He despised the cockiness of its representative sent to enlist his aid. But "that is youth," Bakunin retorted, and it was with youth and revolution that he sided. The alternative? Herzen maintained his position, and saw his influence dwindle and the circulation of *The Bell* plummet by 80 percent. Whatever lessons experience and wisdom had to impart could not be taught by hectoring and lecturing.[19]

For his part, Bakunin was no longer interested in analyzing revolution from afar. As it had in 1847, Poland provided him an entry point to practical politics. Its struggle for national independence broke out once again in 1862, though the movement was split. Some Polish nobles believed national freedom consisted largely of the freedom to expand their landholdings and to exploit the laborers who tilled it. They saw their best chance in cooperating with the Russian government, and hoped only for national autonomy in a state they would control. Other Poles, organized into the Central National Committee, understood with Bakunin that nationalism meant freedom only for the elite if it were not part of the social revolution. This group called for the overthrow of both tsar and Polish landlord, cautiously explored links with the Russian radicals of Land and Liberty and with Herzen and Bakunin, and plotted furiously. So active were their organizing efforts that the Third Section was able to learn all about their plans and to provoke them into premature action. In January 1863, the Russian government ordered a levy of Polish men for military service—in other words, the draft. The order specifically called up workers in the cities, to drain off those who would form the active fighting force of any revolutionary activity, just as poverty and the volunteer army perform the same function today in the United States. In response, the Polish radicals launched an assault on the garrisons.

For many, including Bakunin, it signaled the beginning of a new revolutionary era. Herzen grudgingly agreed, and even Marx and Engels looked for Russian peasants to join with the Poles in a general uprising.[20] For his part, Bakunin secured a passport in the name of a French-Canadian professor, Henri Soulié, and left for Poland by way of Denmark. In Copenhagen he learned that a legion of Polish soldiers had left London in a chartered ship, the *Ward Jackson,* and he hastened to join them in Helsingberg. But the Russian spy network knew all about the *Ward Jackson* and its shipment of men and arms; worse, as the captain became increasingly aware of the risks he was taking, he refused to proceed past Sweden. The Swedish authorities seized the ship, and the vaunted Polish legion was dispersed without firing a shot or even seeing its homeland. The rebels in Poland fared no better. The Russian peasants and workers did not join them and the insurrection was put down firmly. The Russian government, after all, had some experience in that line.

After a short stay in Sweden, where Antonia finally caught up with him, Bakunin decided he had had enough of Poles, Swedes, and winter. Like his father so many years before, he had long thought Italy would provide a more suitable climate, and at the beginning of 1864, he and Antonia headed to Florence. They visited Giuseppe Garibaldi, the patriot soldier who had fought in 1848 first as a republican then as a supporter of Italian King Victor Immanuel II to free Sicily and Naples from the Austrian empire. Garibaldi continued to fight for a unified Italy until Victor Immanuel II, fearing outside intervention, ordered him to abandon his campaign to take Rome and the Papal States and sent the Italian army to defeat Garibaldi at the battle of Aspromonte. Immediately amnestied, Garibaldi was in semiretirement on his island of Caprera when the Bakunins stopped over.

Bakunin too was in semiretirement from revolutionary activities. Herzen's careful plan to influence public opinion had produced little and the Polish insurrection had collapsed. The Russian radicals had been rounded up, and their failure showed that the peasants and workers needed more than a single spark to ignite their revolutionary fervor. Reform was out of the question in nations and empires that had no effective political process. Where the possibility of reform did exist, as in England, it usually served to forestall radical change and undercut revolution. The tsar had made it plain that he would not lead a revolution from above, and national liberation movements did little more than put a native son on thrones vacated by a foreign emperor. Garibaldi's campaign was proof of that; France and its Second Empire too were proof that nationalism was more likely to serve reaction than reform or revolution. It was a time for reflection and writing, and for reconsidering tactics and strategy.

Bakunin had joined the Freemasons in Paris in the 1840s, and he rejoined in Italy. While today's Freemasons are best known, at least in North America, for the fezzes and minibikes of the freewheelin' Shriners, in nineteenth-century Europe they were highly political, reformist, and even revolutionary, challenging the authority of king and pope equally. Bakunin had worked with radical members from several countries while he was in London and he became a member of the Scottish Rite, one of the chapters of the fraternal order; soon, he became a thirty-second-degree Mason. Like becoming a karate black belt, this is usually given much more significance by those unfamiliar with the society than by those in it. The passage through the rites of Masonry is not automatic, but it is not onerous. It indicates that the candidate has proven himself trustworthy, memorized the accompanying rituals, and gone through the appropriate initiation ceremonies. It does not confer secret powers or reveal profound and arcane mysteries of the universe or entry into the cabal that actually runs the world from its undersea headquarters at the North Pole. It was a way to meet like-minded people, to engage in serious but not strenuous political activity, and likely, to have some fun.

His brief involvement with the Freemasons did push Bakunin to reevaluate the relationship of religion and politics. It was a theme he had addressed much earlier, concluding that the state needed religion, if only in the broad sense of a belief that bound people together. Then he had acknowledged that he believed in God and rather than split hairs and his audience, often found it convenient to express a general religious sense or feeling, while the God he referred to might be love, humanity, freedom, nature, or the revolution. Now, however, he rejected the notion entirely, and a passionate atheism would remain part of his revolutionary project. Whatever its alleged ideas, in practice, Bakunin maintained, religion "translates into the tutelage of the church and state, the despotism of princes, and the brutal and hypocritical exploitation of the popular masses for the profit of a corrupt minority. The fundamental principle of all religion, and especially the Christian church, is that the mass of humanity is stupid, wicked, ignorant, anarchic, incapable of producing or sustaining social order, and thus for its own good it must be silenced and governed with a firm hand." Therefore, he concluded, "if God exists, then man is a slave. Man can, must be, free; therefore, there is no God. It is impossible to escape this dilemma—now let us choose." He made his choice. While maintaining a "religious respect" for the right of the individual to hold any belief, Bakunin argued that "the idea of God is incompatible with reason, justice, morality, dignity, and human liberty." In short, "to proclaim the existence of a just and true God," was "to proclaim the universal and permanent enslavement of humanity."[21]

His ideas on religion now resolved, Bakunin moved with Antonia to Sorrento in May 1865 to meet up with his brother Paul and Paul's wife, Natalie, for a short time. The visit was cordial enough, but did nothing to bring Michael back into the family. It was hardly surprising; the two men had never been close. After all, Paul had been only eight when his older brother left for military school, and it had been his sisters Michael had relied upon in those early years. Nonetheless, Antonia painted a pleasant picture of the time in Sorrento. "Life here flows peacefully and regularly as before," she wrote. "We rise early, Michael bathes, then has coffee and grapes . . . The entire morning Michael writes, while I read." At three, he would put down his pen, she her book, to take a short nap followed by a swim. At six they would dine, then go for a leisurely walk, return for tea at nine before Michael would resume writing until one or two in the morning.[22] A few months later, the two moved to Naples, where they would spend perhaps the most pleasant two years of their lives. There Bakunin met Zoe Obolensky, a Russian noble born into one of the wealthiest and most influential families and married into another. However, she loved neither her homeland nor her husband, a prominent general, and took her children with her to Italy, where her personality, love of radical politics, and money soon created an amiable circle of admirers, thinkers, and hangers-on, including the Bakunins. From Naples they accompanied Obolensky to the island of Ischia, near Capri, where they went sailing and Bakunin organized picnics, fired off letters in all directions, and held late-night meetings with mysterious visitors. All in all, it must have seemed like heaven to the revolutionary.[23]

Unlike Florence, radical politics had some following in Naples; there was even a newspaper, *II Popolo d'Italia,* for which Bakunin wrote a few articles. He then founded the International Brotherhood, consisting of a few Italians, including the lawyer Carlo Gambuzzi, and some Slavic radicals. While the activity of the International Brotherhood itself amounted to very little, its members would learn their anarchism well and do much to spread the word. One member, Giuseppe Fanelli, would go on to create branches of Bakunin's later revolutionary organization, the Alliance of Social Revolutionaries, in Madrid and Barcelona; Gambuzzi would start another in Naples. Furthermore, the Brotherhood gave Bakunin the opportunity to write a powerful political manifesto that made public for the first time his essentially anarchist program. While he had written a similar document in Stockholm, nothing seems to have come of it. However, his Italian piece, "Principles and Organization of the International Revolutionary Society," written in 1866, is widely cited as a founding document for the anarchist movement. Better known as the "Revolutionary Catechism" and often confused with a later piece with a similar name, it is an ambitious essay, part critique, part call to arms, and part how-to manual for social change. In it Bakunin wrestled with some of the fundamental questions of political philosophy. What is the relationship between the individual and society? How can the inherent conflict between the rights of the individual and the rights of the group be resolved? How can society ensure the freedom of the individual while pursuing collective goals? How can organizations be democratic and efficient? What is, and what should be, the basis of morality? What would a new society based on anarchist ideas and principles look like?[24]

The essay proclaimed the objective of the secret society was "the triumph of the principle of revolution in the world, and consequently the radical overthrow of all presently existing religious, political, economic, and social organizations and institutions and subsequently of world society on the basis of liberty, reason, justice, and work." In fifty-six pages, Bakunin outlined his principles and ideas and showed how far his politics had evolved since his escape from Siberia. The catechism was much more than a list of do's and don'ts; it was a philosophical treatise that pulled together many themes Bakunin had considered over the years. The first of these was the "denial of the existence of a real, extraterrestrial God, and consequently also of any revelation and any divine intervention in the affairs of the human world." Instead of God, "human reason" would be the single "criterion of truth"; "human conscience" that of justice, and "individual and collective liberty as the only creator of order for humanity." What was liberty? This abstraction had been foremost in his ideas and actions for thirty years. Now he defined it as "the absolute right of all adult men and women to seek no sanction for their actions except their own conscience and reason, to determine them only of their own free will, and consequently to be responsible for them to themselves first of all, and then to the society of which they are a part, but only insofar as they freely consent to be part of it." No idea would be censored or forbidden. The only constraint would be the "natural corrective power of public opinion," tempered with the concomitant freedom to disagree and disavow. Morality too would be an individual matter, and even those associations that aimed at destroying individual and public liberty would be allowed. Obviously in a society without compulsion or force or coercion, such ideas could pose no threat. No one would be forced to work, or even forbidden from "exploiting charity or individual trust," providing only that such "charity and trust be voluntary" and given by adults only.

Would some take advantage of this? Possibly; but the use of legislation and coercion to forbid any activity would lead to a worse problem: the end of liberty. "Liberty cannot and should not defend itself except by means of liberty," Bakunin argued, "and it is a dangerous misconception to advocate its limitation under the specious pretext of protection." Any restriction of liberty in the name of protecting it obviously infringes upon it, a sentiment he shared with Benjamin Franklin, who wrote, "they that can give up essential liberty to obtain a little temporary safety deserve neither liberty nor safety." Furthermore, Bakunin observed, immorality and crime were caused by society, either through poor education, lack of equal opportunity, or unjust organization. "Repression and authoritarianism" could not cure the problem; they could only suppress the symptoms temporarily. The cure was to "moralize society" by tearing down "that entire political and social organization which is built on inequality, privilege, divine authority, and contempt for humanity. Once having rebuilt it on the basis of the utmost equality, justice, work, and an education inspired exclusively by respect for humanity," the root cause of most crime and antisocial behavior would be eliminated.

Still, humanity was not perfect, and it was entirely possible that someone could engage in behavior that infringed on the freedom of others. How could society protect itself from that? First, Bakunin believed, public opinion, not expressed by polls or surveys but by active political life, would exert considerable pressure. Second, while he insisted that all "cruel and degrading punishments, corporal punishment, and the death penalty," would be abolished along with "indefinite or protracted punishments," that implied some punishments would remain. The individual, however, could avoid the imposed sentence by declaring complete independence from the society, at which point society could withdraw from the individual, offering neither shelter nor comfort nor means of life.

Philosophers before and after Bakunin have asserted that the freedom of the individual is limited and bounded by the freedom of others in society. He argued the contrary, that the individual could only be free when all were free, while the "enslavement of any one man on earth . . . is a denial of the liberty of all." Thus liberty required economic equality, for inequality granted one power over another. That meant land and resources would be shared by all so no one could command another to work for him or profit from another's labor. But "equality," he stressed, "does not mean the leveling down of individual differences, or intellectual, moral, and physical uniformity among individuals. This diversity of ability and strength, and these differences of race, nation, sex, age, and character, far from being a social evil, constitute the treasure house of humanity." Nor did it mean the "leveling down of individual fortunes," as long as these were the product of the "ability, productive energy, and thrift" of the individual, not the labor of others or inheritance. For that matter, inheritance would cease to be meaningful in a society that provided for all. His point remained: political equality was irrelevant in the face of economic inequality, and from that observation, Bakunin turned to consider the question of labor.

Sharing the observation of Adam Smith as well as Karl Marx, Bakunin proclaimed "labor is the sole producer of wealth." More, it was the "fundamental basis of dignity and human rights, for it is only by means of his own, free, intelligent work that man becomes a creator in his turn, wins from the surrounding world and his own animal nature his humanity and rights, and creates the world of civilization." Yet under feudalism and capitalism, labor was reduced to a "purely mechanical task, no different from that of a beast of burden." Manual labor left the masses "crushed," for their work was designed "more to deaden than develop their natural intelligence." The separation of labor into intellectual labor, including managerial functions, and manual labor had to be ended. To live off the labor of others was to be a "parasite, an exploiter . . . and a thief," while intellectual labor in present society granted privilege even as it left its practitioners "learnedly asinine," since they rarely had any practical knowledge to complete their academic learning. Such a division also weakened society as a whole, for brutalized workers and impractical intellectuals could not produce as much as integrated labor. "When the thinker works and the worker thinks, free, intelligent labor will emerge as humanity's highest aspiration, the basis of its dignity and law, and the embodiment of its human power on earth—and humanity will be instituted," Bakunin concluded. It was an argument very similar to the one Marx and Engels made in "The German Ideology," where, decrying the division of labor, they wrote that "as soon as the distribution of labor comes into being, each man has a particular, exclusive sphere of activity, which is forced upon him and from which he cannot escape." In a communist society, "each can become accomplished in any branch he wishes," and the well-rounded, unalienated human could "do one thing today and another thing tomorrow, to hunt in the morning, fish in the afternoon, rear cattle in the evening, criticize after dinner, just as I have a mind, without ever becoming hunter, fisherman, shepherd, or critic."[25]

In the new society, Bakunin argued, labor would likely be social and collective rather than individual, for in combination humans are much more productive and create more goods in less time. With such free associations of producers, "human labor, emancipating each and every man, will regenerate the world," ending scarcity and providing leisure for real culture and civilization. In a later article, he would make his position even more explicit. "The isolated labor of a single person, however strong and capable, is never enough to counteract the collective labor of the many who are associated and well organized. What is called individual labor in industry today is nothing but the exploitation of the collective labor of the workers by individuals who are privileged holders either of capital or learning." Even intellectual production was, he maintained, collective and social production. "The mind of the world's greatest genius" was entirely "the product of the collective intellectual and industrial labor of all past and present generations." If this was not readily apparent, he suggested an experiment. Put the "genius" on a desert island as an infant. Would it survive? Would it be little more than a beast if it did? The thought experiment demonstrated more than that it takes a village to raise a child or that you should thank a teacher and the taxpayers who paid for salary and school if you can read this. It showed that whatever potential abilities someone was born with would "remain dead unless they are fertilized by the potent and beneficial activity of the collectivity. We shall say more: The more endowed by nature an individual is, the more that person takes from the collectivity; from which it follows, in all justice, that more must be repaid."[26]

Though he used masculine pronouns throughout the "Revolutionary Catechism," Bakunin included "woman," who, "differing from man but not inferior to him, intelligent, industrious, and free like him, is declared his equal both in rights and in all political and social functions and duties." The "legal family," sanctioned and enforced by law, would be replaced by free marriage, that is, union in which both partners were free and equal, not one that bound women in positions of subservience. No doubt remembering the struggles of his sisters, he insisted "neither violence, passion, nor the rights freely granted in the past may excuse any infringement by one party of the other's liberty, and any such infringement shall be considered criminal." This was much more than a token assertion of equality. While Bakunin usually agreed with Herzen and Ogarev that the people had much to teach intellectuals and others, shortly after writing the "Revolutionary Catechism," Bakunin criticized both men for their failure to understand that the primitive socialism of the peasant commune did not extend to women's rights. The *mir* was host to "the scandalous degradation of women," and whatever the virtues of peasant life, the "absolute negation and total incomprehension of the rights and honor of women" amounted to a "patriarchal despotism" that the revolutionary had to confront.[27] The "Revolutionary Catechism" also included ideas on raising children. Children could be raised by their birth parents, though society would remain responsible for providing for mother and child. But "children belong neither to their parents nor to society but to themselves and their future liberty." They needed to be protected and would not be granted complete license, but they would be nurtured to be independent, rational, and moral, and given more and more freedom to the degree they could make informed decisions.

Bakunin's commitment to women's equality and his radical ideas on liberty and equality put him in the vanguard of progressive thinkers in the nineteenth century, and they stand today as stinging rebukes to the contemporary reign of capital and empire that has some way to go to catch up with him. At the same time, the "Revolutionary Catechism" signaled an end to his short retirement from radical politics. Political events and his own restlessness ensured he would soon make a return engagement on the world stage.

LIBERTY WITHOUT SOCIALISM IS INJUSTICE; SOCIALISM WITHOUT LIBERTY IS SLAVERY

By 1867, Bakunin, always physically, mentally, and politically restive, had had enough of Italy and the relatively quiet activism of writing and politics he found there. There were other reasons to move on, chief among them Obolensky's husband. Appalled in equal measure by her politics and her Polish lover, the general cut off her financial support in 1867 and so forced an end to the Bakunins' Italian island interlude. Forced to economize, Obolensky and several of her circle, including the Bakunins and Gambuzzi, moved to Vevey, Switzerland, near Montreux on the Lake Geneva shoreline, in time for Michael to head to the founding congress of the League of Peace and Freedom. For world events too made it difficult to remain in splendid isolation. Louis Napoleon Bonaparte, who had been calling himself Emperor Napoleon III since 1852, was pushing his luck. The Crimean War and the Congress of Paris had done much to strengthen his rule. He had intervened successfully on Italy's side in war against Austria, though he was disappointed when the Italians kept on going and unified the peninsula; he had annexed Savoy and Nice, helped the British take Canton during the Second Opium War, supported the Polish uprising of 1863, obtained colonies in Senegal and Indochina, and installed Archduke Maximilian as emperor of Mexico. While the Mexican escapade ended in disaster—Montezuma's revenge took the form of a firing squad for the hapless Max—dramatic foreign policy was a useful diversion from domestic problems. Such problems, however, continued to grow, for foreign adventures could not replace progressive policy. The secularizing state angered the Catholic Church; free trade agreements with Britain harmed local industry and French workers; the growth of capitalist industrialism was no smoother in the 1860s than it had been in the 1840s or would be in the twenty-first century, and the displaced, dispossessed, and disaffected were not silent.

At the same time, while French industry was growing, it was growing more slowly than other European countries. That had a dramatic impact on both domestic and foreign policy. By the 1860s, warfare was much more industrialized than it had been during the Napoleonic wars; one lesson of the Crimean War was that sheer numbers of soldiers counted for much less than the arms they had at their disposal. But France's industrial production was increasingly outpaced by its neighbor, Prussia. The German state used this growing productive capacity to build its armies, and used the armies to expand its territory through confederation, annexation, and conquest, all at the expense of neighboring states. This aggression in turn brought in new resources and allowed even greater economic and military expansion. By the 1860s, Prussia had the most formidable war machine in central Europe. It also had a leader keen to use it. Otto von Bismarck, the "Iron Chancellor," assumed the position of premier of Prussia in 1862. Acting under the orders of his king, William I, he dissolved the rudimentary parliament, increased the army substantially, and set out simultaneously to unify Germany and expand its territory. Both of these aims came at the expense of Austria when Prussia declared war on it in 1866. The pundits, just as they would in the first Gulf War, saw two opponents whose very different strengths and weaknesses canceled out, and predicted a long, drawn-out war. The pundits, of course, were wrong in both cases, for the key to both victories was technology. The telegraph and railroad meant Prussia could move men and material much more quickly than could Austria, and in less than two months the German upstart had decisively defeated the empire. While Bismarck took no Austrian territory, he annexed its German allies, including Hanover, Hesse, and Frankfurt, and created a confederation of North German states, headed, naturally, by Prussia. The balance of power in Europe was dangerously out of whack, and the leaders of France and Prussia, with all the moral sensibility of an Al Capone or a Dick Cheney, saw only opportunity in that imbalance.

Reasonable men and women across Europe feared that conflict was imminent and organized to forestall it. In 1867, they convened a congress in Geneva to bring to heel the dogs of war. Activists and intellectuals such as John Stuart Mill, Victor Hugo, Garibaldi, Blanc, and Herzen supported the congress; ten thousand others from across Europe signed petitions and the first conference drew six thousand participants.

One of them was Michael Bakunin. His name was well-known to all, and he was called upon to serve on the executive committee along with Garibaldi and others. He agreed and took his place on the raised dais with the other committee members. As he made his way over, Garibaldi rose from his chair and clasped him in his arms. It was an emotional moment, and as the two comrades embraced, they were saluted with a standing ovation from the delegates.

It was, however, the high point of the congress. It voted to create a League of Peace and Freedom, but the bulk of moderate and liberal delegates had no real plan save to pass motions indicating their opposition to war. Karl Marx observed the proceedings from London and argued that the International Working Men's Association, better known as the International, that he had helped to create in 1864 should not formally join or support the League; instead, he urged his members to attend as individuals to try to inject some political sense into the proceedings. Accordingly, one member, James Guillaume, presented the International's suggestion that the League include the emancipation of workers in its platform. It bewildered many of the cautious delegates, even as Garibaldi's appeal that all adopt the "religion of God" had mystified and divided them. The delegates split on many issues, and little came of their efforts.

Bakunin's attempts to radicalize the League were no more successful. For him, however, there were several benefits to his initial work there. It signified his return to active politics, and he met Guillaume, who would become one of his best friends and chroniclers. Most importantly, it gave Bakunin another opportunity to formulate his ideas and write. Recasting one of his speeches to the League for publication, he asked rhetorically whether he, as a Russian, had the right to address a body convened to work for peace. After all, Russia had smashed brave Poland just a few years earlier. But perhaps, he suggested, as Russia's "most disobedient subject" he had earned the privilege to speak. Unlike many of the speakers, Bakunin understood that simply asking governments not to go to war would not work. The problem was not this or that government, but the very existence of states. The delegates needed to understand that while Russia was perhaps the worst example of empire, the state was virtually the same everywhere. If it was "cynically brutal in Russia," it was "hypocritical and deceitful behind the mask of constitutions in the civilized countries of the west." The state was based on violence: "internal violence under the pretext of public order, external violence under the pretext of equilibrium." Internal violence stemmed from the fact that all European states, including the liberal republics, were "the oppressors and exploiters of the popular masses and workers for the profit of a privileged class." The only way the masses could be kept subjugated was through violence and therefore the states maintained standing armies for use against their own people. These very armies increased the risk of war and each state believed it had to arm itself against its neighbors.

Against the power of governments, the congress was naive to think it was strong enough to ward off the "terrible war that is more imminent than ever." What they could do was articulate the principles that would make peace possible. First and foremost, that meant adopting the principles of international justice instead of "narrow patriotism." He drew a sophisticated distinction between the fact of nations, the reality of people who had different cultures and institutions they wished to preserve, and the recent notion of the "false principle of nationality," an invention of "the despots of France, Russia, and Prussia to suffocate the supreme principle of liberty." Each nation, as opposed to state, large or small, had the "incontestable right to be itself, to live according to its own nature; this right is only the consequence of the universal principle of liberty." From that it followed that empire and conquest were unjust. Therefore, everyone who wanted peace had to renounce "all that which is called national glory, dominion, and grandeur, all the egoistic and vain interests of patriotism." To those who advocated a United States of Europe as an antidote to war, Bakunin pointed out that a federation of "centralized, bureaucratic, and militarized" states would be no improvement. "Universal peace," he concluded, "will be impossible as long as the present centralized states exist." Those who wished for peace had to prepare not for war but for the dissolution of the state and for the creation of "free units, organized from the bottom up, by the free federation of communes into a province, provinces into nations, and nations into the United States of Europe."[1]

He expanded this theme over the next few months in a much longer document, "Federalism, Socialism, and Antitheologism." Like so much of his work, it was part political platform, part manifesto, and part philosophical treatise, designed to convince, cajole, and convert its readers with logic, appeals to emotion, and careful analysis in equal proportions. It is particularly important as a clarification of Bakunin's ideas on class and socialism. As Bakunin realized, radicals and liberals did not differ on the question of political liberty and political equality. Everyone was a democrat now if by that one meant a belief in republican government and an end to monarchy. Yet democratic, republican states could engage in the same foul crimes against humanity as any monarch. The Confederate states were as democratic as those of the North; it was, after all, the Democratic party that insisted on states' rights "to the point of wanting secession." There was only this one little blemish that kept them from being truly democratic and earned them the reproach of humanity, he noted sardonically, the little matter of slavery. That alone indicated that cliches about democracy meant little in the face of economic repression. In words echoing Marx's declaration in the Communist Manifesto that "the history of all hitherto existing society is the history of class struggle," Bakunin argued,

> Citizens and slaves—that was the antagonism in the ancient world as it was in the slave states of the new world, in America today. Citizens and wage earners, that is to say, those who are compelled to work, not by law but by reality—that is the antagonism of the modern world. And just as the ancient states were destroyed by slavery, so will the modern states be destroyed by the proletariat.[2]

His point about class may grate on contemporary ears as many insist that there is no longer a working class. We are all middle class now, the line goes, since it is possible for a plumber to make as much money as a small business operator or because union pension funds own shares in companies and therefore every union member is actually a shareholder and a capitalist. It is a naive argument. Class is not about income; it is about whether you hire people to work for you or have to go to work for someone else; it is about whether you own the company or sell your labor to it. Owning a share in a company, even owning a share directly, as opposed to having it locked in a pension fund administered by someone else, no more confers real ownership and control of the corporation than owning a federal savings bond makes you a member of the government of the United States. But what about the self-employed plumber? Or the independent farmer? The dentist? They aren't workers because they don't sell their labor to someone else, and they aren't capitalists because they don't hire others to produce for them. Quite right; that's why they're called "middle class," because they are somewhere between the working class and the capitalist class. They may dream of becoming the latter, and they may dread becoming the former, but their existence between the two important classes doesn't render the idea of class moot. As Bakunin demonstrated in 1867, such examples do not cancel out class, for "it is in vain that we try to console ourselves that this is a fictional rather than a real antagonism, or that it is impossible to establish a line of demarcation between the propertied class and the disinherited, dispossessed class because these two classes shade into each other by intermediary and imperceptible degrees." He gave an analogy from natural science. There was a point where plant life and animal life were nearly indistinguishable—the slime mold is the classic example today in first-year biology classes—but no one concludes from that observation that all plants are animals and vice versa. For those who missed Biology 101, perhaps another analogy would be more useful. Just because twilight is neither day nor night we do not conclude that day and night do not exist or cannot be distinguished with a high degree of accuracy and utility. So too with classes. Even though there were "intermediate positions that make an imperceptible transition from one level of political and social life to another, the difference between classes is nonetheless clearly marked." The two classes of bourgeoisie and proletariat, employer and employee, owner and worker, were separated by an "abyss," as much in the present day as slave owners and slaves were in antiquity. "Modern civilization," no less than the ancient world, was made up of a "comparatively small minority" whose freedom and wealth was dependent on the "immense majority" forced to work, not by the lash or law but by hunger. He made his point easy to grasp. "Slavery may change its form and its name but its essence remains the same. It may be summed up thusly: to be a slave is to be forced to work for another; to be a master is to live off the work of another." Call them slaves, call them serfs, call them wage workers, they were all forced to work by "hunger as well as the political and social institutions," and by their labor made possible "the complete or relative idleness of others."

It was easy to distinguish the members of classes by ownership of property and by the cultural differences that wealth and control conferred. Today most people can make fairly accurate and subtle class distinctions based on vocabulary, accent, clothing, vehicles, manners, even posture and dentition. One can even take classes in faking class. So too in Bakunin's day was it relatively easy to distinguish the "titled aristocrat from the financial aristocrat, the upper bourgeoisie from the petit bourgeoisie, and each of those from the factory and urban proletariat; the large landowner, someone who lives from his investments, from the peasant proprietor who cultivates the land himself, and the farmer from the agricultural laborer." His point was that whatever one might think about the disappearance of class, people in fact made class distinctions regularly. The important distinction in the modern period could be "reduced to two categories" that were "natural enemies diametrically opposed to each other": those who had all the privileges of "land and capital," and the "working classes without capital or land." In the first category, he also included those with "bourgeois education," arguing that education was a form of capital and privilege denied to workers. Such privilege meant the "work of the most mediocre bourgeois pays three to four times more than that of the most intelligent worker." Here Bakunin introduced a new idea into class theory, and one that is still much debated today. Are professionals such as doctors and professors and lawyers and lower-level managers part of the bourgeoisie? Are they part of a new middle class? A professional managerial class? Perhaps they occupy contradictory class locations and are pulled in two directions at once. Entire books have been written on the topic, and the debate is not resolved yet. In Bakunin's period, university education was much rarer than it is today. Virtually inaccessible to workers, universities were the preserve of the rich. He and Marx were the exceptions, not the rule, in that prison, exile, and genteel poverty went a long way toward erasing their own class privilege. But we might note parenthetically that even today most doctors, lawyers, and professors are the sons and daughters of doctors, lawyers, and professors. The higher education and status of these professions can be a form of capital passed on from one generation to the next, and if it is dwarfed by the capital of the wealthy, it still takes its possessors far from the daily reality of wage labor.

Bakunin's argument about education was also part of his larger debate on the relationship of the intellectual to the working-class movement. He had long argued that workers and peasants had to control the movement for their own liberation. Intellectuals could help, but not lead; they could refine, but not dictate; theory had to give way to practice. By placing them in the class of privilege, he underlined the fact that intellectuals had interests that were different from those of workers and could not be assumed to be on the side of the working class. It was an argument he would soon take up again with Marx.

It was also an important part of his anarchism, for he saw that any privilege was an affront to equality and to freedom. "The state cannot exist a single day without having a least one privileged, exploiting class: the bureaucracy," he wrote to a radical newspaper around the time he finished "Federalism, Socialism, and Antitheologism."[3] Whether admittance to the state bureaucracy was a hereditary right, as in Russia, or one earned through education and promotion, as in Germany, that power and authority divided rulers from the ruled as clearly as class divided capitalists and workers, and with the same terrible effects. It was, after all, the classic argument of the elites to insist that it only made sense that society be ruled by the best and the brightest; it was just coincidence that they also happened to be the best and the brightest. Besides, running the world was harder work than it might appear. Bakunin tackled this argument with gusto. The state and church both assumed that humans were essentially evil and that giving liberty to all would lead to the exploitation and slaughter of the weak by the strong—"just the opposite of what goes on in our model states today," he added sarcastically. Thus church and state assumed a "superior authority" was needed to establish and maintain order and control the worst impulses of human nature. Who was fit to rule? As long as one believed in God and the divine right of kings, it was clear enough. Once humanity got over that idea, however, it became a little more difficult to decide. After all, the whole premise of the social contract was that humans, left to their own devices, would dedicate themselves to pursuing their own self-interest in the most selfish ways possible. How did electing some of them to government change them into altruists?

The conventional answer, Bakunin suggested, was that "the best citizens, that is, the most intelligent and the most virtuous, those who best understood the common interests of society and the need for all to subordinate their particular interests," would be chosen to rule. It wasn't enough that they be the most intelligent, for if they had no virtue, they would use public office for their own interest. Nor could they simply be virtuous, because if they were "without intelligence," their folly would bring ruin. But history suggested that such intelligent and virtuous men were rare; that was why they were made into heroes and role models through the ages. More often, the halls of power were filled with the "insignificant, the dull," and "vice and bloody violence" triumphed. If indeed society depended on selecting the most able rulers, it would have "ceased to exist long ago." Suppose, however, just suppose, that there were enough intelligent and virtuous people to rule. Who would find them and put them in power? Perhaps they would do it themselves, since they would presumably be keenly aware of their suitability to rule. There was a name for people who assumed power on their own: They were usually given the "odious name of tyrants." What if they simply tried to persuade others to put them in power? Unfortunately, the best people were those who were least convinced they were the best and so were not the type to press themselves upon others. The people who were quickest to present themselves tended to be the "bad and mediocre," so self-selection was a little dodgy. If the would-be rulers were not inclined to use persuasion, then they would have to use force, and that took us straight back to despotic rule by the most powerful, not the best. Finally, if the people were actually able to choose the best rulers, did that not suggest that they were smart enough and upright enough to look after themselves?

From there Bakunin argued that any government would, by definition, be the rule of the majority by a minority. Even in the most democratic countries, such as the United States and Switzerland, the "self-government of the masses" was a "fiction. In reality, it is minorities who govern." This is obvious enough; any representative system boils down to minority rule as a handful of elected rule over those who elect them. That in turn meant that "society was separated into two categories, not to say two classes: the one, composed of the immense majority of citizens who submit freely to the government of the elected," and a small minority chosen to govern. Twenty years before Lord Acton decreed that "power tends to corrupt and absolute power corrupts absolutely," Bakunin warned that those chosen to govern, even "the best, the purest, the most intelligent, the most disinterested, the most generous, will always and certainly be corrupted by this profession." How could they avoid "contempt for the popular masses and the exaggeration of their own merit"? After all, hadn't they been selected on the basis of their superiority by others who conceded their own inferiority? It would be natural enough for a leader to conclude that "the people need me, they cannot do without my service . . . they must obey me for their own good." Who could resist this easy conclusion? Certainly not, say, Henry Kissinger, who famously remarked that he could not "see why we need to stand by and watch a country go communist due to the irresponsibility of its people," especially since "the issues are much too important for the Chilean voters to be left to decide for themselves."

Bakunin's arguments were a clever refutation of Rousseau and the social contract theory of government. He demonstrated nicely that claims about the necessity of government were "essentially founded on the principle of authority" and were circular arguments that assumed what had to be proved: that "the people" were "more or less ignorant, immature, incompetent, incapable," little more than *canaille,* or rabble. It was true, he conceded, that "the most imperfect republic is a thousand times better than the most enlightened monarchy." While the people remained economically exploited in a republic, there were at least "brief moments" when they were not politically oppressed. In addition, republics gave citizens some slight experience in public life and political action, and this was useful as rudimentary training in governing themselves. Nonetheless, any form of government, even a republic, that was based on the "hereditary inequality of occupations, wealth, education, and rights, [and was] divided into different classes" remained a state of exclusion that maintained the "inevitable exploitation of the majority by the minority." In fact, "the state was nothing other than regulated and systematized domination and exploitation."

Then and now, some suggest that education is the way to end poverty. Retool, relearn, adapt, work smarter not harder, take up lifelong learning—the buzzwords go on and on. Auto plant shut down? Learn computer programming! Has technological change done away with your job in the sawmill? Become an eco-guide! Is housecleaning or food serving poorly paid? Upgrade to become an entrepreneur! But poverty was systemic, not arbitrary, Bakunin reminded his readers. It was the result of exploitation, not lack of schooling. Ignorance did not cause poverty: poverty caused ignorance. "Improve working conditions, return to labor what justice demands it be given, and in this way give the people security, affluence, and leisure. Then have no doubt, they will educate themselves. They will toss aside all your catechisms and create a more generous, sane, and elevated civilization than yours."

The argument that economic growth, deregulation, and free trade lead to more prosperity for workers was also pretty stale by 1867. Bakunin granted that "free trade and commerce is certainly a very great thing and one of the essential foundations of the future international alliance of all the people of the world." The problem with it, as it is with globalization today, is that capitalist free trade was designed to enrich "a very small portion of the bourgeoisie to the detriment of the immense majority of the population." It was nothing more than the exploitation of workers on a worldwide level as opposed to a local or national level. As long as the "present states exist and labor continues to be the serf of property and capital, this freedom" will only increase the "misery, the grievances, and the righteous indignation of the masses of workers." For proof, one had only to look at the nations of England, France, and Germany. These were the most industrially developed nations and industry there had a freer hand than elsewhere. Yet they were also where the "gulf between the capitalists and the owners, on one side, and the working classes, on the other, appears to have widened to an extent unknown in other countries." In less developed countries, where more people lived on the land, famine was largely unknown, save in catastrophes, and these, then and now, were often caused by capitalist agriculture that exported food for profit while people starved. We might recall that during the Irish famine of the 1840s, Ireland was a net exporter of food. In the "developed" countries, starvation was common because unemployed workers, unlike peasants, could not feed themselves, and because employers, unlike lords or masters, had no responsibility to care for those who could not work. Thus in "the economic state that prevails today . . . the freedom and development of commerce and industry, the marvelous applications of science to production, the machines designed to emancipate the workers and reduce human labor, all these inventions, all this progress . . . far from improving the situation of the working classes only makes it worse and renders it even more intolerable." As Bakunin observed in 1867, the system is rigged for capitalists, not for workers. All its freedoms and technologies are not designed to give all of us a better standard of living and more leisure time; they are designed to increase profits. For the record, while productivity has doubled in North America since 1970, unemployment has gone up while real wages have gone down. Those workers who have jobs are working longer hours; the eight-hour day, first fought for in 1886, is vanishing, and more years are added to working life as retirement is pushed farther and farther into the future. Instead of providing jobs, the United States leads the world in prison populations, with over two million people incarcerated. The trends are perhaps most pronounced in the U.S., but they are worldwide and spreading as more and more people are kicked off the land and out of villages to become an urban proletariat, as the process of globalization finishes what capital began with the Industrial Revolution.[4]

At the time Bakunin wrote, however, it looked to most observers as though the United States would escape the terrible price European workers paid for industrialization and free trade. He noted that American workers were generally paid more than those in Europe and "class antagonism" was much less pronounced; education was more widespread and more citizens participated more fully in the body politic. This idea of American "exceptionalism," that the U.S. was qualitatively and essentially different from Europe and immune to the forces that wracked and shaped that continent, is an old one that still seems to resonate today. In 1630, the Puritan John Winthrop insisted that he and his fellow immigrants would create a "city upon a hill," and the idea of America as uniquely fitted to lead the world into freedom is still popular today, at least in America. In "Federalism, Socialism, and Antitheologism," Bakunin anticipated many of the explanations for this "exceptionalism." America had two advantages over Europe, he argued. The European settlers were free in America. There was little government save what they created. With no "obsessions from the past," they could "create a new world: a world of liberty. And liberty is a great magician, endowed with a productivity so marvelous that inspired by it alone, North America has, in less than a century ... surpassed the civilization of Europe." But Bakunin was too much of a materialist to ascribe American prosperity only to ideas. He pointed out that while it was the material fact of freedom, the absence of government, that attracted immigrants to America in the first place, even more important was the reality of the "immense quantity of fertile land" that America offered. That too attracted immigrants and created prosperity even for workers, for it gave them a choice they did not have in Europe. If they could not find work or their wages were unsatisfactory, they could move "to the far west" to take up farming. "This possibility remains open to all the workers of America and naturally keeps wages higher and gives each an independence unknown in Europe"; as long as capital had to compete with free land, wages would be high. Those high wages in turn explained why class conflict was muted in America. The simple fact was that workers were paid better because they had an alternative to wage work. Bakunin neatly anticipated two important arguments about American exceptionalism: the frontier thesis Frederick Jackson Taylor put forward in 1893, and Werner Sombart's 1906 observation that there was no socialism in America because class consciousness foundered on the "shoals of roast beef and apple pie."

Yet America was not, Bakunin suggested, as exceptional as it thought. The higher price of labor meant industrialists received higher prices for their goods, and that made their products less competitive with those made in Europe. American manufacturers then sought protectionist tariffs to keep out cheaper imports, but that created industries that were artificially propped up by the state. Tariffs also hurt the southern states, which had no industrial base and were forced to pay higher prices for manufactured goods. That in turn fueled their drive for secession and turned many into internal migrants who had to head into the industrial centers to seek work. There they encountered conditions more like those of Europe than not: poverty, overcrowding, unemployment, and hunger. Despite its very great advantages, Bakunin noted, the "social question" was now being posed in America itself. If America was different, it was no exception to the general course of capitalist development, and "we are forced to recognize that in our modern world, no less than in the ancient world, the civilization of a minority is, for all that, still founded on the forced labor and the relative barbarism of the majority."

But capitalists work too! We are always being treated to stories of the long hours the boss puts in, of how hard it is at the top, of how CEOs ruefully wish the eight-hour day applied to their jobs. Yes, Bakunin conceded, the "privileged class is no stranger to work" and it is hard work indeed to "remain at the top of the present order and to know how to profit from and keep their privileges." But "there is this difference between the work of the comfortable classes and that of the working classes. The former is rewarded in an infinitely larger proportion than the latter. And it is given leisure, the supreme condition for human moral and intellectual development, a condition that is never achieved by the working classes." Furthermore, the kind of work each class did was very different. The work of the capitalist involved "imagination, memory, and thought," while the work of "millions of proletarians" was usually physically and mentally stunting. Nor was the wealth and leisure of the privileged classes a reward for intelligence, thrift, ability, or hard work. It was the result of a social structure that reproduced itself and rewarded the accident of birth. That was the insight of class: to show that the world order was not arbitrary or a question of individual merit. It was an economic system that rewarded those few who had control over the means of production, whether that was land, factories, mines, or mills, and with that control could compel others to work for them. Their ownership was not a right but a privilege, one stolen from humanity and protected by the laws, courts, police, and armies of the state. The result was that the "privileged class" received all the benefits produced by society: the "riches, the luxury, the comfort, the well-being, the tranquility of family life, the exclusive political liberty to exploit the labor of millions of workers and to govern them in their own manner and in their own interest." But increasingly, workers rejected the notion that the world had to be as it was. They shook off the "fog of religion" and saw the "abyss" between the classes more clearly. Inspired by historical examples of revolution, increasingly workers developed their own gospel, one that was "not mystical, but rational, not celestial, but terrestrial, not divine, but human: the gospel of the rights of man." Increasingly they asked if perhaps workers too were entitled to the rights of "equality, liberty, and humanity." It was obvious to the masses that these abstract rights were themselves based on material well-being and a respite from work, on "bread" and "leisure" in Bakunin's words, or, to use the slogan of the 1912 Lawrence, Massachusetts, strike, on bread and roses. To obtain these required the "radical transformation of present society," and that, for Bakunin, meant socialism.

Not, however, the technocratic socialism of Fourier or Saint-Simon, Blanc, or Cabet, he clarified. While they had contributed powerful critiques of existing society, the "doctrinaire socialism" that arose before 1848 was "more or less authoritarian," based on the "passion to indoctrinate and organize the future." There was one exception: Proudhon. Unlike the others, he was "the son of a peasant and thus in fact and instinct a hundred times more revolutionary than all the authoritarian and doctrinaire socialists." Proudhon "armed himself with a critique as profound and penetrating as it was relentless" and used it to "destroy their systems." "Opposing liberty to authority," Proudhon distinguished himself from the "state socialists" by calling himself an anarchist, and insisted on individual as well as collective freedom. The "voluntary action of free associations" would replace government regulation and the protection of the state; anarchism would subordinate "politics to the economic, intellectual, and moral interests of society," Bakunin argued.

But hadn't 1848 put paid to these ideas of socialism? Hadn't they been tried and found wanting? This would also be the refrain of later generations of cold warriors. Didn't the tyranny and eventual collapse of the Soviet Union prove that socialism was the god that failed? Bakunin would say no. The events of 1848 demonstrated that republicanism and liberalism were more closely allied with reaction and privilege than with socialism. That year demonstrated that despite its talk about freedom, when the bourgeoisie was "terrified of the red phantom" it would choose a military regime over the "menacing dangers of a popular emancipation." Socialism did not lose an even contest of ideas in 1848; it was smashed by all the power the state and capital could muster. More precisely, Bakunin argued, what lost in 1848 was not "socialism in general," but "state socialism, authoritarian, regimented socialism," the belief that the state could somehow be used to satisfy the "needs and legitimate aspirations of the working classes." The social revolution, the people, had given the state the power to overthrow the old regimes, but instead of recognizing the bill that was owed, the state "proclaimed that it was incapable of paying the debt" and tried instead to kill its creditor. What it had killed, however, was not socialism, but faith in the state, and in the brands of socialism that depended on the state.

It was true that socialism "had lost this first battle." It had lost for a simple reason. While it was "rich in instinct and negative theoretical ideas," it "absolutely lacked the positive and practical ideas that were necessary to build a new system on the ruins of the bourgeois system." The workers who fought for freedom on the barricades were "united by instinct, not ideas; and the confused ideas they did have created a tower of Babel, a chaos that could leave nothing." This passage is an important one, for it indicates that Bakunin did not believe that instinct or moral outrage or passion were enough to build a movement. They were a necessary condition, he would always insist, but not a sufficient one. The lack of ideas had been the cause of defeat, but was it possible from that to conclude that socialism had no future? Hardly. After all, Bakunin pointed out, Christianity had taken several centuries to triumph. Socialism had posed itself a much more difficult task than the church had: "the reign of justice on earth." Surely we might expect that to take a few years.

In the meantime, the reports of the death of socialism were highly exaggerated. Indeed, behind all the diplomatic maneuvering and saber-rattling of governments, it was "the social question" that demanded answering. The question was posed by the people themselves as they built "workers' cooperative associations, mutual aid banks, labor banks, these trade unions and that international league of workers of all countries." It was obvious in the "growing movement of workers in England, in France, in Belgium, and Germany, in Italy, and in Switzerland." All this surely proved that workers had not "renounced their goal or lost faith in their coming emancipation." Their autonomous free associations further demonstrated that they now understood they could not "count on the states or the largely hypocritical aid of the privileged classes." Instead they had to depend on "themselves and their independent, completely voluntary associations."⁵

The struggles of workers had won some reforms in England; they were forcing Napoleon III to the bargaining table; even Bismarck had to design a rudimentary welfare state to consolidate his power. If socialism had been defeated on the streets in 1848, now it was underground and spreading everywhere. Even people "who do not know the word socialism are today socialists," for they "know no other flag but that which announces their economic emancipation." Only through socialism could they be won over to politics, to "good politics." And the reality of modern capitalism was pushing some of the petit bourgeoisie into the working class and making socialism attractive, as "big business, big industry, and especially big and dishonest speculation devoured them and pushed them into the abyss."

From this wide-ranging argument that brought together his ideas on religion, socialism, the state, and class, Bakunin reiterated his political position for the League of Peace and Freedom. The League did not have to declare for "this or that socialist system." But peace depended on everyone having "the material and moral means to develop their full humanity." That in turn meant it was necessary

> to organize society in such a way that every individual, man and woman . . . finds the more or less equal means to develop their different faculties and utilize their labor and to organize a society in which the exploitation of labor is impossible. Social wealth is produced by labor, and no one will share in it unless they have contributed to its production.

He then gave what remains perhaps the best brief description of anarchism: "Liberty without socialism is privilege and injustice; socialism without liberty is slavery and brutality."

The League of Peace and Freedom was not prepared to become a revolutionary society. In truth, it had about run its course anyway. Its 1868 congress attracted only a hundred or so delegates and few were disposed to adopt Bakunin's resolutions. The congress did give him the opportunity to express more clearly what he meant by the socialism he had outlined in "Federalism, Socialism, and Antitheologism" and made clear the break between anarchism and state socialism, or, as he put it, between "collectivism" and "communism." While he believed that property should be owned socially, not individually, that is, by all members of society and not by a privileged few, he agreed with Proudhon that it should not be owned and controlled by the state in the name of the people. In language reminiscent of his differences with Weitling, Bakunin made it plain that

> I detest communism because it is the negation of liberty. I cannot conceive of humanity without liberty. I am not a communist because communism concentrates and absorbs all the powers of society in the state; it necessarily ends with the concentration of property in the hands of the state. I, on the other hand, want the abolition of the state, the radical elimination of the principle of authority and tutelage of the state. Under the pretext of making men moral and civilized, the state has enslaved, oppressed, exploited, and corrupted them. I want the organization of society and collective, social property by free association from the bottom up, not by authority from the top down.[6]

Having made his statement, there was little else to do at the congress. When it ended, convinced that it could play no role in securing liberty, peace, or socialism, Bakunin resigned from the League. He would instead devote his considerable energies to the International Working Men's Association, whose most prominent spokesman was Karl Marx, and to the creation of his own secret societies.

Secret societies? Surely plots, intrigue, and iron discipline are inconsistent with open democracy and anarchism. Clearly the failure of the Soviet Union has discredited the notion of the tightly organized vanguard party operating in the name of the working class. Bakunin's liberal critics have long insisted that his secret societies are a sordid fact that contradict his lofty theories and prove that anarchism was but a disguise for his ruthless ambition, self-aggrandizement, and his mad desire to plunge the world into terror and chaos. After all, didn't Mussolini remark somewhere that an anarchist was simply a fascist who hadn't figured out how to take power? For that matter, Mussolini's father was a Bakuninist, and Il Duce himself went through a brief anarchist phase. Marxist critics have argued variously that Bakunin's secret societies meant he was the forerunner of the Leninist vanguard "party of the new type" and so to be welcomed, cautiously, aboard the Bolshevik ship of state, or that he was a Blanquist conspirator who sought to substitute the putsch for mass movements and the social revolution. Anarchists have often been placed in the uncomfortable position of denying the existence of such societies, none more awkwardly than one of Bakunin's most devoted colleagues, James Guillaume, who denied that there were any Bakuninist secret organizations while he was revealed as belonging to one. There is, however, rather more—and rather less—to Bakunin's secret societies than his critics have insisted or his supporters have feared.

There is no doubt that Bakunin founded a number of societies and organizations, some public and some private. The real question that needs to be examined, however, is not whether such organizations existed but what the context was and what their purposes were. It is, after all, one thing to create a radical book club that one invites only friends to join and quite another to form a conspiracy to install oneself as supreme world leader for life. At the same time, when reading radical literature is illegal, organizing *sub rosa* for innocent ends may be prudent and necessary even though it is technically a crime, while one can hardly be surprised that revolutionaries may, as Marx put it in the Communist Manifesto, carry on a "now hidden, now open fight" as circumstance permits.

Precautions made some sense in this period. The Polish and Russian movements had been infiltrated by spies and smashed before the people could respond; one logical answer was to go underground and organize secretly. Throughout Europe, unions, still illegal even in Britain in the 1860s, were often organized as secret societies to avoid fines, arrest, and imprisonment. In North America, the Knights of Labor, formed in 1869, used elaborate passwords, secret signs, and rituals to protect the order. Fearsome oaths, complicated rituals, and coded language made it more difficult for spies to worm their way in and bound members together with shared knowledge, creating solidarity that could not be forged openly and overtly without drastic reprisals. Italy had a rich tradition of organizing underground for political purposes. Mazzini, for example, had belonged to the Carbonari, a secret society organized in the Abruzzi and Calabria to fight against the power of the Catholic Church and kings, with rituals based on the trade of charcoal makers. Rooted out by the authorities, the Carbonari were no longer a force after 1830, but many of its dispersed members formed other secret societies organized on similar lines. Mazzini created Young Italy and welcomed Garibaldi into its ranks as they fought against Austrian control of the Italian peninsula. Others joined the Freemasons, which granted Carbonari alumni instant membership. Secrecy in itself is not necessarily a reason to condemn a movement or a personality.

At the same time, several of Bakunin's so-called secret societies existed only on paper, as a convenient format for the expression of his political ideas. Instead of crafting a formal essay with a thematic introduction, he would often give his notes a title like "The Secret Statutes of the International Fraternity of Revolutionaries," even when no such organization existed, and then launch into a brilliant discourse on the nature of liberty and justice. On other occasions, Bakunin would, like the Utopian socialists such as Cabet and Saint-Simon, find some pleasure in designing "ideal societies," though in his case, these were designs, rituals, and rules for revolutionary organizations, again usually for societies that did not exist. These complicated schematics were irrelevant, best understood as a sort of hobby. In practice, the revolutionary groups Bakunin belonged to functioned not as secret conspiracies but like the Russian circles and present-day affinity groups, with like-minded individuals coming together, sometimes around social activities, sometimes around particular books, to discuss and debate, to plan and to organize political activity. These circles gave Bakunin meaningful opportunities to develop his political ideas and produce articles, pamphlets, and the like. Furthermore, the circles attracted and educated a number of workers, journalists, students, and political activists, and if these were measured by the scores rather than the thousands, many continued to play important roles in the revolutionary and labor movements of the nineteenth and early twentieth centuries, especially in Italy, Spain, and France.

But what of Bakunin's insistence in the "Revolutionary Catechism" and elsewhere that members of the secret society "must be subject to rigorous discipline"? Anarchism surely implies, even insists, that discipline is an absolute contradiction of the ideals of freedom and equality. Some commentators have gone even further, to insist that such phrases prove that Bakunin was either a proto-fascist or a proto-Leninist, or both simultaneously. Yet a careful reading of what Bakunin actually wrote makes it plain that his arguments about discipline are much more complicated and thoughtful than his critics have suggested. They represent his attempt to work out the practical political problem of how to make an organization both democratic and able to act decisively. In prisons, armies, criminal gangs, governments, and corporations, the problem of democracy seldom arises: you simply obey or suffer punishment. But organizations and societies that wish to hear and incorporate the ideas of their members need to find some balance between free and open discussion and resolution and action. All democratic governments invoke the principle of cabinet solidarity: once a decision has been made, individual members must support the decision or resign. Similarly Bakunin held that a secret society, one pledged to revolutionary action and thus liable to arrest and worse, needed discipline "in the interest of the cause it serves, as well as of effective action and the security of each of its members."

But surely anarchists must be held to higher moral standards than presidents and prime ministers. Bakunin agreed. The "rigorous discipline" of the anarchist, he continued in the "Revolutionary Catechism," "amounts to nothing more or less than the expression and direct outcome of the reciprocal commitment contracted by each of its members toward the other." He put it even more plainly: the "master" of the society was not any individual but the "laws," principles, and decisions "which we have all helped to create or at any rate equally approved by our free consent." Furthermore, he insisted that while different members had different abilities and might make different contributions to the society, whether these were ideas, funds, or influence, none of these were grounds for authority, privilege, or power. Indeed, any appeals to past service or present contributions were "motives for distrust," symptoms of the old world and its habits of obedience and conformity, and potential threats to the freedom of the individuals and the society. "Rigorous discipline" was the free choice to belong to and participate in the society, to obey those decisions one freely participated in and agreed to, and the duty to reject authoritarianism and privilege within the society.

For those who argue that anarchism can mean only the complete absence of guidelines and formal procedures, it might be noted that such an absence does not guarantee democracy in an organization. Without acknowledged and accepted methods for discussion and debate, the result is less likely to be freedom and equality than control by a clique that is virtually inaccessible because its decisions are not accountable or open. It may be argued, for example, that insisting on quorum and a scheduled meeting day are infringements on personal liberty, but without them, the group runs the risk of having a self-appointed faction determine policy with the mass membership *in absentia*.

Yet however we may parse and explain Bakunin, we are left with passages in his writing that suggest he believed not in democratic, social revolutions of the masses but in secret conspiracies, putsches, and coups made by small bands of revolutionaries organized in shadowy, elite vanguards. In 1868, for example, he wrote that the creation of a "secret universal association" was necessary "for the triumph of the revolution." Organized properly as the International Brotherhood, "a hundred powerfully and seriously allied revolutionaries are enough for the international organization of the whole of Europe." In 1870, he again called for the "creation of a secret organization," of perhaps ten and no more than seventy members, to aid the revolution in Russia and form the "collective dictatorship of the secret organization." This organization would "direct the people's revolution" through "an invisible force—recognized by no one, imposed by no one—through which the collective dictatorship of our organization will be all the mightier, the more it remains invisible and unacknowledged, the more it remains without any official legality and significance." That same year, he wrote to a friend, Albert Richard, "we must be the invisible pilots guiding the revolution, not by any kind of overt power but by the collective dictatorship of all our allies . . . all the more powerful as it does not carry the trappings of power." These and similar phrases are chilling in their calculated cynicism. They sound completely contrary to Bakunin's arguments on liberty and equality, community, and democracy, and this sharp contrast has convinced many that these stark pronouncements are the real, dark, covert key to Bakunin's thought and authoritarian designs.[7]

Such an interpretation, however, can be made only if the quotes are ripped out of context and served up on a platitude. Bakunin's 1868 call for a secret, universal association was prefaced by his insistence that such a society "rules out any idea of dictatorship and custodial control." Anarchists were the "natural enemies of these revolutionaries—future dictators, regimenters, and custodians of revolution" who feared the honest, if disorderly, aspirations of the people and were "longing to create new revolutionary states just as centralist and despotic as those we already know." In contrast to the top-down model of revolution, Bakunin held that

> revolutions are never made by individuals or even secret societies. They make themselves, produced by the force of affairs, by the movement of events and facts. They are prepared in the depth of the instinctive consciousness of the masses—then they burst out, instigated by what often appear to be frivolous causes. All that a secret, well-organized society can do is to help at the birth of a revolution by spreading the ideas that correspond to the instincts of the masses and to organize not the revolutionary army—the army must always be the people—but a sort of revolutionary general staff composed of individuals who are devoted, energetic, intelligent, and most impor-

tant, sincere and lacking ambition and vanity, capable of serving as intermediaries between the revolutionary idea and popular instinct.[8]

While the notion of a "revolutionary general staff" is not without significant problems for any anarchist, it is clear from the context that it was to serve only as an "organ in the midst of the popular anarchy" to unite "revolutionary thought and action," rather than an order-giving vanguard, its function restricted to articulating the demands the masses themselves made and exhorting them to refuse to surrender their autonomy.

Bakunin's 1870 call for a "collective dictatorship" was more carefully described in surrounding passages as a "popular auxiliary force" and a "practical school of moral education for all its members." It was to serve as "an organizer of the people's power, not its own, a middleman between popular instinct and revolutionary thought." To attempt to dictate or control the revolution, "to strive to foist on the people your own thoughts—foreign to its instinct—implies a wish to make it subservient to a new state," he warned. "A revolutionary idea," he continued, "is revolutionary, vital, real, and true, only because it expresses and only as far as it represents popular instincts which are the result of history." He explicitly denied the utility, "or even the possibility, of any revolution except a spontaneous or a people's social revolution. I am deeply convinced that any other revolution is dishonest, harmful, and spells death to liberty and the people." Not only was it wrong, Bakunin added, it was also impossible, for the modern state had such power that "all contrived secret conspiracies and non-popular attempts, sudden attacks, surprises, and coups are bound to be shattered against it." Therefore, "the sole aim of a secret society must be, not the creation of an artificial power outside the people, but the rousing, uniting, and organizing of the spontaneous power of the people."

In his letter to Richard, Bakunin was likewise unambiguous. The secret dictatorship, "the only dictatorship I will accept," would not attempt to seize power. It would instead oppose the efforts of "the political revolutionaries, the believers of overt dictatorship," who would call for "order, trust, and submission to the established revolutionary power" and would, ostensibly for "the good of all," install "dictatorship, government, the state." He warned Richard unequivocally against those who would seek to make themselves the "Dantons, Robespierres, Saint-Justs of revolutionary socialism" and would use the masses as a "stepping-stone" for their own glory. Such revolutionaries, Bakunin cautioned, not only "served reaction; they would themselves be reaction." In contrast, Bakunin's revolutionary society would exist not to dominate or control the masses but to prevent them from being co-opted by others. It would not take or exercise power; it would only encourage the people to trust their passions and instincts and resist the attempts of politicos to channel the social revolution into a mere political revolution. For if the revolution of the people led to the "triumph of individuals," the result would not be socialism, but "politics, the concern of the bourgeoisie, and the socialist movement will perish."

In another letter, Bakunin elaborated further on his vision of the role of the secret society. Such a society does not "foist upon the people any new regulations, orders, style of life," he wrote, "but merely unleashes its will and gives wide scope to its self-determination and its economic and social organization, which must be created by itself from below and not from above." The band of revolutionaries he envisioned was to provide inspiration, not directives, in the swirling chaos of a revolutionary uprising, working as the "servant and a helper, but never the commander of the people, never under any pretext its manager, not even under the pretext of the people's welfare." Far from dominating the people or taking the reins of state, Bakunin envisioned the revolutionary organization helping "the people achieve self-determination on a basis of complete and comprehensive human liberty, without the slightest interference from even temporary or transitional power, that is, without any mediation of the state."[9] With no power other than the power of moral suasion, without recourse to the coercive force of the state, Bakunin's revolutionary societies can hardly be called "dictatorships"; his insistence that the people, not individuals or parties, made social revolutions demonstrates plainly he actively opposed the coup and putsch.

What his writings on secret societies do show is his belief that education, rational thought, and sincere discussion were necessary to combine thought and action, theory and practice. What made his formulation different was his insistence that the intellectual should play the junior role in this process, acting, at best, as helpful editor while the writing of the script was the work of the people themselves. Why was such a role even necessary? Bakunin sketched an answer to that question in a later article. What would happen if you, convinced that workers understood that the present system did not and could not satisfy their desire for the good life, showed up at the factory gate or office tower and started talking about abolishing God, capital, and the state? If you made such a proclamation to

> the unlearned workers, crushed by their daily labor, workers who
> are demoralized and corrupted, by design, one might say, by the per-

verse doctrines liberally dispensed by governments in concert with every privileged caste—the priests, the nobility, the bourgeoisie—then you will alarm the workers. They may resist you without suspecting that these ideas are only the most faithful expression of their own interests, that these goals carry in themselves the realization of their dearest wishes, and that the religious and political prejudices in the name of which they may resist these ideas and goals are on the contrary the direct cause of their continued slavery and poverty.

Bakunin too understood that rulers, whether they were kings, lords, prime ministers, or capitalists, put a great deal of effort into creating and maintaining "the prejudices of the masses." But "the masses' prejudices are based only on their ignorance and totally oppose their very interests, while the bourgeoisie's are based precisely on its class interests . . . The people want but do not know; the bourgeoisie knows, but does not want. Which of the two is incurable? The bourgeoisie, to be sure." The "great mass of workers," he continued, were "exhausted by their daily labor" and so were "poor and unlearned." Yet they, despite the

> political and religious prejudices implanted in their mind, are social-
> ist without knowing it; their most basic instinct and their social
> situation makes them more earnestly and truly socialist than all the
> scientific and bourgeois socialists taken together. They are socialist
> because of all the conditions of their material existence and all the
> needs of their being, whereas others are socialist only by virtue of
> their intellectual needs. And in real life the needs of the being are
> always stronger than those of the intellect, since the intellect is never
> the source of being but is always and everywhere its expression,
> reflecting its successive development.

In this we see Bakunin's attempt to find a synthesis that gave sufficient weight both to material conditions and class experience and to reflective thought and more general knowledge. He acknowledged that "the people" were not always right in their views and ideas, but understood that unlike the intellectual, their ideas sprang directly from their experience. Bakunin argued that the role of the revolutionary was to appreciate the anger and frustration that led to prejudice and attempt to show the real causes. For "workers lack neither the potential for socialist aspirations nor their actuality; they lack only socialist thought." They did have the "germ" of such thought, since they could only "be emancipated by the overthrow of all things now existing; either injustice would be destroyed or the working masses will be condemned to eternal slavery." How then should the revolutionary proceed? "Education and propaganda" were the obvious place to start, but "the isolated worker is too overwhelmed by his daily grind and his daily cares to have much time to devote to education." The question of who would educate them also posed a problem. While the "few sincere socialists who come from the bourgeoisie" and, we might add, the university, might be learned enough, they were too few. More importantly, they "do not adequately understand the workers' world because their situation puts them in a different world," and as a result "the workers rather legitimately distrust" them. The best teacher was experience, or, as Bakunin put it, "emancipation through practical action," through "workers' solidarity," through "trade unions, organization, and the federation of resistance funds," through the "progress of the collective struggle of the workers against the bosses." When the worker began "to fight, in association with his comrades, for the reduction of his working hours and for an increase in his salary . . . as soon as he begins to take an active part in this wholly material struggle," he will soon "abandon every preoccupation with heaven" and rely "on the collective strength of the workers."[10]

What Bakunin understood was that workers and peasants could only transform their lives through revolution, that the very conditions of their lives provided the inspiration for protest, and, as the vast majority of society, they had the strength to succeed. But he did not believe that they would spontaneously develop all the ideas and strategies necessary for success. That required reflection, discussion, and sometimes knowledge that went beyond the individual factory or commune. As he had suggested in "Romanov, Pugachev, or Pestel?" the revolutionary had some useful skills of information gathering and generalization that could draw conclusions from the particular and offer them to others. The secret societies could help perform that function. That he deemed such societies important indicates that Bakunin did not blithely assume political consciousness and revolutionary strategy were the direct, inevitable, unmediated results of oppression. Individual resistance might well be as natural as submission, but collective action required tactics and strategies, and they required thought as well as "instinct" and motivation. Collective action required that a militant minority educate, agitate, and organize without any notion of controlling the masses. To claim that Bakunin advocated the coup or putsch is to commit the intellectual sin he warned against, that of chopping and hacking at reality to make it fit preconceived theory. Those who continue to do so should give thanks that it is not possible to be sued for libeling the dead.

Despite, or, more accurately, because of, all the attention paid to the references to secret societies, the substantive ideas Bakunin developed in this period have largely been ignored. In the 1868 statutes for the International Brotherhood, for example, Bakunin elaborated a theory of materialist history and revolution. The aim of revolution was to change the "present order of things," an order that was founded on "property, exploitation, domination, and the principle of authority, be it religious, be it metaphysical and bourgeois doctrinarian, be it even revolutionary Jacobinism." Revolution, however, was not the same as a bloody uprising aimed only at destruction. On the contrary, Bakunin pointed out that the source of oppression was not individuals but "the organization of things" and the "social position" of oppressors. Therefore, violence was not the point of the revolution. It was instead a "disaster," and if the oppression of the masses made such a violent reaction inevitable, it was no more rational, moral, or useful than "the ravages caused by a storm." It was irrational because "the kings, the oppressors, the exploiters" were no more guilty or responsible than the "common criminals," no less the "involuntary products" of the social system, and so punishing them was no more moral than society's punishment of the petty thief. Each human being was the "involuntary product of the natural and social milieu in which he was born," and thus was less responsible for his actions than society as a whole; "the organization of society is always and everywhere the unique cause of the crimes committed by individuals." Nor was such violence moral, for no society, not even the revolutionary one, had the "right to judge and condemn," only the right to self-defense. Revolutionary violence was useless, and for that one had only to look at the French Revolution. To the degree the nobility was vanquished, it was not the result of the guillotine but of the confiscation of property. "Carnage" was less effective against the ruling class because its "power resides less in the individuals than in their positions," in "the organization of things," in "the institution of the state and its natural foundation, private property." For that reason, the aim of the revolution was not to kill individuals but to "attack positions and things," to do away with institutions, to "destroy property and the state." Thus there would be, he pressed, "no need to destroy human life" and provoke the "reaction" that massacres always created. If there was no need for it, he feared that it could well be a "natural, distressing, but inevitable fact." It was inevitable because "the oppressed, the suffering victims," were naturally filled with "hate" and it would not be surprising that the revolution would unleash their anger and give them opportunity to wreak vengeance on their oppressors. Franz Fanon would make a similar point in 1961 in his book *The Wretched of the Earth,* though unlike Bakunin, he would see such catharsis as a positive force. But "the whole secret of the revolution" was not violence against people but the destruction of "property and its inevitable corollary—the state." This distinguished the social revolutionary from the political revolutionaries who did not wish to abolish private property but only to confiscate it in the name of the state. To do so meant they had to capture and use the state, not against institutions in general, but only against those individuals they wished to displace. To take the power and property of the king, one does not abolish the right to rule or distribute property to the people; one simply takes the crown. That did not free the people. It simply led to "military dictatorship and a new master. Thus the triumph of the Jacobins or Blanquists would be the death of the Revolution."

In contrast, the social revolution meant "unchaining what today is called the 'evil passions' and the destruction of what is called in the same fashion 'public order.'" These passions were the passion for liberty and equality, while "public order" was nothing more than the violent suppression of the fight for freedom. Unlike the forces of "order," the social revolutionaries "do not fear anarchy; we invoke it," meaning by this not chaos but "revolutionary organization from the bottom up, not from the center to the circumference in authoritarian fashion." Bakunin then outlined some of the measures the revolution would take. It would abolish public and private debt, end taxes, and dissolve the army, the judiciary, the bureaucracy, and police. Capital and the machinery of production would be turned over to workers; the property of churches would be confiscated and dispersed. Revolutionary committees, democratically selected and recallable, would organize self-defense; and "revolutionary messengers," not "official revolutionary commissionaires with sashes of office," would be sent as envoys to win support in surrounding regions.

Bakunin's careful thoughts on the nature of revolution and organization were, however, overshadowed by his relationship with one of the most repellent characters of the nineteenth-century revolutionary movements. His active work with Sergei Nechaev took up only a few months of Bakunin's life, yet it would have immediate repercussions and would taint Bakunin and anarchism for generations to come.

12

THE REVOLUTIONARY IS A DOOMED MAN

Sergei Gennadievich Nechaev sorely tested Bakunin's belief that society, not individuals, should be held responsible for crimes and transgressions. Nechaev stole money and reputation from the anarchist, inadvertently aided Marx in purging him from the International Working Men's Association, and provided ample, if indiscriminate and inaccurate, munitions to the enemies of anarchism that they are still firing off today. Yet to the degree the historian seeks to provide explanation, not blame, it is useful to sketch the world that thrust up Nechaev.

Despite the best efforts of the secret police and the persuasive effect of prison and exile, revolutionary activity in Russia continued to grow after Young Russia and Land and Liberty had been smashed. Peasants, though formally free, were little better off after emancipation, and if they were largely unable to organize across communes and regions, they still presented a threat to the stability of the regime. Students continued to organize in the face of harsh repression. Confronted with the failure of reform and the impossibility of open political work, convinced that whatever their instincts might be, peasants and workers were not prepared to join the revolution, many radicals concluded that new methods were needed. Some formed cooperatives; others became teachers, hoping to influence the next generation. Still others concluded that tightly disciplined cells were needed if the resistance were to continue, and they went underground to create secret groups very different from the relatively open circles of Herzen's and Bakunin's day. Around 1866, a small number of students, most of them the sons of priests, had coalesced around an informal but secret society named the Organization. Headed by Nicholas Ishutin, the Organization held that reform was dangerous, for it co-opted the revolution; constitutions and parliaments would only speed up the introduction of capitalism. If capitalism meant liberty and wealth for the nobility and merchant class, it would do nothing for peasants save turn them into factory hands and destroy their forms of collective property on which socialism could be based. Members of the Organization took up political propaganda in the provinces and in Moscow and St. Petersburg.

If Bakunin agreed with the Russian radicals on the need for revolution rather than reform, he had long distanced himself from their revolutionary Jacobinism and consistently argued that revolutionaries must not separate themselves from the people. The Organization paid lip service to that ideal, but in practice it functioned as a small sect whose members increasingly spoke only to themselves. In the fetid atmosphere of the underground, an even smaller group split off and abandoned most connections to their earlier lives. Deploring the relatively comfortable existence of student life, they toughened themselves for the coming conflict through a rigid asceticism, to the point of sleeping on hard floors and eating a highly restricted diet. Calling their group Hell, they insisted that the revolutionary could not be bound by any ethics or morality apart from dedicated opposition to the Russian regime. That opposition increasingly took one form: terrorism. Where Bakunin insisted that the revolution sought to destroy institutions, not individuals, the members of Hell talked openly of assassination. On 4 April 1866, Ishutin's cousin, Dimitri Karakozov, did more than talk. Dressed as a peasant and armed with a cheap revolver, he entered the Summer Gardens in St. Petersburg and fired at Alexander II. His shots went astray, and Karakozov was arrested and hanged five months later. As Bakunin had predicted in "The People's Cause: Romanov, Pugachev, or Pestel?" the peasantry rallied around the tsar. Alexander's advisors turned the failed assassination into a public relations coup, claiming that a real peasant had risked his life to grab Karakozov and cause him to miss the target. The story was a complete fabrication, but it was a successful, cynical move. It won the regime some support for its crackdown on radicals and reformers in the "White Terror" headed by the minister of the interior, yet another Muraviev, known as the "Hangman of Vilna" for his bloody repression of the Polish revolt. Thus could Bakunin claim to be the kin of both Muraviev the Hanged, a reference to his Decembrist cousin, and Muraviev the Hanger. Once again newspapers were shut down, the universities placed under stricter surveillance, and those who looked suspicious, including women with short hair, watched carefully. Dozens of radicals were arrested, including Ishutin, who spent several years in prison before dying in exile in Siberia in 1879.

Bakunin agreed with Herzen that the assassination attempt would generate nothing except a wave of public and peasant support for the tsar. Unlike Herzen, however, he refused to attack Karakozov in print, insisting that he would "not throw a stone" at him. To criticize Karakozov's personal motives was to give tacit support to the regime, he argued.[1] Bakunin continued to support the student revolutionaries, and by 1868 a small number made their

way to Switzerland. Together with Bakunin they put out a new Russian journal, *The People's Cause,* in time for a new wave of student unrest. Though
Bakunin worked with them and found much to admire, he was not uncritical of the new student movement. In particular, he was critical of its tendency
toward elitism. Increasingly the new generations of student radicals believed
it was their duty to make the revolution themselves. If populism, socialism,
and anarchism were the ideologies of Bakunin's generation, the students of
the late 1860s were more inclined to nihilism.

Nihilism! The belief in nothing! The amoral, destructive assault on all
beliefs, ideals, and morality! Complete anarchy, plus apathy! The nineteenth-
century equivalent to rock 'n' roll, or heavy metal, or hip-hop! Well, no.
Russian nihilism was very different from the meaning usually ascribed to the
word today. Today it is often used to describe a lack of belief of any kind,
an existential notion of meaninglessness, and thus a moral skepticism, even
amoralism, as summed up in the Coen brothers' movie *The Big Lebowski.*
When the Dude, played by Jeff Bridges, is threatened by self-proclaimed
nihilists, his friend Walter Sobchak, played by John Goodman, exclaims,
"Nihilists! Fuck me. I mean, say what you like about the tenets of National
Socialism, Dude, at least it's an ethos."

Strictly speaking, nihilism refers to an ethos of a Russian intellectual movement in the 1860s. Nihilists were not surrealists or existentialists or insouciant
hipsters. Nihilism was an insistence that one should not believe in anything
that could not be demonstrated to be true. In its essence, it was a critical
approach to virtually everything. It was uninterested in debating art or beauty,
preferring the harsh reality of empirical knowledge to the feeble efforts of
romanticism, sentimentality, or philosophy. More than anything else, nihilism
was a form of literary and political criticism based on a broad definition of
science. In this sense, the nihilist movement had evolved to the position
Bakunin held in 1842, that criticism and destruction were needed before
building could begin. Chernyshevsky gave nihilists literary models in *What Is
To Be Done?* while Turgenev tried to parody the movement with the character of Bazarov in his novel *Fathers and Sons.* To the horror of Turgenev's
generation, one young writer, Dimitri Pisarev, quickly adopted the term and
the characterization of Turgenev's nihilist. He stressed that the fundamental
role of the young intellectual was to criticize and corrode, to assert a fierce,
negative realism that confronted ideas, tradition, and accepted wisdom. In
that, nihilism had much in common with the Bakunin who had insisted that
the passion for destruction was a creative passion. But Bakunin had at the
same time contended that workers and peasants could be, in fact had to be,

revolutionary agents. The nihilists had no such belief in the masses. Their movement reflected the failure of revolution, of political organization, and of the Russian state, and it represented a retreat away from the people to the insulated hothouse and coffeehouse of the academy, resulting in what Abbott Gleason has labeled "bitter militancy, ironic superiority, and general extremism." Like the vulgar postmodernism that superficially resembles nihilism, especially if we replace "general extremism" with "banal liberalism," it had more than a tinge of elitism to it. The "real" revolutionary was the one who rejected the sophistry and deception of tradition, hegemony, and faith. In this rejection, however, nihilism too often also rejected the possibility of real political struggle. If Bakunin agreed in principle with the importance of criticism, he also understood that the first job of the radical was to bring people together in collective action, not to tell them they were idiots. But the self-referential world of the nihilist did not see organizing others as the primary task. Individual emancipation, the freeing of the self from false ideas, and ruthless condemnation applied to all without favor were the guiding principles. This critical realism could be applied as easily to the peasantry as to the tsar, and in a philosophy that stressed individual revolt and the enlightened minority, there was no more of a role for workers and peasants than there was for anyone else who had not seen the light.[2]

Thus the logical politics for the nihilist was less anarchism than it was Jacobinism. Such at least was the conclusion of one young radical, Peter Tkachev, who as much as anyone gave the movement a coherent political expression. Born in 1844 into the lower gentry, he had been involved in the student demonstrations of the early 1860s, knew Ishutin and his organization, and wrote for several radical newspapers. By 1867, he had been arrested several times for revolutionary activity. For him, the logical outcome of economic materialism, the backwardness of the Russian peasantry, the overwhelming power of the Russian state, and the invigorated spirit of the small fraction of radical students, was the vanguard party that would pull the masses into the new world. The revolutionary had to "impart a considered and rational form to the struggle, leading it toward determined ends, directing this coarse material element toward ideal principles." It was far from Bakunin's description of the relationship of the revolutionary to the people and represented a very different political tradition, one founded as much in intellectual elitism and isolation as repression and state violence.[3]

There was more to Tkachev's philosophy than that, of course. But the emphasis on conspiracy was enough to attract one young Russian radical, Sergei Nechaev. In the course of his career, Nechaev insisted that the radical had the right and obligation to engage in any crime, any vice, any monstrous deed that might advance the cause. It was a foul doctrine that he applied in his daily life. He was, in words crafted for another political activist, "a no-good lying bastard. He can lie out of both sides of his mouth at the same time, and even if he caught himself telling the truth, he'd lie just to keep his hand in." The description was of Richard Nixon, made by Harry Truman, but it suits Nechaev nicely. He—Nechaev, that is—extorted and stole money from colleagues and people who had befriended him; he endangered comrades with his carelessness and his unscrupulous machinations; and he attempted to seduce Herzen's daughter solely to extract money from her. When one of the members of his Russian group, Ivan Ivanov, disagreed with his schemes, Nechaev accused him of being an agent of the Third Section and ordered the others to murder him; in the end, Nechaev himself strangled and shot the young man. Later it was revealed that he knew the man to be completely innocent and had made up the charge to rid himself of a competitor, to test the loyalty and squeamishness of his comrades, and to implicate them in a crime so he could more easily control them. When the body of Nechaev's victim was found, it triggered a police dragnet that caught up three hundred revolutionaries, many of whom were tried and sentenced for their role in the radical movement. In the meantime, Nechaev abandoned his comrades and slipped into Western Europe. Yet he managed to dupe many in the revolutionary movement for some time, and Bakunin was no better at ferreting him out than those he betrayed in Russia had been.

Nechaev was born in Ivanovo, sometimes called the "Russian Manchester," a textile mill town about 160 miles from Moscow. His grandparents had been serfs long since freed by the time Nechaev was born in 1847. His maternal grandparents owned a small painting business that often employed his father, and his mother worked as a seamstress. The family was by no means wealthy, but it could afford to give Nechaev a solid education. In 1865, he moved to Moscow to study and take the examination to become an elementary school teacher. He failed, however, and moved to St. Petersburg, arriving there in time to be inspired by Karakozov's attempt to assassinate the tsar. He found his way into the radical student movement as he audited university classes, managing at the same time to pass his teacher's exam and take a job instructing religion. By 1868, he was working with Peter Tkachev, and combined the idea of the elitist party with the asceticism preached by Chernyshevsky's fictional character Rakhmetov and practiced by members of Hell. He added to it a strong dose of class hatred laced with a rich dollop of amorality. He was soon able to give the Carbonari lessons in secrecy and conspiracy and set about making himself a legend in his own mind. He exaggerated stories of his humble origins to appear to be a gifted proletarian rather than an underachieving student, and his prolier-than-thou attitude gave him some cachet among his fellow students. He duped several of his comrades into believing that he had been arrested by the secret police, and when he "miraculously" reappeared, he became renowned as the first revolutionary ever to escape from the Peter and Paul fortress that had held Bakunin for so many years. In fact, he was simply preparing to leave Russia, and while that was no easy feat in itself, it was much less heroic than imprisonment and a daring escape. He had, however, created a successful "backstory" that would gain him entrance into the radical communities in Western Europe.

The story was helpful when Nechaev met Bakunin in Geneva in March 1869. The anarchist, always more trusting and forgiving of individuals than of institutions, was delighted to be in contact with one of the radical Russian students he had heard so much about. Nechaev, thirty-three years Bakunin's junior, seemed to be the embodiment of the model Russian revolutionary youth. He was of the people, and thus understood from personal experience the need for radical change. He was educated and could generalize from his particular situation to understand the difference between rebellion and revolution. Nechaev seemed to Bakunin to be "one of those young fanatics who doubt nothing and who fear nothing" and who had pledged themselves not to rest until the people rose in revolt. The anarchist expressed his admiration in these "believers without God and heroes without oratory," welcomed Nechaev into his circles of friends, and helped him produce several pamphlets between April and August 1869 for distribution in Russia.

The pamphlets have been the center of controversy and legend ever since, for together they outline a cynical program of deceit, wholesale destruction, and implacable revolutionary violence. One, "Principles of Revolution," calls for the "massacre of personages in high places" by lone terrorists on the model of Karakozov. Such actions had, in the past, been undertaken by individual idealists driven by hope and desperation. Now they were to be based on the "severe, cold, and implacable logic" of systematic assassinations committed to create widespread panic among the ruling class. These assassinations would show others that the mighty could fall and would embolden others to take up the bullet and bomb in a "a generalized passion among the youth" and culminate in a "general uprising." Since the revolution was a "battle of life and death between the profiteers and the oppressed," the revolutionary advocated "no other activity than the act of annihilation," using "poison, the knife, the noose." The "revolution" sanctioned all means and all those who fell in combat even as it "darkened the last days of the social leeches"; the "sacred work of the extermination of evil, of purification" by "fire and sword" would finally free Russia and ultimately Europe.[4]

Another pamphlet, "The Catechism of a Revolutionary," distinct from Bakunin's earlier "Revolutionary Catechism," outlined a complicated structure of revolutionary cells, the appointment of secretaries, the notion of distributing information on a "need-to-know basis," and suggestions on how to gather funds and information. It is not, however, the first pages that are of historical interest. It is the section entitled "The Attitude of the Revolutionary Toward Himself" that has continued to resonate with radicals, including Eldridge Cleaver, who "fell in love with" the passage and took it "for my bible."[5] The hook is set with the first sentence:

> The revolutionary is a doomed man. He has no interests of his own, no affairs, no feelings, no attachments, no belongings, not even a name. Everything in him is absorbed by a single, exclusive interest, a single thought, a single passion: the revolution. In the very depths of his being, in words and in deeds, he has broken every tie with the civil order and the entire cultured world, and with all the laws, proprieties, conventions, and morality of this world.[6]

If the above has a romantic sweep to it, the next paragraphs make it clear that revolution is serious business. The revolutionary is the "merciless enemy" of society, and "if he continues to live in it, then it is only in order to destroy it more certainly." The revolutionary has no interest in science or art, save "the science of destruction," especially chemistry, physics, and related fields that could aid in "the quickest and surest destruction of this foul order." The revolutionary "despises public opinion" and feels no constraints of social morality. Instead, morality has only one criterion: That which hastens the revolution is ethical and moral; that which hinders it is evil. The revolutionaries should expect and give no quarter, and in the certain knowledge that the state would do its best to eradicate them, have to prepare themselves to withstand torture.

There was no place for "romanticism, sentimentality, enthusiasm, or excitement" in this movement; even "personal hatred and vindictiveness" were forbidden. Only "cold calculation" dedicated to "merciless destruction" was permitted. The same remorseless logic was applied to friends, colleagues, comrades, and acquaintances as it was to the enemy. Comrades were divided into different groups, depending on their loyalty and utility to the cause. The lower groups were considered to be "revolutionary capital" for the revolutionary to "expend"—expend "economically," of course, with an eye to extracting their "maximum value." If comrades were reduced to commodities, the rest of society fared worse. The Catechism divided people into six categories. The first was made up of government officials who were "especially harmful" to the cause. They were to be executed immediately. Other officials were given a stay of execution so their acts of repression and cruelty would outrage the people and drive them to revolt. The third category consisted of those not distinguished by their intelligence or energy but by wealth and influence. They were to be "exploited in every possible way," their secrets found out and turned against them, their weaknesses used so they could be controlled by the revolutionaries, their power and riches taken from them by extortion and blackmail and used for the revolution. The fourth category held politicians and liberals who could be used by pretending to agree with them while carefully weaving them into radical conspiracies without their knowledge. Once they were deeply entangled, they could be brought under control and sacrificed for the cause as needed. Armchair radicals made up the fifth category: all those "doctrinaires, conspirators, and revolutionaries who chatter in circles and on paper." The best use for them was to push them into foolhardy and dangerous political actions, so the "majority will vanish without a trace and a few will make real contributions to the revolution." The final category was "women." If a few might earn the designation of "comrades" and thus be regarded as "our most valuable treasure," most were to be put into the above third, fourth, and fifth categories, and used accordingly.

The brutal cynicism and violence of the two articles are appalling; they have been accurately described by one anarchist as revolting rather than revolutionary.[7] They are the pieces that earned Bakunin the reputation as the apostle of pan-destruction and are the basis for the accusations that his revolutionary credo consisted of little more than apocalyptic violence and revolutionary terror.

The only problem with this argument is that Bakunin did not write either the "Catechism" or "Principles of Revolution."

Historians have long debated the authorship of the 1869 essays. One was signed by Nechaev, another by Ogarev, a third, "A Few Words to My Young Brothers in Russia," by Bakunin. Four others, including the "Catechism" and "Principles of Revolution," were unsigned. The provenance of the "Catechism" is even more obscure. The original has been lost since 1869. The version that survived was written in code and taken from Nechaev by the Russian police, who deciphered it and made it public. There is no evidence that Bakunin wrote the "Catechism," and it has been attributed to him only through textual analysis, that is, by finding phrases or ideas in it that seem similar to those written by Bakunin. The strongest evidence for his authorship is that it was cast in the form of a "catechism," a stylistic device Bakunin had used previously. But the Nechaev piece was not originally titled a catechism; the name was given to it later by others. It certainly had the form of a catechism, but so did many articles by any number of revolutionaries and radical organizations. Bakunin himself was borrowing an accepted and common practice when he earlier penned his own catechisms, and thus we can draw no conclusions about authorship from the form of the piece.

Drawing conclusions from its content is equally problematic. Some of the ideas are superficially similar to Bakunin's. But those statements that give the "Catechism" its unique amoral cast have no antecedents in Bakunin's thought and the references to violence and destruction are very different from those made by Bakunin before and after the "Catechism" was written. As we have seen, he insisted that revolutionary violence was to be directed against institutions, not people, and nowhere did he advocate terrorism or assassination. The elitism of the "Catechism" and "Principles of Revolution," where the revolutionary exists outside the people and brings the revolution to them, is radically different from Bakunin's insistence that intellectuals learn from the people. In the only article from the seven known to be by Bakunin, he insists on the contrary that the young intellectuals and radicals had to "leave these universities, these academies" and "go among the people. There should be your career, your life, your knowledge. Learn amid these masses whose hands are hardened by labor how you should serve the people's cause." Far from instigating the revolution from above, the "cultured youth should be neither master nor protector nor benefactor nor dictator to the people, only the midwife of their spontaneous emancipation, the uniter and organizer of their efforts and their strength." This was very different from the notion that the revolutionary should spark the inevitable conflagration with poison, knife, noose, or bomb. The idea that women were a "treasure" when they were not to be used without compunction also runs counter to Bakunin's longstanding insistence on sexual equality.

There is one piece of evidence that connects Bakunin to the "Catechism," and on the surface, it is damning. One anarchist, Michael Sazhin, also known as Armand Ross, claimed to have seen a copy of the "Catechism" in Bakunin's handwriting. But eye-witness testimony is often unreliable, and certainly cannot be accepted easily in this case. As best as can be determined, Ross did not meet Bakunin until the spring of 1870 and they were not close until 1872. The earliest Ross could have seen any original manuscript was more than a year after the "Catechism" was written, encoded, and confiscated by the police from Nechaev's Russian colleagues. Since the "Catechism" figured in the trials of Nechaev's comrades, it is highly unlikely that Bakunin would keep such an incriminating piece of evidence on hand for a year. That alone casts considerable doubt on Ross's claim. More importantly, Ross did not come forward with his story until 1904. Thirty-five years is a long time. It is not too long to remember an important event, but it is long enough for the careful reader to require some corroborating evidence before accepting any claim. Nor was it a question of Ross keeping a secret all that time to protect Bakunin. The two had fallen out by 1874, and Ross's animosity did not end with Bakunin's death. To sum up: The only evidence that Bakunin wrote the "Catechism" is an allegation made by an unfriendly witness more than thirty years after the fact that a copy in Bakunin's handwriting existed and then vanished.

Against this claim we have Bakunin's own writings, which are very different in argument, tone, and principle. The "Catechism" and "Principles of Revolution" do resemble the writings of Tkachev and other Russian Jacobins. While Bakunin knew relatively little of them or their work, Nechaev was part of their circle and the "Catechism" is more consistent with their ideas than Bakunin's, suggesting that Nechaev wrote the article himself. Finally, Bakunin formally and explicitly disassociated himself from the "Catechism" in 1870. It was precisely in response to Nechaev that Bakunin, as we have seen previously, insisted that anything other than a "spontaneous or a people's social revolution . . . is dishonest, harmful, and spells death to liberty and the people. It dooms them to new penury and new slavery." It was also where Bakunin pointed out that only a mass social revolution could possibly succeed, for "centralization and civilization," modern communications, arms, and military organization, and the "techniques of administration" rendered secret conspiracies ineffective and obsolete. In particular, the "science and suppression of people's and all other riots, carefully worked out, tested by experiment and perfected in the last seventy-five years of contemporary history" gave the state such power that only the people's revolution could hope to overcome it.

Against Nechaev's hope that assassinations and terrorism would rouse the people, Bakunin argued that "it is impossible to rouse the people artificially." He repeated the point he had made earlier:

People's revolutions are born from the course of events, or from historical currents which, continuously and usually slowly, flow underground and unseen within the popular strata, increasingly embracing, penetrating, and undermining them until they emerge from the ground and their turbulent waters break all barriers and destroy everything that impedes their course. Such a revolution cannot be artificially induced. It is even impossible to hasten it, although I have no doubt that an efficient and intelligent organization can facilitate the explosion. There are historical periods when revolutions are simply impossible; there are other periods when they are inevitable.[8]

Bakunin went further, criticizing Nechaev for his failure to believe in either people or the people, and for his constant attempts to "subdue them, frighten them, to tie them down by external controls . . . so that once they get into your hands they can never tear themselves free." Nechaev was less a revolutionary than an *abrek,* a member of a Caucasus mountain tribe banished from his people for his antisocial behavior and driven to blood feuds. And Nechaev's catechism, Bakunin continued, was "a catechism of *abreks.*" Nechaev did not desire a world of morality; he sought only to make "your own selfless cruelty, your own truly extreme fanaticism, into a rule of common life," and thus he more closely resembled "religious fanatics and ascetics . . . nearer to the Jesuits than to us." Using the methods of the Jesuits, Nechaev sought to "systematically kill all personal human feeling in [other revolutionaries], all feeling of personal fairness," and replace them with "lying, suspicion, spying, and denunciation." While Bakunin had no scruples when it came to dealing with the enemy, he deplored Nechaev for treating "your friends as you treat your enemies, with cunning and lies," hoping always "to divide them, even to foment quarrels," seeking not unity but disunity to protect his own position in the movement.

Nechaev's personal relations were no better, Bakunin continued. His attempt to seduce Natalie Herzen was "repugnant," and Nechaev had embroiled Bakunin himself in a nasty little scandal. Bakunin had been commissioned to translate Marx's *Capital* into Russian. He soon gave up on the job, and of course had long spent the advance. Nechaev wrote a threatening letter to the publisher, without Bakunin's knowledge, complete with intimidating pictures of a knife, a revolver, and the peasant's axe, to "persuade" him to let Bakunin abandon the project and keep the advance. When the letter was made public, many believed, erroneously, that Bakunin was responsible for it. The episode was a blow to Bakunin's reputation and honor, and became a useful tool for those who wished to kick him out of the International. The anarchist would sadly confess later that he had been duped by Nechaev. No one, he wrote to Ogarev, "has done me, and deliberately done me, so much harm as he."[9]

Given his very real and profound differences with Nechaev, why would Bakunin work with him? He even continued to defend Nechaev against the early misgivings of Herzen and others, and supported him even when the younger man denounced him, deprived him of money, and blackened his name. He explained it to Nechaev simply enough. By 1869, he had long been out-of touch with Russian radicals and Nechaev seemed to be a bridge to the youth movement. The aging anarchist welcomed the chance to pitch in. He wrote pamphlets and worked to secure funds for the revolution. In particular, he went after the Bahkmetov fund, named after its donor who, in 1858, established a trust fund of about eight hundred pounds for Russian revolutionary activities. Administered by Herzen and Ogarev, the principle was still available in 1869, when Bakunin lobbied to give it to Nechaev. They reluctantly agreed to give Bakunin half, and he then turned the money over to Nechaev, who promptly made his way to Russia. There his principle accomplishment was the murder of Ivanov in November 1869, after which Nechaev returned to Switzerland, where he was able to conceal public knowledge of his crime for some time.

Even before he was told of the murder, Bakunin began to have doubts about Nechaev. But he put them aside, believing that the ardent radical was sincere and that he shared Bakunin's views. Later he would understand that Nechaev would lie, even to him, to pursue his own goals, and the realization came as a crushing disappointment. Until then, he was willing to overlook Nechaev's flaws, believing, or hoping, they were signs of immaturity he would outgrow and that they were in any case overshadowed by Nechaev's "real and indefatigable strength, devotion, passion, and power of thought" and his selfless dedication. Even when Bakunin broke with him, when he was forced to acknowledge the depth of Nechaev's crimes and treachery, he still held a faint hope that the young man would redeem himself, abandon his nasty creed, and serve the revolution.[10]

To an extent, Nechaev did. Arrested by the Swiss police in 1872, two years after Bakunin broke with him, Nechaev was turned over to the Russian authorities and charged with Ivanov's murder. During his trial, he denounced the court and the Russian empire, insisting that he was a political activist and should be tried as one, not as a common criminal. Despite his protests, he was quickly found guilty and sentenced to twenty years of hard labor in Siberia. He was instead put into solitary confinement in the Peter and Paul fortress. He remained steadfast, refusing to name names or accept an offer of leniency in return for serving as a spy for the Third Section. He remained in solitary for ten years, until his death from scurvy and tuberculosis in 1882. He could not be said to have redeemed himself for his life of treachery and murder, but at the end, he showed something of the mettle that Bakunin had seen in the brutish young man.

Why have historians been so quick to attribute the "Catechism" to Bakunin? The confusion over its authorship has distorted the popular understanding of Bakunin and greatly contributed to the mistaken notion that he was an advocate of terrorism. It has even shaped the way succeeding generations have interpreted Bakunin, leading many of them to trace his life backward from the "Catechism" to find hints of violence and instability in every casual remark and incident. In part, it is a question of evidence. Bakunin's 1870 letter to Nechaev, the strongest evidence that Bakunin did not write or agree with the "Catechism," was not made public until 1966. Yet it is hard to shake the notion that many historians have made a rush to judgment, seeing anarchism only as a threat to be smashed rather than an ideology to be understood. The easiest way to dismiss the ideas of Bakunin and other anarchists, apart from warning that sexual dysfunction would result from reading their pamphlets, was, and is, to preach that it is no more than mindless violence. The "Catechism" was a useful way to make that spurious connection, and too many historians have eagerly insisted Bakunin was its author as part of their campaign to discredit him and anarchism.

It is certainly true that Bakunin advocated revolution. But as we have seen, his idea of revolution was very different from terrorism. It was primarily a social movement that likely would have to resort to violence in self-defense as capitalists and lords fought to retain the property and privileges they had extracted from workers and peasants. That anarchism might be created peacefully was something to hope for, but the grim reality, and one Bakunin had experienced directly, was that the rich and powerful would use any means, however barbaric, to maintain their positions. Furthermore, Bakunin understood that property and power were not individual attributes but social relationships between classes. These social relationships, unlike individuals, could not be destroyed by bomb or axe, but by dismantling social institutions. Throughout his career, he stressed that the revolution was aimed at institutions, not people. For him, revolutionary violence did not mean a strategy of assassination or destruction by an elite group in the hope that the resulting repression would enrage and mobilize the people. On the contrary, Bakunin rejected the so-called "immiseration theory" that held that there is a certain level of misery that people must hit before they revolt. "The most terrible poverty . . . is not a sufficient guarantee of revolution," he observed. Humanity possessed "an astonishing and, indeed sometimes despairing patience," and immiseration, either in the form of greater poverty or greater repression was as likely to produce "obedience" as rebellion.[11]

Nor was violence acceptable as a strategy of eliminating representatives of the regime for the theatrical or propaganda effect, or even to rid the people of a particularly nasty oppressor. Social relationships, not individuals, were the enemy, and if the bourgeoisie and lords and prime ministers and kings would hand over the wealth and power they had usurped, there would be no need for violence. That did seem unlikely, of course, but it meant that the people's violence, aimed at reclaiming what was rightfully theirs, was as justified and moral as the violence of anyone used to resist a thief. At the same time, Bakunin understood human nature enough to imagine that after years of repression, a people prepared to revolt might well commit excesses in a fury of unleashed rage. He deplored such passions even as he recognized them, and more importantly, understood they stemmed not from peasants and workers themselves but from systems of government and economics that were designed to exploit them. Employers and governments sowed the wind; they should not be surprised if the whirlwind reaped them.

Linking Bakunin to the "Catechism" is also a way to dodge the very real question of the relationship of politics to violence. Virtually every political ideology save pacifism has justified violence for its cause while deploring the violence of every other. We may also reflect that adherents of virtually every political ideology have turned to violence at some instance and there is no particular reason why anarchism should be exempt. More often than not, the violence of anarchists is reviled not because it is violence but because it is anarchist. That is, it is the end that is objected to, not the means. If justified violence is a matter of ends, then the old question, "Is it moral to kill Hitler to avoid the death of millions?" opens the door to justify political violence. Many would agree that defending their country from an invader would be justified, even though defense is, obviously enough, violence for political ends. Many have gone further, to rationalize preemptive violence to eliminate the chance of attack on the homeland. Few states or individuals have ever insisted that all violence was equally wrong, and their defense of their own actions is more often special pleading than consistent ethics. The argument that your freedom fighter is their terrorist, your preemptive strike their unprovoked attack, your aerial bombing of innocent civilians self-defense, their suicide bomber a crime against humanity, has become a cliche, but it is one that is still worth remembering in any assessment of anarchist violence.

A sense of perspective is also useful. The violence of capital and the state outweighs that of the anarchists on the order of millions to one. Any American president is responsible for thousands more deaths through wars foreign and native than all the anarchist assassinations put together. Indeed, George W. Bush as governor of Texas oversaw more people executed by the state than anarchists assassinated in the nineteenth and early twentieth centuries. Nor is capital blameless. We may argue that many, perhaps most, wars have been waged to protect its interests and to that toll we may add up the deaths caused by slavery, colonialism, and imperialism. If this seems too remote, then we may calculate the deaths caused by industrial accidents and unsafe procedures, and these too number in the hundreds of thousands. To take one small example: nearly six thousand workers die on the job in the U.S. annually. These are accidents, to be sure, but the fact remains that these deaths, almost entirely preventable, have been whisked out of the category of violence. They are not seen as the result of a particular way of organizing society but as "acts of God." This sleight of hand, the anarchists and labor activists argue persuasively, tells us something significant about the power of the state and capital to define violence against them as a crime and violence against the weak as merely unfortunate and unavoidable. While crimes against the powerful and their property are rooted out with the police and legislation and the courts and prisons, violence against workers goes relatively unchecked. One might make a lofty argument about all life being equal and that the slaughter of thousands in the workplace and millions in war does not justify the taking of a single life by anarchists. We might well agree with this argument and still ask, along with St. Matthew, "Why beholdest thou the mote that is in thy brother's eye, but considerest not the beam that is in thine own?" The answer of course is that the state and capital are not opposed to violence as such but only to violence directed against them, and they have the power to define their violence as acceptable, even honorable. A disinterested analysis, however, would make the question of anarchist violence almost irrelevant on the scales of history. Because it has never had the sanction or the power of the state, anarchist violence has remained small-scale and individual. There have been no anarchist gulags, no anarchist genocide of native peoples, no anarchist concentration camps or death camps, no anarchist atomic bombs or mass bombings of civilian populations, no anarchist poison gas attacks. If the pundit replies that war is different because the state has a monopoly on legitimate violence, anarchists may be forgiven for retorting that that is precisely their point.

The anarchists may legitimately point out that the state does more than kill; it enlists others to do its killing and to die for it, and it usually lies to them about what they are doing. No serious historian today believes that World War I was fought by Britain, France, and their allies to preserve democracy or to end all war. Yet millions of citizens were told precisely that in order to secure their compliance. Purposely deluded about the cause and meaning of the war, they went off to slaughter and be slaughtered. Even those who would argue that such violence was justified may hold that at the bare minimum the organized violence of war, to be moral, requires that those who are being asked to do unspeakable deeds and to die be told the real reasons for their sacrifice.

It was also relatively easy to link Bakunin to the "Catechism" because of the bewildering melange of Russian revolutionaries of the 1860s through the 1880s and several lone assassins operating; in the name of anarchism from 1890 to 1914. As we have seen, Karakozov tried to assassinate the tsar in 1866, and in 1881 another group, the People's Will, succeeded in blowing up Tsar Alexander II. Descended from the student movement of the 1860s and 1870s, the People's Will advocated terrorism and assassination, but it owed little to Bakunin and anarchism. The group was not formed until 1879, three years after Bakunin's death, and called not for anarchism but for a constituent assembly and universal suffrage. The most famous member of People's Will, Vera Figner, commented that while they carried Bakunin "in our hearts as a fighting revolutionary," they were not guided by his ideas. The broad similarities of their program to some of Bakunin's ideas—land to be divided among the peasants, a vague antistate sentiment, and a belief "in the creative abilities of the popular masses to build new and just ways of life"—owed much more to the student movement and the radical organizations of the 1860s and 1870s than to Bakunin. More recent radical groups that adopted violence, ranging from the Black Panthers to the Weather Underground to the German Red Army Fraction, popularly known as the Baader-Meinhoff Gang, identified themselves as Marxists, not anarchists, while Eldridge Cleaver's commitment was to the credo of Nechaev's "Catechism," not Bakunin's thought.[12]

Nonetheless, anarchists have on occasion advocated terrorism, and between 1892 and 1901, a handful of anarchists engaged in a number of such acts. In France, Francois-Claudius Ravachol, Auguste Vaillant, and Emile Henry did as much as anyone to create the image of the anarchist as an indiscriminate, mad bomb-thrower. Ravachol set off an explosion in the apartment building where antilabor magistrates lived, then blew up a restaurant. Vaillant threw a bomb into the French Chamber of Deputies, while Henry bombed a mining company and a Parisian cafe, proclaiming coldly, "There are no innocents." Italian anarchists in particular turned to assassination: In 1894, one stabbed French president Carnot to death; three years later, another killed Antonio Canovas, the prime minister of Spain; the following year, still another killed Austria's Empress Elizabeth. After a number of attempts on his life that he shrugged off as occupational hazards, Umberto I of Italy was finally struck down by yet another Italian anarchist in 1900. Perhaps the most famous anarchist assassin was Leon Czolgosz, pronounced "choll-gosh," who shot and killed U.S. president William McKinley in 1901. But Czolgosz was virtually unknown to contemporary American anarchists such as Emma Goldman. Some of these anarchists, such as Johann Most and Alexander Berkman, had advocated assassination years earlier. Most was famous for an 1885 how-to book entitled *Science of Revolutionary Warfare: A Manual of Instruction in the Use and Preparation of Nitroglycerine, Dynamite, Gun-Cotton, Fulminating Mercury, Bombs, Fuses, Poisons, Etc., Etc.,* and Berkman served fourteen years in prison for the attempted assassination of Andrew Carnegie's lieutenant, Henry Clay Frick, for his role in smashing the Homestead Steel strike of 1892. But Czolgosz had no connection with them or the larger anarchist movement. It is worth noting too that of the four American presidents who have fallen to assassins, only one was killed by an anarchist, and that statistic alone suggests that political violence is not the exclusive preserve of the anarchist. The more important point, however, is that while some anarchists, like advocates of other political ideologies, have advocated terrorism and assassination, Bakunin did not. None of the anarchist assassins or bombers had any connection to Bakunin, or claimed any, and their particular interpretation of anarchism devolved long after Bakunin's death. None could draw inspiration or support for their actions from his writings or his life.

Finally, Bakunin was often linked to Nechaev and viewed as the first theorist of anarchist violence by three connected ideas: direct action, propaganda by the deed, and the criminal as revolutionary. While direct action has today been greatly expanded to include any sort of street protest and demonstration, and though the term has been appropriated by a number of groups that advocate violence against the state and capital, in Bakunin's time it had a very restricted meaning. Direct action was originally used by anarchists in the 1870s to describe economic action taken by workers against their employers. It was the opposite of political, indirect action, which aimed at electing reform politicians or lobbying them to pass laws and regulations to improve wages and working conditions. Workers were exploited by employers, and so it was employers they should be fighting, the direct action-ists held. After all, why talk to the monkey when you could talk to the organ grinder? What did the capitalist revere most of all? Profit. Therefore, the quickest—the direct—way to bring the boss to heel was to attack those prof-its through economic action. That meant measures such as the strike, the boycott, and sabotage, which could range from working to rule and slow-downs to breaking machinery, anything that would put direct economic pressure on the employer. In its original use, direct action had no connection to terrorism or violence against people.[13]

Nor did propaganda by the deed. The phrase has often been attributed to Bakunin, but it appears nowhere in his writings and appears in anarchist lit-erature only after his death. It does find a precedent in one of his letters, written in 1873 to his comrades in the Jura Federation, an organization of workers and anarchists that included James Guillaume and that argued for direct action. "I am convinced that the time of grand theoretical discourse, written or spoken, is past," Bakunin wrote. "Over the last nine years, the International has developed more than enough ideas to save the world—if ideas alone can save the world—and I defy anyone to invent a new one. It is no longer the time for ideas but for deeds and acts." What were these deeds and acts to consist of? Not terrorism or violence, but "the organization of the forces of the proletariat."[14] Subsequent anarchists such as Errico Malat-esta, Paul Brousse, and Peter Kropotkin built on Bakunin's argument that action, not theory, was needed, and developed the doctrine of propaganda by the deed. Their argument was that workers and peasants would not be convinced by words, for they did not have the time to read and so needed practical proof that revolt was possible. Propaganda by the deed meant demonstrations, burning of deeds, titles, and mortgages, and other forms of collective action extending even to insurrections. Only later did it degenerate into terrorism and assassination, and by then it bore no resemblance to Bakunin's tactic. For him, propaganda by the deed could be a bridge between theory and practice, between intellectuals on the one hand and workers and peasants on the other, for it provided concrete examples of how to organize and fight. The peasant commune itself was such an example for future soci-eties, and Bakunin argued that radicals should look to it as a "basic embryo of all future organizations."[15] Furthermore, the peasants had expressed their revolutionary ideal in practice, if not in theory, for "every time the people's rising succeeded for a while," Bakunin explained, "the people did one thing only: They took all the land into common ownership, sent the landowning gentry and the tsar's government officials, sometimes the clergy as well, to the devil and organized their own free communes." As a result of their practical action, "our people holds in its memory and as its ideal one precious element which the Western people do not possess, that is, a free economic community," and with it, "the conviction that this is its indubitable right." This memory was a historical form of propaganda by the deed, and Bakunin believed that radicals could build on these examples and create new ones to show people, rather than preach to them, about revolution.[16]

Bakunin argued that Russian peasants and workers had another revolutionary example they could draw upon: the brigand, or outlaw. By this he meant something very different than a motley crew of gangsters, hoodlums, and thugs. He meant specifically those outlaws who continued the tradition of Stenka Razin and Pugachev, who drew their strength from the peasantry and engaged in crimes against property and lord not to enrich themselves but to aid the poor. In the same way that the legends of Robin Hood resonated among English workers and peasants, so too were the exploits of Razin and Pugachev celebrated in Russia. There, the historical role of the brigand was much more overtly political than the romanticized Hell's Angels or the Mafia of *The Godfather* and *The Sopranos*. Both the motorcycle gang and the mob were little more than capitalist enterprises set up by those excluded from the larger society by ethnicity, class, manners, or status. They functioned largely as businesses, extracting wealth from their workers and customers and funneling it up to the top. The brigand armies of Razin and Pugachev, in contrast, had an overt political aim: the redistribution of land to the peasants. The threat they posed to the regime was not competition for control of vice or the accidental murder of upstanding citizens or the corruption of willing public officials; it was the utter destruction of the social relationship of peasant and lord on which the Russian empire depended. Nor could the brigands hope or wish to parlay their loot into legitimate, respectable businesses and political offices and become virtually indistinguishable from the ruling elite in a generation or two. Successive tsars understood well that the brigands represented a fierce, radical menace to their rule. Nobles, even old Alexander Bakunin at Priamukhino, by all accounts a liberal and kindly lord, had feared the possibility of a peasants' uprising as much as they feared Napoleon's armies, and understood that the same arms issued to the serfs to repel the foreign invader could be turned against the master. For Bakunin, brigandage represented an important peasant tradition that could be drawn upon as further examples of the strength of the people. The songs, stories, and literature of Stenka Razin and Pugachev were proof that alongside the daily practice of deference and obedience, peasants had a culture of liberty and revolt upon which a revolutionary consciousness could be built. The brigands also could be a formidable fighting force that could spread the message of insurrection as they rode from village to village. In Bakunin's words, "the Cossacks and the world of brigands and thieves . . . include both protest against oppression by the state and by the patriarchal society." These groups had "played the catalyst and unifier of separate revolts under Stenka Razin and under Pugachev," and along with the tramps who traveled Russia in search of work and bread, were readymade organizers and "promoters of general popular unrest, this precursor of popular revolt."

Bakunin's faith in the brigand bands, however, was not naive or unqualified. They were a potential revolutionary force, but one with "unquiet passions, misfortunes, frequently ignoble aims, feelings, and actions." The world of the brigand was, he admitted, "far from beautiful from the truly human point of view." But if the brigands were "wild and cruelly coarse people," that was their strength as well as their weakness. Unlike the weary, dispirited proletariat and peasantry, they had a "fresh, strong, untried, and unused nature" that was fertile ground for propaganda. If their ferocity meant that "a Russian revolution will certainly be a terrible revolution," that was because "the Russian world, both privileged state and popular, is a terrible world." Reaction and regime would only reap what they had sowed. After all, Bakunin asked, "who among us in Russia is not a brigand and thief? Is it perhaps the government? Or our official and private speculators and fixers? Or our landowners and our merchants?" Between the "brigandage and thieving of those occupying the throne and enjoying all privileges, and popular thieving and brigandage, I would without hesitation take the side of the latter." In an official Russia marked from top to bottom by a "depravity of thought, feelings, relationships, and deeds . . . the people's depravity is natural, forceful, and vital. By sacrifice over many centuries, they have earned the right to it," for their violence was "a mighty protest against the root cause of all depravity and against the state, and therefore contains the seeds of the future." For that reason, Bakunin declared himself "on the side of popular brigandage" and saw it as "one of the most essential tools for the future people's revolution in Russia." The key was for the radicals and intellectuals to work with the brigands to give them "new souls and arousing within them a new, truly popular aim." If this was, as he admitted, easier said than done, it was nevertheless necessary.[17]

Bakunin's ideas on the nature and purpose of brigandage were considerably more complicated than a desire to set the countryside ablaze and slaughter lords and overseers. Together, peasants, workers, and brigands could form a revolutionary force powerful enough to topple the Russian regime, just as an organized and radicalized proletariat was strategically placed to overthrow capitalism in the West. Bakunin's argument that the Russian brigands represented a potential revolutionary force has led many to conclude that he believed criminals in western nations could play a similar role. More specifically, Bakunin's liberal and Marxist opponents and some anarchist supporters have claimed that he put less faith in the proletariat than the so-called "lumpenproletariat." The term was coined from the German *Lump,* roughly "scoundrel" or contemptible person, from *Lumpen,* that is, "rag" or "ragged," and by extension, one eking out a bare subsistence as a ragpicker or dressed in rags, and *proletariat.* Marx used the word to characterize "a mass sharply differentiated from the industrial proletariat, a recruiting ground for thieves and criminals of all kinds, living on the crumbs of society, people without a definite trade, vagabonds, people without hearth or home . . . as capable of the most heroic deeds and the most exalted sacrifices as of the basest banditry and the foulest corruption." As early as the Communist Manifesto, he made reference to "the dangerous class, the social scum, that passively rotting mass thrown off by the lowest layers of old society," while in "The Eighteenth Brumaire of Louis Bonaparte" he described the lumpenproletariat as consisting of "decayed roués, with dubious means of subsistence and of dubious origin, alongside ruined and adventurous offshoots of the bourgeoisie" together with "vagabonds, escaped galley slaves, swindlers, mountebanks, *lazzaroni* [idlers], pickpockets, tricksters, gamblers, *maquereaus* [pimps], brothel keeps, porters, *literati,* organ-grinders, ragpickers, knife grinders, tinkers, beggars—in short, the whole indefinite, disintegrated mass thrown hither and thither."[18] For Marx, the important point was less who made up the group than its déclassé position. Without a clear class interest, this group could be won over by the right as well as the left. Since it had no obvious allegiance, it was untrustworthy and provided a ripe climate for demagogues and opportunists such as Louis Bonaparte. The lumpenproletariat, in Marx's view, had no particular reason to side with the proletariat, since it had no employer and was not exploited in the same way; relying on handouts, charity, and crime, it was dependent on the existing order and could be employed by the forces of reaction against workers.

To argue that this group was a potential revolutionary class flew in the face of Marxist analysis. To orthodox Marxists, such an argument represents

246 THE REVOLUTIONARY IS A DOOMED MAN

"substitutionism," that is, the belief that groups other than the working class had as much to gain from abolishing capitalism and could in fact form the leading edge of the revolution. C. Wright Mills and Herbert Marcuse, for example, would argue in the 1960s that African-Americans and students, rather than the American working class, would form the real vanguard of radical politics. More recently, "post-Marxists" such as Chantal Mouffe and Ernest Laclau have made similar arguments; much of the so-called "identity politics" and social movement theory that began in the 1980s is explicitly a rejection of class and class analysis.[19] Some anarchists have also found much in this, decrying Marx's reliance on the proletariat as little more than "privileging" a working class that has shown little interest in revolution or progressive politics. Bakunin, it is argued, championed the downtrodden lumpenproletariat along with the déclassé students, intellectuals, peasants, and brigands and so held out a very different vision of how the revolution would be made and who would make it.

Certainly déclassé intellectuals, in Russia and the West, had a role in radical politics. This was as true for Marx as it was for Bakunin, both of whom could be characterized either as men of "dubious means of subsistence and of dubious origin" or the "portion of the bourgeois ideologists . . . [that] goes over to the proletariat" he described in the Communist Manifesto, depending on how one looked at them. But as we have seen, Bakunin's analysis of the Russian peasants and brigands was not a rejection of class so much as a recognition of the reality of the very different Russian class structure and the belief that a spirit and practice of revolt was a critical element of revolution. Did the lumpenproletariat play a similar role in Western Europe? Was it, rather than the proletariat, the class that had nothing to lose and a world to win?

The point of class analysis, as Bakunin had recognized in 1842, when he determined that the revolution would be made by the working class, was not to rule out individuals who might decide to become radicals or to insist that only certain segments of the society could take part in the revolutionary movement. Nor was it to predict which specific individuals might move to the left. As a poster from the late 1970s put it, "Class consciousness is knowing which side of the fence you're on. Class analysis is figuring out who is there with you." Class analysis was to understand which large groups had the potential to become revolutionary. This potential was assessed by asking two questions. The first was, whom is the system exploiting? The answer to that question would indicate who would benefit from toppling the present order. After all, at the level of idealism and possibilities, nothing precludes the Baron Rothschild, John D. Rockefeller, or Bill Gates from becoming anarchists, and some scions of the wealthy have. But by and large, this is not a group from which one expects radical politics simply because it is not in their best, material interests. They benefit just fine from the existing social arrangements. The second question was, which groups were able to make the revolution? That is, which groups were numerous enough and strategically placed to overthrow capitalism? As someone once remarked about student radicals of the 1960s, "If every student radical in the United States were laid end to end, I wouldn't be a bit surprised." The point was not that students could not understand or support radical politics, but that in their social role as students they could not make the revolution. If they all boycotted their seminars, the ruling order would not collapse. By the same token, if every street beggar refrained from begging, little would change. Furthermore, students and beggars make up small, isolated percentages of the population. On the other hand, in nineteenth-century Europe, peasants and workers made up the vast majority of the population, and the moment they withdrew their labor, capital was threatened. Thus for Bakunin and Marx, revolutionary groups were defined less by their potential to learn about revolutionary ideas than their strategic place in the economic and social order.

If Bakunin argued that brigands, with their intrinsic connection to the peasantry, occupied such a place in Russia, there is little evidence that he viewed the lumpenproletariat of Europe in the same way. In fact, he rarely used the word "lumpenproletariat." While he does use the French word *canaille,* this is better translated as "mob" or "rabble." But these are descriptions of how people have organized, not their class position. It was, after all, a mob of middle-class Tories who burned down Montreal's parliament buildings in 1849. When Bakunin does talk about the *canaille* or rabble, he usually refers not to the lumpenproletariat as such but to the poorer sections of the working class. Thus in a famous passage in his *Statism and Anarchy,* often quoted to prove Bakunin held the lumpenproletariat was the revolutionary class, he is not talking about the criminal element or even beggars, but about a section of the working class that is paid much less than skilled workers:

> In Italy [it] is that destitute proletariat to which Marx and Engels, and, following them, the whole school of German social democrats, refer with the utmost contempt. They do so completely in vain, because here, and here alone, not in the bourgeois stratum of workers, is to be found the mind as well as the might of the future social revolution.[20]

While we might translate "destitute proletariat" as "lumpenproletariat," Bakunin himself goes on to define this group as "largely illiterate and wholly destitute," but consisting of "two or three million urban factory workers and small artisans, and some twenty million landless peasants." Clearly Bakunin is referring to a portion of the proletariat and the peasantry, not the lumpen-proletariat. In "The Politics of the International," published in *L'Egalité* in 1869, Bakunin refers to *la canaille* but more exactly to *la canaille ouvriere*, better translated as "the working rabble" than lumpenproletariat. Again, Bakunin makes it clear in the same sentence that it is not the criminal or beggar he is referring to but to "the lowly people whose labor feeds the world." After all, it was impossible to "convert to socialism a noble who covets riches, a member of the bourgeoisie who would like to be a noble, or even a worker who in his soul strives only to be a member of the bourgeoisie!" The point was that "the prejudices of the masses are based only on their ignorance, and are contrary to their own interests, whereas the prejudices of the bourgeoisie are based precisely upon the interests of that class." Instead, one had to organize among the "real workers," "all those who are truly crushed by the weight of labor," who are in "so destitute and precarious a situation," among the "great mass of workers, who, exhausted by their daily labor, are ignorant and miserable." Whatever Bakunin thought about the potential of the Russian brigand, clearly the different historical and economic development of Western Europe meant that workers, not the lumpenproletariat or criminal elements, were the revolutionary class.[21]

It is true that Bakunin often argued that it was the poorest elements of the working class, not the relatively well-paid skilled worker, who were most likely to be revolutionary. Artisans engaged in traditional crafts might well tend to identify less with factory workers than with the small bourgeoisie; they might, he suggested, even consider themselves as "semi-bourgeois." So too might better-paid workers, who because of their "self-interest and self-delusion" might identify with employers and oppose the revolution. This was hardly a point of disagreement with Marx, who had attacked Weitling and others on precisely the same grounds, and, along with Engels, often complained that the "labor aristocracy" was inclined to be less radical than other workers.[22] At the same time, Bakunin held that it was precisely through "trade unions" and the "struggle against the bosses" that workers would come to understand where their interests lay and how their instinct and passion for freedom would express itself in purposeful action.[23] That action, in the West and increasingly in Russia, would be the strike. Strikes were more than a way to bargain with the employer. They showed workers the need for solidarity and unity, for a strike brought them "together with all the other workers in the name of the same passion and the same goal; it convinces all workers in the most graphic and perceptible manner of the necessity of a strict organization to attain victory." At the same time, strikes "awaken in the masses all the social-revolutionary instincts which reside deeply in the heart of every worker" but which were normally "consciously perceived by very few workers, most of whom are weighed down by slavish habits and a general spirit of resignation." The strike, Bakunin continued, "jolts the ordinary worker out of his humdrum existence, out of his meaningless, joyless, and hopeless isolation." The "economic struggle" made workers more receptive to the message of the revolutionary, which was, after all, "the purest and most faithful expression of the instinct of the people." Once the revolutionary message was made clear, provided it represented the "genuine thought of the people," workers would respond positively and resolutely. Strikes had another educational function as well, Bakunin observed. They drew a clear line between worker and capitalist and made it clear that a "gulf" separated the "bourgeois class from the masses of the people." Anyone who believed that the employer and the employees were on the same team would soon learn that in fact "their interests are absolutely incompatible." Still today workers' wages are the employer's expense, and there is still no way to reconcile the fact that capitalism remains a zero-sum game: whatever one side wins, it wins from the other side. Modern labor relations law, industrial relations schools, and sophisticated state intervention ranging from mediation to arbitration to the use of police to break picket lines and, on occasion, heads, try to convince people otherwise, but Bakunin was right: Their interests are not the same, and "there is no better way of detaching the workers from the political influence of the bourgeoisie than a strike."[24]

From all of this, it seems clear enough that neither direct action, propaganda by the deed, nor the social role of the criminal were used by Bakunin to justify violence or terrorism. Nowhere in his work do we find calls for assassination; instead, there are warnings against the harm caused by revolutionary violence. This may be counted as further evidence of Bakunin's distance from, and distaste for, Nechaev's amoral "Catechism" and Jacobin politics. It was, however, evidence that would be conveniently ignored as Bakunin struggled against Marx, this time within the First International.

13

HERMAPHRODITE MAN VERSUS CARBUNCLE BOY IN THE FIRST INTERNATIONAL

The Nechaev affair left Bakunin a great deal to sort out, including his very real poverty when Nechaev made off with funds the anarchist had hoped to share in. His life was always complicated, given his tendency to ride off madly in all directions, and if his dealings with Nechaev were the most toxic of Bakunin's adventures in this period, they were the least important in his development as a political activist and thinker. Much more significant was the four-year fight with Marx in the First International. In part a clash of personalities, in part a replay of their disagreements of the 1840s, in part a minefield of misunderstanding and misinterpretation that both men blundered across, the conflict hinged on ideas of reform, revolution, and state. Yet principled differences soon gave way to unprincipled tactics and the collapse of the International, leaving an acrimony that taints the relationship of Marxists and anarchists to this day.

By 1868, it was clear the League of Peace and Freedom was not interested in radical politics. Bakunin, now living in Switzerland, created a new political organization, the International Alliance of Socialist Democracy, sometimes called the Alliance of Social Revolutionaries, in the fall of that year. The Alliance actively recruited members and functioned openly as a political group, and Bakunin wrote an ecumenical program that outlined its goals and politics in seven points. In the first of these, the Alliance "declares itself atheist; it wants the abolition of cults, substitution of science for faith, and human justice for divine justice." The next two points underscored Bakunin's commitment to gender equality. One called for "political, economic, and social equalization of classes and individuals of both sexes, commencing with the abolition of the right of inheritance." The goal was to establish that "land, [and] instruments of labor, like all other capital, on becoming collective property of the entire society, shall be used only by the workers, that is, by agricultural and industrial associations." The next demanded equal education in "science, industry, and the arts" for "children of both sexes." Bakunin then rejected "any political action which does not have as its immediate and direct aim the triumph of the workers' cause against capital." Point five suggested that even authoritarian states were "reducing their activities to simple administrative functions of public service," and in the future would "dissolve into a universal union of free associations." Next, the Alliance rejected "any policy based on self-styled patriotism and on rivalry between nations," calling instead for the "international or universal solidarity of the workers of all countries." The last point called for the "universal association of all local associations on the basis of liberty."[1]

The program was a concise statement of anarchist principles, and in it Bakunin outlined how a new anarchist society might function, though he was deliberately vague. After all, it would hardly be consistent to argue that future generations could be free only if they obeyed the instructions and designs of long-dead gurus. "We frankly refuse to work out plans for future conditions," he observed elsewhere, "because this does not coincide with our activity, and therefore we consider the purely theoretical work of reasoning as useless."[2] Yet some implications may be drawn from the program of the Alliance. Workers and peasants would no longer be compelled to labor for the profits of others. Instead, they would form free associations of producers, on the land or in factories and artisanal shops. These free associations, owned by the members themselves as cooperatives and communes, would federate with others locally, regionally, and federally as necessary and as useful to provide other needs and wants that they could not supply themselves. With the capitalists gone, class struggle too would disappear. Therefore, there would be no need for the coercive function of the state to maintain exploitive class relations. There would be a need for administration and coordination, from the collectively owned farm to the shop to the region and beyond, but each smaller unit would be organized from the bottom up and would freely affiliate to the larger unit in the same way, with no centralized control or authority. Certainly disputes and differences would arise, but they could be resolved, if not always amicably, at least democratically, in part because there were no competing class interests that guaranteed one side could win only at the other's expense. If this seems Utopian, there are examples of such associations even today in our class-riven and antagonistic societies, from library boards to volunteer fire departments to charities to food and housing cooperatives. These organizations are capable of organizing scores, even hundreds, of people to fulfill the needs of the individual and the collective without recourse to a supreme executive authority, top-down management, or the army. These groups are not free of conflict, and certainly disputes can be rancorous. But anarchists have never claimed that the goal was a world without disagreements, only that there is no need for a boss or government to resolve differences through coercion and violence while exploiting everyone in the meantime. Without hierarchies of power and profit, the collective power of humanity would be devoted to the full and equal development of all.

Turning from the broad sketch of anarchist principles, the program of the Alliance outlined several rules for the organization. Most dealt with the way members would form local and national sections, but the first rule was the most significant. It announced that the Alliance would formally join the International Working Men's Association, better known as the International or the First International.

Though often identified with Marx and Engels, the inspiration for the International came from French and British workers who sought to express their solidarity with the ill-fated Polish uprising of 1863. They were unable to do much for the Poles, but it was obvious that international cooperation was crucial for workers in an age of transnational capital, colonization, and empire. The following year the International Working Men's Association was created, and Marx was asked to join. He was reluctant at first. He had not been active in any political organization since 1850, and though he was living in London, had little involvement with British trade unionists, few of whom would be bumped into in the course of his research at the British Museum. Nonetheless, he accepted the invitation to attend the founding meeting and was soon elected secretary. He was also elected as one of two German representatives to the International and as the corresponding secretary for Germany, even though it had been more than twenty years since he had been in his homeland.

The International was an awkward amalgamation of revolutionaries and reformers. Socialists ranged from leftover followers of Robert Owen to anarchists, Marxists, and radicals such as the Italian republican Giuseppe Mazzini, whose politics had a certain flair but little substance and even less connection to the working class. The bulk of the British trade union members had long given up the radicalism of Chartism for moderate reformism, and they had no interest in revolution. Proudhon's ideas still reverberated in France, where workers had much less success in winning reforms under the Second Republic and Second Empire of Napoleon III and so were less inclined to favor parliamentary politics. It was difficult to know what to make of the German movements. The most important German working-class organization was the General German Workers' Association. But it was the creation of Marx's flamboyant rival, Ferdinand Lassalle, and Marx was disinclined to encourage its members to join the International. Even though Lassalle had been killed in a duel shortly before the International was founded, Marx found it more conducive to harmonious relations to court a much smaller group, the German Workers' Social Democratic Party, led by Wilhelm Liebknecht, a journalist, and August Bebel, a woodworker. Ostensibly more radical than the Association, their group had little to recommend it save its willingness to declare itself opposed to Lassalle and for Marx. Later it would absorb the Lassallean party and adopt much of its program; as the German Social Democratic Party, or SPD, it would have great success in electoral politics, though it would abandon all but the pretense of remaining a revolutionary workers' party until the 1940s, when it abandoned even the pretense.

The first order of business for the International was to constitute its rules and program. Marx was selected to serve on the subcommittee charged with drawing them up, but missed the preliminary meetings. The provisional drafts submitted by the rest of the committee appalled him, and he took over the job of revising through the time-honored practice of extending debate until the rest of the committee was exhausted and happy to let someone—anyone—finish up so they could go home. Marx then wrote a draft that he found eminently satisfactory. The first paragraphs were a model of carefully weighed political ideas, with a nod to virtually every faction. "The emancipation of the working classes must be conquered by the working classes themselves," it started, and no one could object to that. It held that "all social misery, mental degradation, and political dependence" were based on "the economical subjection of the man of labor to the monopolizer of the means of labor, that is, the sources of life," and this materialist explanation found favor with Proudhonists, trade unionists, anarchists, and socialists alike. Marx even threw in some obligatory phrases about "duty and right" and "truth, morality, and justice" to keep everyone happy, though he made sure, as he noted to Engels, to place such meaningless platitudes where they could do no harm. The rules established the International as "a central medium of communication and cooperation" between workers' organizations throughout the world that would "proclaim the common aspirations of the working class," and set out its structure. Individuals would form local associations that in turn would form national federations or sections. These associations, federations, and sections would send delegates to the annual General Congress to decide policy. The General Congress would also elect members to the executive of the International, the General Council, which would direct the affairs of the International between congresses. The General Council would select from its own members the officers such as secretary and treasurer and the corresponding secretaries for the different sections. In his rules and principles for the International, Marx accomplished a difficult trick rather deftly. The finished product was acceptable to all the very different groups and individuals, and he had written a platform that would not scare off the more cautious while leaving room for the revolutionary.[3]

Certainly Bakunin had no objections to the ideas and structure of the International. Nor was there any personal antipathy between him and Marx when the International was founded. After all, they had not seen each other for nearly twenty years. In the meantime, Marx had been pleased to come into possession of some books by Hegel that had once belonged to Bakunin, left behind as he traveled across Europe just ahead of the police and troops. True, in 1863, Marx could not resist passing on to Engels the gossip from a friend that "Bakunin has become a monster, a huge mass of flesh and fat, and is barely capable of walking anymore. To crown it all, he is sexually perverse and jealous of the seventeen-year-old Polish girl who married him in Siberia because of his martyrdom."[4] But when Bakunin returned to London the following year to have a bespoke suit made, he and Marx spent a pleasant evening together. Marx's accusation that Bakunin had been a spy had long since been forgiven, though it could hardly have been forgotten. Since then, Marx had defended Bakunin in the press against similar charges made by a conservative British journalist, coincidentally named Francis Marx, and by David Urquhart, a notorious anti-Russian whose conspiracy theories had occupied Karl for a time. On the whole, the meeting went well, and Marx passed on Bakunin's regards to Engels, along with the observation that "I must say I liked him very much, more so than previously . . . On the whole, he is one of the few people whom after sixteen years I find to have moved forward and not backward." Undoubtedly they talked politics, for Marx had just finished writing the address and rules for the International, and the two parted as friends. Perhaps most significantly, Bakunin made it clear that he had no interest in nationalist causes, and Marx recorded approvingly that "from now on—after the collapse of the Polish affairs—he [Bakunin] will only involve himself in the socialist movement." They exchanged a few more letters and Bakunin agreed to inform Garibaldi of the International and have its program translated into Italian. Marx hoped that Bakunin could "lay some countermines for Mr. Mazzini," and in 1867 deplored the foolish assertion made in *The Diplomatic Review* that the Geneva Peace Congress was a trick of the Russian government and its "well worn-out agent Bakounine." That same year, Marx was still sufficiently friendly to send Bakunin a copy of *Capital* hot off the press. For his part, Bakunin translated the Communist Manifesto into Russian and had it published by Herzen in 1869, and made the stab at translating *Capital* that would end badly, thanks to the work of Nechaev. Though Bakunin would write several years later that he had not been taken in by Marx's friendly overtures, this statement was made after their battles in the International, and it is reasonable enough to believe that both men were originally prepared to give the other the benefit of the doubt.[5]

If their personal relationship had grown closer, so too had their philosophical and political thought. Bakunin had long appreciated that the very real strength of Marx's analysis was precisely the emphasis he placed on economic factors. Marx, he argued, "was on the right path. He established the principle that religious, political, and juridical evolutions in history were not the cause, but the effect, of economic evolution. This is a great and fruitful concept . . . and he is to be credited for solidly establishing it and having made it the base for his economic system." In an unpublished section that precedes Bakunin's best known work, *God and State,* the anarchist explicitly praises Marx's historical materialism for its insistence that where the "idealists claim that ideas dominate and produce reality, the communists, in accordance with scientific materialism, claim on the contrary that reality gives birth to ideas . . . and economic, material reality constitutes . . . the essential base, the principal foundation from which intellectual, moral, political, and social facts are only the necessary derivatives." Even at the height of their conflict, Bakunin would praise Marx for putting socialism on an economic rather than sentimental footing, writing, "There is a good deal of truth in the merciless critique he directed against Proudhon. For all his efforts to ground himself in reality, Proudhon remained an idealist and a metaphysician. His starting point is the abstract idea of right. From right he proceeds to economic fact, while Marx, by contrast, advanced and proved the incontrovertible truth, confirmed by the entire past and present history of human society, nations, and states, that economic fact has always preceded legal and political right. The exposition and demonstration of that truth constitutes one of Marx's principal contributions to science." The anarchist even adapted and incorporated some aspects of the positivism of Auguste Comte into his worldview. The French sociologist—who coined the term—sought to put the study of human nature on a scientific basis and from that standpoint rejected religion and metaphysics. The anarchist was not uncritical of Comte, however; he refused outright the idea that scientists, broadly defined to include economists and sociologists, should make policy or have any authority in the new society. He took from Comte the scientific defense of atheism and the general principle of Comte's positivism, that science could produce "positive," certain, and true knowledge about the world and humanity. No less than Marx, Bakunin was a philosophical realist and a materialist.[6]

Nor were Bakunin and Marx as far apart on their ideas about the relative merits of proletarians and peasants as their critics and supporters have sometimes alleged. While Bakunin argued that peasants should not be ignored, especially in countries where they made up a large percentage of the population, as we have seen he also insisted on the revolutionary role of workers. At the same time, Marx's views on peasants have sometimes been distorted. Marx's remarks in the Communist Manifesto about the "idiocy of rural life" are often quoted as proof he despised peasants, but we must remember that "idiocy" comes from the Greek and originally implied isolation rather than retardation. That peasants were isolated and that isolation was a problem for the revolutionary to overcome were observations Bakunin readily shared. While Marx had no great faith in the land-owning peasantry in France, he would later concede that Russian peasants might well be able to build socialism on the basis of their communal traditions. And both were aware that well-paid workers might be tempted to abandon revolution for reform. Indeed, it was Marx, not Bakunin, who would write that while the "English have all the material necessary for the social revolution," they lacked "the spirit of generalization and revolutionary fervor."[7]

Yet it is often the nature of political groups to fight more ferociously with one's closest competitor than with the mutual enemy. Despite their detente in 1864, Bakunin and Marx did not remain close; indeed, they never met again and the personal and the political soon drove them apart. When Bakunin failed to acknowledge Marx's gift of *Capital* in a timely fashion, Jenny Marx wrote to Johann Philip Becker, a friend of both men, asking, "Have you seen or heard anything of Bakunin? My husband sent him, as an old Hegelian, his book—not a word or a sign. There must be something underneath this! You really can't trust all those Russians. If they don't adhere to the tsar in Russia, then they adhere to or are kept by Herzen, which in the end comes to the same thing. Six of one and half a dozen of the other." Bakunin's oversight rankled Marx too, for some months later, the book still unacknowledged, he cautiously asked a mutual acquaintance if Bakunin still considered him a friend, hoping that the question would be posed discreetly to the anarchist. When Bakunin was told of Marx's inquiry, he immediately fired off a warm letter to "my old friend," assuring him they were, "more than ever, dear Marx," comrades, for he had come "to understand better than ever how correct you were in following and in inviting all of us to advance on the high road of economic revolution." Marx was correct, he continued, to criticize "those of us who were becoming lost on the footpath of national, exclusively political enterprises. I am now doing that which you began to do more than twenty years ago." Bakunin informed Marx that he had parted company with the "bourgeois" League of Peace and Freedom and would now devote himself to the cause of workers. "My country now," he continued, "is the International . . . You see, dear friend, that I am your disciple, and I am proud to be such." Bakunin's letter was fulsome, in part because he had just applied to have the Alliance affiliate directly to the International. Aware of Marx's sensitivity to academic insult, however slight and unintended, Bakunin was undoubtedly concerned that Marx would refuse to admit the Alliance if he were aggrieved, and so the letter was crafted to smooth any ruffled feathers. But the effusive letter arrived just after Bakunin's petition to join the International and had the opposite effect. "I trust no Russian," Marx flatly remarked to Engels, and he dismissed Bakunin's letter as nothing more than an attempt to make a "sentimental entrée" to his good graces and the International. Why would Bakunin wish to affiliate with the International? Marx could conceive of only one reason. "The old acquaintance of mine—the Russian Bakunin—has started a nice little conspiracy against the International," he fumed in a letter to his daughter and son-in-law. The Alliance program, he continued, "would, by a clever trick, have placed our society under the guidance and the supreme initiative of the Russian Bakunin . . . I could not let this first attempt at disorganizing our society . . . succeed."[8]

There was more to Marx's reaction than paranoia, ego, or the state of his famous carbuncles.[9] Modern times called for new forms of organization and new methods. The old sects and secret organizations had had their day. Trade unions were an established fact in nations such as England, even if their legal status was dubious; workers there had shown that they could use the existing political system to win significant gains, such as the Ten Hours Bill that limited the length of the working day. The key to new tactics was the international solidarity of workers, and that was precisely the aim of the International. Such solidarity did not require uniformity of opinion, but it did require an end to the factions and clandestine parties of the past. As Marx put it later, "The International was founded in order to replace the socialist or semisocialist sects by a really militant organization of the working class . . . Sects are (historically) justified so long as the working class is not yet ripe for an independent historical movement. As soon as it has attained this maturity all sects are essentially reactionary." In his view, "the history of the International was a continual struggle of the General Council against the sects and amateur experiments, which sought to assert themselves within the International against the real movement of the working class." Marx's assessment does of course beg the question of whether he had properly divined the real movement of the working class. Nonetheless, it is reasonable to conclude that what Marx sought at first was not to dominate and control, but, in the words of two historians of the International, to provide some "cohesion" to overcome the "centrifugal force" of the different groups in the International. Admitting a separate organization holus-bolus into the International was an invitation to factional infighting and sectarian splits.[10]

Bakunin's reputation as a revolutionary was largely based on 1848 and the old methods, and his delight in secret organizations was no secret. It is hardly surprising that Marx feared that the Alliance would be "established within and established against!" the International.[11] Bakunin's further suggestion that the Alliance would have as its "special mission" within the International "to study political and philosophical questions on the basis of the grand principle of universal and genuine equality of all human beings on earth," was waving a red, or rather, black, flag in front of Marx. Leaving aside the argument that such grand platitudes were largely meaningless, why would the International need a self-appointed subcommittee to examine the very questions the International posed and that had been Marx's lifework? Furthermore, the Alliance proposed, or appeared to propose, that it would set up a parallel structure within the International, even to the point of having separate meetings at the annual congresses. Marx's response to the Alliance's application to affiliate with the International was logical enough, and remarkably restrained given his strong feelings. If, as it claimed, the Alliance had the same aims and goals as the International, there was no need for it to enter as a separate organization. If it didn't agree with the principles of the International, it should not join. The International Working Men's Association was by no means as powerful, international, or associated as its name implied, and it made some sense to avoid the factional disputes that would inevitably follow the admission of another organization. For these reasons, the International declined Bakunin's offer of affiliation, on the grounds that "the presence of a second international body operating within and outside the International Working Men's Association will be the most infallible means of its disorganization." The Alliance members were welcome to join as individuals, and the following year it was agreed that certain sections of the Alliance could join not as affiliates but as newly constituted sections of the International. It was a workable compromise that suggests that while Marx was wary of Bakunin, he was hardly acting in a dictatorial or authoritarian fashion.[12]

He did, however, completely misjudge Bakunin's motives. There was never any question of his taking over the International or creating a secret society or sect within it. Even those biographers friendly to Marx have admitted there is no evidence to support such an allegation. What Bakunin did hope to do was to establish the Alliance as a sort of revolutionary think tank that would develop ideas and strategies and so advance the political ideas of workers once they had joined the International. It was hardly a secret: he had said as much in the Alliance's program, after all, and made it clearer a few years later when he wrote that

> the Alliance is the necessary complement to the International . . . But the International and the Alliance, while having the same final goal, pursue different objects. The former seeks to unify the millions of workers, to overcome the differences of craft and country, into a single immense and compact body. The latter seeks to give these masses a truly revolutionary direction. The programs of the one and the other are not at all opposed. They are different only in the degree of their respective development. The International contains in embryo, but only in embryo, the whole program of the Alliance. For its part, the Alliance is the fullest expression of the International.

Furthermore, if the Alliance joined as a separate affiliate, it would give Bakunin the support of a circle or affinity group; it would bring him into the International as an equal to Marx, and surely he deserved no less.[13]

What Marx objected to was not whether the International would have the dual purpose of bringing workers together and educating them, but who would do the educating. He had, after all, rejected the suggestion that the International have honorary memberships, with the explicit aim of keeping out the French socialist Louis Blanc. And as he noted to Engels, Marx had framed the rules and program of the International "so that our view should appear in a form acceptable from the present standpoint of the workers' movement," understanding that it would "take time before the reawakened movement allows the old boldness of speech." In the meantime, it would necessary to be *fortiter in re, suaviter in modo,"* that is, strong in deed, but gentle in manner. Such a tactic was not necessarily duplicitous. Neither Marx nor Bakunin assumed that workers necessarily understood from their experience how the world worked or how to change it. No one expects someone to become an economist or a carpenter simply by observing the world around them, and it is not necessarily elitist to argue that people do not learn about politics that way either. It is fashionable today to disapprove of anything that hints of "false consciousness," that is, the idea that people do not always understand or act according to their real self-interest. Yet given the truly astounding apparatus of the state, capital, religion, schools, universities, and the media, each capable of misleading people, it would be more surprising if everyone did understand naturally and instinctively how the world works and where their interests lie. No, Marx was wary of Bakunin and the Alliance because they represented a threat to Marx's position in the International and to his belief that political action, not direct action, was the key to workers' emancipation.[14]

From the beginning, Marx insisted that the workers' movement had to make use of the state and participate in electoral politics. In the founding rules he set out for the International, he had carefully played down political action, holding that "the economical emancipation of the working classes is therefore the great end to which every political movement ought to be subordinate as a means." This was just acceptable to the Proudhonists, who tried unsuccessfully to have the clause removed, and it satisfied the more moderate British unionists and German socialists who believed that significant reforms could be won from the state. The Proudhonists regrouped, however, and in 1866, taking Marx at his word that the emancipation of the working class was the job of the working class itself, nearly succeeded in passing a resolution to exclude all nonworkers, including Marx, from the International. Marx counterattacked, and at the General Congress held at Lausanne in 1867, pushed the question of political action. Largely due to Marx's efforts, the Congress resolved that "the social emancipation of the workers cannot be effected without their political emancipation" and that "the establishment of political liberty is absolutely essential as a preliminary step."[15] While these resolutions could hardly be construed as a commitment to parliamentary procedure and capitalist highroading, they shifted political action from being the "subordinate means" to the essential task of the working class. Of such small changes and implications are doctrinal splits and schisms made. Buoyed by his success, Marx decided to push harder at the next congress, scheduled for Brussels in 1868, confiding to Engels that he would "personally make hay out of the asses of Proudhonists."[16] The congress was held in September, before Bakunin applied to join the International, and so Marx had little organized opposition. Though he did not attend personally, Marx made good on his promise to Engels. It was no longer necessary to be gentle in manner, for the world of the artisan, the proprietor, the small landholder, and the skilled, semiautonomous worker that Proudhon spoke to was vanishing. As more people became wage workers, they, unlike Proudhon, increasingly viewed the strike as their best weapon. Nor did they share his hope that workers' co-ops and credit unions could supplant big capital. Thus Marx's resolutions in favor of strike action and the collective ownership of the means of production were strongly supported by the delegates, over half of whom were Belgian workers. Marx's success in having his resolutions passed effectively ended the role of the Proudhonists in the International.

Yet his victory was short-lived. Only a few months after the Brussels congress, Bakunin and the Alliance applied to join the International. For Marx, it was déja vu all over again. If anything, Bakunin was worse, from Marx's point of view. Proudhon had died in 1865, and his movement had no obvious leader to rally around. But Bakunin was a famous and popular figure: the ovation he received with Garibaldi at the League of Peace and Freedom was proof of that. Respected by the Proudhonists, Bakunin, unlike Proudhon, was opposed to private property and so could not be accused of "petit bourgeois" ideology. Bakunin's refusal of the state and of political action was popular among both Proudhonists and workers in countries such as Italy and Spain who did not have the vote or recourse to parliament and so could rely only on direct action. At the same time, his revolutionary rhetoric appealed to those who did not have time to wait for the full development of productive forces and who wanted action and hope in the present, not the far-off future. Bakunin was also well equipped to challenge Marx's position as the brain trust of the International. Engels grasped this immediately and attempted to reassure his friend. Going over the list of Alliance members, he asked Marx rhetorically, "Will we find among them men known to have devoted their whole lives to these questions? On the contrary. There is not a name whose bearer has so far dared as much as to claim to be a man of science . . . I have never read anything more wretched than the [Alliance's] theoretical program. Siberia, his stomach, and the young Polish woman have made Bakunin a perfect blockhead." Though Marx would insist that Bakunin was "devoid of all theoretical knowledge" and "a nonentity as a theorist," that was a demonstrable untruth. Bakunin was not an unsophisticated worker Marx could displace with academic rigor as he had Weitling; he was a competitor for theoretical correctness who also had a gift for reaching nonintellectuals. Unlike Marx, Bakunin would never be the target of a purge of the Poindexters.[17]

But what Marx could do better than anyone was read texts closely and critically. Getting it right was a sacred obligation, not because he was an authoritarian but because he was an intellectual by trade and a meticulous scholar, not to say nitpicker, by nature. He worked his way through the Alliance's program sentence by sentence, hunting out error and deviation with the zeal that leads many to believe the expression "pedantic professor" contains a redundancy. His notes on his copy of the program demonstrate his academic bent and set the tone for the future conflict with Bakunin. "Equality of classes!" he scrawled in the margin when the phrase appeared in the opening paragraph. In Marx's view, classes existed precisely so one could exploit the other; there could be no question of making them equal. Instead, it was "the abolition of classes, this true secret of the proletarian movement, which forms the great aim of the International Working Men's Association." And Marx was right, as Bakunin freely admitted to him. The watered-down statement had been a compromise originally intended for the "bourgeois audience" of the League of Peace and Freedom, he explained, and Marx admitted later that it was clear from the context that the phrase was "a mere slip of the pen." Later, however, in his polemics against Bakunin, he would use the phrase as proof that his rival had no under-standing of economics and that his ideas were but "a hash superficially scraped together from the right and the left."[18]

Where Bakunin declared atheism as a principle of the Alliance, Marx wrote indignantly, "As if one could declare—by royal decree—abolition of faith!" While he was himself an atheist, Marx understood religion as one of the few solaces an oppressed people had. Remove the causes of their oppression, and religion would disappear, at least as a social force; whatever individuals chose to believe privately was entirely up to them. For Marx, religion was "the sigh of the oppressed creature, the heart of a heartless world . . . It is the opiate of the masses," as he put it in the *Introduction to Critique of Hegel's Philoso-phy of Life* in 1844. But this too was Bakunin's position:

> It is not the propaganda of free thought, but the social revolution alone that will be able to kill religion in the people . . . [Religion is] a natural, living powerful protest on the part of the masses against their narrow and wretched lives. The people go to church as they go to the alehouse, to numb themselves, to forget their misery, to imag-ine themselves, if only for a short time, as free and as happy as everyone else. Give them a human existence, and they will no longer go to the alehouse or the church.

Marx's more substantial point was that making atheism a principle of joining the International would alienate potential members who believed in God. But this too Bakunin understood. "We think that the founders of the International were very wise to eliminate all political and religious questions from its program," he wrote. "Their main purpose, before all else, was to unite the working masses of the civilized world in a common movement. Inevitably they had to seek a common basis, a set of elementary principles on which all workers should agree . . ." Hardly an irreconcilable difference, it would appear, but it reinforced, in Bakunin's view, the need for a special committee of the International to consider social questions from an explicitly revolutionary perspective.[19]

Working his way through the Alliance program, Marx bridled at the call for equalization of both sexes, underlining the phrase in the text and writing beside it, "Hermaphrodite man! Just like the Russian Commune!" It is difficult to know why Marx found this objectionable; he was committed to women's equality and had worked hard to provide good educations for his own daughters. It may be that he had his share of Victorian prejudices, or simply that he would reach for any stick to beat a dog. Equally odd was Marx's reaction to Bakunin's call for the abolition of the right of inheritance, a demand Marx had expressed in identical language in the Communist Manifesto. Now Marx dismissed it as "the old Saint-Simon panacea!" Bakunin believed that the right or, more accurately, the law of inheritance maintained class differences. There could be no "level playing field" if the rich could pass on their advantages to their children. Just as abolishing private property did not mean you had to share your toothbrush with the world proletariat on alternate weekends, Bakunin was quick to add that items of great personal meaning but of little monetary value could of course be passed on. Capital and land, however, had to remain "forever the collective property of all productive associations." Personal fortunes would not be passed on, for that would begin anew the division of the world into rich and poor, owners and owned. In a rational, free society, the needs of one's children would be taken care of by society; there would be no need to grant them the savings and investments of their parents. Furthermore, it was clear that anyone who had amassed personal wealth had not done so by their own labor alone; they had benefited from all of society and thus to society their wealth should be returned. Everyone was entitled to the necessities and luxuries of life, but these were to be earned, not bequeathed. Marx, on the other hand, argued that once private property was abolished, the right of inheritance would be meaningless. If Bakunin was instead urging the abolition of inheritance as a short-term, pragmatic goal, much the same could be accomplished through reforms in tax law. That would have the advantage of protecting what small property the poor might possess and would not alienate potential allies who would be frightened off if they believed socialism meant they couldn't keep granddad's pocket watch. Nonetheless, there was no particular reason why both views could not have peacefully coexisted in the International, and it is not clear why Marx would waste a moment on such trifling matters, let alone pen a special "Report of the General Council on the Right of Inheritance" and return to the issue repeatedly over the next few years.[20]

The problem was that each man appeared to represent the political tendency the other despised and feared most. Bakunin proposed that the Alliance join the International as a relatively independent body; Marx could conceive of no innocent reason for such a move and set out to counter what he feared would be a schism. Refusing to admit the Alliance and attacking its program struck Bakunin as authoritarian, while Marx's manipulations to push through his resolutions on political action were reformist and sneaky. The obvious course of action was to organize one's allies openly where possible and covertly where necessary to avoid expulsion. Such organizing in turn would convince Marx that Bakunin was interested either in taking over the International or wrecking it from within—precisely what he had feared from the outset. And so it continued, until the overreactions of each gave the ghosts they conjured in their own minds solid form. The march to folly was exacerbated by the fact that Bakunin and Marx never met again after 1864. Marx attended only one congress of the International, that held in the Hague in 1872, Bakunin only that of Basel in 1869. Their maneuvers were carried out through official pronouncements, secret memos, and dubious intermediaries that practically ensured their exchanges would degenerate into a flame war.

At first, Marx restrained the impulse to intrigue, and was critical of his allies who sought to blacken Bakunin's name. Instead, the first unscrupulous attack on Bakunin was launched by one of Marx's colleagues. Sigismund Borkheim despised Russians in general, and Alexander Herzen in particular. In 1868, he published a series of articles denouncing Herzen, and soon turned his aim on Bakunin. Unaware of or indifferent to Bakunin's current political ideas, Borkheim denounced him as one of Herzen's "Cossacks" whose observation that "the passion for destruction is a creative passion" would be rejected out of hand even by German schoolboys. That Borkheim was referring to Bakunin's 1842 article and to a point of view that Marx and Engels had shared at the time seemed to have escaped him. To their credit, both Marx and Engels tried to rein in Borkheim and rejected his request for permission to reprint the attacks on Bakunin Engels had penned in the 1840s. Their fair-minded behavior, however, soon evaporated and they took no action when other colleagues, notably August Bebel and Wilhelm Liebknecht, began hinting in the press yet again that Bakunin was a pan-Slavist and thus acting in the interest of the Russian tsar, whether he knew it or not. As everyone knew, this was a not very subtle way of once again accusing him of being a Russian police agent, and Bakunin believed that Marx and Engels either acquiesced in the campaign of their lieutenants or were directly responsible yet again for an unprincipled attack on his name and reputation.

First, however, he had other problems to deal with. His wife, Antonia, had developed a romantic liaison with Carlo Gambuzzi, one of the Italian comrades who had followed the Bakunins to Switzerland. Short of postmortem DNA testing—hey, they did it for the Romanovs to determine if Ingrid Bergman was Anastasia—it is impossible to prove paternity, but certainly it was widely believed, even by Bakunin, that Gambuzzi was the father of Antonia's three children. Born in 1868, the same year the Alliance was founded, Carlo lived until 1942; Sophia, born two years later, lived until 1956; Maria, born in 1873, would become a famous chemist and university professor in Italy, and lived until 1960. Gambuzzi would help support Bakunin in the last years of his life. After the anarchist's death in 1876, he would marry Antonia, and the two would have a fourth child, Tanya, together. Such complicated relationships were hardly unknown in the nineteenth century, either in sophisticated, bohemian circles or in the practical world of working people, where short life expectancy, poverty, and love encouraged creative family structures that ranged far outside the boundaries of middle-class morality. Marx, for example, was likely the father of his live-in maid's son, though he refused to acknowledge paternity. Engels gallantly claimed he was the father, which was credible enough, as he might charitably be described, in that quaint bourgeois expression, as a "womanizer." Herzen, his wife, Natalie, and Georg Herwegh tried unsuccessfully to create a triangle of "love and affection" in the 1840s while later Herzen and the Ogarevs maintained a ménage a trois in which Herzen and Natalie Ogarev had three children together. As one historian has concluded, what is most striking about Michael and Antonia's relationship are the "bonds of affection and loyalty that held the marriage together" despite the difficulties they faced.[21]

One of these difficulties was money, and now it was compounded by political fights. The Bakunins had moved from Italy to Vevey with Zoe Obolensky, and the town had become a center for Russian radical émigrés, including two former members of Land and Liberty, Nicholas Utin and Nicholas Zhukovsky, both of whom had met Bakunin in London some years before. Though Obolensky could no longer support the revolutionaries, Zhukovsky's sister-in-law, Olga Levashov, could. She was prepared to invest in the revolution and with her support, the circle launched a radical newspaper, *The People's Cause*. Edited and largely written by Bakunin and Zhukovsky, the first issue came off the presses in September 1868. As a newspaper, it was of little historical consequence. Its real importance soon became apparent: It was a prize in the contest between Bakunin and Marx. At the Geneva congress of the League of Peace and Freedom a year earlier, Utin had reintroduced himself to Bakunin as a dedicated follower of anarchism. However sincere that declaration may have been, Utin broke with Bakunin before the second issue of *The People's Cause* came out and took over the editorship himself. His motives were mixed. Bakunin implied the two had a personal squabble, perhaps because the older revolutionary had not given the young radical his due and so left him miffed. Certainly the resources of Olga Levashov were at stake, as was the prestige of assuming the position of editor; revolutionary integrity is often weighed and measured exceedingly fine. And while Bakunin sniffed that they had not quarreled over political ideas, because his opponent had none, Utin did not need any; those of Karl Marx were ready to hand. Utin broke with anarchism, argued for reform and trade union politics, and shifted the editorial stance of *The People's Cause* to reflect his newfound ideas. The split with Bakunin also represented a split in the working-class movement in the regions around Geneva, where native workers in the highly skilled manufacturing sector, especially the famous Swiss watchmakers, had the vote and were better paid than foreign-born, unenfranchised laborers, and so were much more interested in reform and party politics. Not surprisingly, Bakunin sided with those who had no vote and so were drawn to direct action and extraparliamentary politics as the only way to improve their condition. Utin, following Marx, looked to the reformist workers first.[22]

Whatever the precise admixture of the causes of the dispute, Bakunin found himself removed from the masthead of *The People's Cause,* without a benefactor, and with a wife and another man's child to support. He and Antonia moved to Geneva's working-class district of Montbrillant, literally on the wrong side of the tracks, in October 1868, perhaps in the hope that Herzen, who had moved there earlier, could provide some financial aid. But the two old warriors had quarreled too often and too fiercely; while they met a few times, Herzen had little to do with his former comrade, beyond noting in a letter to Ogarev that "there is no news of Bakunin, except that his trousers have lost their last buttons, and keep up only by force of habit and sympathetic attraction."[23] Bakunin was in danger of losing more than his trousers. In February 1869, he sent off a terse note to his sisters in Priamukhino: "Debts are crushing me. I am facing death from starvation. Help me."[24] No help was forthcoming; somehow he struggled through. In the spring of 1869, Antonia left for an extended visit with Carlo Gambuzzi in Italy; she would return several months later, bearing another child. Perhaps the most profound result of this series of personal and political hardships was that Bakunin was left vulnerable to the blandishments and revolutionary opportunism of Nechaev, who turned up in the middle of the chaos.

There were small pleasures, however, including a banquet in Le Locle where Bakunin was the guest of honor. He still had the aversion to dancing he had noted in his youth, though now it was perhaps forced upon him by his bad heart and weight; in any case, while others danced, he expounded on politics and the seven aspects of human happiness: "first, to die fighting for liberty; second, love and friendship; third, art and science; fourth, smoking; fifth, drinking; sixth, eating; and seventh, sleeping."[25] It is, all things considered, rather a humble list, and yet we still cannot deliver it to most of the world's population. It may also be compared with a list of answers Marx supplied to a parlor game of "Confession," where he noted that his favorite virtue in a man was strength, and in a woman, weakness; that his chief characteristic was singleness of purpose, his idea of happiness to fight, and his idea of misery, submission. Making much of after-dinner testimonials and games is almost as fatuous as psychohistory and cold war histrionics, yet they are suggestive of the two clashing personalities. In any event, by 1869 Bakunin had helped form a new Geneva section of the International, the Fédération Romande, or Romance Federation, and became involved with two new anarchist newspapers, *L'Egalité* and *Progres*.

Like Francis Ford Coppola, Bakunin was not always at his best when given unlimited time and resources to complete a project, and his short pieces in *L'Egalité* have a focus and clarity that are often missing from the long, unpolished writings. He reiterated his belief that "revolutions are not improvised. They are not made arbitrarily either by individuals or even by the most powerful associations. They occur independently of all volition and conspiracy and are always brought about by the force of circumstances. They can be foreseen and their approach can sometimes be sensed, but their outbreak can never be hastened."[26] Could he make it any plainer? Revolution was not a question of will, it was not a matter of wishing, it was not possible anywhere, anytime. It depended greatly on social conditions; on that he and Marx were agreed, though Marx would later deny it. Nor would the social revolution resemble 1848 "in the sense of barricades and a violent overthrow of the political order," for the revolutionaries did not "wish to kill persons, but to abolish status and its perquisites." The "realization on earth of justice and humanity" would come through "a single means: association." Isolated workers were powerless, isolated associations nearly so. Even national workers' associations were not strong enough to resist international capital. Labor needed to organize internationally; it needed the ideas the International could help provide, and more importantly, it needed "solidarity in study, in labor, in public action, and life." Through associations, cooperatives, trade unions, and mutual aid societies, "workers become accustomed to handling their own affairs," and in that prepared the "precious seeds for the organization of the future."[27]

Bakunin's discussion on education remains instructive today as schooling from kindergarten to university becomes more "streamlined" to produce cannon fodder, worker-drones, and lawyers. Art, music, and literature are the first subjects dropped from the curriculum as school budgets are slashed, and education seems largely devoted to replacing critical thought with obedience and curiosity with boredom. From the vantage point of 1869, Bakunin gave a stirring plea for integrated, well-rounded, and equal education for women and men. One of the privileges the bourgeoisie kept for itself, he pointed out, was a "fuller education." It was obvious that the person who is "broader-minded thanks to scientific learning, who grasps more easily and fully the nature of his surroundings because he better understands those facts which are called the laws of nature and society . . . will feel freer in nature and society and . . . will also in fact be the cleverer and stronger . . . The one who knows more will naturally rule over the one who knows less," and if only this difference remained to separate people into classes, humanity would soon find itself again divided into "a large number of slaves and a small number of rulers, the former working for the latter." That was why the privileged called only for "some education of the people," and not "total education." The result of that, as Bob Dylan observed much later, was "twenty years of schoolin' and they put you on the day shift."

Surely Bakunin could not object to the notion that some people should be allowed to devote themselves full-time to intellectual pursuits, for didn't their "scientific discoveries" and "artistic creations" improve life for everyone? He granted that there had been "vast progress" in knowledge and art, just as capitalist industry had created more wealth than the world had ever seen before. But the greater wealth was not distributed equally, and neither were knowledge and education. Furthermore, whatever gains workers had made in absolute terms, they had lost in relative terms. He used a simple analogy to demonstrate his point. If you and I start walking at the same pace and you have a head start of one hundred paces, at the end of an hour, we have both moved ahead an equal amount though we are still one hundred paces apart. If, however, you can make sixty paces a minute to my thirty, at the end of the hour we will be nineteen hundred paces apart. Progress in wealth and education were exactly the same. If workers were better educated than they were before, the gap separating them from the privileged had grown, and as it yawned wider, the "privileged will have become more powerful and the worker will have become more dependent, more of a slave than in the beginning." Just as wealth was increasingly concentrated in fewer hands, so too was education. The net effect of all this "progress" was to "divide the world into a small, excessively affluent, learned, ruling minority and a vast majority of wretched, ignorant, slavish proletarians."

At the same time, much of the so-called progress that resulted from this education was actually designed to oppress workers. The "science of government, the science of administration, and financial science" was nothing more than the "science of fleecing the people without making them complain too much and, when they begin to complain, the science of imposing silence, forbearance, and obedience on them by scientifically organized violence; the science of tricking and dividing the masses of people, of keeping them eternally and advantageously ignorant," so they could never unite, and the science of the military, making it much more powerful "and allowing it to be present, to act, and to strike everywhere."

A common objection to socialism or anarchism is the question, "Who will do the dirty work?" Marx gave one useful answer to one such interrogator. "You will!" he retorted. Bakunin confronted the question as well. If everyone were educated, who would do the necessary but unrewarding work? His response was simple: "Everyone shall work and everyone shall be educated." When manual and mental labor were no longer separated, all work could be more interesting and useful. The more or less equal development of "muscular and mental activities" in each individual "will not impede each other but instead will support, broaden, and reinforce each other." It followed that "in the interest of both labor and science . . . there should no longer be either workers or scholars but only human beings." If that meant there were less time for the rarefied genius to doggedly pursue research, whatever might be lost from that individual would more than be made up by the much greater contributions the rest of society could make. "Certainly, there will be fewer illustrious scholars," Bakunin agreed, "but at the same time there will be infinitely fewer ignorant people. No longer will there be a few who touch the skies, but millions who are now crushed and degraded will walk on the earth as human beings. There will be no demigods, but neither will there be any slaves," for society would see "the former coming down a little, the latter rising quite a bit."

To the argument that not all people were capable of being educated to the same level, Bakunin made the obvious but still often ignored point, that at present "rich but stupid heirs will receive a superior education; the most intelligent children of the proletariat will continue to inherit ignorance . . ." Thus it was often the case that "a very bright worker must stand silent while a stupid scholar gets the better of him, not because the latter has any sense but because of the education denied the worker." Worse, the superior education of the scholar was possible only because "the labor of the worker clothed him, lodged him, fed him, and provided him with tutors, books, and everything else he needed for his education while his stupidity was being scientifically developed in the schools." Until humanity created a society in which wealth, leisure, and education were provided equally to all, there were no good grounds for comparison or determining who could be educated to what level. Once the artificial differences of "upbringing, education, and economic and political standing" were removed, he suspected that most humans would not be "identical, but they are equivalent and hence equal." The differences that remained would be a resource, not a drain. There might still be extreme cases of both "geniuses" and "idiots," but these would be a very small percentage of the population. Those who were unable to learn suffered from illness and would be cared for; with equal health care, nutrition, and resources for all, likely the number would decrease substantially. As for geniuses, they were rare enough one could be forgiven for not losing much sleep over them. Nor was it clear that geniuses were produced by superior education. Many were not called "genius" until they were dead, while many young people of promise failed to deliver. It was just about impossible to predict who might develop into what and that was, Bakunin concluded, another argument to educate everyone well and equally. More to the point, in a society where everyone was well educated, human progress would not depend on isolated, random genius but on the much greater abilities of everyone.

He then outlined briefly the content of education in the new society. It would "prepare every child of each sex for the life of thought as well as for the life of labor," and would provide a general knowledge of all the sciences, including sociology. Since no one could encompass "every speciality of every science," students would, after their general education, choose the particular area of study that "best suits their individual aptitude and tastes." Undoubtedly some would make mistakes, but that was better than streaming children, for no parent or teacher could possibly make the proper decision for a child; Bakunin sided with the child's freedom to choose over "every official, semi-official, paternal, and pedantic tutor in the world." Scientific and theoretical education would be complemented with "industrial or practical instruction," again divided into general and specialized schooling, and instruction, or rather, "a series of experiments" in "human morality." Divine morality, he argued, was "based on two immoral principles: respect for authority and contempt for humanity." Human morality was "founded on contempt for authority and respect for the freedom of humanity." This was not the freedom of free will, for he denied that such existed. "Every so-called human vice and virtue is only the product of the combined action of nature, properly so-called, and society . . . All individuals, at every moment of their life, are, without exception, what nature and society have made them." While this might be cause for existential paralysis in some, for Bakunin it was further proof "that for human beings to be moralized, their social environment must be moralized." Education at present could not do that, for real, integrated, and complete education could not be created in a capitalist society. What was necessary was not a revolution in education, but an education in revolution; once the people had been emancipated, "they will educate themselves."[28]

The ideas and arguments Bakunin put forward in these short articles remain some of his most interesting and provocative. The difficulties and work of these years, however, were put aside in September 1869 as he prepared himself for the Basel congress of the International. As usual, the real battles were camouflaged as resolutions that appeared innocent enough to the uninitiated, and it first seemed that there would be no major schisms. A motion to give the General Council the power to determine which groups would be allowed to affiliate and to suspend sections of the International that threatened unity was passed easily. Even though this would centralize authority in the hands of the General Council, Bakunin sided with Marx and Liebknecht in favor of the resolution. Given his commitment to decentralization, this may seem surprising. But Bakunin sought to protect revolutionary sections of the International, including his own, from attack by national sections, such as the British and German, that tended to be less radical. The General Council, he correctly surmised, would tend to favor radicals over reformers. At the same time, he wanted to fend off an attempt to organize a new Swiss branch of the International that hoped to supplant Bakunin's section, and so was prepared to hand the General Council stronger powers. It is a measure of Bakunin's complete unsuitability for the role of a Machiavelli that these new powers were first used against him.[29]

The second resolution finally ended the long-standing controversy over private property, and Bakunin again voted with Marx to declare that the International stood for collective property. Whether property should be owned by the state or by the people in common was a question that all agreed could wait another day. The next resolution was on the right of inheritance. Everyone understood that more hinged on this than the issue itself: it was the test of strength between Bakunin and Marx. Bakunin had asked to have "the question of inheritance" placed on the agenda of the congress, and Marx had readily agreed, believing that he would win easily and so "be able to hit Bakunin on the head directly."[30] The result shocked Marx. Despite his explicit instructions to his delegates and his carefully written report on the question, backed by the General Council that Marx himself headed, the majority of the delegates sided with Bakunin. Marx did not attend the congress, and Bakunin's personal appearance helped his cause considerably. The anarchist's speech at the congress no doubt convinced many; it was, by all accounts, an eloquent and impassioned oration, an example of Bakunin at his best, and in it, he outlined some of the differences between anarchism and Marxism, or as he called them, collectivism and communism. The Marxists, he thundered, "put themselves right in the future, and in taking collective property as their starting point, find that there is no longer any occasion to speak of a right of inheritance." The anarchists, however, "start off from the present," under the "regime of triumphant individual property, and, while marching toward collective property, we encounter an obstacle: the right of inheritance. We therefore think it is necessary to overthrow it."[31] Though Bakunin's resolution received a majority of votes cast, the number of abstentions and absences meant that it did not receive a clear majority of all the delegates, and so it failed on a technicality. But Marx's own counterresolution was rejected by a clear majority, and the votes showed that Bakunin had much more support than Marx had thought possible. Bakunin won a moral victory and would win a public relations one as well. He demanded that the congress strike a special court of honor to force Liebknecht to put up evidence or shut up his whispering campaign that Bakunin was a Russian spy. Liebknecht had no proof and backed down, claiming he had never made such a charge. He may have been technically correct, but there was no doubt that Liebknecht's innuendoes pointed in precisely that direction. He was severely chastised by the court of honor, which publicly handed Bakunin its written verdict. With an eye to the grand gesture, the benevolent giant rolled up the paper, lit it, then used it as a spill to light his cigar, demonstrating with some flair that he had no need of written proof of Liebknecht's guilt and that he was prepared to forget the entire matter.[32]

The Basel delegates then voted their support of trade unions and of the need for solidarity of workers across nations. A cautious unity was forged, and both Marx and Bakunin declared themselves satisfied with the results of the congress. Subsequent events, however, would reveal that the solidarity was more apparent than real and that neither side would cease its fulminations against the other. Though both Bakunin and Marx could claim tactical victories at Basel, the congress confirmed, or appeared to confirm, the worst fears of both. Each believed he was engaged in a defensive war to protect himself from the unprincipled machinations of the other. From Bakunin's perspective, it seemed that Marx was prepared to take up again the smear campaign he had begun in the 1840s when he could not win through force of argument. Barely three weeks after the congress, another of Marx's colleagues, Moses Hess, who had known Bakunin in the 1840s, published another attack on the anarchist in the French newspaper *Le Reveil*. He accused Bakunin of secret intrigues aimed at destroying the International, and while he veiled his attack by insisting he did not wish impugn the anarchist's revolutionary integrity, he went on to claim, falsely, that Bakunin had associated with another radical accused of being a police agent at Basel. Hess, like Borkheim and Liebknecht, further intimated that Bakunin was a "pan-Slavist." This was more than an accusation of being a Russophile or an acknowledgment of Bakunin's earlier belief in the necessity of Slavic revolt against the tsar. It was shorthand for "supporter of the Russian empire," and carried with it the implication that Bakunin was doing the tsar's bidding. Probably Marx had no prior knowledge of Hess's article, just as he had no knowledge of Liebknecht's earlier whispering campaign against Bakunin. But he worked closely with both, and to Bakunin, it would have be the height of naïveté not to suspect that Marx was the puppeteer.

The campaign of innuendo and slander infuriated Bakunin. Believing he had finally cleared up the muck at the Basel congress with the public renunciation of Liebknecht, Hess's renewed assault in *Le Reveil* provoked Bakunin into penning a lengthy response. In it Bakunin did not counter this campaign by advancing anarchist thought so much as attempt to discredit his critics. Some of his criticisms were accurate enough, but he also attacked Marx, Hess, and Liebknecht as Jews. This anti-Semitism was a vile and disturbing theme in some of his writings in this period. It is especially disheartening in the work of a thinker who proclaimed himself in favor of freedom and equality, and no rationalization can expiate it. Since the term "anti-Semitism" may be applied to a wide range of ideas and behaviors, from preferring a Jewish doctor because one believes "Jews are smart" to participating in pogroms, it is necessary to distinguish between these poles to make sense of the charge, disturbing though the notion of a spectrum may be. In an age when it was common to ascribe physiological, mental, and cultural characteristics to such a dubious concept as "race," racist language was common. Even Marx, for example, referred to the socialist Ferdinand Lassalle as "the Jewish nigger" and occasionally attributed his political maneuvering to his genetic origins, just as he insisted that Bakunin's "Russian blood" made him a born conspirator. Marx even categorized his son-in-law, Paul Lafargue, as a "nigger" whose romantic excesses in courting Marx's daughter were attributable to his "race." As a young man, Bakunin occasionally had used the Polish word *zhid,* that is, "yid," to refer to Jews. In nineteenth-century Russia, the word was considered much less offensive, at least in genteel, gentile circles, than it is today, and was used in official government documents and literature, often without overt or conscious pejorative intent. That tells us something very important about the pervasiveness of anti-Semitism in Russia. But precisely because the use of the word was so prevalent and deep-seated, it is not in itself proof of virulent anti-Semitism. In fact, on some occasions Bakunin has been badly served by translators who turned his use of the French *juif* or "Jew" into *zhid.* In his letter to *Le Reveil,* Bakunin made repeated references to the "German Jewish journalists" who accused him of being a tsarist spy as he reached for the old, despicable tropes and rationalizations of anti-Semitism. Noting sardonically that some might think him capable even of cannibalism, Bakunin asserted that he was "neither the enemy nor the detractor of the Jews," and that he did not support such a barbaric position. On the contrary, he continued, "all nations are equal in my eyes," since each was "a product of historical ethnography and consequently not responsible for either its defaults or merits." In a later note, Bakunin expanded on this idea to suggest that by "national characteristics" he meant not genetic or attributed racial traits but "the individual temperament and character of all races and peoples, which are themselves the product of a host of ethnographic, climatological and economic, as well as historical causes," a claim that in itself was much more enlightened than contemporary discussions of inherent racial characteristics.[33] Furthermore, in the letter to *Le Reveil* he added that while historical, political, and social reality influenced people, they did not precisely determine outcomes and ideas. As a negative example, he pointed out that "in the heart of democratic America" one also found "the singularly passionate tendency toward imperialism." As a positive example, he pointed out that not only had Judaism given the world Christ, Saint Paul, and Spinoza, it had also produced "the two most eminent socialists of our day: Marx and Lassalle." Moses Hess, however, could not be included among such giants; he was instead one of the "Jewish pygmies" who resorted to character assassination rather than the frank exchange of political differences.

Bakunin then argued that the history of the Jews had given them an "essentially mercantile and bourgeois tendency" that meant, "taken as a nation," they were "preeminently the exploiters of the labor of others." While he insisted he did not categorize all Jews as exploiters and that to do so "would be an injustice and a folly," and while he made later references not to the broad category of "Jews" but to "bourgeois Jews and Germans," it is clear he was making a disreputable argument about ethnicity as much as an argument about class. Because they exploited workers, "Jews" had "a natural horror and fear of the popular masses" and despised them, "either openly or in secret," and their interests were "entirely contrary to the interests and the instincts of the proletariat." Jews constituted "a real force in Europe today," for they "reign despotically in commerce and banking." This was a widespread notion in the nineteenth century, shared even by Karl Marx, who wrote in 1844, "Let us look for the secret of the Jew not in his religion, but let us look for the secret of religion in the actual Jew. What is the secular basis of Judaism? Practical need, selfishness. What is the secular cult of the Jew? Haggling. What is his secular god? Money. Well then, an emancipation from haggling and money, from practical, real Judaism would be the self-emancipation of our age." When Bruno Bauer argued that the Viennese Jew "controls through his money the fate of the whole Empire," Marx agreed that "this is no isolated fact. The Jew has emancipated himself in a Jewish manner, not only annexing the power of money but also because through him and also apart from him money has become a world power and the practical spirit of the Jew has become the practical spirit of the Christian people."[34] The debate over whether or to what degree Marx was anti-Semitic continues today, and it is no defense of Bakunin to point out that others too were anti-Semitic. Nor is provocation a defense, though the fact that Bakunin's outbursts were a knee-jerk response to a persistent and malicious campaign of slander may be mitigating. His remarks make up a deplorable but miniscule part of his thought, never becoming a consistent theme in his writing or turning into generalized attacks on Jews. It is hardly the case, as one historian has asserted, that Bakunin's anti-Semitism was "enough to corrupt his message irredeemably."[35]

Ironically, labeling his foes as "journalists" may have been the greatest insult at the time. Journalism, especially in Germany, was widely regarded as the career choice of the educated but unsuccessful, the uninspired and disaffected who could not find gainful employment. Coming from Bakunin, such a charge was rather hypocritical, but it emphasized his belief that he was the victim of an unprincipled personal attack from the lesser lights of the left.[36] And in drawing attention to their German nationality, Bakunin emphasized that his detractors shared the prejudice of many Western Europeans against his homeland and, by extension, against him. The bulk of the thirty-eight pages he penned dealt with the specific charges made by Hess and Marx's other supporters. While Bakunin frankly admitted his passionate belief in the Russian people, there was no stronger critic of the Russian empire than himself. After all, who among his accusers had suffered at the hands of the tsar as he had? The allegations of "pan-Slavism" were clearly false, prompted, he suggested, by the traditional German fear of Russia and Russians. Bakunin reaffirmed his support for the International and its principles, pointing out the errors and half-truths told by those who accused him of being a splitter, and he described in detail how the court of honor at the Basel congress had unanimously championed him against Liebknecht's smears.

He then launched into a discussion of Garibaldi and Mazzini before sending the letter, unfinished, not to the newspaper, but to Herzen for his comments, with the abashed acknowledgment that the "polemic against the German Jews will seem too raw and coarse to you" and the hope that Herzen might help edit it. Herzen was appalled by the letter and penned a defense of Bakunin for *Le Reveil* that he sent off instead. Long himself the target of Marx's venom, he did wonder why Bakunin had largely ignored Marx in his diatribe, and the anarchist's answer is worth quoting at some length, for it illustrates how Bakunin was torn in the larger struggle in the International. Marx had been spared, he wrote, because

> leaving aside all the foulness he has spewed against us, we cannot ignore, at least I cannot, the great service he has rendered to the socialist cause for twenty-five years. Undoubtedly he has left all of us far behind in this. He is also one of the first founders, if not the cre-

ator, of the International. This is of enormous worth, in my view, and whatever his attitude toward us, I will always acknowledge this . . . Marx is undeniably a very useful man in the International. Up to now he has been a wise influence and has been the strongest bulwark for socialism, the strongest obstacle against the invasion of bourgeois ideas and tendencies. And I could never forgive myself if I destroyed or weakened his beneficial influence for the mere aim of personal vengeance.

However, he continued, it was likely that the two would soon clash, not on personal grounds but on a question of principle, that of state communism. Openly attacking Marx now would probably fail; better to pick off some of his weaker disciples first. This argument, however, was probably unconvincing to both men.[37] Herzen, quite correctly, believed that Bakunin had no ability as a political intriguer. Bakunin himself, for all his fondness for secret codes and paper organizations, had neither talent nor taste for internecine battles and infighting. Perhaps it reflected his generosity of spirit; perhaps it reflected his particular cast of mind that immediately grasped the broad strokes of a situation or argument and was happy to leave the details to others; perhaps he got bored easily. Despite his feuding with Marx, Bakunin took up the task of translating *Capital* into Russian shortly after the Basel congress. The publisher's advance of three hundred rubles let him leave Geneva for Locarno on Switzerland's Lake Maggiore; it would also prove to be the critical weapon for his opponents in the International.

14

THE ONLY LIBERTY
DESERVING OF THE NAME

That *Capital* can be a challenging read is hardly news; the fact that there are several books offering to introduce Marx, explain him, make him easy, or let the beginner understand it is proof enough. Rendering it from German to Russian soon became loathsome toil for Bakunin. "Marx's frightful work, *Das Kapital,* 748 pages in tiny letters," was "terribly difficult" to translate, he admitted to Ogarev; he was lucky to get through five pages a day. Later he would call it an "extremely important, learned, and profound, if very abstract" work, but in the meantime, it was tough going.[1] He did have a few other things on his mind. In December 1869, Antonia returned from Italy to join him in Locarno. Pregnant and seasick, she arrived two days late, due to a storm in the Mediterranean. Bakunin had waited anxiously for her and young Carl, but her return was not an unmixed blessing, for their complicated relationship was strained, as Bakunin noted in a letter to Ogarev. "Dear friend," he wrote, "I will explain to you once and for all my relationship with Antonia and her veritable spouse. I did something frightfully stupid, even more, I committed a crime, in marrying a woman almost two and a half times younger than me." Antonia is "a gentle being and a beautiful spirit, and I love her as much as a father could love his daughter." Thus when she found "her true love" in Gambuzzi, Bakunin insisted that whatever the cost to himself, Antonia had to be "entirely free" to follow her heart. He hoped she would choose to stay with him, but he would not oppose her if she went to Gambuzzi, especially since her lover was his friend and a fellow revolutionary. The letter describes how Antonia hid the love affair, the subsequent pregnancy, and the birth of Carlo from Bakunin, how she was torn between two very different men and two very different relationships, how the three of them tried to resolve the situation, and how each genuinely cared for the others. Bakunin had finally put the matter plainly; Antonia could renounce Gambuzzi's love while remaining his friend and return to Switzerland, where Bakunin would accept "my son and future child," or stay with Gambuzzi, who would openly acknowledge Antonia as his spouse and the children as his. Gambuzzi, according to Bakunin, was not keen on formally recognizing his paternity or raising the children, and this outraged Antonia; at the same time, she had grown accustomed to Bakunin and could not consider living without him. Respecting her decision to live with him, Bakunin told Ogarev, "I have adopted Gambuzzi's children, without denying his incontestable right to take responsibility for, and to direct, with Antonia, their education." Gambuzzi promised to send money for them, and "we remain together, Antonia and I, as long as the revolution doesn't call me. Then I shall belong only to the revolution and to myself."² It was entirely in keeping with his commitment to women's rights and the lessons he had learned from the struggles of his sisters so long ago, though, like most of life's lessons, not without considerable pain and perhaps some self-deception.

It was a lesson reinforced by a criminal act facilitated by the state. In July 1869, Zoe Obolensky's husband, with the connivance of the Swiss authorities, kidnapped their children from their mother and spirited them away to Russia. Bakunin sprang to her defense in a lengthy pamphlet entitled "The Bears of Berne and the Bears of St. Petersburg." He defended Zoe Obolensky as a mother who had left oppressive Russia to raise her children in liberty. In doing so, she had forfeited all the wealth she had brought to the marriage to live in relative poverty in Switzerland. That Swiss and Russian governments alike had upheld the so-called "rights of husband and father" and allowed him to "use force to kidnap, if not the mother, then at least the children," revealed the true, oppressive nature of both republic and autocracy. Further complicating Bakunin's work and life was the association with Nechaev that had begun in March 1869. While Bakunin would finally break with him by June 1870, their relationship was hardly conducive to the peace and tranquility needed for translation. Indeed, much of "The Bears of Berne and the Bears of St. Petersburg" was aimed at the Swiss authorities who harassed the Russian radical community, including Nechaev.³

The final difficulty came from an expected quarter. Marx had resumed his campaign against Bakunin immediately after the Basel congress. Among Marx's allies—by now Bakunin was undoubtedly thinking of them as "known associates" and "henchmen"—was Nicholas Utin, who pressed his attack on the Swiss front. A sincere revolutionary in his student days and a devoted Marxist after his break with Bakunin, Utin would break with the revolutionary movement in 1875. Unlike Bakunin in his "confession," Utin did write the tsar in repentance, and in return received a pardon. Allowed to return to Russia, Utin went into the family liquor business and diversified, becoming rich as a contractor to the tsar's war machine. In the meantime, he engineered a split in the Fédération Romande and requested the General Council in London to recognize his new faction as the official Swiss affiliate of the International, with the right to keep the original name. Since this was essentially an appeal to Marx in a cause Marx supported, the request was granted with unseemly haste. That Marx used the powers that Bakunin himself had voted to give the General Council was undoubtedly a bit of delicious and bitter irony, respectively. Utin also took over the editorship of *L'Egalité* just as he had *The People's Cause* earlier. He then created a Russian section of the International in Geneva, offering Marx the position of corresponding secretary of the new section, a proposal that Marx agreed to with alacrity. With the Federation Romande now officially a Marxist group, Bakunin and his supporters regrouped and formed the Jura Federation of the International.

For his part, Marx sent a lengthy "Confidential Communication on Bakunin" to his friend Ludwig Kugelman, an influential member of Liebknecht's German Social Democratic Workers' Party, in March 1870. Ostensibly a justification of the General Council's decision to acknowledge Utin's splinter group as the legitimate Swiss section of the International, the letter was a calculated and outrageous misrepresentation of Bakunin and the Alliance. Repeating once again the veiled accusation that Bakunin was a Russian spy, Marx charged that members of the League of Peace and Freedom had kept an eye on Bakunin as a "Russian suspect." He added that in a speech to the League, Bakunin had "denounced the Occidental bourgeoisie in the same tone that the Muscovite optimists use to attack Western civilization in order to minimize their own barbarism." This odd comment was more serious than it sounds, for it played to the deeply rooted German fear that Russian hordes would sweep across from the steppes and destroy Western civilization, with Bakunin as their point man. In the twentieth century, this same fear would fuel Germany's two aggressive wars. Bakunin was an opportunist, Marx railed, who had deliberately introduced to the League radical resolutions he knew would fail so he could storm out and enter the International in a burst of revolutionary élan. The program of the Alliance was nothing more than an *"olla podrida* [roughly, "mulligan stew"] of polished commonplaces," and the Alliance itself an organization of "Bakuninist private mysticism."

Marx then launched into the indictment he and subsequent Marxists would make for generations to come: that Bakunin had joined the International to split it and sow dissension for his own self-aggrandizement. The Alliance, Marx insisted, had only one function, that of "a machine for the disorganization of the International," while Bakunin was "one of the most ignorant of men in the field of social theory," and worse, nothing more than a "sect founder." Ignoring his own eagerness to put the motion on the floor, Marx then suggested that Bakunin's resolution on inheritance at Basel had been a cunning ploy to take over the International, for if it had passed, it would "show the world that he has not gone over to the International, but the International has gone over to him." Since Bakunin had failed to get his way, he was now attacking the General Council in *L'Egalité* and *Progres* and was agitating to move it from London to Geneva, where it would fall under the control of the anarchists. These allegations were simply untrue. While some anarchists did agitate to move the General Council and reduce its powers, Bakunin himself declared publicly that this would be a great mistake. He was not even in place to take advantage of such a move, for he had already moved to Locarno. Nor did Bakunin critique the General Council in the anarchist press. His articles on the International predated Basel, and were restrained and generally supportive; where he was critical of the International at this time, he expressed his differences in the mildest terms. The only pieces of his that appeared in the anarchist papers after the congress were the texts of two speeches he had made at the congress, and neither was critical of the International. That other writers were more hostile was no reason to paint Bakunin with the same brush, but undoubtedly Marx believed he had detected the hand of his archenemy in the articles. Finally, Marx added an outright fabrication, probably passed on to him by Utin, who was regarded by Marx as uniquely positioned to expose the intricate dealings of the Russian expatriate community. Alexander Herzen had died in early January 1870. Marx claimed Herzen had received twenty-five thousand francs a year, a very significant sum, from a Russian pan-Slavist group. Marx then accused Bakunin, "despite his hatred of the right of inheritance," of appropriating this money from Herzen's estate. This was a distorted account of the Bahkmetov money that Herzen helped administer and that Bakunin had used to fund Nechaev, but any anti-Bakunin reader could be counted on to connect the dots and conclude from these falsehoods that Herzen and Bakunin were in league together, that both were supporters of the Russian empire, that both were in essence little more than agents of the tsar, and that Bakunin was a thief. Marx finished his letter by noting that the next step of Utin's brandnew Russian branch would be "to tear off Bakunin's mask publicly, because that man speaks two entirely different languages, one in Russia and one in Europe. Thus the game of this highly dangerous intrigant—at least on the terrain of the International—will soon be played out."[4]

Marx's hostility reflected more than personal antipathy, though that certainly gave his polemic a particularly unscrupulous and nasty edge. The brutal fact was that the International was growing only in those regions where Bakunin had some influence. Its nominal strength numbered in the tens of thousands, but that was misleading, for it represented union members who had been affiliated to the International by their leadership and who probably neither knew nor cared about it. They certainly didn't pay dues or a per capita levy; if one counted paid-up members, the International listed only a few hundred. The English were losing interest and feuding with Marx. The Germans were split between the Lassalleans, whom Marx disliked and distrusted, and Liebknecht's much smaller Social Democratic Workers' Party. These two groups were more interested in fighting each other than building the International; anyway, creating sections of the International was illegal under German law, and that made organization difficult. France was the strongest national section, but it largely ignored the General Council and could not be counted on. The only real growth was taking place in Switzerland, Belgium, and especially Spain and Italy. There conditions made Bakunin's message much more appealing. Spain and Italy had only recently begun the process of industrialization, and the shock treatment of capitalism left workers militant and radical. Nor had the newly created wealth trickled down to create a significant layer of labor aristocrats who would counsel against revolution or who could afford to take the long view of reform. Furthermore, workers had no legal means to press their demands. Trade unions were banned, the vote was restricted, and workers' political parties were nonexistent. Reformism and political action, therefore, seemed both irrelevant and impossible, and so the antipolitical, direct action of anarchism made a great deal of sense. Bakunin's colleagues had been active in Italy and in Spain, and had received a warm reception. There was little doubt that the influence of anarchism in the International would grow by the next congress, set for September 1870 in Paris, and Marx worked hard to counter this growing tendency.

His efforts had to be put on hold, for the French government was cracking down on radicals and unionists, and discretion dictated the congress change its venue to Mainz, Germany. The new plan, however, was rendered impossible by the outbreak of the Franco-Prussian War on 19 July 1870.

The war had long been predicted. Bismarck eagerly sought the conflict, seeing in war the best chance to bring into Prussia's fold the German states, such as Bavaria, that preferred to remain politically independent. Victory over France would also bring Germany control of the Alsace-Lorraine, greedily eyed for its vineyards, and, perhaps nearly as important for the emperor, its rich coal and iron deposits. Pushing into the region would also improve Germany's strategic position. France had little territory or resources to gain from war with its neighbor, but Napoleon III had long played on nationalist sentiment and hysteria to blunt the socialist and labor movements and his political opposition. War seemed an easy way to whip up popular support for himself and his government. The pretext for the conflict was a dispute over the succession to the Spanish Queen Isabella II. France prevailed upon the obvious candidate, a Hohenzollern, to decline, and pressed its luck by demanding that Germany promise not to support his candidacy in the future. It was an offer that Bismarck and Wilhelm I were delighted to refuse, and when they did so in most insulting terms through the so-called Ems dispatch, Napoleon III declared war.

French socialists opposed the war, while the German parties split on the issue. The socialists elected to the Reichstag overwhelmingly supported the war, believing, or claiming to believe, that Germany was fighting a defensive war. To their credit, Liebknecht and Bebel, both sitting in the Reichstag, abstained from voting for war credits. Their abstention, however, mattered little. The German military machine smashed through the French lines, trapping an entire army of 155,000 men at Metz on 19 August and another of 130,000, including Napoleon III himself, at Sedan on 1 September. Three days later, Parisian crowds took over the local government, declared the fall of the Second Empire, and proclaimed a republican Government of National Defense. But by 20 September, Paris was surrounded by the invader. Attempts to rally the provinces to relieve the city won initial support, but were quickly defeated. When the national government signed an armistice, Paris remained recalcitrant and decided to hold out against the German army and the French government.

From his home in Switzerland, Bakunin began a series of "Letters to a Frenchman" in August 1870, outlining the failure of France's government and demonstrating that the same politicians and *raison d'etat* that had brought the nation to disaster could not possibly extricate it. What could France do? It could surrender, of course, or it could launch a people's war against the German invader. "No army in the world, however well organized and equipped with the most extraordinary weapons" could hope to defeat thirty-eight million people, he argued. But it was crucial that the people's army wage a revolutionary war at the same time. Only if they truly believed they had a new world to win would the people mobilize effectively. A people's army, however, would not be considered by the bourgeoisie or the aristocracy, who feared the masses even more than they feared Germany. Nor could they lead a regular army; they had already proved themselves unequal to that task. Even worse, the so-called leaders of France were happy to treat with Bismarck's Germany, for they preferred to serve in hell rather than create a heaven on earth that would cost them their privilege and profit.

The people's army could not be organized from Paris, Bakunin insisted, for Paris had to defend itself. At the same time, it could not rely on its old habit of issuing orders to the provinces, for they had no wish to remain under the yoke of the capital city, however revolutionary it might be. Only free uprisings throughout the country could save France. These would be spearheaded by workers in the larger cities such as Lyon, Marseilles, and Rouen, and by peasants in the countryside. The peasants, Bakunin admitted, were problematic. They occupied a very different social and economic position than the Russian peasants who had saved their homeland from the invader. French peasants were small landowners, more like independent farmers than serfs or agricultural laborers. Because they tended to see themselves as rural proprietors, they often hated and feared urban workers. It was, after all, the peasants who had originally elected Napoleon III and supported his reactionary policies. Nonetheless, Bakunin maintained that they could be enlisted in a people's war. While they were property owners, they were not wealthy and had little privilege to defend. As small property owners, they felt the pressure of big capital and despised the large absentee landowners. Finally, if the peasants' sense of possessing the land translated into a fierce patriotism, it could easily become a hatred of the German invader.

The slogans and ideas that rallied urban workers would not work on peasants, Bakunin warned. Their experience was different and it was important not to tread too heavily on their traditions and prejudices. Attacking Napoleon III, for example, would bring cheers in Paris, but would anger the peasants who had seen in him their only protection from the local authorities and capitalists. Talk about collectivizing the land would outrage them and was unnecessary anyway, as peasant proprietorship was not the same as capitalism and need not be abolished to make the social revolution. Ordering peasants to rebel and rally to the revolution in the cities, as generations of radicals from 1789 on had done, was utterly unproductive. Worse, it was precisely the sort authoritarianism that workers themselves were fighting. Urban radicals had to dispel their own prejudices about the peasantry and understand that it was a constituency to organize and ally with. While historically the peasants had often been won over to the side of reaction, they still had "socialist passions." It was, after all, the peasants' desire for freedom and equality that Napoleon III had played upon to win their support. What the revolutionary had to do was to "direct these same passions toward their true goal, toward a goal that conformed to those profound instincts." There was no doubt that the peasants' instinct was "profoundly socialist," because it was in essence the hatred shared by "all workers against all the exploiters of labor." And that economic fact was at the heart of all "elementary, natural, and real socialism." The systems, doctrinaire thought, and abstract theory of too many socialist thinkers tended to cloud that fact; strip them away to that essence and the revolutionary would find the peasantry ready for revolution. But not for any socialism that promised centralization and state control; that the peasants would always reject. Part of the appeal of Napoleon III was his promise, always broken, that he would reduce government regulation, taxes, and supervision. Only free socialism—anarchism—would win the peasants over.[5]

It was a masterful document that showed Bakunin's deep understanding of the peasantry, and he was, at first, content to comment on events from afar. He was, after all, fifty-seven years old and had never recovered from the blows to his health he suffered in prison. But when the bell of revolution rang out, the old fire horse responded. When the last French army surrendered at Sedan, Bakunin determined to join his comrades at Lyon in the hope that workers there would launch an insurrection as a preliminary round in the people's war and the social revolution. He had already argued that the only hope for France lay in the insurrection of the cities, and if cooler heads reckoned it a faint hope, he still knew which side he was on. By the time he arrived at Lyon on 15 September 1870, the city, like Paris, had proclaimed itself a republic. Drawing on the tradition of the French Revolution of 1789, it created an emergency Committee for Public Safety to replace the defunct government and held free elections. Factories were nationalized into democratic workshops and charged to provide full employment rather than profits for the capitalist. It was not the revolution, as Bakunin admitted frankly, but it was an example of propaganda by the deed, an instance of people organizing themselves freely from the bottom up the moment official "order" collapsed and surrendered.

Keeping the momentum going was more difficult. While other uprisings broke out across France in the aftermath of the German invasion, they were not coordinated or well planned. In Lyon, Bakunin helped organize a Committee for the Saving of France and organized public demonstrations that called for increased taxation of the wealthy and the free election of military officers. A manifesto announced that people's justice would now replace the state's judicial system. Taxes, save for those on the rich, and mortgages were abolished and the Committee would begin to prepare to defend France. The ideas were largely Bakunin's, and they met with popular support in demonstrations and parades. But Lyon was not as unified as it first appeared, and differences in opinion soon became deep fissures. Bakunin, who had some experience in these matters, argued that it was necessary to arrest those who were organizing to crush the newborn republic. Some of his colleagues balked at such a drastic step and so left a fifth column in their ranks. Worse, the municipal council cut the wages in the workshops, a move that virtually guaranteed spontaneous rallies to oppose the republic. At one demonstration called to protest the wage cuts, Bakunin and several score other people took over the hotel where the council met and proclaimed a new provisional government. But time had run out for the Lyon republic. The French National Guard arrived and marched on the hotel while the city's military commander quickly remembered a previous engagement and retired from the scene. Bakunin was arrested, but in the chaos and the halfhearted efforts of the National Guard, was quickly freed by his friends and made his way back to Switzerland by the end of September.

Lyon of 1870 was not Paris of 1848 and it was not the social revolution. Bakunin's critics have been quick to denounce his involvement as quixotic and reckless, a foolhardy attempt that endangered the lives of others who were swept away by his rhetoric. There is no question that the Lyon insurrection failed. Yet those who believe that "resistance is futile" turn the dismal pronouncement into a self-fulfilling prophecy. Thomas Jefferson and Lenin might well have stayed in bed if they had weighed the odds meticulously; it is relatively easy to take up the fray when you know you are going to win and easier still to denounce failed efforts from the vantage point of history. One of those critics was Karl Marx. The day after the Franco-Prussian war broke out, he declared to Engels, "The French need a drubbing." A Prussian victory, he went on, would centralize state power and aid in the "centralization of the working class." It would also mean that Germany would replace France as the "center of the working class movement in Western Europe." This, Marx believed, would be a good thing, since "the German working class is theoretically and organizationally superior to the French." Furthermore, a Prussian triumph would "mean at the same time the superiority of our theory over Proudhon's."[6] Upon reflection, he would temper this considerably, but he continued to argue that the war was a "defensive war" for Germany, even if Prussia remained responsible for it by allowing the corrupt Bonapartist regime to flourish and adopting all its vices for its own. The real issues, he realized, were whether German workers could prevent the state from shifting the war from a defensive one to an aggressive one, and

whether German and French workers would unite across national boundaries to ultimately "kill war" itself.[7] As for the insurrection at Lyon, "At first
everything went well," Marx wrote. "But those asses, Bakunin and Cluseret,
arrived at Lyon and spoiled everything." Both he and Engels opposed the
very idea of workers' insurrections to combat the German invasion, believing that such action would set them back twenty years, or perhaps fifty.[8]

Events in Paris would soon force Marx and Engels to reevaluate their predictions and their politics. The French national government was increasingly
reactionary and there was certainly no indication that the German army was
about to return home and advance the socialist revolution. But the working-
class population of Paris was determined to hang on to the freedom it had
won by declaring the republic, and it reasserted its revolutionary tradition.
On 18 March 1871, the citizens of Paris refused to allow the French army to
remove its artillery from the city. Instead, they created their own militia,
declared Paris a free city—the Commune—and raised the red flag over the
Hotel de Ville. Fearing a repeat of 1848, when French troops had gone over
to the rebels, the national government ordered its army out of the city. The
Communards organized soup kitchens, hospitals, a newspaper, and municipal
services. Equally important, they created a new political structure for the city,
one based on universal suffrage and representative wards. All government
positions were elected, and all officials were immediately responsible to and
recallable by the voters. There was no distinction between the legislature and
the executive: Elected representatives all shared in the work, and were paid
the same salaries as ordinary workers. The people of Paris called for other
cities to join them in insurrection against the German invaders and the French
government that had betrayed them, and they prepared to defend the city, not
from the German army that was still in place, but from the French government that was positioning its army for an assault on its own citizens.

On 11 April 1871, the French army attacked, and though they had been
under siege for months, the volunteers of the Commune now took on the
same troops and government that had surrendered to Germany. They fought
in the streets and boulevards until munitions, food, and time ran out and the
army could claim victory. The so-called "Reign of Terror" during the French
Revolution had sent perhaps twenty-five hundred aristocrats to the guillotine over several months; *la Semaine Sanglante*, "the Bloody Week" of 21-28
May, saw over twenty thousand Communards slaughtered, many after they
had laid down their arms and surrendered. It was gory proof of Bakunin's
observation that reaction was always more violent than the revolution could
ever be.

The Paris Commune was, as Eric Hobsbawm has noted, "extraordinary, heroic, dramatic, and tragic." That it was also brief did not reassure its enemies or tarnish its importance to the left. Both sides understood that it represented the power of the working class and the promise of the future. That promise is repeated in the verses of the left-wing hymn "The Internationale," written by Eugene Pottier, a Proudhonist member of the First International who had been on the barricades of 1848 and returned to them during the Commune. "Arise, ye prisoners of starvation!" it dares. "We have been naught, we shall be all." Another Communard, Jean-Baptiste Clement, had written "Le Temps des Cerises" five years before the Commune. Covered by contemporary artists ranging from Yves Montand to Juliette Greco to Nana Mouskouri, the haunting lyrics were sung by the workers who fought in the streets of Paris and promised that none would forget the time of the cherries. The Commune continues to intrigue and inspire; in 2000, Peter Watkins used it as the subject of a six-hour film to comment on politics and the media in the new millennium. But the Commune was not an explicitly Marxist or anarchist uprising. While anarchists such as Louise Michel and Élisée Reclus participated, Marxists, Jacobins, and Blanquists played an equal role. Probably the largest political contingent was comprised of Proudhonists, and it was as difficult to slot them as it is to slot Proudhon himself. While the International was often blamed for the Commune, and while it was often pleased to take credit for it, in fact it had little to do with it, though some of its members were found on the governing council and undoubtedly more were found among its dead.

Nonetheless, the Paris Commune, Bakunin argued, was the first attempt to realize the principles of revolutionary socialism and to replace the state with the self-organization of the people. It was true that it had not even made explicit, let alone created, socialism; neither were most Communard socialists. And yet the people of Paris, without aid of, or more to the point, in opposition to, the central government, organized, fed, and armed a population of hundreds of thousands under the siege guns and bayonets of two armies. Could the Commune have gone further? Undoubtedly; but to reproach it for failing to create socialism ignored the gulf between the ideal world of the theoreticians and the practical world of the people, Bakunin argued. The social revolution could not be decreed from above, and the socialism of the Commune lay not in programs or theories but in the "spontaneous action of the masses, of the popular groups and associations." That was the lesson of the Commune: The future society must be made "from the bottom up, by the free association and federation of workers, first in their unions, then in communes, then in regions and nations, and finally in a great international and universal federation," with neither God nor state nor master. Bakunin wrote as a "fanatical lover of liberty," not that "formal freedom granted, measured, and regulated by the state," but "the only liberty which is truly deserving of the name, the liberty that consists of the full development of all the material, intellectual, and moral powers latent in everyone." But freedom required equality, he reminded his readers, and these could only be achieved by the "voluntary organization of work and collective property, of freely organized and federated associations of producers in communes." These could not be accomplished through the state, he warned, and it was precisely this point that divided the "socialists or revolutionary collectivists" from the "authoritarian communists." Their goals were the same: the "creation of a new social order, founded solely on the organization of collective labor," economic equality, and "the collective appropriation of the instruments of labor," or, more loosely, the means of production. But the authoritarian socialists believed this could be achieved by the "development and organization of the political power of the working classes." Anarchists insisted that it could obtained through the "development and organization not of political power but the social, and so in consequence, antipolitical, power of the working masses of the cities and country." While the authoritarian socialists spoke of capturing state power, the anarchists demanded instead the "destruction" or the "liquidation" of the state. Both groups believed in rationality and science, but where authoritarian socialists sought to impose it, anarchists sought to propagate it. The revolutionary, anarchist socialists understood that "humanity has let itself be governed long enough, too long, and that the source of its unhappiness does not lie in this or that form of government but in the principle and the very fact of government itself."⁹

Bakunin's analysis was aimed as carefully at Marx as it was at capital and the state. Marx himself was initially as unenthusiastic about the Commune as he had been about Lyon. In part, his skepticism was based on a realistic assessment of its chances. At the same time, the Paris Commune was a powerful counterargument against his analysis of reform, the German working class, and the state. He alternately criticized the Communards first for rising and then for failing to go far enough soon enough; throughout the Commune's brief existence, the official voice of the International remained silent. But if the Lyon uprising could be safely ignored, the Paris Commune could not. Lyon and Paris were social experiments, arguably the most important European working-class actions since 1848, and they pushed Marx to rethink some of his ideas in a pamphlet called *The Civil War in France.* Originally commissioned to outline the International's position on the Commune, the essay was not finished until the conclusion of *la Semaine Sanglante*: it was not a birth announcement for the revolution but an obituary. As Samuel Johnson noted, one is not on oath in such circumstances, and historians have argued how accurately Marx's stirring words reflected his considered thought on the subject. Nonetheless, the essay shows him at his most libertarian, and it is an effective antidote to those who work so hard to draw a straight line from *Capital* to the gulag. In it, Marx, like Bakunin, praised the autonomous action of the Paris workers and heralded their democratic self-organization as the model for future socialist societies. Certainly the Commune pushed Marx to rethink some of his ideas on the state. As he noted in the preface to a new edition of the Communist Manifesto, published a year after the Paris uprising, the Commune proved that "the working class cannot simply lay hold of the ready-made state machinery and wield it for its own purposes"; the machinery so well-adapted for the rule of the bourgeoisie could not provide the model for socialism.[10]

"That's just what I've been on about!" Bakunin exclaimed. The old foes eyed each other warily until the realization sunk in. Then each extended his arms, crying out "Comrade!" as they embraced in a particularly hairy hug that, to be honest, left both men feeling a little awkward. "But I thought you . . ." "I was a fool to put it that way . . ." "No more than I!" "How could we have been so . . . ?" Reconciled at last, they agreed to work together and use that dynamic tension that had so divided them to build a united socialist movement and well and truly launch humanity's history anew.

Perhaps in a parallel universe. The opportunity the Commune offered for unity was soon squandered in another wave of mutual distrust and maneuvering. War, insurrection, and repression made it impossible to convene a congress of the International. Instead, the General Council, headed by Marx, was given the authority to arrange the next meeting as it saw fit. It opted for a private conference in a small London pub in September 1871. In essence by invitation only, fewer than twenty-five delegates attended the sessions. While it was undoubtedly difficult for European delegates to make their way to England in the wake of reaction—"Business or pleasure trip, sir?" "Bit of both, really, just off to smash the state"—there was no attempt to represent the general membership of the International. Thirteen of the delegates were members of the General Council; Utin was asked to represent Switzerland while the Bakuninist Jura Federation was excluded; there were no German delegates, and the few French participants were refugees who represented only themselves. Though the conference was authorized only to deal with administrative questions, the small showing made it possible for Marx to control the agenda and resolutions, and he did so with enthusiasm. The London conference, in other words, looked a lot like a secret organization within the International, of the type Marx claimed to abhor, and in fact, it was.

The conference set out, depending on which side one was on, to put an end to sectarian squabbling or to smash legitimate dissent. It resolved that none of the branches, sections, or groups that made up the International could "designate themselves by sectarian names such as positivists, mutualists, collectivists, communists, etc., or form separatist bodies under the name of sections of propaganda, etc., pretending to accomplish special missions, distinct from the common purposes of the Association." This was obviously a slap at Bakunin's Alliance and its avowed mission to study political and philosophical questions. If there was any doubt about who this was aimed at, a subsequent resolution identified the Alliance by name and reiterated that the General Council had the right to refuse the admittance of any new group or section to the International. For good measure, the conference reaffirmed the General Council's recognition of Utin's faction as the official Swiss branch of the International and, singling out the anarchist papers *Progres* and *Solidarité*, warned that the General Council would "publicly denounce and disavow all organs of the International" that discussed "questions exclusively reserved for the local or Federal Committees and the General Council, or for the private and administrative sitting of the Federal or General Congresses."

Finally, the conference decided to resolve the question of political action once and for all. With few anarchists or Proudhonists in attendance, it was easy enough to do. Marx gave a potted history of the International to insist that it had always been in favor of political action. He reminded the delegates that his original rules held that the "political movement" was a subordinate means for economic emancipation. His inaugural address of 1864 had upped this to making conquering political power "the great duty of the working class," while the 1867 congress had resolved that "the social emancipation of the workmen is inseparable from their political emancipation." A subsequent declaration of the General Council, moved by Marx, had announced that the "special mission" of all branches of the International was "to support, in their respective countries, every political movement tending toward the accomplishment of our ultimate end, the economical emancipation of the working class." Political action had always been part of the International's brief, Marx maintained, and anyone who denied that was relying on "false translations" and "various interpretations which were mischievous to the development and action of the International." Therefore, he

now insisted, "the working class cannot act, as a class, except by constitut-
ing itself into a political party, distinct from, and opposed to, all old parties
formed by the propertied classes." Furthermore, he continued, the "constitution of the working class into a political party is indispensable in order to
ensure the triumph of the social revolution and its ultimate end—the abolition of classes." Now, he concluded, "in the militant state of the working
class, its economical movement and its political action are indissolubly
united." Engels weighed in for good measure, insisting that "complete
abstention from political action is impossible." The "only means" to abolish
classes, he finished, "is political domination of the proletariat."[11]

This interpretation of the history of the International was disingenuous
and distorted. Political action had not been the creed of the International; it
had been the subject of intense debate and dispute from the very beginning.
For all the talk about opposing sects and splitters, Marx and the London delegates had, in a particularly high-handed and undemocratic way, imposed a
narrow political program on the International and made dissent punishable
by expulsion. Whatever their intentions, the predictable result of forcing such
a program was to split the International. Numerous sections registered their
protest at the actions of the General Council and several resigned en masse.
Others determined to counter what seemed to be—indeed, what could hardly
be interpreted otherwise—as the growing authoritarianism of the General
Council. Anarchists hastily arranged a congress at Sonvillier, Switzerland,
and pulled together sixteen delegates from nine of twenty-two sections, rival-
ing the London conference in size despite the short notice. While Bakunin
did not attend the congress, the Sonvillier Circular it produced clearly bore
his influence. It condemned the London conference and its decisions, even
though the anarchists were prepared to accept that the General Council had
acted in "good faith." For whatever its motives and beliefs, the actions of
the General Council were proof of the anarchist contention that "it is
absolutely impossible for a man who wields power to remain a moral man."
It was, they continued, only to be expected that people in authority would
confuse their interests with those of the greater community and would seek
to impose their ideas on others. The membership of the General Council
rarely changed and was not accountable between congresses, and so naturally would come to have a proprietary interest in the International and to
view competing ideas as sacrilege. Furthermore, the Sonvillier Circular
insisted, it was entirely consistent, if completely mistaken, for those who
sought the "conquest of political power by the working class" to wish to
transform the International "into a hierarchical organization directed and

controlled by the General Council." In a sense that was the core argument of anarchism. Precisely because humanity was not made up largely of saints, it was necessary to create institutions and organizations that prevented anyone taking power. Thus it was necessary to counter the tendency toward authoritarianism by dismantling the apparatus of authority the General Council had created for itself. The new society that all desired required new forms of organization, for it was impossible "for an egalitarian society to emerge out of an authoritarian organization." Acknowledging that there was still a need for a coordinating body, the anarchists called for a new congress of the International to be held as soon as possible, and for the General Council to be reorganized, its powers reduced to that of a correspondence and statistics bureau, no greater or less than any national federation.[12]

In response, Marx and Engels penned a circular of their own entitled "Fictitious Splits in the International," where they laid out their side and denounced the work of the "Sonvillier Sixteen" and Bakunin, the "Pope of Locarno." They repeated all their intimations about the Alliance doing the work of the police, Bakunin's "makeshift program" and the "economic and social equalization of classes," and the "old Saint-Simon rubbish" of the inheritance question. This time they went further and accused Bakunin of mailing letters stamped "secret revolutionary committee" on the envelopes to Russian comrades and so identifying the recipients to the Russian Third Section. The screed then turned on those anarchists and others who had opposed the actions taken at the London conference, launched a general attack on the historical origins and futility of sectarianism, including that of Lassalle, and then intimated that the Alliance and Bakunin were effectively, if not knowingly, doing the work of the police. Marxists and anarchists alike regrouped for the next congress of the International, planned for the Hague in 1872.[13]

In truth, the anarchists did little to prepare for what would be the last meaningful gathering of the International. Bakunin wrote, furiously, to make his position clear and to urge others to weigh in, but he was more concerned with elaborating anarchist ideas, and produced some of his most interesting work in the middle of this fray. The Marxist contingent, on the other hand, spared no effort to rid the International of its last internal opponents.

Its chief tactic was to try to prove that some secret form of the Alliance existed, contrary to the orders of the London conference. This became the primary charge leveled against Bakunin and his followers at the congress of the Hague, and has been used ever since by his critics on the left and the right. The Alliance itself declared itself officially dissolved in a letter to the

International in August 1871. Did secret anarchist organizations remain in the International, as Marx charged? Undoubtedly, though this was often denied, even by those who belonged to the groups and groupuscles. Many of the organizations were probably a secret kept from Bakunin, as no one felt it necessary to report to Anarchist HQ whenever two or more gathered together in his, or anyone's, name.

The question, however, is an entirely misleading one. Until the resolutions of the London conference, Bakunin and his colleagues had a perfect right to create any sort of group they wished, from a book club to a newspaper, within the International, without advertising for members or announcing meeting times from a bullhorn. They had the right, moreover, to be critical members. They even had the fundamental democratic right to try to stack meetings, as long as the members were selected and appointed according to the rules of the organization. But the General Council now had the self-granted power to summarily expel any group calling itself the "Alliance," anyone who belonged to such a group, anyone who was organizing or publishing without the express and explicit consent of the General Council, or was involved in a "secret" organization as defined by the General Council. Engels, Paul Lafargue, and others were soon dispatched across Europe to hunt up proof—testimony, letters, anything—that some sort of secret, now illegal, Alliance existed with Bakunin's knowledge or support. Given Bakunin's capacity to generate reams of letters, manifestos, catechisms, instructions, and paper organizations, such proof would not be hard to find. More importantly, the London conference made any organized work by Bakunin and his comrades illicit by definition. Previously allowed activities were now officially banned. This proved especially difficult for the anarchists in Spain. When Giuseppe Fanelli went there in 1868, he, like Bakunin, believed that the Alliance would be accepted into the International without difficulty, and organized workers into both associations. The Alliance and the anarchist program were much more successful than the International or Marxism, and Fanelli, caring little for titular niceties or sectarian squabbles taking place far away, went with the flow. The situation in Italy was similar. There Mazzini had denounced the Paris Commune, and Bakunin had fired off lengthy ripostes that made it clear the anarchist rejected Mazzini's idealism, mysticism, and republicanism in equal measure. Bakunin's arguments and the organizational efforts of other anarchists garnered a great deal of support, and, as in Spain, this support was to the ideas of the Alliance, not the International. To abandon the Alliance because of an ukase of the General Council would be folly.[14]

Furthermore, Marx and the General Council guaranteed, practically by definition, that opposition to their undemocratic actions and resolutions would have to be taken in secret. It was clear—or it seemed clear—that despite his talk about democracy and letting a thousand flowers bloom, Marx would expel groups with whom he disagreed on the narrowest of pretexts. In that situation, it was crucial to organize caucuses and gather delegates for the next congress in order to be heard, and there was no reason, or ethical, moral, or political imperative, to broadcast this intent and get purged before the congress. Keeping the caucus a secret became a matter of self-defense, not conspiratorial intrigue. In this way, Marx created what he claimed he most feared: the rending of the International into opposing factions.

The important question of Bakunin's "secret organizations" is not whether they existed. They did, in various forms, ranging from circles of friends to affinity groups to fantasies to caucuses within the International. The real question is, what was the purpose of these groups? As members of the International, they did not have a right to organize a coup or to unilaterally change the rules or principles of the organization. And they did nothing of the sort. Even Marxist critics have acknowledged there is no evidence that Bakunin ever wanted or tried to take over or destroy the International. There was no secret conspiracy to take over the International undemocratically, to split the organization through nefarious means, or to wrest control from the General Council unilaterally. But the London conference had defined heresy and given the General Council the power to root it out.

The International's 1872 congress presented the opportunity to use that power. Early plans to hold the congress in Geneva were abandoned in favor of the Hague, and a map of Europe suggests why. It was easy enough for the German, British, and French supporters of Marx to make it to the Hague, and rather more difficult for the Swiss, Italian, and Spanish anarchists. The Italian sections, strongly Bakuninist, boycotted the congress and resigned from the International in protest. The tally of the delegates confirms the geographic reality: of the sixty-five seated delegates, nineteen came from Germany and four from Switzerland. Twenty-one were members of the General Council itself, while the Bakuninists could count only twenty-five of their adherents. It was the only congress Marx attended, but both he and Engels showed up for the showdown. Bakunin could not make it, for he was broke and risked arrest if he entered France or Germany on his way to Holland. After considerable wrangling over who would be confirmed as a delegate, for control of the credentials committee is crucial for political schemers of every persuasion, the congress settled down to business. Among the first

THE ONLY LIBERTY DESERVING OF THE NAME **297**

items was the appointment of a special five-person "Commission to Investigate the Alliance." It was chaired by Theodore Cuno, who had been briefed, inaccurately, on Bakunin by Engels in a long letter months before the congress. Another member of the commission, ironically enough, turned out later to be a spy for the French police. Engels submitted a twelve-page report along with the letters and testimony he and Lafargue had gathered up, and the commission rendered its verdict on the last day of the congress. Despite the best efforts of Marx, Engels, Lafargue, and others, they had produced no smoking gun. With one member of the commission dissenting from the majority report, the commission declared that the secret Alliance "has existed, but it has not been sufficiently proved to the commission that it still exists." On Bakunin's role, it reported that it was convinced that "this citizen has attempted, perhaps successfully, to found in Europe a society called the Alliance, with rules completely at variance, from the social and political point of view, with those of the International Working Men's Association."

From the social and political point of view? What the hell did that mean? Read in the context of Engels's report, it clearly meant that whatever traces had been found of the Alliance were in violation of the London resolutions. That was hardly surprising, because the London resolutions had been drafted precisely to purge Bakunin and the Alliance. Even more odd, the commission then called for the expulsion of James Guillaume and another anarchist, on the grounds that the two belonged to an Alliance the commission was not sure existed. The travesty continued, for the commission threw in another charge against Bakunin: that he had "resorted to dishonest dealings with the aim of appropriating the whole or part of another person's property, which constitutes an act of fraud. Furthermore, in order to avoid fulfilling his contract, he or his agents have resorted to intimidation." The commission did not produce any evidence for this charge, asking instead only for a vote of confidence in its findings. It did not produce evidence, for there was none. The charge was a reference to the advance Bakunin had received for translating *Capital* and to Nechaev's letter to the Russian publisher, which threatened terrible consequences if Bakunin was not released from the contract. Failing to return an advance or complete the work is not a nice thing, but it is hardly a capital or even a *Capital* offense; nor was it one Marx was innocent of. As for Nechaev's threat, while the publisher declared himself happy to help discredit Bakunin, he made it plain there was no proof the anarchist even knew of the letter. Though Marx was informed of this before the congress, he did not hesitate to read Nechaev's note to the commission and imply that Bakunin had instigated it.[15]

The slander over the advance and Nechaev's intimidation was only part of a larger campaign undertaken by Utin. He had been given the task of investigating the entire Nechaev affair, and he took it up with great enthusiasm and no scruples. With his ties to the Russian movement and émigré communities, he was well placed to gather every bit of gossip, lie, and innuendo to build a dossier against Bakunin. In the end, his report to the congress blamed Bakunin for all of Nechaev's activities. Utin, without adducing any evidence, attributed authorship of the notorious "Catechism" to Bakunin alone and held him indirectly responsible for the murder of Ivanov. Not content to restrict himself to the recent past, Utin accused Bakunin of adding falsely to his street cred by claiming his sentence in Siberia was to hard labor, rather than simple exile. Bakunin was then charged of first sucking up to the Siberian governor-general, his cousin Muraviev-Amursky, and then of betraying his trust. Coming from a revolutionary pledged to the overthrow of the tsar, the accusation of lying to the tsar's agent to make his escape was a little rich. Utin continued to pile on the charges, though even Marx rolled his eyes at the accusation that Bakunin borrowed large sums of money. In a final document that filled 114 typescript pages, Utin scoured Bakunin's writings looking for any heresy he could find, regardless of when it was written or of context, ranging from sexism to pan-Slavism to brigandage, to, yes, once again, hints that Bakunin was a Russian spy.

The lies and distortions in Utin's report were obvious, but in the hostile atmosphere of the congress, little could be done to defend Bakunin or anarchism. The delegates who remained—over a third had already left—voted to expel Bakunin and Guillaume. The congress had already voted to increase the powers of the General Council, yet again, and to insist on political action; the banishment of the anarchists was both unnecessary and a foregone conclusion. What did surprise the delegates was the motion by Marx and Engels to transfer the General Council from London to New York. Despite their victory at the Hague, the two understood that the anti-Marxist forces, ranging from British trade unionists to Blanquists to anarchists, were gaining in strength; furthermore, Marx was eager to return to his study and his studies, and was not content to let the International find its own way in his absence. The Blanquist contingent walked out when the resolution was narrowly passed and condemned the move, writing, "Called upon to do its duty, the International collapsed. It fled from the revolution over the Atlantic Ocean." And they were right. While the International staggered on until 1876, Marx noted that it was dead in England by 1874, and Engels observed in the same year that "the old International is anyhow entirely wound up and at an end."

In another reflection, Engels made it clear that he and Marx had had no intention of building unity, fearing that if the congress had "come out in a conciliatory way," the "sectarians, especially the Bakuninists, would have had another year in which to perpetrate, in the name of the International, still greater stupidities and infamies." Better to destroy the International in order to save it, in other words; in Engels's own words, "a party proves itself victorious by splitting and being able to stand the split." That the International did not survive the split was a point that seemed to escape him. Unity at any price may not be a virtue, but it might be thought a tad hypocritical to ban a group for sectarianism while working doggedly to engineer a split. In any case, the determined efforts of the Marxists to ram through their own political agenda and fracture the International was further proof to the anarchists of the pitfalls of authoritarian socialism and political maneuvering.[16]

In response to their purge, the anarchists created their own International at a founding convention at St. Imier, Switzerland, a week after the Hague congress adjourned. There they repudiated the old International and voiced their solidarity with Bakunin, Guillaume, and the others. Particularly outraged by the continuing personal attacks on Bakunin, one comrade suggested they might pay Marx and Engels back in kind and launch a slanderous assault of their own. In the words of one witness, the prominent anarchist Errico Malatesta, "Bakunin rose up like a wounded lion" to his full height and shouted, "What are you saying, you wretch! No, it is better to be slandered a thousand times, even if people believe it, than to shame oneself by becoming a slanderer." Malatesta remained a Bakunin partisan and related the story years later; it may have improved with age, but it captures the respect the venerable anarchist had earned among the comrades and their sense that they had acted always from principle and never from expediency. The St. Imier convention then moved from the personal to the political. Not surprisingly, it rejected the resolutions and policies of the old International and structured itself on the basis of free association and autonomy. It further determined that it was "absurd and reactionary" to attempt to impose a political program on the working class," and that all political organizations were "the organization of rule in the interests of a class and to the detriment of the masses." Even if the proletariat would seize the state, it would then itself "become a ruling and exploiting class."[17]

Bakunin dashed off a number of letters and notes defending himself and the Alliance and putting forward his own version of the fight in the International. These included a long letter for *La Liberté,* written in October 1872 but never sent. In it he suggested that the Marxists "are worshipers of state power, and so also prophets of political and social discipline. [They are] the champions of order established from the top down, always in the name of universal suffrage and the sovereignty of the masses, for whom they reserve the fortune and honor of obeying the commanders, the elected masters." Unlike the Marxists, Bakunin continued, the anarchists rejected the idea, even as a transitional phase, of "national conventions, constituent assemblies, or so-called revolutionary dictatorships," for such concentrations of power in a few hands "inevitably and immediately become reaction." This was the fundamental point on which anarchists and Marxists differed, and it was one Bakunin would return to in his last major works.[18]

15

WE DETEST ALL POWER

It is tempting to reduce the fight between Bakunin and Marx to a personality conflict. Despite their occasional overtures, they did not much like each other and there was never any warmth or affection between the two. They shared many ideas, though both were loath to admit it. They were devout atheists; they called for the abolition of private property; they understood the necessity of revolution, though they had different timetables and disagreed on precisely who was likely to make it. But their struggle in the International reflected more than personal dislike. It was in part the result of the political strategy both adopted. Bakunin and Marx each exaggerated their differences in a strategy of polemical brinkmanship that forced people to take sides. Both accentuated their differences to make the choice clear and unequivocal. This political strategy was necessary precisely because the two sides had much in common and because they differed on two important and related issues: that of reform and that of the state.

Bakunin was not unalterably opposed to reform. He was, however, much less enamored of the process than Marx. Bakunin was keenly aware that measures such as the ten-hour day could be won, that such efforts required organization, and that such relief meant much to those who received it. He also rejected the version of the immiseration theory that insisted all reform should be refused on the grounds that it would take the edge off the workers' need and desire for revolution; neither did he hold that things had to get much worse to inspire people to rebel. Reformism made him wary, not because it was impossible but because it was partial and incomplete. Shortening the working day did not stop the exploitation of workers any more than a kinder and gentler slavery—say, one where whippings were restricted by law to every second Tuesday—would make slaves free. The point was not to reform the system, but to overthrow it. If reforms came from the agitation for revolution, fair enough; but there were reformers aplenty already, and Bakunin preferred to work for revolution.

There were other reasons to be suspicious of reform. Reform meant compromise with the very authority that oppressed workers and peasants. That compromise legitimated authority by acknowledging its right to exist and control. Compromise could have a corrosive effect on reformers as well. Capital and the state were not interested in dealing with "the people" at the bargaining table; they spoke to representatives. These representatives were only recognized if they made it clear they were ready to cut a deal and that they had the power to make such deal and hold the people to it. Put plainly, it meant that power had shifted from the people to the delegates, from the masses to an elite. Once tangled up in the spirit of negotiating, bargaining, and conceding, it was easy to forget just what the real point was; in the eagerness to come to an arrangement, it was easy to put too much on the table. Furthermore, the rewards of status, power, and position made it easy for reformers themselves to be corrupted. For all these reasons, reform had a way of becoming an end itself; instead of building toward the revolution, reform too often replaced it. That was, according to Bakunin, in keeping with Marx's evolutionary model of historical change that stressed the need to wait until economic development had reached a certain point. It meant always postponing the revolution, always settling and coming to an agreement with the enemy. There were examples enough to point to. Lassalle, after all, had given up revolution when he courted the Prussian state; for all their denials, the leaders of the SPD, including Liebknecht and Bebel, and later Kautsky and Bernstein, went down the same road. They were so eager to put the top down and floor it that one critic, Robert Michels, in his 1915 book, *Political Parties,* asked of these socialist leaders, "What interest for them has now the dogma of the social revolution? Their own social revolution has already been effected." The chance for political power and status corrupted and made leaders more conservative, Michels argued, following closely the argument made by Bakunin years earlier.[1]

Was Bakunin's criticism applicable to Marx? Surely Marx on the state was a little too Pollyanna-like when he insisted that immediate reforms could "only be effected by converting social reason into social force, and, under given circumstances, there exists no other method of doing so, than through general laws, enforced by the power of the state. In enforcing such laws, the working class do not fortify governmental power. On the contrary, they transform that power, now used against them, into their own agency."[2] Yet Marx rejected Lassalle's political opportunism and took several opportunities over the years to distance himself from Liebknecht. He said a great many things about revolution and reform, and it is possible to read him in many different ways. Thus we may look for and find both a revolutionary and a reformist Marx, just as we may find a Marx who insisted history was a fairly mechanical process of economic development and one who said it was moved by class struggle, that is to say, by humanity. The real question for activists is perhaps not "Which is the real Marx?" but "Which Marx is useful to us and for what purpose?"

The question of reform is not so easily resolved as many revolutionaries have held, and Bakunin's own arguments were rather more complicated. For anarchists, the question may be, must the anarchist also be a revolutionary? Not just in the sense of intellectually realizing that a society without exploitation and domination would be revolutionarily, radically different from our own, but in the sense of insisting revolution is the only acceptable short-term and long-term tactic and goal? If the Paris Commune showed that workers could organize autonomously, surely it also demonstrated that insurrection was likely to be futile, at least in the short term. If insurrection was not a realistic tactic, what then was left for the revolutionary to do? When Noam Chomsky suggests that the present-day state might be strengthened and democratized—that is to say, reformed—to defang the particularly brutal capitalism we face today, he is not calling for immediate social revolution. Does that mean he has abandoned anarchism? Or is the question of means and ends more complicated than Chomsky's anarchist critics insist? Furthermore, as Bakunin observed, oppression often divides people and sends them to find sanctuary in the church, the pub, and authority. Fears alone are not enough; people need community and confidence to build movements. Reform can forge the links and small successes that are necessary to build self-reliance. When the insurrection fails, reform may be a way to salvage something. The all-or-nothing strategy too often leads to isolation and retreat, especially among intellectuals who wagered everything on the struggle. Thus the wave of anarchist bombings and assassinations between the late 1880s and early 1900s represented despair rather than hope, as some radicals falsely concluded that the working class could or would do nothing. Desperate, futile acts, they resolved, had to replace organization, for there was nothing else to do. Similarly, the flight of intellectuals from radical politics to postmodernism, "identity politics," and resignation, reflected their disappointment after May 1968. The mistaken conclusion was again that the working class had somehow failed its prescribed historical mission, and so could now be abandoned, ignored, or explained away.

This was not a mistake Bakunin made. He did not believe the masses required only a single spark to ignite the prairie fire, and he understood that their fears and conservatism were where the movement started, not where it gave up. Therefore strikes, cooperatives, propaganda by the deed or leaflet, and reform were important for their educational value as much as for their revolutionary potential. Anarchists could take part in nonrevolutionary activities and advocate measures other than unrelenting revolt. Even elections and parliament could be useful on occasion, Bakunin suggested, when he urged Carlo Gambuzzi to seek election in Naples during the Franco-Prussian War. Aware that this advice would surprise Gambuzzi, given that Bakunin usually advocated abstaining from such action, he argued that winning political office was important, for "times have become so grave that it is necessary for all good men to step into the breach" where they could exert as much influence as possible. In 1872, he argued that anarchists should not hesitate to help the left-wing Spanish political parties, without diluting their own anarchist position; later, as the movement developed, there would be time to abstain from the parliamentary struggle. The trick was to work for reform without sacrificing revolution. If we may conclude that it is possible for a consistent anarchist to consider tactics other than outright revolution at a given moment, then it is possible to argue that the divide between anarchists and Marxists is not necessarily the question of reform versus revolution.[3]

For Bakunin, the chief difference between them could be summed up in two words: the state. If this seems clear enough, misinterpretations fueled misunderstanding and needless animosity. Engels, for example, was just flat-out wrong to claim that Bakunin "maintains that it is the state which has created capital, that the capitalist has his capital only by the grace of the state. As, therefore, the state is the chief evil, it is above all the state which must be abolished and then capitalism will go to blazes of itself."[4] What Bakunin did argue was that the social revolution had to be launched against the state and capitalism simultaneously, for the two reinforced each other. Instead of viewing capital as the creation of the state, as Engels alleged, Bakunin saw that "exploitation and government are two inseparable expressions of all that is called politics. The first gives the means of governing and makes up both the necessary base and the goal of all government. Government in turn guarantees and legalizes the power to exploit." This was the reciprocal relationship of lord and state, fogged by religion until the French Revolution. The Revolution displaced religion, but it also brought to power the bourgeoisie, who, "tired of being the anvil, became in turn the hammer" and "inaugurated the modern state." "Exploitation," Bakunin concluded, is "the visible body of the bourgeois regime, and government is its soul."[5] It was not a question of the state creating capital, or vice versa, but their reciprocal—dare one say dialectical?—relationship. The most vulgar of Marxists, who hold that the state is completely determined by economic structures and

interests, might argue that this formulation gave the state too much autonomy and moved away from historical materialism. But Bakunin reinforced
his commitment to materialist history, arguing that "the base of all the historical, national, religious, and political problems, for workers and all other
classes, and even for the state and church, the most important, the most vital
of all, has been the economic problem." At the same time, more sophisticated Marxists, including Marx himself, stressed precisely the reciprocal
relationship between state and economy that Bakunin sketched.[6] It is a mistake to insist Marx argued that the economic "base" completely determines
the "superstructure" of the state, ideology, and culture. It is true that Engels
and Marx would argue in the battles against Bakunin that "the abolition of
capital is precisely the social revolution" and when capital had been
destroyed "the state will collapse of itself."[7] Taken at face value, this remark
suggests that the two believed that the state was just a reflection of the economic system and had no independent existence. That argument led both to
reformism and political revolution. In the first case, it implied that little could
be done politically until the economic system had evolved and changed. In
the second case, it implied that revolutionaries could take over the state in a
coup, effect changes in the economic system, and see these changes render
the state irrelevant. Yet throughout their writing, Marx and Engels avoided
such a simplistic, one-way analysis of the relationship between capital and
the state. Even as early as the Communist Manifesto they argued that the
"executive of the modern state is but a committee for managing the common
affairs of the whole bourgeoisie." The use of the word "manage" clearly
implies that the state has some coercive power over capital and is not simply
its tool any more than it is a neutral arbiter between capital and labor. A
strand of Marxism that rejects both social democracy and the vanguard has
usually—save when battling anarchists—argued that the state has some "relative autonomy" and is not a direct, simple reflex of a given economic
system.

Having conceded all this, there still remained important differences
between the anarchist and the revolutionary Marxist conception of the state.
Anarchism is opposed to the state. Bakunin insisted that representative
democracy was essentially a swindle that promised freedom to all but in
practice empowered the liberal bourgeoisie. Even a workers' state would, by
definition, have a government, which is to say, a minority ruling a majority,
and that power would corrupt those who wielded it. "We certainly are all
sincere socialists and revolutionaries," Bakunin observed, "and yet, if we
were given power, if only for a few months, we would not be what we are

now. As socialists we are convinced . . . that social environment, social position, and conditions of existence, are more powerful than the intelligence
and will of the strongest and most energetic individual. It is precisely for this
reason that we demand not natural but social equality of individuals as the
condition for justice and the foundation of morality. And that is why we
detest power, all power, just as the people detest it."[8]

Even revolutionary Marxism is statist, in that it does not hold that capital
and the state must be abolished simultaneously. It argues instead that the state
can be seized, perhaps altered drastically, and then used by workers and their
allies. The state may wither away or it may not, but there is no question of
abolishing it on the first day of the revolution. For his part, Bakunin summed
up "the difference between us, a difference that digs an abyss between us"
precisely. Marx and his followers wanted "the transformation of private property into collective property to be accomplished by the power of the state. We
claim on the contrary that it can be only be effected by the abolition of the
state." When Marxists "agitated the people for the reconstitution of states,"
the anarchists agitated "the masses with a view to the destruction of all
states." That single difference led to important consequences far beyond the
quarreling in the International, and Bakunin would spend the years between
1870 and 1873 developing and refining his position.[9]

Much of this time was spent writing a document entitled "The Knouto-
Germanic Empire and the Social Revolution." It is a sprawling manuscript of
nearly one thousand pages, some of them concise, even elegant arguments
that break off in midsentence, others polished sections that stand alone, still
others fragmented notes, corrections, and additions, none of it well organized
and little of it edited. It was a work Bakunin intended to leave as his philosophical and political testament. The title suggested he would concentrate
on the political repression that followed the Franco-Prussian War: the
"knout" was a reference to the reactionary role Russia played once again,
now in conjunction with Prussia, and that was a theme that ran through the
manuscript. But it became only one theme among many. In the end, the project was an attempt to sum up Bakunin's vast, wide-ranging analysis of the
historical connections between religion, the state, science, and economic
exploitation, of modern philosophy, political thought and action, and the
differences between anarchism and Marxism.

Little of it made its way to print. Of the pieces that did, the hundred pages
titled by his editors *God and State* are the most famous. Published six years
after his death, it restates Bakunin's materialism, atheism, and critique of intellectuals powerfully and dramatically. It does not deal much with economic

exploitation, so the publication of this fragment may have reinforced the notion that Bakunin saw the state as the primary problem of contemporary society. But the piece left no doubt that Bakunin was a strong materialist. "Who are right, the idealists or the materialists?" it opens. "The question once stated in this way, hesitation becomes impossible. Undoubtedly the idealists are wrong and the materialists right. Yes, facts are before ideas; yes, the ideal, as Proudhon said, is but a flower, whose root lies in the material conditions of existence. Yes, the whole history of humanity, intellectual and moral, is but a reflection of its economic history."[10] Humanity was not something separate from the world or an ideal construction; it was "the highest manifestation of animality" and thus bounded by the laws of nature that were increasingly being revealed by science. But unlike animals, "man has emancipated himself." That emancipation, as even biblical accounts of the Garden of Eden acknowledged, began a "distinctively human history and development by an act of disobedience and science—that is, by rebellion and thought."[11]

From there he segued to a critique of religion. Science had exposed it as a lie, but the question remained: "How comes an intelligent and well-informed man ever to feel the need of believing in this mystery?" He elaborated on the arguments he had made earlier. The people "are still very ignorant, and are kept in ignorance by the systematic efforts of all the governments, who consider this ignorance, not without good reason, as one of the essential conditions of their own power. Weighted down by their daily labor, deprived of leisure, of intellectual intercourse, of reading . . . the people generally accept religious traditions without criticism and in a lump." The traditions were sustained by a professional caste of priests and laymen and became "a sort of mental and moral habit, too often more powerful even than their natural good sense." There was, of course, a material cause for this as well: "the wretched situation to which they find themselves fatally condemned by the economic organization of society in the most civilized countries of Europe." They had three escape routes: "the dramshop and the church, debauchery of the body or debauchery of the mind; the third is the social revolution," and if the people "have no reason to believe, they will have at least a right."

Oppression and ignorance explained why the masses believed in God; what of the educated? Many did not, but found it expedient to pretend to believe, Bakunin noted. This group was made up of "all the tormentors, the oppressors, and all the exploiters of humanity; priests, monarchs, statesmen, soldiers, public and private financiers, officials of all sorts, policemen, gendarmes, jailers and executioners, monopolists, capitalists, tax leeches, contractors and landlords, lawyers, economists, politicians of all shades, down to the smallest vendor of sweetmeats." They believed in religion as a "safety valve," as a way to stifle the independent thought that would lead to revolt. Thus they "will repeat in unison those words of Voltaire: 'If God did not exist, it would be necessary to invent him.'" But for Bakunin, "the idea of God implies the abdication of human reason and justice; it is the most decisive negation of human liberty, and necessarily ends in the enslavement of mankind, both in theory and practice." Bakunin's conclusion was clear: "I reverse the phrase of Voltaire, and say that, if God really existed, it would be necessary to abolish him."

But if humanity were merely the highest expression of animality, as Bakunin had asserted, did it make sense to speak of human liberty? If we are bound by natural laws, then we are bound, not free. Nice return by the idealists, but Bakunin spiked it right back. Yes, we are bound by natural laws of physics, biology, chemistry, and the like. But obviously these constitute our existence. They are not external to us; they are us. We must breathe; this is a natural fact or law. That fact does not oppress us, it defines us, and so, "Yes, we are absolutely the slaves of these laws. But in such slavery there is no humiliation, or rather, it is not slavery at all. For slavery supposes an external master, a legislator outside of him whom he commands, while these laws are not outside of us; they are inherent in us; they constitute our being, our whole being, physically, intellectually, and morally; we live, we breathe, we act, we think, we wish only through these laws. Without them we are nothing, we are not. Whence, then, could we derive the power and the wish to rebel against them?" The only liberty humanity could achieve within the realm of natural laws—and again, it is clear he meant the laws that govern the functioning of the universe—was to increase our knowledge of them so we did not waste time and effort in needlessly opposing these physical limits. That required science, broadly defined to include all aspects of human knowledge, and it required complete and thorough education of all members of society.

Human laws, however, were a very different phenomenon. These were not a reflection of natural law but a distortion of it, and so "the liberty of man consists solely in this: that he obeys natural laws because he himself has recognized them as such, and not because they have been externally imposed upon him by any extrinsic will whatever, divine or human, collective or individual." Even if the lawgiver were right, that did not give the authority to govern or to rule. That was true equally of the scientist who discovered laws of nature, the philosopher who identified laws of human development, and the revolutionary who invented laws for a new society. Why not let these people rule? First, human science, Bakunin observed, "is always and necessarily imperfect," and any attempt "to force the practical life of men, collective as well as individual, into strict and exclusive conformity with the latest data of science" condemned society "to suffer martyrdom on a bed of Procrustes," the mythological thief who stretched or amputated his visitors so they would fit the bed he offered them. Furthermore, any legislation from the scientists that was imposed rather than freely accepted—or rejected— would be imposed in the name of a science that the rest of humanity "venerated without comprehending," and such a society would be one "not of men, but of brutes." Finally, the power invested in this scientific caste would soon corrupt the scientists themselves. "It is the characteristic of privilege and of every privileged position to kill the mind and heart of men," even those of science. Once given the authority to decide and rule, they would soon divert their energies into finding ways to perpetuate their privilege.

If that were true of Bakunin's hypothetical scientific managers, it was equally true of existing "constituent and legislative assemblies, even those chosen by universal suffrage." Elections might change the composition of a legislature—though the flagrant gerrymandering in the United States has almost eliminated such changes in our day—but that would not prevent legislators of all stripes from forming a "political aristocracy or oligarchy," devoted to maintaining its privilege. Consequently, liberty and equality demanded "no external legislation and no authority—one, for that matter being inseparable from the other, and both tending to the servitude of society and the degradation of the legislators themselves."

That did not mean that Bakunin rejected knowledge or specialized skills. "In the matter of boots," for example, "I refer to the authority of the bootmaker; concerning houses, canals, or railroads, I consult that of the architect or engineer." No one could possibly become a master in all branches of knowledge, and humanity advanced in part because of the division and association of labor, mental as well as physical. But freedom meant that "I allow neither the bootmaker nor the architect nor the savant to impose his authority upon me." One listened, compared, evaluated; and then one made a free, informed decision. One must "recognize no infallible authority," for such "faith would be fatal to my reason, my liberty . . . it would immediately transform me into a stupid slave, an instrument of the will and interests of others." One hears an echo of Fichte here: "Each directs and is directed in his turn. Therefore there is no fixed and constant authority, but a continual change of mutual, temporary, and above all, voluntary authority and subordination." In short, Bakunin explained, we accept all natural authorities and all influences of fact, but none of right; for every authority or influence of right, officially imposed as such, becoming directly an oppression and a falsehood, would inevitably impose upon us . . . slavery and absurdity. In a word, we reject all legislation, all authority, and all privileged, licensed, official, and legal influence, even though arising from universal suffrage, convinced that it can turn only to the advantage of a dominant minority of exploiters against the interests of the immense majority in subjection to them. This is the sense in which we are really anarchists.

This argument had to be applied even against the positivism of Comte. And it especially had to be applied against the "doctrinaire school of German Communism," by which he meant Marx and Engels. Science, even that of political economy, dealt with abstraction, the general case, the broad argument. It could not, by definition, consider the individual; it was in the business of determining the general law. For that reason, Bakunin preached "to a certain extent, the revolt of life against science, or rather against the government of science," not to "destroy science," but to "remand it to its place." History had been the "perpetual and bloody immolation of millions of poor human beings in honor of some pitiless abstraction—God, country, power of state, national honor, historical rights, political liberty, public welfare." The role of science, especially social science, was to "point us with faithful and sure hand to the general causes of individual suffering," including the subordination of people to abstractions, and to show "the general conditions necessary to the real emancipation of the individuals living in society." It should do no more than indicate the path, for "it is time to have done with all popes and priests; we want them no longer, even if they call themselves Social Democrats."

God and the State returned to its critique of idealism in its remaining pages as Bakunin explored the roots of religious belief and metaphysics and traced the development of the state. He noted that by 1830, France had replaced the old landed aristocracy with "an aristocracy of capital," and it too used religion to underpin its rule. He anticipated Antonio Gramsci's theory of hegemony, arguing that while "the state is force," force alone "is not sufficient in the long run. Some moral sanction or other is absolutely necessary" to "convince the masses" so they "morally recognize its right." That was the role of religion, and thus "there cannot be a state without religion." Different economic systems required different religions and more than thirty years before Max Weber, Bakunin declared Protestantism "the bourgeois religion par excellence."

It was in another fragment of "The Knouto-Germanic Empire" that Bakunin clarified his arguments about capitalism. "Is it necessary to repeat the irresistible arguments of socialism, the arguments that no bourgeois economist has succeeded in destroying?" he asked rhetorically. "What is property, what is capital, in their present form? For the capitalist and the property owner, it is the power and the right, guaranteed and protected by the state, to live without working. Since capital and property produce absolutely nothing unless they are made productive by labor, this is the power and the right to live off the work of others, to exploit the work of those who, having neither property nor capital, are forced to sell their productive power to the lucky owners of one or the other." Since capitalists and property owners "did not live by their own productive labor, but from the rent of their land, the rent of their buildings, and the interest of their capital," or from "speculation" or by the "commercial and industrial exploitation of the manual labor of the proletariat," they "live at the expense of the proletariat." Yes, he granted, "speculation and exploitation undoubtedly constitute a sort of work, but work that is entirely unproductive. By this reckoning, thieves and kings work as well." He then pointed out that while the folklore of capitalism held that workers and employers came together freely in the marketplace for their mutual advantage, workers were compelled by hunger to seek employment. If capitalists were "forced" to hire labor, they entered the market with much greater resources and so could insist on exploitive terms of work; if the price of labor meant they would make no profit, the capitalists could invest somewhere else or simply live off their savings. Workers had no such options and so were forced to take what was offered. "If there were equality between the necessity to purchase labor and the necessity to sell it, the slavery and the poverty of the proletariat would not exist," he explained. Furthermore, there would be "neither capitalists and property owners nor proletarians, neither rich nor poor; there would only be workers. The exploiters are only possible because this equality does not exist."

Bakunin conceded that administration was work, and necessary work at that. There was, however, no need to put this work in the hands of the capitalist or to pay more for this work than for any other labor. Workers' cooperatives had already shown that the proletariat was competent to administer complex affairs. The truth was that capitalists and managers were paid more because they had the power to pay themselves more, always at the expense of their employees. But weren't profits the reward for taking risks? The worker was assured of wages, at least, and so traded wealth for security; the capitalist gambled, and so deserved greater compensation. "Yeah, right," Bakunin replied, in an incredibly loose translation. More precisely, he pointed out that workers risked even more than capitalists did. The conditions of work and relative poverty meant that an employed worker risked accident and ill health at the best of times; no capitalist faced those problems as a term of employment. Even a ruined capitalist was usually left with greater resources than an employed worker. Family connections, class ties, and greater education made it possible for the bankrupt capitalist to find work in management, the civil service, or even in the higher-paid jobs in the proletariat, if worse came to worst, while unemployment meant instant hardship for workers. The collapse of the company usually meant workers were thrown out of work with wages still owing, since then, as now, wages were not paid as the work was performed but a week or more after. If he were a capitalist, Bakunin continued, "and if I wanted to be sincere, and if I were well guarded," he would say to workers,

> Look, my dear children, I have here some capital, which strictly speaking, can produce nothing because a dead thing can produce nothing; it is labor that makes it productive. Since once I have consumed it, I have nothing left, and so there is nothing to be gained from using it unproductively. But thanks to the social and political institutions we have, and which are all in my favor in the present economic system, my capital is supposed to produce as well; it gives me interest. From whom this interest must be taken—and it must be taken from someone, since in reality, by itself it produces nothing at all—is not something that concerns you . . . In addition to the pleasures I want it to provide, I also want my capital to increase. How will I achieve this goal? Armed with my capital, I propose to exploit you, and I propose that you let yourself be exploited by me. You will work and I will collect and I will appropriate and I will sell for my own benefit the product of your work. You will be left only what is absolutely necessary for you to keep from dying of hunger today so that tomorrow you can work again for me under the same conditions. And when you are worn out, I will throw you out and replace you with others. Understand clearly that I will pay you the lowest wage possible and I will make you work as long a day as possible under the most severe, despotic, and harshest conditions possible. This is not from spite; I have no reason to hate you or harm you. It

is from the love of wealth and to enrich myself quickly, because the less I pay you and the more you work, the more I gain.

This is what is said implicitly by every capitalist, every industrial entrepreneur, every business head, everyone who requires labor from the workers they recruit.

And in case the reader has forgotten, workers were forced to take this offer because they had no other options; they had no money to invest and had "the terrible threat of starvation" facing them. Implicitly hearkening back to the theme of alienation he had addressed as a young man, just as Marx did in much of his work, Bakunin pointed out that unlike the capitalist who sold things, the worker sells "his labor, his personal service, the productive force of his body, mind, and spirit that is found in him and is inseparable from him; it is his own self." Despite the fact that workers, unlike serfs, were free and had the right to quit, this amounted to a "theoretical freedom" at best, since they still had to sell their labor to someone. In reality, "the whole life of the worker is nothing other than a grievous succession of terms of legally voluntary but economically forced servitude, momentarily interrupted by liberty accompanied by starvation, and consequently a real slavery."[12]

Bakunin returned to his critique of "German Communism" and social democracy in other pieces of "The Knouto-Germanic Empire," especially in the short essay known as "The Paris Commune and the Idea of the State." His most trenchant critique of Marx, however, was made in his book *Statism and Anarchy*. Written in 1873, the book may be Bakunin's most polished work, but it suffers greatly from its strains of anti-Semitism and what Marshall Shatz has labeled "virulent Germanophobia," the result undoubtedly of Bakunin's experience of German prisons and liberals, the Franco-Prussian War, and Marx.[13] These are sometimes repellent and irrational screeds, and it is no defense to point out that these were common assumptions held by many of his generation and class. They are also more subtle in places than one might expect, and are woven among trenchant and perceptive criticisms. For the most part, his arguments are directed not against the German people, but against the policies and tendencies of the German government. Bakunin's criticisms of Bismarck's militarism, totalitarianism, and alliances with big business were accurate and foreshadowed kaiserism, fascism, monopoly capitalism, and the military-industrial complex.[14] Written in Russian for a Russian audience, much of the book went over ideas and arguments Bakunin had made earlier. The bulk of the book was a criticism of the rise and power of the German state in the light of its victory over France in the Franco-Prussian War. Bakunin argued that Bismarck's state was but the clearest expression of the modern state; what one saw in Prussia in its extreme form there was only the logical extension of the essence of all states. "The sole objective" of the modern state, he warned, was to "organize the most intensive exploitation of the people's labor for the benefit of capital concentrated in a very small number of hands." In order to develop fully, "modern capitalist production and bank speculation require enormous centralized states, which alone are capable of subjecting the many millions of laborers to their exploitation." Representative democracy, the "latest form of the state, based on the pseudo-sovereignty of the people in sham popular assemblies," combined the centralized state and the subordination of the people to the intellectual minority "supposedly representing them but invariably exploiting them." The modern state was also "necessarily a military state." Just like the capitalist company, it had to grow or be crushed; it was propelled into war with its competitors by its very nature.

The sections of particular interest, however, were the critique of Marxism and the outlines of anarchist theory. Both were provided in more concrete language than Bakunin usually employed. The attack on Marx made an especially bold claim. Where Marx claimed to be a rigorous materialist, Bakunin suggested that the crucial problem with his theory was that he had failed to move far enough away from the metaphysics of the German idealists and Hegel. Whether Marx stood Hegel on his head, or, as Marx himself insisted, stood him on his feet to plant social criticism firmly on the ground, or remained within the confines of Hegelian thought, is still debated today. Bakunin's argument is interesting, not least because many later Marxists have maintained that authoritarian socialism traced its way from the Marx who believed he had found a science of materialism. Searching for a humanist, libertarian socialism, they turned instead to the Hegelian Marx. Bakunin, however, found a root of authoritarianism precisely in that Hegelianism as well as in Marx's positivism.

Science, Bakunin said, was essentially inductive. That is, it began "from the real fact to the idea that encompasses it, expresses it, and thereby explains it." That too was the method of the anarchist social revolution, to proceed "from life to thought." Metaphysicians and idealists, however, began with thought and abstraction and tried to fit reality into their ideas. They moved "from thought to life." Thus metaphysicians were not just those who studied the philosophical field of metaphysics; these, mercifully, were rather rare. Nor were they simply those who followed Hegel. It included "positivists" and the "present-day worshipers of the goddess science," indeed all those who "have created for themselves an ideal social organization" that they wished to "force the life of future generations" into. This was the problem with Marx, Bakunin held. In another essay, he made the point more concretely. A consistent Hegelian, and Marxist, Bakunin suggested, would have to conclude that the Roman empire represented a positive advance over the Greek civilization it replaced. Rome was, for all its barbarism, a necessary step in human development, and in that sense had to be applauded as progress, in this conception of history. Bakunin disagreed. True, the materialist understood that "the conquest and destruction of Greece and its comparatively higher development of liberty by the military and civic barbarism of the Romans was a logical, natural, and absolutely inevitable fact. But this does not prevent me from taking, retrospectively and very resolutely, the side of Greece against Rome in that struggle. I find that humanity has gained absolutely nothing by the triumph of Rome." Only the idealist who sought to impose a particular theory on the real world could see Rome's victory as both inevitable and progressive, Bakunin held. And that idealism was a dangerous political philosophy, for it legitimized the rule of the theorists who insisted they had determined how history, and the future, worked.[15] This repeated the theme he had addressed in *God and State,* that scholars and scientists, academics and intellectuals, could not be trusted to rule humanity. "Power should no more be given to them than to anyone else," he emphasized in *Statism and Anarchy,* "for anyone who is invested with power by an invariable social law will inevitably become the oppressor and exploiter of society."

For that reason, revolutionaries could not make use of the power of the state. By definition, "every state power, every government, by its nature and by its position stands outside the people and above them, and must invariably try to subject them to rules and objectives which are alien to them." Anarchists, in marked contrast, "have neither the intention nor the least desire to impose on our own people or on any other an ideal social organization that we have drawn from books or thought up on our own." Instead, they understood that "the masses bear all the elements of their future organizational norms in their own more or less historically evolved instincts, in their everyday needs, and their conscious and unconscious desires"; anarchists sought "that ideal within the people themselves." "Doctrinaire revolutionaries," by which Bakunin particularly meant Marx in both his Hegelian and positivist incarnations, insisted that science had to be "the point of departure for social upheavals and reconstructions." Since "thought, theory, and science, at least for the present, are the property of a very few individuals," it logically followed that "those few must be the directors of social life. They must be not only the instigators but the managers of all popular movements," and managing the revolution meant not "the free union" of people and associations "from below upward," but "solely by means of the dictatorial power of this learned minority which supposedly expresses the will of all the people."

Thus theories of "revolutionary dictatorship" were, in their essence, identical to classical justifications of the state. Both meant "the government of the masses by an insignificant handful of privileged individuals," elected or not. Both meant "the same government of the majority by a minority in the name of the presumed stupidity of the one and the presumed intelligence of the other," and both were "equally reactionary." For that reason, Marxists could "never be enemies of the state." At best, they were "enemies only of existing governments, because they want to take their place," enemies of "existing political institutions because these preclude the possibility of their own dictatorship." They remained the "most impassioned friends of state power," because without the state, the social revolution would simply sweep the intellectuals aside as the masses created their own free institutions and associations.

Whether this was true of Marx himself is still a matter of debate, not least among the competing schools of Marxism themselves. But it was certainly an accurate prediction of what would become "actually existing" Marxism, from the German Social Democratic Party to the Bolsheviks, from the Second International of Social Democracy through the Third International of Communist Parties to the Fourth International of the Trotskyists. Nor did the Chinese Communists, with their reliance on the peasantry instead of the proletariat, counter Bakunin's argument. Bakunin, however, insisted that it did apply to Marx and his theories. He was unable, however, to make his case solely by logic and demonstration. He attributed it also to Marx's character, his personality, and his religious and national origins. Whatever the provocation, such tactics are shameful. Bakunin was on much stronger ground when he pointed out that the class origins of many left-wing intellectuals led them to put their faith in the state. The "bourgeois-radical party," as he described Marx's politics, "is separated from the mass of laborers by the fact that it is profoundly, one might say organically, tied to the exploiting class by its economic and political interests and by all its habits of life, its ambition, its vanity, and its prejudices. How, then, can it have any desire to use the power it has won for the benefit of the people, even if it has won it with the people's help?"

Did such an analysis apply to Bakunin himself with his aristocratic roots? His point was not that class origins were destiny but that without careful attention, they would influence political thought and lead to political action that favored one's class, knowingly or not. The answer for those who were "bourgeois by origin but not by convictions or aspirations" was to "immerse themselves in the people, solely in the people's cause. If they continue to exist outside of the people, they will not only be useless to them but positively harmful." This was a very different role than that of the "radical party," which constituted "a separate party, living and acting outside of the people."[16]

With all his criticism of Marx, Bakunin could still appreciate the considerable achievements of his antagonist. Among these he counted Marx's vast knowledge and study of economics. Again Bakunin insisted that where Proudhon was wrong to start from the "abstract idea of right" and proceed from there to "economic fact," Marx "advanced and proved the inconvertible truth, confirmed by the entire past and present history of human society, nations, and states, that economic fact has always preceded legal and political right. The exposition and demonstration of that truth constitutes one of Marx's principal contributions to science." But he remained a scholar who believed that his possession of truth entitled him not just to be listened to, but to instruct and to lead. After all, there was no point in figuring out the course of history and then being ignored. That was, in Bakunin's view, why Marx remained a statist; it was the only way a minority of intellectuals could direct history in the direction they believed it had to go. It was also why Marx believed peasants were, for the most part, reactionary. Peasants had a strong distaste for and distrust of the state; a peasant revolution, like any popular revolution, was "by nature anarchistic and leads directly to the abolition of the state." Again, taken at face value as an accurate criticism of what Marx thought about the role of the state and peasants, it is an oversimplification. Yet for all that, it contains more prescience than Marx might care to concede.

Bakunin then turned to a logical dissection of the claims made by those socialists who believed they could take over the state and use it to create free socialism. They had, Bakunin observed, only two ways to do that. They could make a political revolution, that is, a coup d'etat, or they could advocate a "legal popular agitation for peaceful reform." Either way, such socialists had, "if not as their ultimate ideal, then at least as their immediate and principal objective, the creation of a people's state." This, in their mind, would be "the proletariat raised to the level of a ruling class." But "if the proletariat is to be the ruling class, it may be asked, then whom will it rule?" After all, to rule is to rule over someone else; "if there is a state, then necessarily there is domination and consequently slavery," and this new state could be no different. What exactly did it mean to raise the proletariat to a ruling or governing class? Bakunin asked. Did it mean that the entire proletariat would head the government? Would all forty million Germans, say, be members of the government? Obviously not, Bakunin concluded, and therefore socialists who looked to the state had to fall back on arguments of "popular government," which actually meant "government of the people by a small number of representatives elected by the people." But that was the line of liberals and the bourgeoisie; when voiced by socialists, it still remained "a lie behind which the despotism of a ruling minority is concealed, a lie all the more dangerous in that it represents itself as the expression of a sham popular will."

But wouldn't a socialist government be made up of workers? Wouldn't that make the difference? So the Marxists claimed, Bakunin responded. But in fact, it would be a government of "former workers, who, as soon as they become rulers or representatives of the people will cease to be workers and will begin to look upon the whole workers' world from the heights of the state. They will no longer represent the people but themselves and their own pretensions to govern the people." It would be even worse if the elected representatives were the educated radicals who spoke of "scientific socialism," for, as Bakunin had already suggested, a "government of scholars" was perhaps the most oppressive government of all precisely because its members were convinced by their objective science that they were right. To the counterargument that such a dictatorship would be temporary, lasting only until the people were educated enough to govern themselves and thus make government unnecessary, Bakunin pointed out the obvious contradiction. If that provisional socialist government were "truly a people's state, then why abolish it? But if its abolition is essential for the liberation of the people, then how do they dare call it a people's state?" Any call for a "transitional state," a people's state, a dictatorship of the proletariat, amounted to little more than claiming "for the masses to be liberated they must first be enslaved." In contrast, Bakunin put forward the anarchist position: "Liberty can only be created by liberty, by an insurrection of all the people and the voluntary organization of the workers from below upward."

That in turn meant the anarchists had to break completely with all governments and bourgeois politics, leaving the "social revolution" as the only tactic and strategy. It was a logical outcome of his argument against Marx, but it is not so clear that it resolved the issue as cleanly as Bakunin implied. What of his own argument that it could be useful to have some say in governments between now and the social revolution? Given the immense problems of organizing the social revolution, to which Bakunin's entire life was testament, was it less Utopian than Marx and Engels's hope that the state would eventually "wither away"? At the same time, was Bakunin's prediction not largely borne out by the Russian Revolution and the triumph of the Bolshevik Party? This is not the same as the argument of anarchists, liberals, and social democrats alike that Marx was the theorist of Stalinism or the architect of the gulag. It is to argue that Bakunin raised crucial questions of revolutionary tactics and strategy that are more substantial than his critics on the left and the right have usually acknowledged. His answer—the social revolution—is not as complete or useful as he implied, but no one on the left has yet found a serviceable solution. Perhaps Bakunin's real answer is that we ourselves should resolve the issue, and if that is not helpful, it is at least hopeful.

Marx in turn advanced his own criticisms of *Statism and Anarchy* in a copy of the book he annotated thoroughly. Some of the comments echoed his earlier reactions to Bakunin's work. "Schoolboyish rot!" Marx exclaimed unhelpfully in one margin. "The will, not economic conditions, is the basis of his social revolution . . . A radical social revolution is connected with definite historical conditions of economic development; the latter are its prerequisites." Bakunin "has no idea of social revolution, knows only its political phrases; its economic conditions have no meaning for him." As we have seen, this is a blatant misinterpretation, but it was not proof of Bakunin's accusations that Marx was essentially a metaphysician who believed he had divined the secrets of history. They were not Marx's final words on historical materialism, and given the animosity between the two radicals, it pays to be cautious in putting too much weight on them.

Where Bakunin asked over whom the proletariat would rule if it were the ruling class, Marx suggested that as long as other classes, especially the capitalist class, still existed, the proletariat would need "coercive means, hence governmental means," to protect itself. This is not a refutation of Bakunin's argument, but it is a more sophisticated defense of the state than the one Bakunin attacked. Marx also noted that in countries where peasants made up an important segment of the population, the revolution had to be careful not to alienate them and the proletariat had to avoid colliding with their interests. Less helpfully, he suggested that the revolutionary government had to both improve the conditions of the peasantry and "facilitate the transition from private to collective property in land so that the peasant himself is converted for economic reasons." This is a far cry from Stalin's forced collectivization of the peasantry; though it is tempting to connect the dots, it would be a mistake to do so, for Marx would continue to develop his ideas on the peasantry and would end up much closer to Bakunin's position.

More interesting was Marx's reaction to Bakunin's rhetorical question of whether all forty million Germans might be members of the government. "Certainly," Marx snorted, "for the whole thing begins with the self-government of the commune." "Exactly!" Bakunin might have replied and ordered drinks all around. Yet their essential difference reasserted itself later. The anarchist had argued that a government of workers would in fact be a government of ex-workers. Marx replied that since a manufacturer did not cease to be a capitalist when he was elected to municipal council, why would a worker cease to be a worker? One response consistent with Bakunin's reasoning might be that such an answer firstly proves that government is about maintaining class privilege. Secondly, it dodges the argument that governments evolve their own interests, which often differ from the precise interests of capitalists as a class or as individuals. Workers would be no less immune to such a process, especially if they came to prefer electoral office to the factory floor. Finally, Marx suggested that Bakunin needed some work experience, perhaps as a "manager in a workers' cooperative." That would "send all his nightmares about authority to the devil." Given that Marx was, if anything, further removed from the workplace than Bakunin, this can hardly be considered a definitive counterargument. What Marx's annotations do suggest is that fruitful debate between Marx and Bakunin might have developed the arguments of both in provocative and useful ways. That such a debate was impossible tells us less about the potential relationship and critiques of anarchism and Marxism than it does about the vagaries of history, less about the incompatibility of the two ideologies than the very different approaches of Bakunin and Marx.[17]

Bakunin had no opportunity to respond to Marx's scribbled criticisms of *Statism and Anarchy*. The book marked his last sustained political writing. Bakunin's life following the congress at the Hague was filled with chaos and instability, but that will hardly come as a surprise by now. In June 1872, Antonia had left for Russia with the two children, Carlo and Sophia, to visit her family after the death of her last surviving brother. "Separation," Bakunin wrote in his diary, "for how long? For a year? Forever?"[18] After seeing them off from Basel, Bakunin went on to Zürich, where another generation of Russian émigrés gathered as they had earlier in Geneva. The group included Michael Sazhin, better known as Armand Ross, and Zamfiri Ralli, better known as Zamfiri Ralli, though his original name was Arbore. Both had worked with Nechaev, and both had broken with him; Ross, one of many inspired by Chernyshevsky, had been a founder of Land and Liberty, and had taken part in the Paris Commune. Both men were active in the Jura Federation and soon became close, if temporary, political allies and friends of Bakunin.

For the old anarchist still had the power to compel attention and interest. "Everyone fell silent and turned their eyes to him" when Bakunin strode through the door of the inn, recalled Elizabeth Litvinova, a Russian student in Zürich. Followed by a revolutionary entourage, Bakunin swept through the room, completely at ease with the stares he attracted, some awed and some challenging. As he took his place at the table, one woman was so intimidated by the presence of the famous revolutionary that her shaking set all the glasses clinking until Bakunin addressed her with "I say, my good mother!" and the room broke out in laughter. Litvinova was impressed with Bakunin's "thick lion's mane of hair, his handsome face," his red cheeks, and his piercing yet somehow guileless eyes. Admittedly, Litvinova, twenty-two years old that Zürich summer, suffered from myopia, but the presence of the anarchist stirred her deeply as he spoke of the International and reminisced about Russia. After dinner, Bakunin borrowed a cigarette and lit up. When one of the women took a glass of wine, he wrinkled his brows and announced that he did not really approve of women drinking. This triggered a discussion on the rights of women, and Litvinova recalled that "certainly Bakunin acknowledged these rights, but . . . he did not like to see women drinking or smoking." Every idol has feet of clay, though Litvinova seems to have forgiven Bakunin his old-fashioned lapse, perhaps because she observed that he retained another old habit, that of handing out money freely to others in need. He became well-known in the city, easily spotted by his size, his penurious generosity, a large, broadminded group of colleagues, and a large, broadbrimmed straw hat complete with a red—naturally—ribbon.[19] The summer seems to have been pleasant enough, but there and at Locarno, where Bakunin moved in October 1872, much of his time was spent on petty squabbles. The big debate in Zürich was over Bakunin's ideas and those of Peter Lavrov, an exiled Russian, formerly a mathematician in an artillery college, whose approach to politics was as introverted, careful, and precise as Bakunin's was extroverted, imprudent, and sweeping. The two did not much like each other. Their attempts to form an alliance quickly failed, and each became further isolated from the Russian revolutionary movement. The group Bakunin had formed with Ross, Ralli, and others foundered as well, largely due to personal disputes between Ross and the others, who accused him of acting as an authoritarian. He seemed to prove the allegation when he resolved a dispute over a printing press, the chief material and strategic asset of any radical group, by the simple, direct action tactic of locking everyone else out of the building. Though most of the anarchists refused to work any further with Ross, Bakunin sided with him and so alienated the others. The incessant bickering left Bakunin exhausted, and his health was degenerating quickly. He was terribly overweight, and he needed to reduce the eating, drinking, and smoking. This he refused to do. Unlike many of those today who work so hard on their bodies and neglect their brains, Bakunin actually had something important to say, and his poor health cut this short. A visitor to Locarno noted that Bakunin "smoked like a locomotive," and the floor of his home was "covered with ash and cigar butts." While he took his medications, including the strychnine prescribed by his doctor, observed a diet that avoided flour, and carefully trimmed the fat from the meat, he would then augment the regime with enormous quantities of risotto and macaroni served with butter, washed down with brandy, tea, or black coffee at home and in the cafes where many of the political discussions took place.[20] Between the asthma that made it difficult to breathe and a swollen prostate gland that had him up twenty times a night to urinate, he was unable to get much sleep, and congestive heart disease left him breathless with any physical exertion.

His condition was greatly aggravated by the publication in September 1873 of a pamphlet put together by Marx, Engels, and Lafargue. Titled "The Alliance of Socialist Democracy and the International Working Men's Association," it was little more than a rehash of the accusations, exaggerations, and outright fabrications outlined by Marx in his "Confidential Communication" to Kugelman and those compiled by Utin for the International. It was a tawdry effort that blew back on its creators, for even Marx's supporters and biographers have winced with embarrassment at the lies and unprincipled personal attacks. There was nothing new or surprising in the pamphlet. Bakunin's reaction to the latest outrage, however, was remarkably restrained and made no political statement. It simply pointed out that the offensive pamphlet contained many errors and lies, and was just the latest in a string of slanders that dated back to the 1840s.

Bakunin did throw a bomb in at the end, and it was an entirely unexpected one. "I admit that I am profoundly disgusted with public life," he wrote. "I have had enough of it, and having spent my entire life in struggle,

I am tired of it." Age and heart disease made life "more and more difficult," and it was now time for a younger generation "to take up the work." He was no longer able to "push the rock of Sisyphus against the reaction that is triumphant everywhere," and asked his comrades for only one thing: that they forget him. He followed this declaration with another to his comrades of the Jura Federation, announcing his resignation from it and the anarchist International. There were several reasons to retire from the fray, but the most important one was political. "By birth and personal position, though not by sympathies or inclinations, I am only a bourgeois," he wrote. "As such, the only thing I can do among you is theoretical propaganda. But I am convinced that the time for grand theoretical discourse, in print or in speeches, is past . . . The most important task today is to organize the forces of the proletariat. But this organization must be the work of the proletariat itself." If he were young, he ventured, he would join the workers as one of them and take up the struggle to organize. His age and health, however, made this impossible; he was now "an obstacle, not an aid, in the camp of the proletariat," and there was, and rightly so, no room in the movement for "sinecures or honorary positions." He warned of the danger he believed both Marx and Bismarck represented to anarchism, and urged the comrades to "hold firm to the idea of popular liberty and to continue to organize the workers in all trade and in all countries." Above all, he concluded, "remember that however infinitely weak you may be as individuals, in isolated communities or nations, you will be an immense, irresistible force as a worldwide community."[21]

CONCLUSION

Bakunin had fewer than three years to live when he announced his retirement from the struggle. How to live, however, was still an issue, and he was still scrabbling. When an Italian comrade, Carlo Cafiero, came into a substantial inheritance, he and Bakunin devised a plan they hoped would give him some financial security. They purchased a villa near Locarno, or more accurately, Cafiero purchased it, and transferred the title to Bakunin. The villa, named Baronata, had once been a monastery, and the anarchists relished the opportunity to turn it into something more useful. Its land would make it self-sustaining, through harvesting timber, growing crops, and raising livestock, and Baronata would become a refuge for radicals on the run and for superannuated revolutionaries too old to pursue their trade, providing a pension for Bakunin and stability for his wife and the children. The financial improvement was matched with a familial one. Antonia returned from Russia to Switzerland in July 1873, with her sister, her parents, and a third child. Bakunin greeted them with an impressive fireworks display, which, oddly enough, has not been widely cited by historians as evidence of his apocalyptic pyromania. But Baronata failed miserably. Extensive renovations drove up the cost, nearly bankrupting Cafiero, and the fiasco drove apart the two friends. It had further consequences for Bakunin. He had led Antonia to believe that he had bought Baronata with a legacy from Priamukhino and that their future was secure. Now he was forced to sign the villa over to Cafiero, and the family would be homeless. The entire episode left him utterly despondent. Unable to face Antonia with the truth, he set out for Bologna in July 1874 to take part in a final insurrection, undoubtedly hoping to find there a heroic death on the barricades in an attempt to have life imitate the art of *Rudin*.

It would have been a fitting end. But the insurrection quickly failed, and there was nothing left to do but return to Baronata and confess. Angry and without resources or money, Antonia moved to another Swiss town, Lugano, though she soon wrote to Bakunin asking him to join her. He set off as quickly as he could in September 1874, and resumed his old patterns as best he could: long discussions in the cafes, reading, writing, surviving through borrowing money when he could, depending on the kindness of strangers and comrades alike, his health steadily worsening. Perhaps most disconcerting to one who had, for better or worse, made his life from words, he was becoming deaf. His letters increasingly concentrated not on politics but on money and medical matters as each became more dire.

The aftermath of the Paris Commune did as much to dampen his spirit as his ailments and poverty. The social revolution was as necessary as ever to save humanity from the "sewer," but there was no "thought, hope, or revolutionary passion to be found in the masses." European reaction had never been "so formidably armed against any movement of the people," while "repression was a new science taught systematically to lieutenants in military schools of all nations. And what do we have to attack this impregnable fortress? The unorganized masses." The "revolution has for the moment returned to its bed, and we have relapsed into a period of evolution, that is, one in which revolution is underground, invisible, and often even imperceptible," he wrote to his friend and fellow anarchist Élisée Reclus. "Poor humanity!" he exclaimed. It was, however, necessary to keep the revolutionary work going. Propaganda was "something, without doubt," though he admitted that he was "too old, too sick, and, I must tell you, too disillusioned" to fight on. The comrades in Jura and Belgium, the "last Mohicans of the International," who plugged away in the face of reaction and apathy, even though they would not see the results, were a small source of hope. "Their labor will not be wasted," he explained, for "drops of water may be invisible, but they form the ocean nonetheless." But if that were all that could be done, "humanity would rot ten times over before being saved." There remained, however, another even grimmer possibility, he concluded: "world war. These immense military states must destroy each other and devour each other sooner or later. But what a prospect!" His despairing prediction would of course be fulfilled within forty years.[1]

Bakunin then turned to more prosaic matters. He wrote to his family in Russia, expressing his desire to see them and their children and imploring them to come and visit. His last chance for financial security remained the legacy he believed due him from Priamukhino, and he asked his brothers and sisters to sell his portion of the estate and forward the money as quickly as possible. He used the promise of the legacy to borrow enough money to purchase another house, Villa Bresso, and once again, the plan was to make it self-sufficient. Cafiero cheerfully forgave him and continued to lend him money, and Bakunin turned as energetically as possible to planting. This venture too flopped, and when the money from Priamukhino finally arrived, it was too little too late. In the summer of 1876, he and Antonia left the villa before they were evicted. They planned to go to Naples, perhaps to live with Gambuzzi, who was still advancing them funds, and Antonia headed to Italy to make the arrangements while Bakunin detoured to Berne to meet up with his friend and doctor, Adolf Vogt. Bakunin had known Vogt, then a child, from the days when his father hung with Weitling, and now he hoped the doctor could find some relief from his ailments. But when Bakunin arrived on 14 June 1876, Vogt checked him out and then immediately checked him into a hospital.

The old anarchist could fight the laws of capital and the state, but the inexorable laws of nature ground away. A few friends visited regularly, including Vogt and Adolf Reichel, a musician Bakunin had known since the Berlin days of the early 1840s. Reichel wrote to Gambuzzi at length about Bakunin's last days. The two talked philosophy, and Bakunin read Schopenhauer in his hospital bed. He showed some of the old spirit when he remarked to Reichel that "all of our philosophy starts from a false premise. It always begins by taking man as an individual, rather than a being who is part of a community. That's where most of the philosophical errors that lead to either pie in the sky [literally, happiness in the clouds] or the pessimism of Schopenhauer and Hartman come from." As he declined, however, they abandoned philosophy for reminiscences. "It's a pity, Bakunin, you never found time to write your memoirs," Reichel gently chided one day. "Why would you want me to write them?" he responded. "It is not worth wasting the breath. Today, the people of all nations have lost the instinct of revolution. They are all too content with their situation and the fear of losing what they have makes them harmless and inert. No, if I regained some of my health, I would write an ethic based on the principles of collectivism, without reference to philosophical or religious phrases." They spoke of music, and Bakunin expressed his preference still for Beethoven, opining that Wagner, whom he remembered from the Dresden barricades, was deficient in both character and musical taste. At the end, he slept more and more; even his famous appetites left him. The man who had once looked as though he could devour the world could now manage only some spoonfuls of *kasha,* or groats, prepared in the Russian manner by Reichel's wife, Maria. He refused bouillon, murmuring without opening his eyes, "I have no need; I have finished my task." At noon 1 July 1876, Bakunin died an ordinary death in stark counterpoint to an extraordinary life.[2]

About forty mourners attended the funeral service at the Berne cemetery two days later. As he had in life, in death Bakunin pulled a bigger crowd than Marx would when he died six years later, and no doubt the anarchist would have liked that. A final small irony linked the two men, and probably would have amused them both, or at least confirmed the suspicion that the other was irredeemably petit bourgeois. The two sworn enemies of capital were each described in their death certificates as "rentier," that is, someone who lived off investments. If only! they might have muttered. Lack of money had never kept the anarchist fixed in place, and he remained restless even after his interment: The cemetery was made into a park, and Bakunin's remains were transferred to a plot in Friedhof Bremgarten outside the city center. Undoubtedly the inscription, REMEMBER ONE WHO SACRIFICED EVERYTHING FOR HIS COUNTRY,

would set him off on a ferocious argument, though the stone itself, large and rough-hewn, plain and striking, seems apt enough.

Bakunin had failed to make or even see the social revolution, though hardly for lack of trying. Most of his writings were never published in his lifetime; much of what did see print after his death was circulated only in small anarchist circles. He was never much appreciated by intellectuals in the academy, who found much more to argue about in hermeneutic readings of Marx and Engels. His impact, however, is more profound than many have acknowledged. In Russia, succeeding generations of radicals—ranging from student radicals who went "to the people" in the manner advocated by Bakunin, to a new Land and Liberty group, to Narodnaya Volya, or "The People's Will," to the social revolutionaries—were not anarchists, but they owed many of their ideas to Bakunin. The anarchist movement itself continued to grow as it was developed by a new generation of thinkers and activists including Peter Kropotkin and Errico Malatesta. That generation lived to see many of Bakunin's predictions and theories prove correct: 1914 brought the world war he had feared and with it, the destruction of empires; 1917 saw Russian peasants and workers make the social revolution. They built on the peasant commune and created workers' associations, or Soviets, and without waiting for the full development of the material forces of production, overthrew the tsar's regime. Bakunin's more dire predictions came to pass too. The reactionaries caused more bloodshed than the revolution as they launched a civil war, and foreign troops landed on Russian soil to, as Winston Churchill put it, strangle the baby of socialism in its cradle. Bakunin was largely correct in his warnings about authoritarian or state socialism as well. The social revolution was quickly turned into a political one, with new red rulers at the head of a new state. Bakunin's warnings of the nature of the state, even the revolutionary state, were soon proved correct. Like Marx, the Bolsheviks had little sense of or respect for the peasantry, and their clumsy attempts to force them to produce food for the cities quickly backfired. Through a policy of repression and reform, the stubborn resistance of the peasants was worn down, but at a terrible cost. Radical workers too soon discovered that they did not control the state that acted in their name. The Bolshevik state found it expedient to turn their secret police, the Cheka, against anarchists soon after they came to power, shutting down their newspapers, breaking up their meetings, and throwing them into some of the same prisons the tsar had used for them. The events at Kronstadt in 1921, when the Red Army was ordered to turn its guns on revolutionary workers, were as disillusioning to radicals of that day as the tanks sent in to Hungary and Czechoslovakia and Tiananmen Square were to later generations.[3] Marx and Engels soon had the status of prophets of a state religion and their writings took on an importance they had not had during Marx's life. But the new god was a jealous god, and other revolutionary figures were soon deemed false. Soon after Boris Korolev was commissioned in 1918 to create a Cubo-Futurist sculpture commemorating Bakunin, the statue fell afoul of political and artistic orthodoxy and was destroyed a few months after it was unveiled in Moscow.[4] When later Soviet scholars undertook to publish the collected works of Bakunin, the project was halted before the collection made it past 1861. While other attempts were made by anarchists and sympathizers, not until 2000 would a definitive, complete edition appear, on CD-ROM.

In the United States, France, Italy, Spain, and Belgium, anarchism, in its individualist, terrorist phase and, more important, as a tendency in labor movements, was much more significant than Marxism until the early twentieth century. Ten years after Bakunin's death, anarchists played a crucial role in the fight for the eight-hour day in the U.S.; four were rewarded for their efforts by a show trial and the hangman's noose in the aftermath of Chicago's Haymarket affair. One of the four hanged on 11 November 1887 left a young widow, Lucy Parsons, who helped found the most important American expression of anarchism, the Industrial Workers of the World, in 1905. In their call for the general strike, their insistence that it would be the poorest workers who would become the most radical, and their rejection of political action, the Wobblies drew heavily on anarchist ideas pioneered by Bakunin. A different strand of anarchism, represented in the United States by Emma Goldman and Alexander Berkman, was less influential in the labor movement but was significant enough that the American government had to use its secret police, the fledgling FBI, to shut down their newspapers, break up their meetings, throw them in jail, and deport them in 1919.

As the left regrouped and reorganized in the 1920s, communism, or whatever one prefers to call the Bolshevik state, and social democracy overshadowed anarchism, as it appeared that pursuing state power could be an effective stand-in for the social revolution. Anarchism did not disappear, but survived largely as a philosophy that offered a moral and political critique rather than an alternative. It appeared to be largely irrelevant as a political or social force, so much so that Alexander Berkman committed suicide in 1936, made despondent by illness and by the apparent futility of remaining an anarchist in a world dominated by fascism, Bolshevism, and militarism. But only a few weeks after his death, anarchism again asserted itself as a powerful social movement. With the outbreak of the Spanish Civil War, anarchists quickly formed militias to fend off the fascists, phalangists, Catholics, and assorted reactionaries who threatened the Republic. Without the anarchist militias, Madrid would have fallen in the first months of the war. The anarchists did more. In the regions where they had some strength, they took over factories and ran them according to anarchist principles. They collectivized the land and abolished rent, rank, and religion. Servers in restaurants still did their jobs, but without a trace of the stroking and servility that marks the trade even to this day. Spain provided a clear, living example of anarchism in action as workers and peasants ran industries, agriculture, and armies as collective, free associations. But the experiment was smashed as Spain was abandoned by the democratic nations that preferred fascism to revolution and by Stalin's Soviet Union, which sought to treat with the Western powers. Reaction won in Spain, as it had won in Germany and Italy, and again anarchists, along with communists, socialists, and liberals, were rounded up, imprisoned, and executed. Shortly after the Spanish Civil War, capital and states once more formally expressed their preference for world war over the social revolution.

In the wake of World War II—and in particular the working-class pressure for reform that accompanied it, with liberalism, relative prosperity, and state intervention in the capitalist democracies—radicalism, the pundits claimed, was no longer relevant. It was the "end of ideology," they claimed, except of course for the Cold War, the new imperialisms, and the anticolonialism that opposed them. But as Bakunin had pointed out, the fight for anarchism was not just a fight for more; it was a fight for justice, for equality, for freedom. If capitalism had provided better paying jobs for part of its workforce in some nations, this was the result of struggle, not generosity, and still had not addressed the very real problems of a social system based on exploitation. For that reason, the "end of ideology" was just a prelude for what has become known as "the Sixties," when again students, workers, and intellectuals demanded revolution. It is chiefly remembered as a cultural movement, sometimes as little more than a fashion statement; even blue-tinted eyeglasses made a comeback. But the core of "the Sixties" was revolt, and the radicalism of the period owed as much to Bakunin as it did to Marx, both directly, in the case of the avowed anarchists, situationists, and yippies, and indirectly, among those whose revolt was more "instinctive" than learned but no less expressive or important for that. Paris in May 1968 looked more like an anarchist movement than anything else as workers seized factories and students seized the streets. If the feminist movement owed nothing directly to Bakunin, surely he would have counted himself as a supporter. Anarchism even got some attention in academia. One anarchist theorist has argued that the liberal Isaiah Berlin borrowed from Bakunin, noting that Berlin's famous notion of "negative" and "positive" freedom may be found in the anarchist's writings, though they are not so credited.[5] Philosophers such as Paul Goodman and Robert-Paul Wolff gave anarchism serious thought; literary figures and historians such as George Woodcock and James Joll treated it as an important movement. Its libertarian ethos inspired educators ranging from A. S. Neill and his Summerhill School to Neil Postman. One can find traces of Bakunin in the thought of Herbert Marcuse and E. P. Thompson, the first in his argument that other groups along with workers could be revolutionary agents, the second in his understanding that workers have class experiences and so class consciousness, even though these may not resemble an official party program. As Marxism sought to reinvent itself in the academy and sought to correct for the reformism of social democracy, the calamity of Soviet Marxism and its derivatives, the oversimplifications of strict economism, and the sterility of orthodox communism, it moved closer to Bakunin than many Marxists suspected. Intellectuals such as Michel Foucault talked about power and floated over ground first trod by Bakunin, though the anarchist would have scoffed at the rejection of materialism, class, and political action often adopted by postmodernists and post-Marxists.

Does Bakunin have any relevance today? He certainly reappeared as a bogeyman after September 11, but his casting as the grandfather of terrorism was an exercise of mystification rather than explanation. Of more credence is the claim that he has been one of the inspirations of the movement against "globalization," better rendered as the protest against "global capitalism." Bakunin's critique of capitalism and the state has lost none of its force. After all, these institutions took on their modern shape during his life. If they have changed dramatically since then, their essential character as methods of exploitation has not. Anarchists have garnered much of the attention at the large protests around the world, and Bakunin would undoubtedly approve of their sentiments, if not always of their tactics. As contemporary anarchists grapple with questions of tactics and strategy, a reexamination of Bakunin may be useful, for his arguments against "spontaneity" and random violence, and his arguments for organization and class struggle still need to be addressed by those who are serious about building a mass movement. There is something instructive for all on the left in Bakunin's observation that workers and peasants understand, viscerally and fundamentally, that they are oppressed. If they do not react in the way intellectuals and activists hope they will or expect they should, the answer is not to blame them for their own oppression but to seek to understand their experience and build on it. Marxists too may find there is less to quarrel over with anarchists than they think. Both sides have focused on and exaggerated the narrow, if sharp, differences between them. But with the main protagonists now long dead, it may be possible to consider the similarities and find ways to pose the differences as a progressive, dynamic, and creative tension as we confront the problems of the twenty-first century.

For those who are less interested in the questions of political change, Bakunin still remains of some interest and importance as a historical political thinker and actor whose ideas continue to influence world events. His ideas also have considerable utility in daily life. Ernest Hemingway once remarked that every writer needs a "built-in shock-proof shit detector." So do we all. Bakunin reminds us that shit runs downhill. It comes from those who rule, lead, employ, and manipulate us. He reminds us that our anger and protest must be linked with others and directed upward. Today as much as ever Bakunin holds out a vision of a world of freedom and equality against which the present reality may be measured and found wanting.

BIBLIOGRAPHIC GUIDE

The citations in each chapter will guide the reader to the sources used in this book. This essay is offered as a guide to some of the English-language work most useful in interpreting Bakunin and to indicate more generally the material I have drawn upon. Excellent annotated bibliographies and useful explanatory notes on Bakunin may be found in Paul McLaughlin, *Mikhail Bakunin: The Philosophical Basis of His Anarchism*, New York: Algora, 2002; *The Basic Bakunin: Writings, 1869–1871*, Robert M. Cutler, trans., ed., New York: Prometheus Books, 1992; and *Michael Bakunin: Statism and Anarchy*, Marshall Shatz, trans., ed., Cambridge: Cambridge University Press, 1990. The latter two books also offer useful introductions to Bakunin's life and ideas.

The standard biography is E. H. Carr's *Michael Bakunin*. First published in 1937, it is an elegant book full of charming details and anecdotes, but it does little to explain the social context of the world Bakunin inhabited. Nor does it say much about his ideas; Bakunin's book, *Statism and Anarchy*, is not even mentioned. K. J. Kenafick's *Michael Bakunin and Karl Marx*, Melbourne: A. Mailer, 1948, covers much more ground than his title implies. An anarchist activist himself, Kenafick argues that Bakunin and Marx had much in common and he offers a significant counter to Carr's interpretation. Kenafick rejects the psychohistory hinted at in Carr and launched a preemptive strike against two biographies of Bakunin published in the 1980s, Arthur P. Mendel's *Michael Bakunin: Roots of Apocalypse,* and Aileen Kelly's *Mikhail Bakunin: A Study in the Psychology and Politics of Utopianism.* Mendel has read Bakunin's letters closely and reveals much detail, but makes dubious psychological interpretations that stem from his acute distaste for the man and the ideas. The two books are critiqued in Brian Morris's 1997 work, *Bakunin: The Philosophy of Freedom*, Montreal: Black Rose Books, 1993, a short volume written with considerable empathy and intelligence. It relies heavily on secondary sources, but is a provocative and lively introduction to the life and ideas of Bakunin. Paul McLaughlin launches several well-aimed attacks on Mendel, Kelly, Carr, Isaiah Berlin, and Marxist critics of anarchism in *Mikhail Bakunin: The Philosophical Basis of His Anarchism*. His analysis of Bakunin's relationship to Hegel and Fichte is a useful corrective to those scholars who find nothing of value or interest in German idealism. McLaughlin also explores Bakunin's interest in Comte. McLaughlin and I draw on the invigorating and sophisticated work of Martine Del Giudice. Her dissertation, "The Young Bakunin and Left Hegelianism: Origins of Russian Radicalism and the Theory of Praxis, 1814–1842," Ph.D. thesis, McGill University, 1981, and the article drawn from it, "Bakunin's Preface to Hegel's *Gymnasia! Lectures:* The Problem of Alienation and the Reconciliation with Reality," *Canadian-American Slavic Studies,* 16, no. 2, 1982, are crucial to understanding Bakunin's work in philosophy and the turn to Hegel. Another Ph.D. thesis, John Wyatt Randolph's "The Bakunins: Family, Nobility, and Social Thought in Imperial Russia, 1780–1840," University of California, Berkeley, 1997, is an invaluable guide to the early years at Priamukhino and the dreams, realities, and conflicts that shaped the family. Both these theses, though very different in approach and conclusions, are models of scholarship and offer vital and well-argued analyses.

In addition to translating *Statism and Anarchy,* Marshall Shatz is responsible for much of the debunking of the myths surrounding Bakunin. His "Michael Bakunin and His Biographers: The Question of Bakunin's Sexual Impotence," in *Imperial Russia, 1700–1917: State, Society, Opposition: Essays in Honor of Marc Raeff,* Ezra Mendelsohn and Marshall Shatz, eds., DeKalb: Northern Illinois University Press, 1988, exposes the impotence fallacy. The notion that Turgenev's character Rudin is a useful way to understand Bakunin is effectively refuted in "Bakunin, Turgenev, and *Rudin,*" in *The Golden Age of Russian Literature and Thought,* Derek Offord, ed., New York: St. Martin's Press, 1992. Shatz illuminates the relationship of Bakunin to his sisters and the revolts at Priamukhino and establishes his early commitment to women's rights in "Mikhail Bakunin and the Priamukhino Circle: Love and Liberation in the Russian Intelligentsia of the 1830s," *Canadian-American Slavic Studies,* 33, no. 1, spring 1999, pages 1–29.

Paul Avrich is the leading American scholar of anarchism, and his important essays, "The Legacy of Bakunin," "Bakunin and the United States," and "Bakunin and Nechaev," may be found in his book, *Anarchist Portraits,* Princeton: Princeton University Press, 1988. Bakunin's time and influence in Italy are carefully examined in T. R. Ravindranathan, *Bakunin and the Italians,* Kingston and Montreal: McGill-Queen's University Press, 1988, and in Nunzio Pernicone, *Italian Anarchism, 1864–1892,* Princeton: Princeton University Press, 1993. Richard B. Saltman explores Bakunin's anarchism at great length in *The Social and Political Thought of Michael Bakunin,* Westport: Greenwood Press, 1983. He outlines nicely Bakunin's critique of Hegel, though his argument that Bakunin was essentially a Lamarckian is not, to my mind, convincing. His careful analysis of Bakunin's ideas is a spirited critique of much of the liberal and right-wing scholarship on Bakunin. Stephen Porter Halbrook argues in "The Marx-Bakunin Controversy: Intellectual Origins, 1844–1870," Ph.D. thesis, Florida State University, 1972, that Marx was essentially a reformist and Bakunin a violent revolutionary, and if the latter claim is vividly overstated, there is much useful information and several interesting arguments here.

The fights between anarchists and Marxists are taken up by Paul Thomas, *Karl Marx and the Anarchists,* London: Routledge and Kegan Paul, 1980. Generally friendly to Marx, Thomas still states much of the anarchist case well. A thoughtful analysis that disagrees with Thomas on some significant interpretative points is Alvin Gouldner, *Against Fragmentation: The Origins of Marxism and the Sociology of Intellectuals,* Oxford: Oxford University Press, 1985.

BAKUNIN'S WRITINGS

Anarchists have rarely been considered good commercial risks by mainstream publishers. Nor have there been friendly states eager to subsidize the production of their collected works, as was the case with Marx and Engels. As a result, several attempts to publish the collected works of Bakunin were begun and abandoned over the years. The complete works of Bakunin were finally made available on CD-ROM in *Bakounine: Oeuvres completes,* Amsterdam: International Institute of Social History, 2000. This is a wonderful research tool that contains all of Bakunin's writings in all languages, and has translated everything into French where that was not the original language. Many manuscript versions are reproduced, and the collection will make possible continued study and revision of Bakunin's life and ideas. Of the English collections, none is complete. Robert M. Cutler's *The Basic Bakunin: Writings, 1869–1871,* first published as *From Out of the Dustbin,* offers Bakunin's short journalism, which contains some of his most engaging work. *Bakunin on Anarchism,* Sam Dolgoff, trans., ed., Montreal: Black Rose Books, 1980, has a useful introduction and a biographical sketch by James Guillaume. The translations vary in accuracy, and the pieces are often edited and added to in order to increase their polemical value. *Michael Bakunin: Selected Writings,* Arthur Lehning, ed., London: Jonathan Cape, 1973, is a sympathetic collection designed to show Bakunin at his best. *The Political Philosophy of Bakunin,* G. P. Maximoff, ed., New York: The Free Press, 1953, is a labor of love. The biographical sketch by Max Nettlau, along with Lehning, the most important of Bakunin's European biographers, is useful, but the collection itself is an odd project. Maximoff cut and pasted together thematic sections based on paragraphs from all of Bakunin's work. Thus a section on any particular theme may be composed of material written at very different times and with very different emphases in the original. The strength of the book is Maximoff's detailed knowledge of Bakunin's writings and his use of sources that until the publication of *Bakounine: Oeuvres completes* were obscure, but the result is a tricky pastiche that must be sorted through cautiously to avoid errors of consistency and chronology. The best translation of Bakunin's final work is *Michael Bakunin: Statism and Anarchy,* Marshall Shatz, trans., ed., Cambridge: Cambridge University Press, 1990.

NOTES

1. G. B. Trudeau, *Doonesbury*, 16 June 1988.
2. Alexander Cockburn, Jeffrey St. Clair, *5 Days that Shook the World: Seattle and Beyond*, London and New York: Verso, 2000.
3. *Utne Reader*, May-June 2001, page 49.
4. See, for example, Donald Harstad, *Eleven Days*, New York: Doubleday, 1998, pages 239-40, where the only thing worse than anarchists in the Iowa countryside must be the local Satanists. Anarchism has fared a little better in the comic books. Batman was confronted by a new foe, Anarky, in 1989. Unlike the protector of Gotham City, Anarky took on corporations and governments that destroyed the environment and displaced the homeless to build bank towers. The Caped Crusader vanquished him, naturally, but admitted that Anarky's "cause was just" and "he only wanted to set the world straight." *Detective Comics*, nos. 608 and 609, 1989. Anarky appeared in other comics and had his own for a time. The original two-part series owed much to a British graphic novel of the early 1980s, *V for Vendetta*, by Alan Moore and David Lloyd, set in a bleak fascist Britain of the 1990s. The protagonist, V, announces to a statue of Justice that it was her infidelity, her "little fling" with "a man in uniform . . . with his armbands and jackboots," that drove him into the arms of Anarchy. *V for Vendetta* was republished in the U.S. in a ten-part series in 1989 and has been published more recently in book form. It has been made into a movie.
5. Lewis Lapham, "Drums Along the Potomac: NewT War, Old Music," *Harper's Magazine*, November 2001, pages 35-41. John le Carre, "We Have Already Lost," *Globe and Mail*, 13 October 2001. The article by David Ignatius, perhaps the most egregious, may be found in the *International Herald Tribune*, 29 October 2001; like le Carre's article, it was widely reprinted. Ian Brown, "The Next Step Is This: What Goes On in the Mind of a Terrorist?" *Globe and Mail*, 22 September 2001.
6. The contemporary transliteration of his full name is Mikhail Aleksandrovich Bakunin. Russian custom is to give children a patronymic, or father's name, as a middle name. Michael's father was Aleksander, thus Mikhail Aleksandrovich; Aleksander's patronymic was Mikhailovich, after his father, Mikhail. Each of Michael's brothers, including Aleksander, had Aleksandrovich as a middle name. His sisters had the patronymic Aleksandrovna and used the feminine form Bakunina as their surname. I have Anglicized common names such as Mikhail and Aleksander throughout, while using Russian forms for names that are less common to the English reader, such as Sergei or Vassily. I would like to thank my colleagues Ilya Vinkovetsky and Jerry Zaslove for their helpful suggestions on usage and Russian history. I have also changed the capitalization of nouns such as "state" and "revolution" used by Bakunin and sometimes his translators, for consistency and to reflect modern usage.
7. E. H. Carr, *Michael Bakunin*, 1937, New York: Vintage Books, 1961; Aileen Kelly, *Mikhail Bakunin: A Study in the Psychology and Politics of Utopianism*, London: Oxford University Press, 1982, page 3. Arthur P. Mendel, *Michael Bakunin: Roots of Apocalypse*, New York: Praeger Publishers, 1981. The most recent incarnation of what must be considered an historical urban legend is Shlomo Barer in *The Doctors of Revolution: 19th-century Thinkers Who Changed the World*, London: Thames and Hudson, 2000. It is worth repeating that this myth has never had any evidence to support it and was thoroughly debunked by Marshall S. Shatz in "Michael Bakunin and His Biographers: The Question of Bakunin's Sexual Impotence," in *Imperial Russia 1700-1917: State, Society, Opposition*, DeKalb: Northern Illinois University Press, 1988. It is hard to get rid of the suspicion that this story is repeated as a cautionary tale to warn off potential anarchists from reading those dirty

books. For the cautious reader, let me state unequivocally that there is no medical evidence to suggest a causal connection between anarchism and impotence.

8. Howard Zinn, *Marx in Soho,* Cambridge, Mass.: South End Press, 1999, pages 31-41. E. J. Hobsbawm, "Reflections on Anarchism," in *Revolutionaries: Contemporary Essays,* 1973, reprint, London: Quartet Books, 1977, pages 82-94. His conclusion is on page 84. Despite my criticism of his point, this is a fascinating and thoughtful article.

9. E. P. Thompson, "The Poverty of Theory or an Orrery of Errors," in *The Poverty of Theory and Other Essays,* London: Merlin, 1978, page 192.

1: WEREWOLVES, NOBLES, AND THE IDYLL OF PRIAMUKHINO

1. The description of Bakunin is based on his self-portrait of 1829 and a portrait of him printed in *Der Leuchtturm* in 1849. He is described as a "giant" in much of the literature, probably as a result of his strong personality as much as his size. K. J. Kenafick, on page 41, gives his height as six feet, four inches. A police report from Konigstein dated 1850 lists his height as six feet, five and a half inches, his eyes as gray-blue, his build as "powerful, colossal." Cited in *Bakounine et les autres: Esquisses et portraits contemporains d'un revolutionnaire,* Arthur Lehning, ed., Paris: Union General e d'Editions, 1976, page 176.

2. See, for example, the *National Post,* 9 December 2000, page B3, for such a characterization.

3. Simon Dixon, *The Modernisation of Russia, 1676-1825,* page 93. Peter Kolchin, *Unfree Labor: American Slavery and Russian Serfdom,* Cambridge, Mass.: Harvard University Press, 1987, pages 39-40.

4. Dixon, pages 221-55.

5. Jerome Blum, *Lord and Peasant in Russia from the Ninth to the Nineteenth Century,* 1961. Princeton: Princeton University Press, 1971, pages 345-66. For the continuing importance of lineage and the shift to education, see Valerie A. Kivelson, "Kinship Politics /Autocratic Politics: A Reconsideration of Early-Eighteenth-Century Political Culture," in *Imperial Russia: New Histories for the Empire,* Jane Burbank and David L. Ransel, eds., Bloomington and Indianapolis: Indiana University Press, 1998, pages 5–31.

6. For this and the following description of the Bakunin family, see John Wyatt Randolph, "The Bakunins: Family, Nobility, and Social Thought in Imperial Russia, 1780–1840," Ph.D. thesis, University of California, Berkeley, 1997, and Carr, pages 1–6.

7. Carr, pages 3–4.

8. Although there is some doubt about the year of Alexander's birth, both Carr and Randolph believe it was 1768 rather than 1763, and I have chosen to follow their reckoning.

9. For Stephen Bathory's attendance at Padua, see Jonathon Woolfson, *Padua and the Tudors,* Toronto: University of Toronto Press, 1998, page 4. Paul's remark to the Swedish ambassador is cited in Nicholas V. Riasanovsky, *A History of Russia,* third edition, Oxford: Oxford University Press, 1977, page 358.

10. Eric Hobsbawm, *The Age of Revolution, 1789–1848,* 1962, reprint, London: Abacus, 1995. This book remains the best English-language overview of the period and I have relied on it for this section. See also his *Echoes of the Marseillaise: Two Centuries Look Back on the French Revolution,* New Brunswick: Rutgers University Press, 1990. For an interesting and different analysis, see George C. Comninel, *Rethinking of the French Revolution: Marxism and the Revisionist Challenge,* London: Verson, 1987. For the Haitian revolt, see C. L. R. James, *The Black Jacobins: Toussaint L'Ouverture and the San Domingo Revolution,* New York: Vintage Books, 1963.

11. See Carr, pages 3–6, and Randolph, pages 64–7.

12. Carr, pages 3–4; Randolph, pages 73–6.

13. For the description of Priamukhino, see Carr, pages 3–6; Randolph, pages 75-7 and 150-7.

14. Richard Wortman, "The Russian Imperial Family as Symbol," in *Imperial Russia,* page 61. The question of Paul's madness is debated, as successive tsars, especially his son, and their historians have preferred to depict him as insane for their own reasons.

15. Alexander Bakunin to Michael Bakunin, 4 April 1801, cited in Randolph, page 80.

16. Randolph, pages 67–8, 76–8, 101–2, and 119. Alexander's reflections on his status cited in Carr, page 8.
17. *Bakounine: Oeuvres completes,* "Histoire de ma vie," 1871, Amsterdam: International Institute of Social History, 2000, CD-ROM. (Hereafter *Bakounine: Oeuvres completes.)* Unless otherwise stated, translations from *Bakounine: Oeuvres completes* are by the author. I would like to thank my colleagues Rod Day and Mary Lynn Stewart for their help.
18. Jessica Tovrov, "Mother-Child Relationships Among the Russian Nobility," in *The Family in Imperial Russia: New Lines of Historical Research,* David L. Ransel, ed., Urbana: University of Illinois Press, 1978, pages 15–43. Barbara Alpern Engel, "Mothers and Daughters: Family Patterns and the Female Intelligentsia," in *The Family in Imperial Russia,* pages 44–59. Engel, *Mothers and Daughters: Women of the Intelligentsia in Nineteenth-Century Russia,* Cambridge: Cambridge University Press, 1983. Margaret H. Darrow, "French Noblewomen and the New Domesticity, 1750–1850," *Feminist Studies,* 5, no. 1 (spring 1979), pages 41–65. Randolph, pages 120–60.
19. Alexander Bakunin writing about his mother and his resolve to do better cited in Randolph, pages 160–1; see also Mendel, pages 14–6. Marshall Shatz, "Mikhail Bakunin and the Priamukhino Circle: Love and Liberation in the Russian Intelligentsia of the 1830s," *Canadian-American Slavic Studies,* 33, no. 1 (spring 1999), pages 3–5.
20. *Bakounine: Oeuvres completes,* "Histoire de ma vie," 1871.
21. *Bakounine: Oeuvres completes,* letter to his father, 15 December 1837; letter to his family, 4 February 1852; Shatz, "Mikhail Bakunin and the Priamukhino Circle," page 5; Mendel, pages 14–5; Carr, pages 7–9. 22. *Bakounine: Oeuvres completes,* letter to his father, 18 October 1823; letter to his grandfather, 29 June 1824; letter to his mother, 18 September 1824; letter to his father, 18 October 1824.

2: WAR, SLAVERY, AND SERVICE

1. Philip Larkin, "This Be the Verse," in *High Windows,* London: Faber and Faber, 1974.
2. Karl Marx, "The Eighteenth Brumaire of Louis Napoleon," in David McLellan, *Karl Marx: Selected Writings,* second edition, Oxford: Oxford University Press, 2000, page 329.
3. Curtis Cates, *The War of the Two Emperors: The Duel Between Napoleon and Alexander: Russia, 1812,* New York: Random House, 1985, page xviii.
4. Randolph, pages 155–6.
5. The myth that blue-collar workers were the fiercest supporters of American involvement in Vietnam still persists. John Strausbaugh, for example, repeats the mistake in his otherwise delightful book, *Rock 'Til You Drop: The Decline from Rebellion to Nostalgia,* London: Verso, 2001. In his chapter, "Up Against the Wall, Mother Hubbard!" he argues that the American new left of the sixties foundered on the shores of "patriotism and deep personal commitment many working-class Americans felt toward winning the war" (page 82). In fact, as James W. Loewen has pointed out, opposition to the war was always strongest among the working class. See *Lies My Teacher Told Me: Everything Your American History Textbook Got Wrong,* New York: The New Press, 1995, pages 297–303.

A similar misconception surrounds the Luddites. The term is still used to label someone who is afraid of new technology, who cannot adapt to progress, revealed by the telltale blinking "12:00" on their VCR or DVD player. The Luddites who smashed machinery in Britain between 1811 and 1816 were not afraid of new technology. They were textile workers who used the most sophisticated machinery of the day to give Britain its industrial revolution and create the wealth of empire. They understood technology better than their employers, and unlike their employers were not afraid or unable to use it. The Luddite rebellion was about unemployment. Employers brought in new equipment that enabled them to replace workers with machines. Attempts to negotiate the change failed; savvy workers then smashed the new looms to keep their jobs. They were defending their livelihood and their lives; what they feared was unemployment and starvation, not machinery. In response to their attack on property, many were hunted by the army and machine-breaking was made a capital offense. Lord Byron's first speech in the House of Lords, on 27 February 1812, was a spirited, damning indictment of the government and the employers who were responsible for the plight of the Luddites.

6. Randolph, page 158.
7. Elaine Epstein, *Pushkin,* London: Weidenfeld and Nicolson, 1998, pages 139–40; W. Bruce Lincoln, *Nicholas I, Emperor and Autocrat of All the Russias,* London: Allen Lane, 1978, page 82.
8. Walter Arndt, *Pushkin Threefold: Narrative, Lyric, Polemic, and Ribald Verse,* New York: E. P. Dutton, 1972, page 27.
9. Lincoln, *Nicholas I,* page 236; the censor is cited in Sidney Monas, *The Third Section: Police and Society in Russia Under Nicholas I,* Cambridge, Mass.: Harvard University Press, 1961, page 142.
10. Lincoln, *Nicholas I,* pages 58–70; quotes cited here.
11. *Bakounine: Oeuvres completes,* "Histoire de ma vie," 1871.
12. Cited in Randolph, page 195; for Shishkov, see Randolph, page 172.
13. *Bakounine: Oeuvres completes,* "Histoire de ma vie," 1871.
14. *Bakounine: Oeuvres completes,* letter to his father, January 1836.
15. David Moon, *The Russian Peasantry, 1600–1930: The World the Peasants Made,* London: Longman, 1999, pages 21 and 77; Kolchin, *Unfree Labor,* pages 366 and 3; Blum, *Lord and Peasant in Russia,* pages 420–1.
16. *Bakounine: Oeuvres completes,* "Histoire de ma vie," 1871.
17. Kolchin, *Unfree Labor,* chapter 4.
18. Esther Kingston-Mann, "In the Light and Shadow of the West: The Impact of Western Economics in Pre-emancipation Russia," *Comparative Studies in Society and History,* 33, no. 1 (January 1991), pages 86–105.
19. Karl Marx, *Capital,* volume I, Moscow: Progress Publishers, 1983, page 669; the general argument is laid out in Part VIII, "The So-Called Primitive Accumulation." Eric Hobsbawm, *The Age of Revolution, 1789–1848,* chapter 2.
20. Geoffrey Hosking, *Russia: People and Empire, 1552–1917,* London: Fontana, 1998, pages 175–6.
21. See Randolph, pages 100–13.
22. Alexander Bakunin, cited in Randolph, page 101.
23. Cited in Randolph, page 188.
24. *Bakounine: Oeuvres completes,* "Histoire de ma vie," 1871.

3: RULES, REBELLION, AND ROMANCE

1. Alexander Bakunin's poem is from Randolph, page 195.
2. Carr, page 10; *Bakounine: Oeuvres completes,* letter to his aunts, 9 December 1828; for Michael's initial delight, see *Bakounine: Oeuvres completes,* letter to his father, 15 December 1837; for the tsar's dash, see Lincoln, pages 186–7; *Bakounine: Oeuvres completes,* letter to his sisters, spring 1829; Varvara Bakunin cited in Randolph, page 199.
3. *Bakounine: Oeuvres completes,* letter to his sisters, 17 March 1830.
4. *Bakounine: Oeuvres completes,* "Histoire da ma vie," 1871.
5. Carr, page 10; *Bakounine: Oeuvres completes,* "Histoire da ma vie," 1871, letter to his father, 15 December 1837.
6. See John L. Keep, *Power and the People: Essays on Russian History,* New York: Columbia University Press, 1995, especially "The Military Style of the Romanov Rulers," pages 189 209, and "From the Pistol to the Pen: The Military Memoir as a Source on Social History of Pre-Reform Russia," pages 239–66. See also his *Soldiers of the Tsar: Army and Society in Russia, 1462–1874,* Oxford: Clarendon Press, 1985, pages 323–47. Robert F. Barsky, *Noam Chomsky: A Life of Dissent,* Toronto: ECW Press, 1997, page 9.
7. See Lincoln, *Nicholas I,* pages 54–62; Keep, *Soldiers of the Tsar,* page 323; Keep, "The Military Style of the Romanov Rulers," pages 190–1.

8. See Keep, "From the Pistol to the Pen," pages 253–6, for military salaries; Keep, *Soldiers of the Tsar,* pages 335–40, for the costs of military service and the death rate from illness.
9. This judgment of Michael is cited in Keep, "The Military Style of the Romanov Rulers," page 196; Keep, *Soldiers of the Tsar,* page 347.
10. Keep, *Soldiers of the Tsar,* page 243; Lincoln, pages 54–5; Keep, "From the Pistol to the Pen," pages 256–60; Randolph, page 151.
11. *Bakounine: Oeuvres completes,* letter to his parents, 20 September 1831. For the translation of Pushkin, I have relied on Arndt, *Pushkin Threefold,* pages 44–5.
12. *Bakounine: Oeuvres completes,* letter to his sisters, spring 1831.
13. See Marshall Shatz, "Mikhail Bakunin and the Priamukhino Circle," pages 7-8; Andrew Baruch Wachtel, *The Battle for Childhood: Creation of a Russian Myth,* Stanford: Stanford University Press, 1990.
14. For Russian military school students in general, see Keep, "From the Pistol to the Pen," page 257. For Bakunin on his anxieties regarding his studies and his illnesses, see *Bakounine: Oeuvres completes,* letters to his parents, 16 March 1830 and 6 December 1831. For other complaints and work habits, see letter to sisters, May 1832; letters to parents, April 1832, 27 May 1832, 17 June 1832, 17 September 1832, 5 November 1832, 17 January 1833, 12 July 1833, 15 December 1837.
15. *Bakounine: Oeuvres completes,* letter to his parents, 16 March 1830.
16. For cadets and lies, see *Bakounine: Oeuvres completes,* letter to his father, 15 December 1837; also *Bakounine: Oeuvres completes,* letter to his parents, 30 August 1831; Mendel, page 20; *Bakounine: Oeuvres completes,* letter to his parents, April 1832.
17. *Bakounine: Oeuvres completes,* letter to his parents, 12 July 1833; letter to his father, 15 December 1837. See Marshall S. Shatz, "Michael Bakunin and His Biographers: The Question of Bakunin's Sexual Impotence."
18. Carr, pages 10-11; *Bakounine: Oeuvres completes,* letter to his parents, 12 July 1833.
19. *Bakounine: Oeuvres completes,* letter to his sisters, 2 March 1830; Mendel, page 5; *Bakounine: Oeuvres completes,* letter to his sisters, 16 April 1832, 2 February 1833.
20. Contrary to popular belief and thousands of buttons and T-shirts, it appears Emma Goldman never made the famous remark. It is, however, certainly in keeping with her belief that revolution should be joyous rather than dour. For an account of how the slogan became attributed to Goldman, see Alix Kates Shulman, "Dances with Feminists," *Women's Review of Books,* 9, no. 3 (December 1991). For letters outlining Bakunin's pastimes outside military school, see *Bakounine: Oeuvres completes,* letters to his sisters, summer 1830 and 5 May 1831; letter to his parents, 29 December 1831; letter to his sisters, 6 January 1832; letter to his parents, 16 April 1832; letters to his sisters, 17 January 1833 and 2 February 1833; letter to his parents, 11 February 1833; letters to his sisters, 11 February 1833, 17 March 1830, summer 1830, and 5 May 1831; letters to his parents, 30 August 1831 and 6 December 1831; letters to his sisters, 29 December 1831 and 6 January 1832; letter to his parents, 6 February 1832. His dislike of dancing is in letter to his sisters, 28 August 1832.
21. *Bakounine: Oeuvres completes,* letter to his parents, 17 January 1833; letters to his sisters, 17 January 1833 and 28 March 1833; letter to his father, 15 December 1837.
22. *Bakounine: Oeuvres completes,* letters to his sisters, 11 February 1833 and 28 March 1833; letter to Varvara, 5–8 March 1833.
23. *Bakounine: Oeuvres completes,* letter to Varvara, 5–8 March 1833. Esteban Buch, *Beethoven's Ninth: A Political History,* Richard Miller, trans., Chicago: University of Chicago Press, 2003.
24. *Bakounine: Oeuvres completes,* letter to Varvara, 5–8 March 1833.
25. *Bakounine: Oeuvres completes,* letter to Varvara, 5–8 March 1833.
26. *Bakounine: Oeuvres completes,* letter to his parents, April 1832.
27. *Bakounine: Oeuvres completes,* letter to his father, 15 December 1837.
28. For the Romantics in general, see the splendid overview in Hobsbawm, *The Age of Revolution, 1789–1848,* pages 307–35.

4: SHOOTING BLANKS

1. Randolph, pages 232–5.
2. See Randolph; Marshall Shatz, "Mikhail Bakunin and the Priamukhino Circle," pages 1–29.
3. Randolph, pages 241–5; Shatz, "Mikhail Bakunin and the Priamukhino Circle."
4. *Bakounine: Oeuvres completes,* letter to his parents and Varvara, 11 June 1833.
5. Cited in Randolph, page 239; letter to Beyer sisters, 18 December 1832.
6. *Bakounine: Oeuvres completes,* letter to his sisters, September 1833.
7. *Bakounine: Oeuvres completes,* letter to Liubov, autumn 1833.
8. Shatz, "Mikhail Bakunin and the Priamukhino Circle."
9. Bakunin, letter to his sisters, 26 January 1834, cited in Randolph, pages 288–9.
10. *Bakounine: Oeuvres completes,* "Note extraite d'un resume d'histoire," April-July 1834.
11. Mendel, pages 18-9; Carr, pages 16–7.
12. *Bakounine: Oeuvres completes,* letter to his parents, 19 December 1834.
13. *Bakounine: Oeuvres completes,* letter to Beyer sisters, 11 July 1834.
14. *Bakounine: Oeuvres completes,* letter to his parents, 4 October 1834; letter to his sisters, 19 December 1834, again indicates his loneliness and desire to be with his family; in the same letter he also comments on bad shape of his uniform and staving off depression; letter to Sergei N. Muraviev, end of January 1835.
15. *Bakounine: Oeuvres completes,* letter to Muraviev, end of January 1835.
16. *Bakounine: Oeuvres completes,* letter to J. M. Neverov, 15 February 1836.
17. *Bakounine: Oeuvres completes,* letter to Neverov, 15 February 1836; see Shatz, "Michael Bakunin and the Priamukhino Circle," page 9.
18. *Bakounine: Oeuvres completes,* letter to Varvara, 15 March 1840.
19. Aksakov, Annenkov, and Belinsky, cited in Martine Del Giudice, "The Young Bakunin and Left Hegelianism: Origins of Russian Radicalism and the Theory of Praxis, 1814–1842," Ph.D. thesis, McGill University, 1981, pages 85–6.
20. Ivan Turgenev, *Rudin,* Richard Freeborn, trans., London: Penguin Books, 1975, page 98.
21. Shatz, "Michael Bakunin and the Priamukhino Circle."
22. Turgenev cited in Marshall Shatz, "Bakunin, Turgenev, and *Rudin,*" in *The Golden Age of Russian Literature and Thought,* Derek Offord, ed., New York: St. Martin's Press, 1992, page 108.
23. Cited in Carr, page 42.
24. Edward J. Brown, in *Stankevich and His Moscow Circle, 1830–1840,* Stanford: Stanford University Press, 1966, outlines the relationships clearly, as does Shatz, in "Michael Bakunin and the Priamukhino Circle." Brown also argues, correctly, that it is a mistake to attribute the rebellions of his sisters to Michael's interference. Belinsky cited in Randolph, pages 342–53.
25. Lydia Ginzburg, *On Psychological Prose,* Judson Rosengrant, ed., trans., Princeton: Princeton University Press, 1991, pages 58–107.
26. Belinsky cited in Shatz, "Bakunin, Turgenev, and *Rudin,*" page 107.
27. See Mendel, pages 117–21; Shatz, "Bakunin, Turgenev, and *Rudin*"
28. *Bakounine: Oeuvres completes,* letter to Stankevich, September 1838; cited in Mendel, page 123.
29. Cited in Randolph, pages 260 and 332.
30. *Bakounine: Oeuvres completes,* letter to Varvara, 11 October 1836, cited in Shatz, "Michael Bakunin and the Priamukhino Circle," pages 13–4. In this letter, Bakunin was making reference to Liubov, who was faced with another potential suitor at the time.
31. *Bakounine: Oeuvres completes,* letter to Varvara, 9 March 1836; see also Randolph, page 289.
32. See Randolph, page 314; Shatz, "Michael Bakunin and the Priamukhino Circle."
33. *Bakounine: Oeuvres completes,* letter to Alexandra and Natalie Beyer, 22 April 1835, cited in Shatz, "Michael Bakunin and His Biographers: The Question of Bakunin's Sexual Impotence," page 223. The section that follows borrows heavily on this work.

34. Shatz, "Michael Bakunin and His Biographers: The Question of Bakunin's Sexual Impotence," page 224; Mendel, pages 142–3; Carr, pages 81 and 86–8.
35. I am indebted to Randolph and Del Giudice, "The Young Bakunin and Left Hegelianism," and especially Paul McLaughlin, *Mikhail Bakunin: The Philosophical Basis of His Anarchism*, New York: Algora Publishing, 2002, for this argument. Berlin's take may be found in his article "A Remarkable Decade," in *Russian Thinkers*, Henry Hardy and Aileen Kelly, eds., Harmondsworth: Penguin Books, 1978. Martin Malia, *Alexander Herzen and the Birth of Russian Socialism*, Cambridge: Harvard University Press, 1961. Kelly, *Mikhail Bakunin*.

5: THE MAIN ILLNESS OF OUR GENERATION

1. Paul McLaughlin, in *Mikhail Bakunin*, has argued convincingly that many of Bakunin's critics, including Isaiah Berlin, have completely misinterpreted Bakunin and the German idealists. His critique, much of which takes place in his extensive footnotes, is provocative and original, based on a close and nuanced reading of primary texts, and delivered with a scathing wit and accuracy. Brian Morris, in *Bakunin: The Philosophy of Freedom*, Montreal: Black Rose Books, 1993, similarly argues that the Berlin school has got these philosophers about as wrong as possible.
2. Johann Fichte, "Some Lectures Concerning the Vocation of the Scholar," *Fichte: Early Philosophical Writings*, Daniel Breazeale, trans., ed., Ithaca: Cornell University Press, 1988, page 150. The subsequent quotations are from this work.
3. Terry Pinkard, *Hegel: A Biography*, Cambridge: Cambridge University Press, 2000, page ix.
4. Tony Smith, "Hegel: Mystic Dunce or Important Predecessor? A Reply to John Rosenthal," *Historical Materialism: Research in Critical Marxist Theory*, 10, no. 2 (2002), pages 191–206.
5. Pinkard, page 659.
6. Bill Watterson, *Scientific Progress Goes (CBoink,"* Kansas City: Andrews and McMeel, 1991, page 27.
7. G. W. F. Hegel, *Reason in History: A General Introduction to the Philosophy of History*, Robert S. Hartman, trans., New York: Macmillan, 1953, page 24. This volume is the introduction to Hegel's *Lectures on the Philosophy of History*.
8. Peter Singer uses this example in *Hegel: A Very Short Introduction*, Oxford: Oxford University Press, 2001, pages 42–4. I have been guided by his interpretation in this section.
9. Singer, pages 49–50.
10. *Bakounine: Oeuvres completes*, letter to Beyer sisters, 13 March 1838, cited in Del Giudice, page 240.
11. Cited in Del Giudice, page 424. Where Del Giudice has translated *genii* as "genies," I have translated it as "geniuses." Unlike most of the work on Bakunin's Hegelian period, Del Giudice's thesis and her article, "Bakunin's Preface to Hegel's *Gymnasium Lectures*: The Problem of Alienation and the Reconciliation with Reality," *Canadian-American Slavic Studies*, 16, no. 2 (1982), pages 161–89, are models of scholarly insight and integrity. I draw heavily upon her interpretation here. McLaughlin, *Mikhail Bakunin*, also follows Del Giudice.

6: CONTRADICTION IS THE SOURCE OF MOVEMENT

1. I rely here on the translation of "On Philosophy" by Martine Del Giudice in her thesis, page 442, and the French translation in *Bakounine: Oeuvres completes*. This chapter draws heavily on the analysis she advances in her article and thesis and on McLaughlin, *Mikhail Bakunin*.
2. Belinsky and Kraevsky cited in Del Giudice, page 341.

3. Herzen, *My Past and Thoughts: The Memoirs of Alexander Herzen,* trans. Constance Garnett, rev. by Humphrey Higgens, New York: Knopf, 1968, volume 2, page 399.
4. Herbert Marcuse, *Reason and Revolution: Hegel and the Rise of Social Theory,* Boston: Beacon Press, 1960, page vii.
5. Cited in Marcuse, page vii.
6. Marcuse, page xiv.
7. *Bakounine: Oeuvres completes,* letter to Stankevich, 11 February 1840.
8. *Bakounine: Oeuvres completes,* letter to Alexandra Beyer, 22 February 1840.
9. Belinsky cited in Del Giudice, Ph.D. thesis, page 32.
10. *Bakounine: Oeuvres completes,* letter to his parents, 24 March 1840.

7: THE PASSION FOR DESTRUCTION IS A CREATIVE PASSION

1. *Bakounine: Oeuvres completes,* letter to Beyer sisters, 25 July 1840.
2. Turgenev cited in *Bakounine et les autres,* page 82; Bakunin cited in Shatz, "Bakunin, Turgenev, and *Rudin,*" page 104.
3. Ivan Turgenev, "Letter to M. A. Markovich," 16 and 28 September 1862, *Letters,* volume 1, letter 158, page 217, David Lowe, ed., Ann Arbor: Ardis, 1983. Herzen, *My Past and Thoughts,* volume 3, page 1357.
4. Shatz, "Bakunin, Turgenev, and *Rudin,*" page 112.
5. Ludwig Feuerbach, *The Essence of Christianity,* chapter 1, section 2, "The Essence of Religion Considered Generally," in *The Young Hegelians: An Anthology,* Lawrence S. Stepelvich, ed., Atlantic Highlands, N.J.: Humanities Press, 1997, page 155. Bruno Bauer, "The Trumpet of the Last Judgement," in *The Young Hegelians,* page 179.
6. *Bakounine: Oeuvres completes,* letter to Varvara and Paul Bakunin, 27 October 1841.
7. Bauer, "The Trumpet of the Last judgement," chapter 4, in *The Young Hegelians,* page 183. Arnold Ruge, "Hegel's 'Philosophy of Right' and the Politics of Our Times," in *The Young Hegelians,* page 211.
8. Engels erroneously claims Bakunin took "a great deal from Stirner," and that Bakunin "blended [Stirnerl with Proudhon and labeled the blend anarchism," in "Feuerbach and the End of Classical German Philosophy," 1886, Marx and Engels, *Selected Works,* volume 3, Moscow: Progress Publishers, 1977, pages 343 and 360.
9. E. E. Cummings, *Selected Letters of E. E. Cummings,* letter to his sister, 3 May 1922, F. W. Dupee, George Stade, eds., New York: Harcourt, Brace, and World, 1969, page 84. I am indebted to Professor Norman Friedman for this citation. Joseph Schumpeter, *Capitalism, Socialism and Democracy,* reprint, New York: Harper, 1975, pages 82–5.
10. Paul McLaughlin suggests that Thomas Kuhn's model of "paradigm shift" is also appropriate to describe Bakunin's view of revolutionary change in *Mikhail Bakunin,* pages 42–5.
11. The reference to the "old mole" is from *Hamlet,* act 1, scene five. Likely it comes to Bakunin by way of Hegel's *Lectures on the History of Philosophy,* section three, "Recent German Philosophy," where the master writes, "For in this lengthened period, the Notion of Spirit, invested with its entire concrete development, its external subsistence, its wealth, is striving to bring spirit to perfection, to make progress itself and to develop from spirit. It goes ever on and on, because spirit is progress alone. Spirit often seems to have forgotten and lost itself, but inwardly opposed to itself, it is inwardly working ever forward (as when Hamlet says of the ghost of his father, 'Well said, old mole! canst work i' the ground so fast?') until grown strong in itself it bursts asunder the crust of earth which divided it from the sun, its Notion, so that the earth crumbles away. At such a time, when the encircling crust, like a soulless decaying tenement, crumbles away, and spirit displays itself arrayed in new youth, the seven league boots are at length adopted." Or, "Shit happens, even when you don't think there's much going on." Marx makes a similar reference to the old mole in 1852, in "The Eighteenth Brumaire of Louis Napoleon."
12. The quote has been rendered in several ways. In this chapter, I draw from "The Reaction in Germany: A Fragment from a Frenchman," Mary-Barbara Zeldin, trans., in *Russian Phi-*

losophy, volume 1, James M. Edie et al., eds., Chicago: Quadrangle Books, 1965. Other English translations render it as "The urge for destruction is a creative urge," "The desire to destroy is also a creative desire," and variations thereon. In *Bakounine: Oeuvres completes,* the French translation is given as "La volupte de detruire est en meme temps une volupte creatrice." The original German version is given there as "Die Lust der Zerstorung ist zugleich eine schaffende Lust."

13. *Bakounine: Oeuvres completes,* letter to Arnold Ruge, 11 and 19 March 1843.
14. The standard English biography of Weitling is Carl Wittke, *The Utopian Communist: A Biography of Wilhelm Weitling, Nineteenth-Century Reformer,* Baton Rouge: Louisiana State University Press, 1950.
15. Marx, "Critical Notes on the Article 'The King of Prussia and Social Revolution, by a Prussian,' *Vorwarts* 7–10 August 1844," cited in Boris Nicolaievsky and Otto Maenchen-Helfen, *Karl Marx: Man and Fighter,* reprint, Harmondsworth: Pelican Books, 1983, page 83.
16. *Bakounine: Oeuvres completes,* letter to Ruge, 19 January 1843.
17. *Bakounine: Oeuvres completes,* "Der Kommunismus" (Le Communisme), *Der Schweizerischer Republikaner,* 2, 6, and 13 June 1843. *Bakounine: Oeuvres completes,* letter to Ruge, 19 January 1843.
18. *Bakounine: Oeuvres completes,* "Der Kommunismus" (Le Communisme).
19. Michael Bakunin, *The Confession of Mikhail Bakunin,* Robert C. Howes, trans., Ithaca: Cornell University Press, 1977, page 38.
20. Randolph, page 356.

8: GAY PARIS

1. Cited in Carr, page 130.
2. Pierre-Joseph Proudhon, *What Is Property? An Inquiry into the Principle of Right and of Government,* Benjamin Tucker, trans., reprint, Dover: New York, 1970. Tucker translates Proudhon's *vol* as "robbery"; I have substituted "theft," the more usual translation.
3. Cited in George Woodcock, *Pierre-Joseph Proudhon: His Life and Work,* New York: Schocken Books, 1972, page 129.
4. Proudhon, *General Idea of the Revolution in the Nineteenth Century,* John Beverly Robinson, trans., London: Pluto Press, 1989, page 294.
5. *Bakounine: Oeuvres completes,* "Freres de 1'Alliance en Espagne," 12–13 June 1872. Weirdly enough, Proudhon, Bakunin, and Marx have each been accused of Satanism. In an otherwise insightful article, Eric Voegelin states confidently, though without evidence, that Bakunin openly embraced Satanism. An entire book has been written to "prove" that Marx worshipped the devil. Voeglin's remark is in "Bakunin's Confession," *Journal of Politics,* 8, no. 1 (February 1946), page 38. Marx's alleged obeisance to His Satanic Majesty is explored fully, if crazily, by Pastor Richard Wurmbrand in *Was Marx a Satanist?* Glendale, Cal.: Diane Books, 1977. Among Wurmbrand's evidence is the fact that Marx had a beard. Radicals often spoke of Old Nick as the first rebel, appreciating the spirit of revolt in his insistence that it was better to rule in Hell than to serve in Heaven. Bakunin's reference to Proudhon and Satan is a literary, not a literal, one.
6. *Bakounine: Oeuvres completes,* "Federalisme, socialisme, et antitheologisme," 1867–1868. I have translated *spontanee* not as "spontaneous" but as "voluntary." The French word conveys both meanings, depending on context, as does the English word. Bakunin's critics have often criticized him for believing in the "spontaneous" rise of the masses. Since he insisted on the role of education, propaganda, and experience in creating revolutionary consciousness, it is clear that he did not believe that a "spontaneous" revolt would be one without external incitement. Thus "voluntary" is a much more accurate translation.
7. *Bakounine: Oeuvres completes,* letter to Rienold Solger, 18 October 1844.
8. *Bakounine: Oeuvres completes,* letter to Sergei N. Muraviev, end of January 1835.
9. *Bakounine: Oeuvres completes,* letter to *La R forme,* January 1845.

10. Franco Venturi, *Roots of Revolution: A History of the Populist and Socialist Movements in Nineteenth Century Russia,* New York: Grosset and Dunlap, 1966, pages 64–6.
11. Bakunin, *Confession,* pages 50–1; *Bakounine: Oeuvres completes,* letter to *Le Constitutional,* 6 February 1846.
12. Bakunin, *Confession,* page 52.
13. *Bakounine: Oeuvres completes,* "Discours: 17th anniversaire de la revolution polonaise," 29 November 1847.
14. For interesting discussions of the relationship of anarchist and Marxist thought, see Anthony D'Agostino, *Marxism and the Russian Anarchists,* San Francisco: Germinal Press, 1977; and Paul Thomas, *Karl Marx and the Anarchists,* London: Routledge and Kegan Paul, 1980. These books are rather more favorable to Marx than Bakunin. K. J. Kenafick, *Michael Bakunin and Karl Marx,* Melbourne: A. Mailer, 1948, presents Bakunin in a more sympathetic and thoughtful light. Alvin Gouldner, *Against Fragmentation: The Origins of Marxism and the Sociology of Intellectuals,* Oxford: Oxford University Press, 1985, offers an insightful discussion on this subject, arguing that Bakunin was the first post-Marxist.
15. *Bakounine: Oeuvres completes,* "Rapports personnels avec Marx. Pieces justicatives," 1871.
16. *Bakounine: Oeuvres completes,* "Rapports personnels avec Marx. Pieces justicatives," 1871; letter to Georg Herwegh, end of December 1847.
17. Marx cited in P. V. Annenkov, *The Extraordinary Decade: Literary Memoirs,* Irwin R. Titunik, trans., Arthur P. Mendel, ed., Ann Arbor: University of Michigan Press, 1968, page 169. For other examples see Stephen Porter Halbrook, "The Marx-Bakunin Controversy: Intellectual Origins, 1844–1870," Ph.D. thesis, Florida State University College, 1972. Marx's works contain numerous unflattering references to Russia and Russians. *Bakounine: Oeuvres completes,* letter to Georg Herwegh, end of December 1847.
18. Karl Marx and Friedrich Engels, "The German Ideology," *Karl Marx: Selected Writings,* second edition, David McLellan, ed., Oxford: Oxford University Press, 2000, pages 180-1. Emphasis added.
19. Marx to P. V. Annenkov, 28 December 1846, in *The Poverty of Theory: Answer to the "Philosophy of Poverty" by M. Proudhon,* Moscow: Progress Publishers, pages 177-8. Proudhon cited in Woodcock, *Pierre-Joseph Proudhon,* page 102.
20. "German Ideology," page 195; Marx and Engels, *The Communist Manifesto: A Modern Edition,* London: Verso, 1998, page 47. Alvin Gouldner makes this argument in greater length in *Against Fragmentation.* He also develops the argument that follows about the competition between artisans and intellectuals in the 1840s.
21. Annenkov, pages 168-79; Gouldner, pages 93–100; Wittke, pages 104–20.
22. Proudhon to Marx, 17 May 1846, in *Selected Writings of P. J. Proudhon,* Stewart Edwards, ed., Elizabeth Fraser, trans., Garden City: Anchor Books, 1967, pages 150–1.
23. Marx, "For a Ruthless Criticism of Everything Existing," *Deutsch-Franzosische Jahrbiicher,* 1844, in Robert C. Tucker, ed., *The Marx-Engels Reader,* second edition, New York: Norton, 1978, pages 14–5.
24. Marx, "Toward a Critique of Hegel's *Philosophy of Right:* Introduction," McLellan, pages 80–1.
25. Gouldner, *Against Fragmentation,* page 139.
26. *Bakounine: Oeuvres completes,* letter to P. A. Annenkov, 28 December 1847.
27. Marx, "Theses on Feuerbach," *Selected Works,* volume 1, Moscow: Progress Publishers, 1977, page 15.
28. Marx, Montesquieu LVI, *Neue Rheinische Zeitung,* pages 21–2, January 1849, in Marx and Engels, *Articles from the Neue Rheinische Zeitung, 1848–49,* Moscow: Progress Publishers, 1972, page 225.
29. Marx and Engels, "Address of the Central Committee to the Communist League," in *Selected Works,* volume 1, 1977, pages 175–85. See Gouldner, *Against Fragmentation,* pages 126–37.
30. Marx, "Communism and the *Augsburger AUegemeine Zeitung,*" in McLellan, pages 25–6.

31. Marx, "Toward a Critique of Hegel's *Philosophy of Right:* Introduction," McLellan, 81; Marx and Engels, *The Communist Manifesto,* pages 76–7.

32. Marx, *A Contribution to the Critique of Political Economy,* 1859, Moscow: Progress Publishers, 1970, page 21; Marx, *Capital: A Critique of Political Economy,* volume 1, 1867, Moscow: Progress Publishers, 1983, chapter 22, "Historical Tendency of Capitalist Accumulation," page 715.

33. Meghnad Desai, *Marx's Revenge: The Resurgence of Capitalism and the Death of Statist Socialism,* New York: Verso, 2004.

34. Marx and Engels, *The Communist Manifesto,* page 40.

35. *Bakounine: Oeuvres completes,* "La situation en Russe—le people," April 1849.

36. *Bakounine: Oeuvres completes,* "Rapports personnels avec Marx."

37. For a contemporary observation of the two different projects of anarchists and Marxists, see David Graeber, *Fragments of Anarchist Anthropology,* Chicago: Prickly Paradigm Press, 2004.

9: BARRICADES PILED UP LIKE MOUNTAINS

1. Cited in Charles Breunig, *The Age of Revolution and Reaction, 1789–1850,* New York: Norton, 1977, pages 254–5.

2. *Bakounine: Oeuvres completes,* letter to *La Reforme,* March 1848; Bakunin, *Confession,* pages 54–7.

3. *Bakounine: Oeuvres completes,* letter to *La Reforme,* March 1848.

4. *Bakounine: Oeuvres completes,* letter to P. V. Annenkov, 17 April 1848.

5. Carr, pages 154–5.

6. Bakunin, *Confession,* page 67.

7. *Bakounine: Oeuvres completes,* Letter to Herwegh, 1–15 August 1848.

8. *Bakounine: Oeuvres completes,* "Appeal to the Slavic Peoples by a Russian Patriot," October-November 1848.

9. *Bakounine: Oeuvres completes,* "Appeal to the Slavic Peoples by a Russian Patriot," October-November 1848.

10. Herzen, *My Past and Thoughts,* volume 3, page 1353.

11. *Bakounine: Oeuvres completes,* "Appeal to the Slavic Peoples by a Russian Patriot," October–November 1848.

12. Karl Marx, George Sand, *Bakounine et les autres,* 20 July and 3 August 1848, pages 136–7.

13. Lawrence D. Orton, "The Echo of Bakunin's Appeal to the Slavs (1848)," *Canadian-American Slavic Studies,* X, no. 4 (winter 1976), pages 489–502.

14. Engels, "Democratic Pan-Slavism," *Neue Rheinische Zeitung,* 14 February 1849, Marx and Engels *Collected Works,* volume 8, page 362.

15. Marx, letter to the editorial board of the *Otechestvenniye Zapiski,* November 1877, in Marx and Engels, *Selected Correspondence,* Moscow: Progress Publishers, third rev. ed., 1975, pages 291–4; Marx to Vera Zasulich, McLellan, pages 623–4.

16. Engels to Joseph Bloch, 21–2 September 1890, in Marx and Engels, *Selected Correspondence,* pages 394–6.

17. Bakunin, *Confession,* page 135.

18. Engels, "Revolution and Counter-Revolution in Germany," in Marx and Engels, *Selected Works,* volume 1, page 381; Bakunin, *Confession,* page 146.

19. Bakunin, *Confession,* page 148.

20. Peter Kropotkin, *Memoirs of a Revolutionist,* reprint, Montreal: Black Rose Books, 1989, page 320.

21. Bakunin, *Confession,* page 33. See Orton's introduction for a sophisticated analysis of the confession and its historians.

22. Bakunin, *Confession,* pages 82–95.

23. *Bakounine: Oeuvres completes,* letter to Tatiana, February 1854; letter to Alexander Herzen, 8 December 1860.

24. *Bakounine: Oeuvres completes,* letters to Tatiana, beginning of May 1854 and February 1854.

25. *Bakounine: Oeuvres completes,* letter to Varvara, 19 July 1854.

26. *Bakounine: Oeuvres completes,* letter to Alexander II, 14 February 1857.

10: WITHOUT ORGANIZATION, WE WILL NEVER GAIN VICTORY

1. *Bakounine: Oeuvres completes,* letter to Alexander Herzen, 8 December 1860. See also Shatz, "Michael Bakunin and His Biographers," for a detailed analysis of the marriage and how Bakunin's biographers have depicted it.

2. *Bakounine: Oeuvres completes,* letter to Sergei Nechaev, 2-9 June 1870.

3. *Bakounine: Oeuvres completes,* letters to Alexander Herzen, 7–15 November 1860 and 8 December 1860; Kropotkin, *Memoirs of a Revolutionist,* page 158.

4. See Philip Billingsley, "Bakunin in Yokohama: The Dawning of the Pacific Era," *International History Review,* 20, no. 3 (September 1998), pages 532–70. Several details in this paragraph are from this account.

5. *Bakounine: Oeuvres completes,* letter to Michael Semenovich Korsakov, 10 September 1861.

6. Robert M. Cutler, "A Rediscovered Source on Bakunin in 1861, The Diary of F. P. Koe and Excerpts from the Diary of F. P. Koe," *Canadian Slavonic Papers/Revue canadienne des slavistes,* 35, nos. 1–2 (March-June 1993).

7. *Bakounine: Oeuvres completes,* letter to Herzen, 15 October 1861, cited in Paul Avrich, "Bakunin in the United States," *Anarchist Portraits,* Princeton: Princeton University Press, 1988, page 16.

8. Oscar Handlin, "A Russian Anarchist Visits Boston," *New England Quarterly,* 15, no. 1 (March 1942), pages 104-9; See also Robert M. Cutler, "An Unpublished Letter of M. A. Bakunin to R. Solger," *International Review of Social History,* no. 33 (1988), pages 212–7. The letter is also in *Bakounine: Oeuvres completes.*

9. David Hecht, "'Laughing Allegra' Meets an Ogre," *New England Quarterly,* 19, no. 2 (June 1946), pages 243–4. See also Avrich, "Bakunin in the United States," pages 16–31.

10. Herzen cited in Carr, page 243; Carr relates the shirt story on page 248; *Bakounine: Oeuvres completes,* letter to Antonia Bakunin, 21–7 October 1862. Bakunin's travel expenses and the hope that his memoirs would prove profitable are in *Bakounine: Oeuvres completes,* letter to his family, 3 February 1862.

11. *Bakounine: Oeuvres completes,* letter to Alexander Bakunin, 7 December 1862.

12. Herzen, *My Past and Thoughts,* volume 3, page 1352.

13. *Bakounine: Oeuvres completes,* "Aux Russes, Polonais, et tous les amis slaves," 2 February 1862.

14. Herzen, *My Past and Thoughts,* volume 3, pages 1357 and 1366.

15. Cited in Venturi, pages 292–3.

16. Cited in Abbott Gleason, *Young Russia: The Genesis of Russian Radicalism in the 1860s,* New York: Viking Press, 1980, page 172.

17. Cited in Gleason, page 110. See also Herzen's article, "The Superfluous and the Jaundiced," first printed in *The Bell* in 1860, and in *My Past and Thoughts,* volume 4, pages 1574–84.

18. *Bakounine: Oeuvres completes,* "La cause du people: Romanov, Pugachev, ou Pestel?" June-July 1862.

19. Herzen, *My Past and Thoughts,* volume 3, pages 1370–1.

20. Carr, page 278; Engels to Marx, 11 June 1863, *Selected Correspondence,* pages 131–2.

21. *Bakounine: Oeuvres completes,* "Fragments d'ecrits sur la Franc-Maconnerie," summer and fall 1865, fragment E. He made similar arguments in 1864—see *Bakounine: Oeuvres completes,* "Societe internationale secrete de la Revolution. Programme provisoirement arette par les freres fondateurs," September–October 1864.

22. Antonia Bakunin, cited in Mendel, page 299.

23. See Carr, page 315.

24. Michael Bakunin, "Principles and Organization of the International Brotherhood," *Selected Writings*, Arthur Lehning, ed., Steven Cox, trans., London: Jonathan Cape, 1973, pages 64–93; and *Bakounine: Oeuvres completes*, "Principes et organisation de la societe internationale revolutionnaire," March 1866. It is called "Revolutionary Catechism," 1866, in the Dolgoff collection, pages 76–97.
25. Marx and Engels, "The German Ideology," *Selected Works*, volume 1, pages 35–6. The manuscript was written in 1845–1846 but remained unpublished until 1932. That Bakunin would raise very similar arguments suggests how close he and Marx often were in their thought. Furthermore, "The German Ideology" was a key document in the humanist revisiting of Marx that placed more emphasis on his ideas about alienation than historical materialism and political economy, and thus suggests how readings of Marx other than the strictly orthodox ones favored by Soviet and German Social Democratic Marxists move toward anarchism.
26. *Bakounine: Oeuvres completes*, "Les endormeurs," June–July 1869; I have also used the translation in Robert M. Cutler, *The Basic Bakunin: Writings, 1869–1871*, Buffalo: Prometheus Books, 1992, page 78.
27. *Bakounine: Oeuvres completes*, letter to Herzen and Ogarev, 19 July 1866. See Shatz, "Bakunin and the Priamukhino Circle," pages 27–8.

11: LIBERTY WITHOUT SOCIALISM IS INJUSTICE; SOCIALISM WITHOUT LIBERTY IS SLAVERY

1. *Bakounine: Oeuvres completes*, "Discours prononce au Congres de la Paix et de la Liberte, deuxieme seance," 10 September 1867.
2. *Bakounine: Oeuvres completes*, "Federalisme, socialisme et antitheologisme," 1867–1868.
3. *Bakounine: Oeuvres completes*, letter to *La Democratic*, March–April 1868.
4. See, for example, Pietro Basso, *Modern Times, Ancient Hours: Working Lives in the Twenty-first Century*, New York: Verso, 2003.
5. Again, I have translated "spontaneous" as "voluntary"; it is clear from the context that Bakunin does not mean such associations would spring from the void.
6. *Bakounine: Oeuvres completes*, "Deuxieme discours au deuxieme Congres de la Paix et de la Liberte," 23 September 1868.
7. *Bakounine: Oeuvres completes*, "Statuts secrets de l'Alliance: Programme et object de l'organisation revolutionnaire des Freres internationaux," autumn 1868. Parts are translated in "Programme and Purpose of the Revolutionary Organization of International Brothers," in *Selected Writings*, Arthur Lehning, ed., page 172; it is also available in Dolgoff, "The Program of the International Brotherhood," which gives the date as 1869. Bakunin, letter to Nechaev, 2 June 1870, in *Daughter of a Revolutionary: Natalie Herzen and the Bakunin-Nechayev Circle*, Michael Confino, ed., Hilary Sternberg and Lydia Bott, trans., LaSalle, III.: Library Press, 1973, pages 259–63; *Bakounine: Oeuvres completes*, letter to Albert Richard, 1 April 1870. This letter is abridged in Lehning, *Selected Writings*, pages 178–82, and Dolgoff, pages 178–81.
8. *Bakounine: Oeuvres completes*, "Statuts secrets de l'Alliance: Programme et object de l'organisation revolutionnaire des Freres internationaux," autumn 1868.
9. Bakunin, letter to Nechaev, 2 November 1870, in *Daughter of a Revolutionary*, pages 258–9.
10. *Bakounine: Oeuvres completes*, "La politique de l'Internationale," August 1869; I have also used the translation in Robert M. Cutler, *The Basic Bakunin: Writings, 1869–1871*, Buffalo: Prometheus Books, 1992, pages 100–3.

12: THE REVOLUTIONARY IS A DOOMED MAN

1. *Bakounine: Oeuvres completes*, letter to Herzen and Ogarev, 19 July 1866.
2. Venturi, pages 316–30; Gleason, *Young Russia*, page 72.

3. Cited in Venturi, page 423.

4. *Bakounine: Oeuvres completes,* "Les principes de la revolution," spring/summer 1869.

5. Eldridge Cleaver, *Soul on Ice,* New York: Dell, 1970, page 25.

6. *Bakounine: Oeuvres completes,* "Le catechisme du revolutionnaire," 1869. I have been guided by the translations in *Daughter of a Revolutionary,* pages 221–30; and Philip Pomper, *Sergei Nechaev,* New Brunswick: Rutgers University Press, 1979, pages 90–4.

7. Nicolas Walter, cited in Avrich, *Anarchist Portraits,* page 38.

8. See Avrich, "Bakunin and Nechaev," *Anarchist Portraits,* for an excellent elaboration of the debate around authorship of the "Catechism." Confino, *Daughter of a Revolutionary,* makes the argument that Nechaev was the sole author of the "Catechism" and draws attention to the parallels between the "Catechism" and the Russian manifestos and catechisms of the period; the "Catechism" and Bakunin's letter to Nechaev of 2 June 1870 are also translated in this volume. Philip Pomper, in *Sergei Nechaev,* argues that Bakunin collaborated with Nechaev, but is unconvincing. K. J. Kenafick, *Michael Bakunin and Karl Marx,* pages 130–1, provides important information on Sazhin/Ross's claim that he had seen a manuscript of the "Catechism" in Bakunin's handwriting.

9. Bakunin, letter to Ogarev, 2 November 1872, in Confino, page 323.

10. Bakunin, letter to Nechaev, 2 June 1870, in Confino, page 242.

11. Bakunin, *Statism and Anarchy,* Marshall Shatz, trans., ed., Cambridge: Cambridge University Press, 1990, pages 31–2.

12. Vera Figner, *Studencheskie gody, 1872–1876,* cited in *Bakounine et les autres,* page 400.

13. See Caroline Cahm, *Kropotkin and the Rise of Revolutionary Anarchism, 1872–1886,* Cambridge: Cambridge University Press, 2002, pages 213–30; and David Miller, *Anarchism,* London: J. M. Dent, 1984, pages 124–40.

14. *Bakounine: Oeuvres completes,* "Letter to the Comrades of the Jura Federation," 1–15 October 1873.

15. Bakunin, letter to Nechaev, 2 June 1870, Confino, page 256.

16. Bakunin, letter to Nechaev, Confino, pages 251–6.

17. Bakunin, letter to Nechaev, Confino, pages 252–6.

18. Marx, "The Class Struggles in France," in *Selected Works,* volume 1, pages 219–20; *The Communist Manifesto,* page 48; "The Eighteenth Brumaire of Louis Bonaparte," in *Selected Works,* volume 1, page 442.

19. For a compelling critique of identity politics and new social movement theory, see Ellen Meiksins Wood, *The Retreat from Class: A New "True" Socialism,* London: Verso, 1986.

20. Bakunin, *Statism and Anarchy,* Marshall Shatz, trans., Cambridge: Cambridge University Press, 1990, page 7. Eugene Pyziur, *The Doctrine of Anarchism of Michael Bakunin,* Chicago: Gateway, 1968, page 81, uses this passage to argue that Bakunin held that the lumpenproletariat was the revolutionary class, apparently unaware that his own translation renders the passage as "wretchedly poor proletariat," and so obviously a section of the working class. Similarly, the Marxist Paul Thomas, in *Karl Marx and the Anarchists,* pages 290–2, is mistaken to assert that Bakunin "turned away from the proletariat" to fix his hopes on "the peasant, the rural brigand, and the bandit."

21. *Bakounine: Oeuvres completes,* "L'Politique de 1'Internationale"; Cutler, pages 99–101, gives a slightly different interpretation, including translating *l'politique* as "the policy." See also *The Political Philosophy of Bakunin,* G. P. Maximoff, ed., New York: The Free Press, 1964, pages 312–5.

22. *Bakounine: Oeuvres completes,* "L'Alliance Universelle de la Democratic Sociale. Section russe. A la jeunesse russe," March 1870; "Lettre a un Francais," continuation III, 27 August 1870. See also Richard B. Saltman, *The Social and Political Thought of Michael Bakunin,* Westport: Greenwood Press, 1983, pages 137–8. There is a vast literature on Marx and Engels and the labor aristocracy. See Mark Leier, *Red Flags and Red Tape: The Making of a Labour Bureaucracy,* Toronto: University of Toronto Press, 1995, pages 102–8, for a brief discussion.

23. *Bakounine: Oeuvres completes,* "L'Politique de 1'Internationale."

24. *Bakounine: Oeuvres completes,* "L'Alliance Universelle de la Democratic Sociale. Section Russe. A la jeunesse russe," March 1870. See also Maximoff, page 384.

13: HERMAPHRODITE MAN VERSUS CARBUNCLE BOY IN THE FIRST INTERNATIONAL

1. I have taken Bakunin's program from Karl Marx, "Programme and Rules of the International Alliance of Socialist Democracy," in *Documents of the First International,* volume 3, 1868–1870, London, Moscow: Lawrence and Wishart, Progress Publishers, n.d., pages 379–83. Lehning, *Michael Bakunin: Selected Writings,* pages 174–5, has a different version based on a revision printed in 1873. The chief difference is the substitution of the phrase "abolition of classes" for "equality of classes," a change of some importance, as discussed in the body of this chapter.
2. Cited in Pyziur, *The Doctrine of the Anarchism of Michael A. Bakunin,* page 113.
3. Marx, "General Rules of the International Working Men's Association," *Selected Works,* volume 2, pages 19–21. Marx to Engels, 4 November 1864, *Selected Correspondence,* pages 137-40.
4. Marx to Engels, 12 September 1863, *Marx-Engels Collected Works,* volume 41, page 491.
5. Marx to Engels, 4 November 1864, *Marx-Engels Collected Works,* volume 42, page 11. Marx to Engels, 14 January 1858, *Selected Works,* page 93. *Bakounine: Oeuvres completes,* letter to Karl Marx, 7 February 1865. Marx to Engels, 11 April 1865, *Collected Works,* volume 42. Marx to Engels, 4 September 1867, *Collected Works,* volume 42, page 420. Marx to Engels, 4 October 1867, *Collected Works,* volume 42, page 434. *Bakounine: Oeuvres completes,* "Rapports personnels avec Marx. Pieces justificatives," December 1871.
6. *Bakounine: Oeuvres completes,* "Freres de l'Alliance en Espagne," 12–13 June 1872. The appreciation of historical materialism is in *Bakounine: Oeuvres completes,* "L'Empire Knouto-Germanique et la Revolution Sociale. Suite. Dieu et l'Etat," 1 November 1870 to April 1871. Bakunin's support of Marx over Proudhon is in Bakunin, *Statism and Anarchy.* I believe the influence of Comte on Bakunin has been somewhat exaggerated; my reading is that Bakunin took from Comte what fit his own ideas rather than being shaped by Comte in any profound sense. For other views, see McLaughlin, *Mikhail Bakunin,* especially section 2.19; Gouldner, *Against Fragmentation,* pages 148–153; and Saltman, *Bakunin,* pages 72–9.
7. Marx's remark is in "The General Council to the Federal Council of Romance Switzerland," 1870, in *Documents of the First International,* volume 3, page 402.
8. Jenny Marx to Johann Philip Becker, 10 January 1868, Marx and Engels, *Collected Works,* volume 42, page 582. *Bakounine: Oeuvres completes,* letter to Marx, 22 December 1868 and "Rapports personnels avec Marx. Pieces justificatives No. 2," December 1871. Marx to Engels, 13 January 1869, *Collected Works,* volume 43, page 201. Letter to Paul and Laura Lafargue, 15 February 1869, *Collected Works,* volume 43, page 216.
9. Carbuncles are awful, and Marx nearly died from one attack. Nonetheless, his boils and carbuncles have garnered undue attention from generations of writers. Wheen references them eight times in the index to *Karl Marx,* Otto Riihle four times in the index of *Karl Marx: His Life and Work,* Eden and Cedar Paul, trans., New York: New Home Library, 1943. Robert Payne, *Marx: A Biography,* New York: Simon and Schuster, 1968, has an entire section entitled "The Boils."
10. Marx to Friedrich Bolte, 23 November 1871, *Selected Correspondence,* page 253. Jacques Freymond and Miklos Milnar, "The Rise and Fall of the First International," in *The Revolutionary Internationals, 1864–1943,* MiloradM. Drachkovitch, ed., Stanford: Stanford University Press, 1966, page 22.
11. Marx, "Remarks to the Programme and Rules of the International Alliance of Socialist Democracy," in *Documents of the First International,* volume 3, page 379.
12. Marx, "Remarks to the Programme and Rules of the International Alliance of Socialist Democracy," page 379. Marx, "The International Working Men's Association and the

International Alliance of Social Democracy," *Documents of the First International,* volume 3, pages 387-9.

13. *Bakounine: Oeuvres completes,* letter to Tomas Gonzalez Morago, 21 May 1872. See also Dolgoff, page 157.

14. Marx to Engels, 10 December 1864, cited in Gouldner, *Against Fragmentation,* page 144. Marx, "General Rules of the International Working Men's Association," *Selected Works,* volume 2, pages 19–21. Marx to Engels, 4 November 1864, *Selected Correspondence,* pages 137–40.

15. Marx, "General Rules of the International Working Men's Association," *Selected Works,* volume 2, pages 19–21, cited in G. M. Stekloff, *History of the First International,* Eden and Cedar Paul, trans., London: Martin Lawrence, 1928, page 104. Julius Braunthal, *History of the International,* volume 1, 1864-1914, Henry Collins, Kenneth Mitchell, trans., New York: Praeger, 1967, page 130.

16. Cited in McLellan, *Karl Marx: His Thought and Life,* New York: Harper and Row, 1973, page 380.

17. Marx to Friedrich Bolte, 23 November 1871, *Selected Correspondence,* pages 253—4. Engels to Marx, 18 December 1868, *Collected Works,* volume 43, page 191.

18. Marx, "Remarks to the Programme and Rules of the International Alliance of Socialist Democracy," page 379. *Bakounine: Oeuvres completes,* letter to Marx, 22 December 1868. Marx and Engels, "Fictitious Splits in the International—II," *Selected Works,* volume 2, pages 253–4. Marx to Friedrich Bolte, 23 November 1871, *Selected Correspondence,* pages 253–4.

19. *Bakounine: Oeuvres completes,* "Letter to My Italian Friends," 19–28 October 1871; "La politique de l'Internationale," August 1869; I have also used the translation in Robert M. Cutler, *The Basic Bakunin: Writings, 1869-1871,* Buffalo: Prometheus Books, 1992, page 98.

20. *Bakounine: Oeuvres completes,* "Rapport de la commission sur la question de l'heritage," August 1869; see Cutler, pages 126–30. Marx, "Report of the General Council on the Right of Inheritance," 1869, *Documents of the First International,* volume 3, pages 322–4. Marx went through each of these points of the Alliance's program again in 1870 and 1871. See Marx to Ludwig Kugelman, "Confidential Communication on Bakunin," 28 March 1870, *Collected Works,* volume 21, pages 112–24, and his letter to Friedrich Bolte, 23 November 1871, *Selected Correspondence,* pages 253–4.

21. Shatz, "Bakunin and His Biographers," page 232.

22. Kenafick, *Michael Bakunin and Karl Marx,* page 118.

23. Herzen, cited in Carr, page 334.

24. *Bakounine: Oeuvres completes,* letter to his sisters, 4 February 1869.

25. Cited in Carr, page 356.

26. *Bakounine: Oeuvres completes,* "La politique de l'Internationale," August 1869; in Cutler, page 109.

27. *Bakounine: Oeuvres completes,* "La double greve de Geneve," April 1869; see Cutler, pages 145–50; the quotation on abolishing status is in *Bakounine: Oeuvres completes,* "Les endormeurs," June–July 1869; see Cutler, page 71.

28. *Bakounine: Oeuvres completes,* "L'instruction integrale," July–August 1869; see Cutler, pages 111–25.

29. Stekloff, page 140.

30. Marx to Ludwig Kugelman, "Confidential Communication on Bakunin," 28 March 1870, *Collected Works,* volume 21, pages 112–24.

31. James Guillaume, *VInternationale: documents et souvenirs, 1864-1878,* 1905, reprint, New York: Burt Franklin, 1969, four volumes in two, volume 1, pages 202–3.

32. Stekloff, page 144.

33. *Bakounine: Oeuvres completes,* letter to *Le Reveil,* 18 October 1869, "Profession de foi d'un democrate socialiste russe, precedee d'une etude sur les Juifs allemands." Bakunin, "A Letter to the Editorial Board of *La Liberte,*" 5 October 1872, in Lehning, *Michael Bakunin: Selected Writings,* page 256.

34. Marx, "On the Jewish Question," in McLellan, page 66.

35. Mendel, page 426. The charge is also made by anarchists today who wish to disassociate themselves from "classical" anarchism in favor of a new wave, new age anarchism. For a useful critique of this variety of anarchism, see Murray Bookchin, *Social Anarchism or Lifestyle Anarchism: An Unbridgeable Chasm*, Edinburgh: AK Press, 1995.
36. See Lenore O'Boyle, "The Problem of an Excess of Educated Men in Western Europe, 1800–1850," *The Journal of Modern History*, 42, no. 4 (December 1970), 471–95, and "The Image of the Journalist in France, Germany, and England, 1815–1848," *Comparative Studies in Society and History*, 10, no. 3 (April 1968), pages 290–317.
37. *Bakounine: Oeuvres completes*, letters to Herzen, 18 October 1869 and 26 October 1869.

14: THE ONLY LIBERTY DESERVING OF THE NAME

1. *Bakounine: Oeuvres completes*, letter to Ogarev, 16 December 1869; "Rapports personnels avec Marx. Pieces justificatives," no. 2, December 1871.
2. *Bakounine: Oeuvres completes*, letter to Ogarev, 16 December 1869.
3. *Bakounine: Oeuvres completes*, "The Bears of Berne and the Bears of St. Petersburg," March 1870.
4. Marx to Ludwig Kugelman, "Confidential Communication on Bakunin," 28 March 1870, *Collected Works*, volume 21, pages 112–24. See Franz Mehring, *Karl Marx: The Story of His Life*, London: George Allen and Unwin, 1936, pages 421–2, for Bakunin on moving the General Council and his articles on the International.
5. *Bakounine: Oeuvres completes*, "Lettre a un Francais, Continuation III," 27 August 1870. Bakunin's draft was polished and edited by James Guillaume; his edited version is titled "Letters to a Frenchman on the Present Crisis."
6. Marx to Engels, 20 July 1870, cited in Mehring, page 438, and McLellan, page 389.
7. Karl Marx, "First Address of the General Council of the International Working Men's Association on the Franco-Prussian War," *Selected Works*, volume 2, page 192.
8. Engels to Marx, 12 September 1870, *Selected Correspondence*, page 234; see McLellan, pages 389–90.
9. Usually titled "The Paris Commune and the Idea of the State," this article is a fragment of Bakunin's *The Knouto-Germanic Empire and the Social Revolution. Bakounine: Oeuvres completes*, "L'Empire Knouto-Germanique et la Revolution Sociale. Preambule pour la seconde livraison," 5–23 June 1871. See also Dolgoff, pages 259–73, and Lehning, *Michael Bakunin: Selected Writings*, pages 195–213.
10. Marx and Engels, The Communist Manifesto, "Preface to the German Edition of 1872," *Selected Works*, volume 1, page 99.
11. *Documents of the First International*, volume 4, 1870–1871, pages 440–50. That Marx initiated the motion on the "special mission" of the working class is noted in *Documents of the First International*, volume 3, 1868–1870, pages 231–2. Engels, "Apropos of Working-Class Political Action," *Selected Works*, volume 2, pages 245–6.
12. The text of the Sonvillier Circular may be found in James Guillaume, *L'Internationale: Documents et souvenirs*, volume 2, pages 237–41. See Kenafick, pages 261–5; Dolgoff, pages 44–5; Carr, page 427; Steklov, pages 250–2; Thomas, pages 321–7.
13. Marx and Engels, "Fictitious Splits in the International," *Selected Works*, volume 2, pages 247–86.
14. For Bakunin in Spain, see George R. Esenwein, *Anarchist Ideology and the Working Class Movement in Spain, 1868–1898*, Berkeley: University of California Press, 1989, and Temma Kaplan, *Anarchists of Andalusia, 1868-1903*, Princeton: Princeton University Press, 1977. For Italy, see T. R. Ravindranathan, *Bakunin and the Italians*, Kingston and Montreal: McGill-Queen's University Press, 1988.
15. "Report of the Commission of Inquiry into the Alliance Society," *The Hague Congress of the First International, September 2–7, 1872, Minutes and Documents*, Moscow: Progress Publishers, 1976, pages 481–3. See Engels to Cuno, 24 January 1872, *Selected Correspon-*

dence, pages 257–62. For the publisher's note to Marx, see Nikolaj Ljubavin to Karl Marx, 8 August 1872, in *Bakounine et les autres,* pages 308–10.

16. The Blanqui pamphlet is cited in Mehring, page 490. See McLellan, page 410, for Marx and his studies, and Marx's note that the International was dead. See Engels to Sorge, 12 September 1874, *Selected Correspondence,* page 270, and Engels to Bebel, 20 June 1873, *Selected Corresepondence,* pages 265–8.

17. See Guillaume, *LTnternationale: Documents et souvenirs,* volume 3, reprint, New York: Burt Franklin, 1969, pages 1–11, for the St. Imier program. See Errico Malatesta, in *Bakounine et les autres,* pages 315–6, for Bakunin's rejection of the slander campaign. I am grateful to Davide Turcato for bringing this story to my attention.

18. *Bakounine: Oeuvres completes,* letter to the journal *La Liberte de Bruxelles,* 1–8 October 1872.

15: WE DETEST ALL POWER

1. Robert Michels, *Political Parties: A Sociological Study of the Oligarchical Tendencies of Modern Democracy,* reprint, Glencoe: Free Press, 1962, pages 283–4.

2. Marx, "Instructions for Delegates to the Geneva Congress," 1877, in *The First International and After,* David Fernback, ed., Harmondsworth: Penguin, 1974, page 89.

3. *Bakounine: Oeuvres completes,* letter to Gambuzzi, 16 November 1870; letter to Ceretti, 13–27 March 1872; see also Dolgoff, pages 218–9.

4. Engels to Theodore Cuno, 24 January 1872, *Selected Correspondence,* page 257. This, together with the charges that anarchists paid no attention to material, economic development, dumped the working class in favor of criminals, and were petit bourgeois, became a Marxist mantra, repeated most viciously perhaps by Georgy Plekhanov, the "father of Russian Marxism," in a nasty little book, *Anarchism and Socialism,* translated into English and prefaced in nasty sectarian prose by Marx's daughter Eleanor. Thanks to Todd McCallum for a splendid copy of the 1907 Charles H. Kerr edition and for much help with this project.

5. *Bakounine: Oeuvres completes,* "L'Empire Knouto-Germanique et la Revolution Sociale. Suite. Dieu et l'Etat. 4," November 1870–April 1871.

6. *Bakounine: Oeuvres completes,* "La science et la question vitale de la revolution," March 1870.

7. Engels to Theodore Cuno, 24 January 1872, *Selected Correspondence,* pages 257–8.

8. *Bakounine: Oeuvres completes,* "Lettre a mes amis d'ltalie," 19–28 October 1871.

9. *Bakounine: Oeuvres completes,* letter to Anselmo Lorenzo, 7 May 1872.

10. Michael Bakunin, *God and the State,* New York: Dover, 1970, page 9.

11. Bakunin, *God and State,* pages 9–12.

12. *Bakounine: Oeuvres completes,* "L'Empire Knouto-Germanique et la Revolution Sociale. Manuscrit qui precedait le manuscript de l'appendice," November 1870.

13. Bakunin, *Statism and Anarchy,* Marshall Shatz, ed., trans., page xxiv. The quotations from *Statism and Anarchy* that follow are taken from this translation.

14. Kenafick, page 306, makes this observation.

15. *Bakounine: Oeuvres completes,* "Ecrit contre Marx," November-December 1872.

16. Bakunin, *Statism and Anarchy,* pages 132–7 and 178–84. These ideas on the class position and politics of intellectuals were taken up later in greater detail by the Polish radical Jan Waclaw Machajski. See Marshall Shatz, *Jan Waclaw Machajski: A Radical Critic of the Russian Intelligentsia and Socialism,* Pittsburgh: University of Pittsburgh Press, 1989.

17. Marx, "From Comments on Bakunin's Book, *Statehood* [sic] *and Anarchy,*" in Marx and Engels, *Selected Works,* volume 2, pages 411–2; "On Bakunin's *Statism and Anarchy,*" *Karl Marx: Selected Writings,* McLellan, ed., pages 606–9.

18. Cited in Carr, page 444.

19. Elizaveta Litvinova, in *Bakounine et les autres,* pages 304–6.

20. Nicolaj Sokolov, in *Bakounine et les autres,* pages 325–8.

21. *Bakounine: Oeuvres completes,* letter to the *Journal de Geneve,* second fortnight of September 1873; letter to the *compagnons de la Jederation jurasienne,* first fortnight of October 1873. Engels made reference to the "The Alliance of Socialist Democracy and the International Working Men's Association" pamphlet in a series of newspaper articles that attacked the Bakuninists in Spain. The articles largely repeated the old charges made against anarchists and anarchism, especially the complaint that "Spain is such a backward country industrially that there can be no question there of immediate complete emancipation of the working. Spain will first have to pass through various preliminary states of development and remove quite a number of obstacles from its path." See Marx and Engels, *Revolution in Spain,* London: Lawrence and Wishart, 1939.

CONCLUSION

1. *Bakounine: Oeuvres completes,* letter to Elisee Reclus, 15 February 1875.
2. Adolf Reichel to Carlo Gambuzzi, *Bakounine et les autres,* pages 380-7.
3. No book on anarchism is complete without a reference to the events of Kronstadt in 1921, where the Red Army, led by Trotsky, destroyed the left-wing resistance to the Bolsheviks. I tend to follow the line on Kronstadt set out by my friend Charles Demers, which is, "My line on Kronstadt is, if you have a line on Kronstadt, I don't want to hear it."
4. See John E. Bowlt, "A Monument to Bakunin' Korolev's Cubo-Futurist Statue of 1919," *Canadian-American Slavic Studies,* 10, no. 4 (winter 1976), pages 577–90.
5. McLaughlin, *Mikhail Bakunin.*

INDEX

Moscow and, 21, 25, 27
Napoleon III. *See* Louis Napoleon
national assembly, German, 150, 151
nationalism, 12, 153, 181, 190
    German, 150
nationality, 44, 56, 100
National Post, 2
necessity, 78, 79, 80
Nechaev, Sergei, 224–25, 231–34, 237–38,
    241, 249, 251, 268, 280, 297–98, 321
    character of, 229–30
    criticism of, 234–36
negation, 97–98
negative, 97, 114, 115, 212, 227
Neill, A. S., 331
Neue Rheinische Zeitung, 155, 160
The New York Review of Books, 159
The New York Times, 2
Nicholas I, 11, 28–29, 30, 44, 56, 127, 163,
    164
    brutality of, 128, 130
    death of, 169–70
    military of, 45, 47
nihilism, 227–28
Nilovs (aunt and uncle), 44–45, 52, 54
Ninth Symphony (Beethoven), 53, 77
Nixon, Richard, 97, 229
nobility, 7, 8, 10, 11, 28, 59, 73, 129, 165,
    185
    role of women in, 18, 58, 170
    Russian, 8, 128–29
    serfdom and, 33–41
Northern Society, 28, 31
Notes of the Fatherland, 93

obedience, 44, 46, 47, 54, 86
objectivity, 94, 95, 107
Obolensky, Zoe, 267, 280
    circle around, 192, 199
Observer, 91, 92
"Ode to Joy" (Beethoven/Schiller), 77
"Ode to Liberty" (Pushkin), 56
officer training school, 46–48, 49–50, 63
Ogarev, Maria, 72, 232, 279–80
Ogarev, Nicholas, 58, 72
"On Philosophy" (Bakunin, Michael), 93, 97
oppression, 50, 55, 131, 154, 165, 214, 270
order, 3
    new social, 289, 290
    to return to Russia, 121, 153
    world, 211
Organization, 225–26
organization(s)
    from bottom up, 224, 318

of future, 211, 225, 258, 332
political, 299
of proletariat, 323
secret, 296, 297
self, 289
voluntary, 290, 318
orthodoxy, 3, 11, 44, 56, 58, 67, 75, 86, 100
Orwell, George, 5
Ottoman Empire, 23, 169
Owen, Robert, 135, 253
ownership, 34, 155, 203, 204, 211, 243

pan-Slavism, 151–52, 274, 277, 282
Paris, 121, 123
    Congress of, 199
    insurrection of, 288
    treaty of, 26, 27
Paris Commune, 288, 290, 295, 303, 313,
    321, 326
    Marx and, 290–91
"The Paris Commune and the Idea of the
    State" (Bakunin), 313
parliament, 6, 125, 153, 188
    democracy and, 89
    Frankfurt, 149, 150, 151, 160
    French, 7
Parsons, Lucy, 329
passion, 7, 54, 114, 124, 125, 130, 158,
    196, 213, 224
    for destruction, 111, 116, 227
patriotism, 48, 91, 153, 202, 252
Paul I, 12, 14
Payne, A. B., 2
peace, 86, 115, 202, 213, 237
peasants, 110, 159, 165, 169, 257, 285–86,
    316, 317
    commune of, 242–43
    labor and, 55
    modernization and, 35, 36, 147
    resistance of, 328–29
    revolt of, 36–37, 129–30
    self-sufficiency of, 34
people, 12, 22, 34, 44, 87, 93, 100, 119,
    125, 168, 188, 244, 315
    definition of, 28, 116
    dignity of, 120
    direct representation of, 173
    education of, 81
    February Revolution and, 149–50
    history and, 110, 120
    militia of, 148
    politics and, 85
    radicals and, 185–86
    revolution of, 235
    Russian, 129, 131, 165–66

ABOUT MARK LEIER

Mark Leier received his PhD from Memorial University of Newfoundland in 1992. Currently he is the chair of Simon Fraser University's history department and lives in North Vancouver. He has written three books on Canadian labor history and is the director of SFU's Centre for Labour Studies.

ABOUT SEVEN STORIES PRESS

Seven Stories Press is an indepedent book publisher based in New York City, with distribution throughout the United States, Canada, England, and Australia. We publish works of the imagination by such writers as Nelson Algren, Russell Banks, Octavia E. Butler, Assia Djebar, Ariel Dorfman, Coco Fusco, Barry Gifford, Lee Stringer, and Kurt Vonnegut, to name a few, together with political titles by voices of conscience, including the Boston Women's Health Collective, Noam Chomsky, Angela Y. Davis, Human Rights Watch, Derrick Jensen, Ralph Nader, Gary Null, Project Censored, Barbara Seaman, Gary Webb, and Howard Zinn, among many others. We believe publishers have a special responsibility to defend free speech and human rights, and to celebrate the gifts of the human imagination, wherever we can. For additional information, visit www.sevenstories.com.